T0355128

The Opening of the Protestant Mind

The Opening of the Protestant Mind

How Anglo-American Protestants
Embraced Religious Liberty

MARK VALERI

OXFORD
UNIVERSITY PRESS

OXFORD
UNIVERSITY PRESS

Oxford University Press is a department of the University of Oxford. It furthers
the University's objective of excellence in research, scholarship, and education
by publishing worldwide. Oxford is a registered trade mark of Oxford University
Press in the UK and certain other countries.

Published in the United States of America by Oxford University Press
198 Madison Avenue, New York, NY 10016, United States of America.

© Oxford University Press 2023

Library of Congress Cataloging-in-Publication Data
Names: Valeri, Mark, author.
Title: The opening of the Protestant mind : how Anglo-American Protestants
embraced religious liberty / Mark Valeri.
Description: New York, NY, United States of America : Oxford University Press, [2023] |
Includes bibliographical references and index.
Identifiers: LCCN 2023005071 (print) | LCCN 2023005072 (ebook) |
ISBN 9780197663677 (hardback) | ISBN 9780197663691 (epub) | ISBN 9780197663707
Subjects: LCSH: Protestants—United States—Attitudes—History. |
Religion and state—United States—History. | Toleration—United States—History.
Classification: LCC BR520.V36 2023 (print) | LCC BR520 (ebook) |
DDC 261.088/2804—dc23/eng/20230501
LC record available at https://lccn.loc.gov/2023005071
LC ebook record available at https://lccn.loc.gov/2023005072

DOI: 10.1093/oso/9780197663677.001.0001

Printed by Sheridan Books, Inc., United States of America

For longtime friends in Richmond, Virginia
David Clarke and Pam Clarke
Fritz Kling and Val Kling

and St. Louis, Missouri
Alan Boggs and Katie Boggs
John Holmes and Veeda Holmes
Amanda Lothman and Carl Lothman
And, of course, Lynn Valeri

Contents

Preface

The American public square is awash in provocative claims about religion and the nation and about the moral criteria by which public controversies ought to be resolved. Some politicians embrace a Christian nationalist agenda, or a White Christian Nationalism, lacing their assertions about the nation's well-being with evangelical Protestant rhetoric. Many commentators imply that partisan loyalties, even devotion to a single outsized public figure, supersede common notions of moral virtue or veracity in debates about policy. Critics on the extremes of the political spectrum contend that Americans with different social or ethnic backgrounds hold such irreconcilable moral assumptions that it is futile to appeal to a shared moral sense or conscience as a means of mutual understanding or constructive debate. Such claims reduce politics to a contest for power among competing interest groups, privileging sheer polemic over public reason.

Many of these issues—the religious identity of the nation, moral reasonableness as an adjudicator in public debate, and the meaning of moral conscience—are addressed in this book, albeit in seventeenth-century and eighteenth-century contexts and languages. This study is focused on the ways Protestants in England and America described non-Protestant religions, as well as the nature of the choice of one religion or another, during the British colonization of America. Although it is chiefly a historical work, it concerns religious and moral dilemmas, and proposals, that might illumine by way of comparison and contrast some of the rhetoric that occupies today's headlines. For all of their peculiarities and contradictions, late seventeenth-century and eighteenth-century conceptions of moral reason and religious choice raise questions about some of the constricted notions that often beset our public life today. As the reader will find out, there is plenty to question about those early modern discourses. Yet they might hold our interest long enough to cause us to ponder how they could inform our thinking about religion and politics or at least provide an angle of reflection on our contemporary polemics.

Acknowledgments

In producing a study that touches on such vexed issues as the intersection of religious viewpoints and national agendas, the meaning of religious liberty in a settler-colonial society, and the relation between ideas of moral reason and western racial typologies, I have relied on a wide range of historical sources along with the wisdom of many colleagues who have helped me to interpret them. None of these issues lend themselves, at least to my mind, to simple analyses. Along the way, friendly critics have raised issues, recommended readings, and proposed formulations that have enriched the following account. It is time to give at least a partial reckoning for such help.

Several colleagues have given time and attention to this work in various stages. Theo Calderara welcomed it to Oxford University Press with cheerfulness, enthusiasm, and confidence that it could have a wide audience. Many other readers have slogged through my prose and suggested ways to rethink and clarify. Doug Winiarski, a long-time conversation partner, offered candid critique and advice on the whole, as did an anonymous reader for OUP. Other readers have given counsel on chapters that address topics in which they have special expertise. I thank in particular Ann Braude, Richard Cogley, Jill Cook, James Calvin Davis, Sarah Barringer Gordon, Jonathan Koch, Rachel Wheeler, and Steven Zwicker. The remaining faults with my descriptions and analyses are due to my missteps despite their advice. As a research assistant, Gwyneth Henke has made keen suggestions for better prose and more accurate annotations, and provided sorely needed technical expertise in the preparation of the manuscript. So too, Emily Cosgrove has masterfully helped with images and the process of submitting the manuscript to OUP. Katie Lofton has been a welcomed conversation partner about titles good and bad.

Gathered with the support of Washington University in St. Louis, an amiable cohort of scholars known as the religion in America writing group has read chapter after chapter during the past few years, always alert to flawed arguments and misleading formulations. The members of this group have been a steady source of camaraderie along with scholarly advice: Fannie Bialek, John Inazu, Laurie Maffly-Kipp, Kate Moran, and Abram van Engen (our de facto organizer). I also have benefited from feedback given by two other reading groups at Washington University in St. Louis: the Eighteenth Century Salon and the Early Modern Reading Group. The monthly colloquium of the John C. Danforth Center on Religion and Politics, including home faculty, visiting colleagues, postdoctoral fellows, and friends to the Center, has been a lively setting for mutual exchange about several chapters. Indeed, my fellow faculty in the Center have buoyed me throughout the past several years with their willingness to share insights about the tougher aspects of religion and politics in America: Tazeen Ali, Fannie Bialek, Marie Griffith, John Inazu, Laurie Maffly-Kipp, and Leigh Schmidt. My colleagues in the Center exemplify the best in humanistic scholarship and congenial conversation.

I note too the academic institutions away from St. Louis that have hosted me for lectures and provided forums for discussion of this work as it was in progress. I express my gratitude to the Huntington Library, which offered me an incomparable archive and a place in several workshops and conferences at which I presented the work in progress. Among those conferences was the *William and Mary Quarterly* and USC-Huntington Early Modern Studies Institute Workshop on "Religions in the Early Americas," organized by Peter Mancall and Joshua Piker, and convened by Catherine Brekus, at which Rachel Wheeler gave incisive comments on an early draft of my argument. Two years after this conference, I gave a public lecture at the Huntington, which allowed me to introduce a more developed version of my work and receive helpful feedback. Most of the research into books on travel and comparative religions was conducted when I was the 2017–2018 Los Angeles Times Distinguished Fellow at the Huntington. Many thanks are due to Steve Hindle, the Huntington's research director at the time, and to my fellow year-long fellows, who formed a gracious and incisive scholarly community during the year.

I was fortunate to be able to present parts of this study at other venues as well. These include Duke University Divinity School, where I gave the David and Virginia Steinmetz Lecture and enjoyed the kind hospitality of Kate Bowler and Lauren Winner; the University of California at Berkeley, where Ethan Shagan, Mark Peterson, and Jonathan Sheehan led a workshop on early modern alternatives to the nation as sites for collective identities; the McNeil Center for Early American Studies at the University of Pennsylvania, where Dan Richer conducted a spirited discussion of an early chapter; the Early Modern Studies Institute at the University of Tübingen, where Lionel

Laborie hosted me for a keynote address at a conference on funding religion during the eighteenth century; the Center for American Studies at the University of Heidelberg, where I addressed the Baden-Wûrtenberg seminar under the leadership of Jan Stievermann; the Getty Research Institute, at which Edward Sterrett and David Brafman hosted me for a special seminar on eighteenth-century images of religion; the American Religions Workshop at Stanford University, directed by Kathryn Gin Lum; Claremont-McKenna College, where I delivered an Athenaeum Visiting Lecture under the direction of Esther Chung-Kim; Azusa Pacific University with the generosity of Mark Eaton; the Presbyterian Scholars Conference convened by Jeff McDonald; Dartmouth College, at which Henry C. Clark led an engaging conference for the 250th anniversary of the college; the Center for Early Modern Studies at the University of Minnesota, where J. B. Shank organized a lecture series on Bernard Picart and Frederic Bernard; and the Library Company of Philadelphia, which valiantly kept up its programming during the worst of the COVID-19 period through an online webinar.

The primary research for this work was conducted at several archives. I thank especially the experts who allowed me access to and advised me on their collections of diaries, letters, rare books, old dictionaries, and even playing cards: the Beinecke Library of Yale University, the Rauner Special Collections Library at Dartmouth College, the Library Company of Philadelphia, and the Massachusetts Historical Society. Jill Cook graciously introduced me to the eighteenth-century room and its back corridors at the British Museum. Mallica Kumbera Landrus entertained my questions at the Ashmolean Museum. I also benefited from a visit to the Pitt Rivers Museum in Oxford. Ken Minkema helped me to handle the online Jonathan Edwards sermons at the Jonathan Edwards Center at Yale University.

Finally, but certainly not in the least, the John C. Danforth Center on Religion and Politics at Washington University in St. Louis provided financial support for research, travel, leave, and research assistance.

This book is dedicated to friends who do not share a professional academic calling but who nonetheless have shared their love and encouragement over the years. They are kindred spirits who have taught me to discern a higher calling in the thick and thin of life.

Introduction

Benjamin Webb, a Harvard graduate and pastor's son from Braintree, Massachusetts, served as an itinerate schoolteacher in the villages around Boston during the 1750s. Throughout his travels, he toted around a commonplace book, in which he took notes on books from which he taught: Latin grammars, classical poetry, Locke's *Essay on Human Understanding*. He also devoted one page of his notes to "The Articles of the Mahometan Faith." If Webb taught his students from those notes, then rural New England children learned about what he believed to be the eight tenets of Islam—on God, Muhammad, purity rites, prayer, alms, fasting, pilgrimage, and prohibitions against alcohol and gambling—as well as Islamic teaching on such subjects as the difference between male and female souls. His notes demonstrate curiosity, not hostility.[1]

In the mid-eighteenth century, many New Englanders sought out information on the various religions of the world. Jacob Bailey, another Harvard graduate and schoolteacher, who eventually converted to the Church of England and became a missionary pastor, traveled through Nova Scotia during the same period that Webb was teaching school in Massachusetts. Bailey carried notes on Islam and Japanese religions even as he recorded observations of Indigenous traditions and the Catholicism of the Acadians.[2] The minister in Grafton, Massachusetts, Aaron Hutchinson, a Yale graduate, devoted a part of nearly every Sunday service to praying for the conversion of non-Protestants. By the reminiscences of the Baptist elder John Leland, who attended Hutchinson's congregational church as a child, Hutchinson's prayers were exhausting, "about fifty-nine minutes long" in Leland's painful memory. They went into great detail about Muslims, the "pagan" inhabitants of North America and Asia, Jews, and Roman Catholics.[3]

Knowledge of other religions went hand in hand with curiosity about conversion from one tradition to another. England and New England were saturated with tales in which people from far-flung corners came together, often to trade, and in the process switched religious allegiances. Boston newspapers provided breathtaking accounts of interreligious conversions

The Opening of the Protestant Mind. Mark Valeri, Oxford University Press. © Oxford University Press 2023.
DOI: 10.1093/oso/9780197663677.003.0001

especially during the 1720s through the 1750s. They reported on Jews and Muslims who had come to "Embrace the Christian Religion" while in Rome and Amsterdam, and on Christians who had professed Islam in Algeria. They gave accounts of French missions among the Iroquois and of Mohawk sachems who walked the streets of Montreal "wearing Crucifixes." They relayed several narratives of the Christianization of Russia. They noted the conversion of Catholics to Protestantism in Hanover, Frankfurt, Salzburg, London, and Montpellier. They provided authoritative-sounding statistics from Jesuit missions in China: precisely 69,318 converts and 400 priests ordained since the first mission. A trickle of reports became a flood. From the front page they conveyed the notion that religious faith could be a deliberate choice rather than an inheritance.[4]

This was not merely a scholarly preoccupation. London's political essayist Thomas Gordon was so struck by Britons' interest in conversion that in 1719 he authored a tract that featured a fictional German doctor, living in England, who foresaw a worldwide deluge of religious change. The doctor predicted that Italian bishops would renounce the papacy, the French church embrace the Reformation, the people of Sweden and Scotland become Muslim, Genevans reunite with Rome, England become atheist, the Dutch entertain hundreds of religions, and the people of Africa convert to Christianity. It was pure parody, reflecting Gordon's opinion that the rage for conversion had gotten out of hand.[5]

Anglo-American Protestants' infatuation with conversion grew in the midst of a transformation in the ways that they thought about other religions. That transformation is the subject of this book. It focuses on writers who understood England's Protestant tradition to encompass not only the Church of England but also some forms of dissent from the church—such as the majority of churches in New England—that expressed loyalty to England and traditional Protestant teaching. These Protestants can be called "magisterial," meaning that they held a high regard for established laws and civil government—the magistracy.[6] As used in this study, "Anglo-American Protestants" accordingly stands as shorthand for these broad-minded, magisterial, and often transatlantic-oriented Protestants. They produced the bulk of the period's writing on conversion, the world's religions, and the state, and this book relies on a variety of texts from their hands.

This narrative begins in 1653, when, in the aftermath of the English civil wars, the first systematic publications on non-Christian religions appeared in English. It ends in 1765, when the imperial crisis between Britain and

America began to reframe ideas about liberty of choice and reconfigure the political meaning of Protestant missions to Native Americans. Focused on London and Boston (and its environs)—two centers of Anglo-Protestant thought and of missionary activity—this study describes shifting stances especially toward Roman Catholicism, Islam, the indigenous religions of western Africa, and northeastern Native American traditions, with modest attention to East Asian religions.[7]

The Opening of the Protestant Mind offers a narrative of change. From the 1650s through the Restoration of the Stuart monarchy (1660–1688), Anglo-American Protestants understood England and its American colonies as a confessional order. They maintained that the health of the state depended on a post–civil war religious confession that would alleviate the disorders of the Interregnum (the period from 1649 to 1660, when England had no monarch). To be sure, Anglicans and non-Anglican Protestants often differed on the scope of that confession. Many Anglican ecclesiastical officials denied the presumption that any church outside the Church of England represented true English Protestantism. Such sectarian jealousies among Protestants were important, but most of the subjects of this study nonetheless promoted a broad Protestant consensus for the sake of England's stability.

Even as an elusive ideal, the notion of a Protestant confession or theological consensus provided a lens through which Anglo-American Protestants saw the world's religions. Anglicans and dissenters alike rejected all non-Protestant religions as illegitimate, dangerous, and demonic. They described conversion, then, chiefly as the submission of individuals to a version of Christian teaching, particularly Protestant doctrine, that was integral to England's identity. With their emphasis on the national character of religious confessions—England as Protestant, Spain as Catholic, Ottoman Turkey as Islamic—they only rarely contemplated the possibility of choosing one's religion. In religious missions, they believed that becoming English, at least in social and cultural terms, was a prerequisite for becoming Christian.

Beginning with the revolution of 1688, Anglo-American Protestants changed their orientation toward non-Protestant religions. They supported a regime in London, known by the moniker Whig, that relied on cooperation among an increasingly diverse collection of Anglicans, dissenters, and loyal Catholics. They depended on overseas commercial interactions with Muslims. They also attempted to form alliances with Native American communities in the midst of war with France. Whigs defended the revolution of 1688 with appeals to republican constitutional principles, including religious toleration, that implied a distinction between loyalty to the kingdom and conformity to any one creed. Partly in response to these shifting political circumstances, the figures discussed in this book jettisoned a confessional approach. They minimized theological orthodoxy as a prerequisite for patriotism. Instead, they thought that whiggish moral virtues would unify the kingdom. They valorized sects or movements within a variety of traditions—Protestant, Catholic, Islamic, Native American—that sustained what they deemed as republican ideas of toleration and moral virtue. They critiqued religious authorities within any tradition who, by their account, utilized state power or mystery-laden ceremonialism to coerce adherence. They offered a new interpretation of the religions of the world.

Anglo-American Protestants accordingly changed their ideas about conversion and their strategies for the evangelization of non-Christians. During the first half of the eighteenth century, they came to idealize conversion as an uncoerced choice, grounded in whiggish notions of moral liberty. In their missions to Native Americans, for example, they de-emphasized older demands for "Englishness" in favor of what they presumed were innate and universal moral principles that spanned English and Indigenous cultures. Protestants across a wide theological spectrum came to promote persuasion as the most appropriate means of evangelization. To be sure, they pursued their mission in the context of the imperial struggle for North America. Their evangelistic ideas often functioned to justify the subjugation of Indigenous people. Yet those ideas nonetheless contradicted imperial ideologies that dehumanized Native Americans by portraying them merely as unwitting and irrational: incapable of reason, civic virtue, and moral agency—and undeserving of religious liberty.

This study touches on many issues—such as religious toleration, Enlightenment moral thought, evangelicalism, imperial agendas, the state and secularism, missions, and racial ideologies—that in themselves have each been the subject of a large and contested body of scholarship. They do not, however, drive its narrative. Instead, this book focuses on changing Anglo-American Protestant views of other religions and the importance of conceptions of moral liberty to that difference. The discourse itself is the central subject.

Political factors loom large, however, in this intellectual history. Shifting perceptions of the means of political stability and prosperity led to changes in the ways that Anglo-American Protestants thought about religion in the public sphere. They considered a religion legitimate if they judged it to be beneficial to England's public order. That is not to deny that intellectual and theological convictions shaped political agendas. Religious ideas and political agendas developed in tandem, even though this narrative gives a leading role to the politics.

In tracing these Protestants' shifting ideas, this study admittedly addresses only part of the story of political power and religious comparison before American Independence. It describes the views of separatist-radical Protestants, French Catholics in Canada, or Muslim teachers who had conversations with Protestants, in only a few instances. It attends to the voices of Indigenous adherents to traditional practices as well as converts to Christianity chiefly by way of parsing Protestant accounts of those voices. As incomplete as it is, however, the following study may help us to understand an important feature of the religious history of Anglo-America: the mind of those Protestants who often exercised power over the religious "other" in their spheres of influence.

The resulting account offers a reading that differs in some respects from recent interpretations of the history of Protestant views of other religions.[8] Intellectual historians have often emphasized the importance of what we can call, for short, an Enlightenment agenda. They focus on seventeenth- and eighteenth-century critiques of dogmatic Protestantism and support for a religion of reason—a secularized approach that was equally critical of all religious traditions. From this perspective, the central story concerns the triumph of reasonableness over theological stubbornness.

One argument within this school of thought holds that a leading edge of Protestant scholars in the seventeenth century attempted to produce a genealogy of religious phenomena free from dogmatic bias and confessional strife. Early English deists in particular, these scholars maintain, valorized a natural religion shorn of what they held were the doctrines and ceremonial accretions, as well as institutional obligations, that had corrupted pure devotion and aroused controversy in post-Reformation Europe. This natural religion consisted chiefly of a small number of fundamental theological assertions, such as the existence of God, and moral teaching. Historians who have worked within this paradigm maintain that their seventeenth-century subjects, especially in England, promoted the notion that beneath the plurality of religions in the world, including ancient forms of devotion, was a common phenomenon, "religion," that deserved recognition. The discovery of a natural "religion" at the core of all religions was, as this interpretation goes, integral to an open-minded and irenic approach to religious comparison.[9]

Other scholars have emphasized eighteenth-century turns within an Enlightenment agenda, stressing a skeptical assault on all forms of orthodoxy. Historians who subscribe to this narrative contend that the emergence of a "modern" and reliable study of religions during the 1720s and 1730s reflected a "resolutely secular" mindset. They contend that the figures they have studied broke from seventeenth-century orthodoxies and fashioned a popular version of religious comparison that elevated dispassionate and impartial description over Christian apologetics. Other historians have argued that eighteenth-century books on world geography made advances from their predecessors with their reliance on empirical methods and taxonomic proficiency.[10]

While drawing on this body of scholarship, the following study recasts the seventeenth-and eighteenth-century narrative in several ways. First, it attends to a vernacular version of religious commentary rather than to the erudite commentary—chiefly from progressive or rationalist quarters—that has drawn the attention of other scholars. It focuses on popular observation and opinion, the stuff of middling intellectual culture: religious geographies and dictionaries, wondrous illustrations, travel accounts, diplomatic reports, merchants' and soldiers' diaries, sermons, and missionary tracts. By so doing, it recovers political and social agendas that sometimes go unarticulated by the specialized scholars of the seventeenth and eighteenth centuries. It sets the intellectual history in cultural and political context.[11]

It suggests, second, that many of the innovations of the period ought to be read not as efforts to craft a secular alternative to Protestantism but as attempts to articulate the criteria by which religions could be judged as politically acceptable. Such criteria often accorded with traditional versions of what counted as orthodoxy within Protestant churches. Concerns for England's welfare explain how a broad coalition of Protestants—including Calvinists in England and New England, broad-minded Anglicans, and deists—took shape during the second half of the seventeenth century. A similarly expansive Protestant coalition, including evangelicals, was drawn together after 1688 by a discourse of religious liberty and reasonableness.

That discourse provided standards by which to measure forms of devotion throughout the world. According to its advocates, religious practices were laudable if they evinced sociability, reasonableness, and regard for others' liberty of conscience: qualities, in their view, that made for a healthy state.

Religio-political regimes in which a priestly class used elaborate ceremony to awe people into adherence, by contrast, were deemed suspicious. This moral discourse allowed for an appreciation of difference within religious traditions of any sort. Justification for the empire thus rested not on the received dogma of any one tradition as a whole but on public virtues upheld by some groups within those traditions. Eighteenth-century Britons on both sides of the Atlantic understood traditional Protestantism to be compatible with Enlightenment social mandates that sustained loyalty to Britain.[12]

Yet again, there is an abundant literature about the history of the discipline of religious studies in which several scholars have contended that writings on other religions from the late sixteenth through the eighteenth centuries reflected a largely unchanging and theologically inflected criticism of cultures outside of Protestant western Europe. Such was the case, these scholars hold, until the emergence of the academic study of religion in Germany and England during the mid-nineteenth century—the creation of what German scholars called the "science" of comparative religions, or *Religionswissenshaft*. Such contemporary historians of the discipline treat the story of the seventeenth and eighteenth centuries—quite briefly—as a tale of continuity. According to them, eighteenth-century commentators accumulated data about different traditions and developed a classification scheme for major Asian traditions—varieties of Buddhism, Confucianism, and Indian religions—but otherwise conformed their accounts to Protestant polemic: Judaism as an archaic predecessor to Christianity, Catholicism as a superstitious corruption, Islam as a violent deviation, indigenous traditions as irrational primitivism, and Asian religions as exotic idolatries.[13]

These historians of the field of comparative religions, along with theoretically oriented scholars of religion such as Jonathan Z. Smith, focus their attention on the development of generalized concepts of religion and its antithesis, the secular, as a post-eighteenth-century development. According to these scholars, Enlightenment-era notions of natural religion merely anticipated, in a shadowy form, the nineteenth-century notion of "religion" as a discrete phenomenon. By this account, nineteenth-century scholars developed the category of religion as a means of comparing different forms of devotion in an objective fashion. Yet, as this argument goes, the object called "religion" was nonetheless freighted with Protestant assumptions. As defined by English and German intellectuals, it minimized rituals as mere accidents that varied by tradition and maximized common theological beliefs as the essence of religion, with little explicit admission that such a definition elevated a Protestant emphasis on an individual belief at the expense of non-Protestant concerns for traditional, embodied, and communal practice.[14]

In a parallel interpretation, several contemporary critics have claimed that the category of the "secular"—the implied opposite of the term "religion"—was promoted in the post-Enlightenment west as a way to define a public sphere shorn of theological agendas and contentions. These critics argue, furthermore, that the "secular" carried an imperial and often racialized agenda. The rhetoric of western civility and non-western barbarity inflected its use. Western powers wielded the supposed superiority of their secularized politics as an instrument of control over non-western nations and indigenous peoples.[15]

Other scholars within the field of religious studies have contended that the persistence of claims for the superiority of Christianity inflected western imperialism and racism more powerfully than did the emergence of the "secular." Kathryn Gin Lum, for example, has fastened on the trope "heathen," used especially by missionaries, as a Protestant devaluation of non-White, non-western, non-modern, and non-Christian throughout the modern period. From this perspective, seventeenth- or eighteenth-century ideas of religious comparison can be portrayed merely as one phase in a continuous story of White supremacy that culminated in the nineteenth-century American conquest of the continent and overseas empire.[16]

The Opening of the Protestant Mind does not dispute the whole of this overarching narrative. Recent studies of Protestant missions and of the rise of the study of comparative religions demonstrate multiple ways in which Protestants blended notions of White Protestant superiority, civility, and moral agency to justify their enslavement of African captives and their attempts to dominate indigenous people. Many of the purveyors of the discourse of religious comparison claimed empirical objectivity and moral reasonableness, but their comparisons often served colonial power in a variety of settings, including southern Africa, colonial America, the southwestern United States, and Hawaii.[17]

Several scholars have shown that the implications even of the turn to moral liberty—a central theme of this study—were contradictory. The language of liberty of choice cut against the grain of the customary presuppositions that peoples' inherited identities, including race, determined their religious and moral character. At the same time it reflected an imposition of western notions of liberty on non-western peoples. The history of Protestant discourses about non-Protestant religions and of North American missions belongs to a larger story of settler colonialism, racial construction, and slavery—a story that surfaces in this book especially in the sections on Protestant descriptions of African and Indigenous American religious practices.[18]

I have framed these issues, however, within an account of changes in the discourses about religion and conversion, thereby challenging some of the implications of the interpretations I have sketched here. Those changes complicate accounts of continuity within, or an ideological essence to, Anglo-American Protestantism in this period. The discourse around the religious "other" was not fixed, nor did it have univocal political implications. Some recent scholarship can give the misleading impression of an essentialized Protestantism—an irony for scholars who critique the notion of an essentialized religion—throughout the modern period.[19] By indicating the importance of variation in the discourse of religion and conversion, often contingent on shifting political contexts, this study prompts us to resist the notion of a single Anglo-American "Protestant" approach to religion, race, and empire. It calls into question the presumption that seventeenth- and eighteenth-century discourses were mere prelude to or anticipations of the fully developed and explicit racial ideologies that informed British and American colonial projects during the nineteenth century.

In its focus on contingency and change, *The Opening of the Protestant Mind* also suggests that Anglo-American Protestant ideas offered alternatives as well as concessions to colonial ideas. It demonstrates, to mention just one example, that notions of a universal religious consciousness (and therefore some conception of "religion") underwent several reformulations through the mid-eighteenth century. Seventeenth-century puritan discussions of "true" religion often rested on Reformed ideas of right doctrine and an individual's awareness of their own depravity and need for saving faith. Eighteenth-century Protestants came to parse religious consciousness more expansively: as an experience of anxiety and relief, fear and hope, affiliation and disaffiliation, which, at least by their lights, reflected traditional communal concerns. Protestant conceptions of religion were not always individualistic nor centered on cognitive beliefs. This book also uncovers contestation about the legitimacy of non-Protestant religions, the rightness of accepting non-Protestant cultural and social practices, or the utility of western theological language in non-western contexts. In recounting such complexities, this study suggests that Protestant discourse, like those of other religious traditions, could at times call into question or at least buffer imperial and racialized agendas, and could convey the need for exchange across cultural divides, just as it could serve as an instrument of cultural chauvinism and colonialist power. It worked both ways.

My intent, then, is to expose the paradoxes of Protestants' ideas about non-Protestant religions, conversion, and religious liberty. The post-1688 monarchy and its imperial extensions, the leaders of the Hanoverian Empire and its slave-based economies, or the White benefactors of the early American nation with its designs on the conquest of North America: they all deployed some of the discourse described in this book to hegemonic ends. The discourse did not resolve religious factionalism, create a pan-Protestant unity, or give a voice to those dissenters—especially separatist Protestants—who fell outside of a magisterial Protestant consensus. Yet, as the early modern historian Carlo Ginzburg has contended, eighteenth-century writers on the world's religions often recognized the moral contradictions of their ideas.[20] Their conceptions of reasonableness and virtue, for all of their imperial uses, prompted critical diagnoses of racial bias and colonialism. Enlightenment ideas about human proclivities to irrational prejudice, along with Protestant tenets of human self-deceptiveness, mandated self-critique, including mistrust of assumptions about Anglo-Protestant superiority. For us to make claims about the social effects of a discourse, to posit a continuity of ideas about religion and race, or to expose discrepancy between discourse and social reality, we must first understand the discourse on its own terms and appreciate its ambiguities. That is the aim of this book.

1

Disorder and Confessionalism

In 1683, London's Nathaniel Crouch produced one of his many books of curiosities: *The Strange and Prodigious Religions, Customs, and Manners, of Sundry Nations*. Known as a hack publisher, Crouch often plagiarized from previous publications on religious practices, conversions, and the nation, favoring stories of ruthless villains and pious heroes. Published under his name or various pseudonyms, Crouch's small books were inexpensive and sold well. Although his fascination with the occult sometimes scandalized puritan divines, his works appealed to lower and middle-class Londoners and erudite readers alike, including Alexander Pope, and to American intellectuals such as Benjamin Franklin, who collected a copy of nearly every one of Crouch's titles.[1]

One of the first of the crude illustrations in *Strange and Prodigious Religions* concerned "The Manner of the Antient [i.e., Indigenous] Virginians in their Worshiping of Idols" (Figure 1.1). The drawing offers a mélange of images. At the center are three classical columns, pedestals for each of three idols: an ancient pagan (Egyptian) snake, the golden calf of Exodus 32, and the largest and most prominent, the figure of a devil. To the right of the idols, Crouch pictured a group dancing around a fire. According to the text, "the Devotions" of the Virginia Natives "consisted in howling and dancing about Fires." There is a walled town in the background, a group of devotees gesturing toward the idols, and a crowd of people, animated as they jostle each other, in the foreground.[2]

Crouch's prose elucidates this peculiar tableau of idolatry and social disorder. He subsumed Native American religions under the banner of "*Paganism*," which also included ancient religions, Judaism-gone-awry (the golden calf), and the religions of Asia. He asserted that western Catholics and non-western pagans participated in the same sorts of sacrilege, which explains his reliance on images from Catholicism to describe Indigenous American and Asian religions. The "Religion of *China*" included "Fryers, and many Monasteries of Idolaters," and huge cathedrals with thousands of idols, one of which "was as big as a Popish St. *Christopher*." Crouch's report

The Opening of the Protestant Mind. Mark Valeri, Oxford University Press. © Oxford University Press 2023.
DOI: 10.1093/oso/9780197663677.003.0002

Figure 1.1 Crouch, idol worship

Credit: R. D. [Nathaniel Crouch], *The Strange and Prodigious Religious Customs, and Manners of Sundry Nations* (London, 1683), image facing A3.

of a "Religious House" and "Chappel" in Canton that featured "the Image of a Woman with a Child hanging about her Neck" and images of "he and she Saints" held "in great Veneration, with long Legends of their Lives," evoked Catholic devotion to the Virgin Mary and other saints.[3]

According to Crouch, idolatry in all its forms led to evil, inhumane behaviors. Worship of false deities induced "ridiculous," "cruel," and "abominable" practices, from chicanery to the ritual sacrifice of children. He encapsulated all non-English and non-Protestant devotion in the figure of a devil at the center of his drawing.[4]

Crouch's observations on idolatry abroad expressed his concern for political order—and therefore religious uniformity—at home. This explains the curious appearance of the people and the town in the background. In other works, Crouch included illustrations of Native Americans who wore breechcloths or no clothing. Here he dressed the "idolaters" in English garb, pictured them as rabble, and offered the prospect of an English town to suggest the implicit subject of his book: the idolatry and disorder that had afflicted England in the past and continued to do so in the present. His survey of alien religions was a commentary on England itself.

Crouch's apprehensions were rooted in the political crises of the mid-seventeenth century. The division of England into royalist and parliamentary factions during the 1640s, followed by the chaotic government of the Commonwealth during the 1650s, had disrupted civic affairs and nearly ruined the nation.[5] Religious diversity played a role in the upheaval. Disputes and contests for power among different religious parties intensified divisions. Crouch had long lamented the combination of what he considered to be religious deviance, crypto-Catholicism, and political unrest during the Interregnum. In 1681 he wrote about the spread of radical Protestantism, sectarian violence, and political chaos as fresh memories: the "madness," "Confusions," "Treason," "breach of Trust," "Armed factions," "Subverting," and "Miseries we have lately suffered." The kingdom's only true hope, whether in old England or English America, he insisted, was the "preservation of the Protestant Religion" in the face of an onslaught of different, competing creeds, from Quakerism and millenarian frenzy to Native American spiritual practices.[6]

Crouch projected England's afflictions onto non-Protestant religions everywhere. He used the same rhetoric to depict the people of his *Strange and Prodigious Religions* as he used to describe England in turmoil. Wherever they took hold, false religions produced a people "confused," a society suffering from "Disorder," political leaders in the throes of "Fury," and religious enthusiasts spreading falsehoods through their "Prophecyings." He likewise described Native resistance to New England colonists during what the English called the Pequot War (1636–1638) and King Philip's War (1675–1676) in the same terms that he had characterized the chaos of England at midcentury: uprisings, betrayals, deceptions, and misrule. Invectives against non-Christian religions served as a warning against the religious and political disunity that still tempted the people of England, whether in Britain or America.[7]

Crouch's portrait of the "Antient Virginians" and their "Idols" gave a commercialized and sensationalized presentation of ideas that dominated English commentary on religion, the nation, and non-Protestant traditions from the crises of the mid-1640s through the Restoration (1660–1688). An astute reader of popular tastes, Crouch recognized that non-Protestant religions, and cultural geography more generally, were something of a fad. The appearance in London of new dictionaries and geographies of religion, informed by accounts from merchants throughout the Atlantic and the Levant, and by reports from colonists in America, gave evidence of widespread curiosity.

Political concerns peculiar to post-civil-wars England, moreover, animated and informed interest in non-Protestant religions. Commentators, such as Crouch, fastened on the idea that the unity and strength of England depended on the hegemony of a single religious confession—what Crouch called "the Protestant religion"—throughout the realm. His language suggested the importance of a broad Protestant coalition, even though he and his contemporaries knew that English Protestants disagreed on the extent or institutional form of that coalition. Anglicans and dissenters often quarreled over ecclesiastical politics and even the legality of dissent or nonconformity.[8] Yet they did concur on the importance of the Reformation inheritance for England—its power to tame factionalism and hold England together. This conviction produced a heavily politicized reading of other religions: not merely as false or spiritually dangerous but as powerful threats to the nation. Reflecting what Jonathan Sheehan has called "the polemics of distinction," observers divided the world's religions into two sorts: English, magisterial Protestant, and true; and non-English, sectarian or separatist, non-Protestant, and idolatrous or false.[9] The state—whether a parliamentary Commonwealth or restored monarchy—and its exercise of sovereignty depended on England's rejection of idolatrous confusion and its affirmation of religious order in a Protestant mode.

The following discussion of that discourse diverges from recent arguments that Anglo-Protestant critiques of different religions developed merely as justifications for transatlantic colonization: an international "Protestant interest" arrayed against Catholic powers in Europe and the Americas and against Indigenous peoples in North America.[10] As this chapter shows, internal political matters—as well as imperial-colonial projects—affected Protestant interpretations of the world's religions. Anglo-American Protestants transformed the discourse of religious difference according to political circumstances at home as well as to colonial designs. Many of the writers discussed here, who produced England's most widely read accounts, viewed other religions according to their perceptions of the kingdom's need for political and ideological order. This helps to explain how Protestants during the seventeenth century gave new, political meaning to the language of idolatry, superstition, and devilry.[11] They applied those idioms across a broad sweep of cultures—from ancient Greece and Persia to the Americas, the Levant, and contemporary Europe.

This chapter focuses on several predecessors to and contemporaries of Crouch who wrote for popular audiences.[12] The central cast of characters includes Alexander Ross, an Anglican scholar of the world's religions; John Ogilby, a political propagandist and apologist for Stuart power in the American colonies; and Crouch, a critic of the Stuarts. Despite the different genres and political sympathies represented by these characters, they shared common convictions we can characterize under the rubric of a confessional order.

Sources for Restoration-Era Writers

We must begin, however, with the early seventeenth-century sources from which these writers drew: narratives of journeys through Europe and the Levant by the likes of Edwin Sandys and William Lithgow, stories of first exchanges between English adventurers such as Thomas Harriot and the Indigenous peoples of America, and edited compilations of such accounts by scholars such as Richard Hakluyt and Samuel Purchas. Travel writers and compilers often provided ambiguous interpretations of non-western cultures. They did not integrate their stories into consistent and comparative analyses of different traditions—nothing like the comprehensive approach of successors such as Ross. Eyewitness accounts in themselves were episodic, shaped as they were by the vicissitudes of travel: personal exchanges, hardships, pleasures, misunderstandings, encounters.[13] Ross, Ogilby, and Crouch repurposed these accounts to sustain a coherent, confessional ideology according to which all non-Protestant religions threatened England's stability and prosperity.

Restoration-era writers inherited from early seventeenth-century observers and compilers two conventions for reading religion. First, each state, country, or sovereign territory could be identified with a particular religion or religions. Purchas conveyed this impression throughout his works. A chaplain to the Archbishop of Canterbury, he produced multivolume compilations of histories and travelogues: his 1613 *Purchas His Pilgrimage*, a theologically inflected introduction to ancient paganism, Judaism, and the religions of Asia, Africa, and America; and the five-volume, 1625 *Purchas His Pilgrimes*, a redaction of travel accounts into a political, economic, and cultural survey of lands outside of Europe. The sheer volume and diversity of Purchas's sources made his books compendiums of culture, geography, and history. He listed some 1,100 writers from whom he drew observations about religious practices: biblical writers, Greek historians, Roman poets, medieval theologians, papal historians, Protestant theologians, Catholic polemicists, scientists, travel writers, Jesuit and Dominican missionaries, explorers, and merchants.[14]

Purchas assembled snippets from these sources in an unsystematic manner yet conveyed the impression that he had uncovered connections among national histories, religious beliefs, and social practices. He did not define or categorize "religion" as a discrete subject, as did later writers. He organized his material by empires, nations, or colonies rather than by religious tradition. He defined his subjects—the religion of the Turkish Empire, China, or New France, for example—in ways that comingled civil and religious practices. He aggregated theological histories, geographical features, and local political practices.[15]

Second, pre-civil-wars writers turned such reflections on civil and religious co-identities into a running assumption about England: Protestantism was integral to its character as a nation. Purchas, like the sources he used, never elucidated the meaning of Protestantism in theological detail. He did, however, affirm that Reformation Christianity could be defined in part by its opposition to Catholicism. "I hope to shew," he wrote in the introduction to his *Pilgrimage*, "the Paganism of Antichristian Poperie, and other Pseudo-Christian beliefes, and the Truth of Christianitie as it is now professed and established in our Church." He also assured his readers that England had been a special repository for Protestant verities, or, as he put it, that "every English-man may see cause to praise God continually for the light of his truth, communicated to us." He most often associated that truth with the Church of England but did not make fine distinctions among England's

Protestants, except to imply that Reformed traditions, including puritanism, were encompassed by England's "Evangelicall Charter." He defined Protestantism broadly.[16]

Purchas invested traditional Protestant charges of Catholic superstition or idolatry with contemporary political meanings. Catholicism was, in his view, a threat to England's security, and Catholic clergy were treacherous, violent, and abusive. He excerpted the philosophical and moral arguments of Edward Brerewood, who had constructed a history of European languages that equated Catholicism with confusion and heathenism at every turn.[17] Yet Purchas chiefly turned to writers who reported on the political dimensions of Catholic perfidy. He especially drew from Hakluyt's compendium of travel accounts. An Anglican priest and chaplain to Robert Cecil, secretary of state for Elizabeth I and James I, Hakluyt selected his narratives, published in 1600, to emphasize the tyranny of Catholic power and conflicts between English-Protestant and Spanish-Catholic forces throughout the Atlantic world. Relying on Hakluyt, Purchas maintained, for example, that Catholic adventurers were "crueler" than "Savages" as they butchered their way through the Caribbean and America, having been taught by the Inquisition to employ torture.[18]

Many of Purchas's favorite travel writers reached for the most severe idioms—idolatry and evil—to position Catholicism as completely antithetical to all things English. For example, Edwin Sandys—England's envoy to Germany, a member of Commons, and associate of Purchas—wrote of Catholic states in politically delicate terms in his diplomatic work. Yet in his reflections on his travels through Europe, he stressed the frightening economic and political strength of Rome and emphasized how alien Catholicism was to English ways of politics and faith—how devilish in its practices and use of power.[19]

So too did William Lithgow, a pious Scottish Presbyterian with a flair for tale-telling whose works were excerpted by Purchas and read widely in their own right on both sides of the Atlantic. Lithgow recounted three journeys that took him through Europe to Constantinople, Jerusalem, Egypt, Tunis, and Spain. No place appalled him as much as Rome, filled with "Christians" in name only who were more debauched and ignorant than the "Pagans" he had encountered on his travels. He also found what he called "superstitious idolatrie" in pilgrimage sites in the Italian countryside, which evidenced "braine-sicke knowledge," the reign of "Sathan," and "darke ignorance." He repeatedly contrasted English-Protestant rule to "the Cruelties of the Papists, which far exceeded any of the Heathen Countries."[20] Purchas, and the travel writers from whom he drew, portrayed Catholicism as illegitimate top to bottom, a readily visible foe of England and of Protestantism.

Travel writers such as Sandys and compilers such as Purchas gave, by contrast, equivocal descriptions of non-Christian religions. Purchas, for example, gave mixed reports on Islam, with the criticisms of Christian theologians tempered by English merchants' friendly posture toward Ottoman Turks with whom they hoped to trade. Purchas also relied on travelers—again, Sandys and Lithgow—who deplored Islamic theology and complained of run-ins with unscrupulous Muslim businessmen yet extolled hospitable and civil Muslim hosts, were befriended by good (Muslim) Samaritans, appreciated the wisdom of medieval Islamic philosophers, and commended Islamic moral codes.[21]

Purchas and his fellow travelers gave particularly ambiguous descriptions of Native American traditions, a muddle of straightforward empirical observation, religious critique, and political conjecture. English Protestants who promoted colonial agendas, such as Purchas (who had vested interests in the Virginia Company) and Hakluyt, claimed that Indigenous inhabitants were willing to cooperate with English settlers and shared some moral ideas and even concepts of God, an indication that they might make reliable allies. Purchas and Hakluyt also maintained that the same inhabitants were irrational and prone to hostility, which justified military expansion in North America. Yet again, they also claimed that Native people were captivated by idolatry, a rationale for missions. Each of these images served as an argument for colonization. They also implied a confusion of colonial agendas: the establishment of trading partnerships, swift and violent conquest, and evangelization.[22]

The eyewitness account of Thomas Harriot, excerpted by Purchas, illustrates such complexity.[23] An astronomer and experimental scientist who learned the Algonquian language, Harriot joined the 1585 English expedition to Roanoke as its official geographer, working with the illustrator John White. Harriot hinted at potential connections between Algonquian and English people. He portrayed the Indigenous inhabitants of "Virginia" as humane and pious, "ingenious" and friendly. "Their priests," as Harriot put it, had showed him that "some religion they have already."[24] The people he met were "farre from the truth," yet they appeared eager to learn and amenable to both Christianization and colonization.[25]

Figure 1.2 De Bry, Algonquian dance

Credit: Thomas Harriot, *A briefe and true report of the new found land of Virginia* (Frankfort, 1590), Plate XVIII.

Harriot's text appeared in several editions, one of the most widely reprinted of which, first produced in 1590, included illustrations by Theodor De Bry, a Belgian Protestant engraver and publisher living in exile in London.[26] De Bry made his engravings after watercolor paintings by White, which were re-markable for their unelaborate representation of Carolina Algonquians. De Bry's stylized modifications of White's paintings included text from Harriot as captions.

One such image concerned a ceremonial dance, most likely part of an agri-cultural festival performed in Secotan, an Algonquian village on the Pamlico River near today's Outer Banks of North Carolina (see Figure 1.2).

The image features male and female figures, dancing around wood poles carved with faces at the tops. Three people embrace in the center of the circle, evoking the classical Muses. The dancers are spaced carefully, posed as participants in a choreographed ritual.[27]

Figure 1.3 De Bry, Secotan

Credit: Thomas Harriot, *A briefe and true report of the new found land of Virginia* (Frankfort, 1590), Plate XX.

In another engraving, of the central part of Secotan, De Bry—again, after White—placed a small image of the dance in a telling location (Figure 1.3).

The people of Secotan conducted their ceremony at the end of a row of three corn fields, each at a different stage of maturity. The image, at the lower right, includes a line of seated worshippers just outside the dance circle, looking in. White and De Bry identified the "place of solemn prayer" for the village, a circle in the ground with a fire, across a central pathway from the dance. Other villagers prepare a communal meal in the middle of the pathway. The corn abutted by an orderly ceremony, the ceremony attended by worshipful villagers, the common meal: together, these images reflected a logic of communal order, religious devotion, and agricultural fecundity. The artists portrayed Secotan religion as intelligible in English terms.[28]

Yet, in the hands of Purchas, the portrayal took on a more sinister cast. While he included observations of genuine religious sentiment and social virtue—"the Indians" (he named only the "Naragansetts" in passing), for example, believed in a supreme creator—Purchas's conclusion was harsh. Alarmed by reports of increasing Native hostility to English settlers in Virginia, Purchas claimed that the ordinary devotions of the Algonquian people tended toward the diabolical: the real "power they worship, whom they call Hobbamock," as he cribbed from John Smith's reports, was "the Devill," who appeared to control only malevolent forces and wield them ruthlessly.[29] Native idolatry caused social degeneracy, from rampant adultery and mistreatment of women to child sacrifice and arbitrary rule by powerful sachems. Like Harriot, however, Purchas presented a mélange of observations, not yet fixed into a consistent portrait of Native Americans.[30]

England's Confessional Ideology

Post-civil-wars writers took the raw material from Purchas (and his sources) and constructed relentlessly pejorative accounts of non-Protestant religions. They produced an apology for magisterial, patriotic, and socially responsible Protestantism and dismissed all other traditions, including radical Protestantism, as sources of disorder and disloyalty to the kingdom: alien, illegitimate, and unworthy of consideration. They crafted an ideology of religious difference.[31]

What prompted this hardening of Protestant rhetoric, a refusal to probe for any trace of religion or social virtue among Indigenous people? As this chapter's initial discussion of Crouch suggests, in the wake of the calamities of midcentury—the crises of the monarchy during the early 1640s, the failure of Parliament to establish a stable government, the trials of the Commonwealth during the early 1650s—many Protestants in England had turned their attention from the promotion of overseas ventures to internal affairs. Moreover, by some accounts, Oliver Cromwell's policies of religious toleration exacerbated factionalism among Protestants who competed for power: Presbyterians, Fifth Monarchists, Independents, Quakers, and Anglicans. Observers who claimed to be loyal to the government—to England—worried that the incoherence of England's religious order threatened to exacerbate political instability as well as to allow the growth of heresy and Catholicism. They urged parliamentary leaders and pastors to reinforce the constitution of the state by subduing factionalism within England and its colonies.[32]

Many European states had suffered through similar periods of violent upheaval, from the Wars of Religion in France (1562–1598) through the Thirty Years' War in central Europe (1618–1648). English writers knew well that several governments had, through regulation of religious practice, reestablished order, brought a measure of peace, and strengthened their rule. Such control often focused on the assertion of a confession—Catholic, Lutheran, or Reformed—that bound subjects together under the sovereign. What historians of Germany have called "confessionalization" often included toleration for dissent. It required dissenters, however, to obey the government, remain loyal to their country, and recognize the political legitimacy of the sovereign and the established confession. The Treaty of Westphalia, which ended the Thirty Years' War, encoded confessional mandates even as it obliged signatories to tolerate different confessional regimes in other states.[33]

From the early 1650s through the early 1680s, English Protestants such as Ross, Ogilby, and Crouch embraced the idea that England's welfare rested on common religious convictions: an English version of a confessional order.[34] Confessional claims predated 1640, to be sure, but they reemerged with urgency especially after the Interregnum. They came from several perspectives. In his 1651 *Leviathan*, Thomas Hobbes contended that the purpose of government was to reduce threats of violence from civil war, invasion, or crime and thereby secure peace—the protection of property and life. If, he argued, a national religion diminished religiously based discord and prompted obedience to the government and its laws, then such an establishment was indeed proper. The French Protestant theologian Moises Amyraut, whose works were translated into English and appeared in London beginning in 1660, made similar observations, tuned to broad Protestant sympathies. Lancelot Addison, the Anglican chaplain to English merchants in Tangier, who traveled through the Maghrib, claimed that the power of Islamic teachers had prevented civil war in the region. This offered a lesson for English people: supported by the government, a common religious tradition suppressed violence, encouraged virtue, united people, and therefore was, as he put it, "the only method to make a State happy."[35]

William Temple also provided evidence for the importance of a national confession. A career diplomat, Temple was appointed ambassador to the Netherlands following the second Anglo-Dutch War in 1665 and subsequently analyzed the strengths and weaknesses of the Dutch republic. Reputed to be a religious skeptic, he nonetheless contended, with reference to the Netherlands, that the strength of "a State" derived in part from the government's recognition of the religious character of its people. Much of his argument echoed Hobbes. Because religious consensus inhibited civil strife, war, and tyranny, he contended, governments were obliged to establish a confessional order. Temple observed that the nations he visited enjoyed prosperity to the extent that they promoted such an order. He cautioned, however, that no government could establish it by sheer fiat. It served best when it emerged gradually, from the ground up. The inscrutable wisdom of providence, he asserted, had made "the Reformed Profession" the creed in England, Scotland, Denmark, and Holland. It also had made "the Roman Catholique" profession dominant in France and Flanders. Whenever religious outsiders had attempted to "change" the "Religion in a Countrey, or Government" without a slow, providential transformation—"a general conversion of the people"—civil war ensued: "the miserable Effusion of Human Blood and the Confusion of all Laws, Orders, and Virtues." Temple mentioned France's Wars of Religion and gestured toward England's own civil wars.[36]

The Netherlands stood for Temple as the paradigmatic counterexample. Once the people as a whole embraced the Reformation, he argued, the Dutch government wisely made the tenets of the Reformed Church the official religion of the republic. Dutch magistrates had no call to prosecute any group for their particular theological beliefs as long as that group did not attempt to overthrow the official church or disavow allegiance to the republic. This condition excluded Catholics, who, according to Temple, were disloyal to the republic, but it allowed the government to tolerate Jewish congregations and nearly any Protestant "Sect," including Anabaptist groups. Temple's recommendation of the Dutch model of toleration was unusually prescient, anticipating post–Glorious Revolution developments.[37]

To be sure, it was no simple matter to define the boundaries of England's confession. Most subjects in England identified with the established church—its Prayer Book liturgies, episcopal polity, and creed as defined in its Thirty-Nine Articles—even as dissenting groups grew during this period. Anglicans and non-Anglican Protestants often debated the legal status of nonconformity during the 1660s and 1670s. Pressed by highly placed Anglican officials, Parliament passed several statutes from 1661 to 1665, together called the Clarendon Code, intended to restrict dissent. The Code required municipal officeholders to take the sacraments at their local Anglican church, excluded dissenters from official clerical status, and criminalized nonconforming worship that included more than four nonresidents. Widespread debate about such measures, however, along with frequent neglect to enforce the Clarendon Code at the local level, reflected disagreement, even faction. Parliament considered and nearly passed several bills that would have enhanced legal protections for dissenters (chiefly Presbyterians and Independents) who confirmed the legitimacy of an established Church of England. Confessional consensus was a lofty conceit amid the rough and tumble of ecclesiastical politics.[38]

Anglo-American Protestants nonetheless constructed the ideal of a broad Protestant confession as an answer to faction, a remedy for disunity. They meant it as a consensus, a cultural norm, to which Anglicans and dissenters alike could agree despite sometimes fierce arguments over liturgies, bishops, and parliamentary regulations. They claimed that England might be held together by orthodox Protestant theology and loyalty to the kingdom: a capacious definition of English Protestantism that better served England's interests than did strictures such as the Clarendon Code. In such terms, Anglo-American Protestants thought, a Protestant confession, even without a formal creed to which all parties consented, merited popular credence and support by the government. It included Anglicans, Presbyterians, moderate Independents (later called Congregationalists), other Reformed traditions, and proto-deists. These were all Protestants who—again, the term magisterial fits—respected the national government and its monarchy as divinely appointed institutions. Such a definition excluded millenarians such as the Fifth Monarchists, who conducted ill-fated rebellions in 1657 and 1661, as well as Quakers. Many New Englanders voiced discontent with the colonial policies of the restored Stuart regime and valorized the idea of godly resistance to tyrants but nonetheless feared disorder and recognized the legitimacy of the monarchy, at least as a court of appeal for colonial complainants. Confessional observers on both sides of the Atlantic looked to their churches, established or not, to promote national solidarity in the aftermath of political revolution and constitutional crises.[39]

Protestant confessionalism informed Parliament especially in 1680, when several members proposed a bill that would have excluded Roman Catholics from the throne—a proposal aimed at Charles II and his presumed successor, the Duke of York (the future James II), the latter of whom was suspected to have converted to Catholicism. This bill failed, but the Exclusion Crisis heightened confessional zeal, especially in the form of anti-Catholic outcries over papal aggressions against Protestants in Europe, intimations of Jesuit plans for a coup d'état, and rumors of a papal conspiracy to assassinate Charles—the so-called Popish Plot. Demands for Protestant and political solidarity eclipsed the efforts of Stuart apologists, who attempted to refurbish ideas of toleration for Catholics and liberty of conscience that had circulated for decades (more on the Stuarts and the issue of toleration in Chapter 3).[40]

Confessional Descriptions of the World's Religions

Fixed on a confessional remedy to England's disorders, Protestant writers from the end of the civil wars through the Restoration built the ad hoc observations of Purchas and his predecessors into a systematic critique of non-Protestant religions. They tarred all such traditions with the same brush—superstitious, idolatrous, and disorderly. This was not just theological polemic or an imperial justification for the subjugation of indigenous people. It was a warning to loyal subjects that all religions outside of magisterial Protestantism fomented misrule and disunity.

Alexander Ross, the most influential writer about the world's religions during the Interregnum, shaped much of his work to confessional concerns. Ross's 1653 *Pansebia: Or, A View of the Religions of the World*, offered non-technical descriptions of the world's religions.[41] It echoed through a range of later Protestant texts, including travel accounts, encyclopedias or dictionaries of religion, geographies, and sensationalistic chap books such as Crouch's *Strange and Prodigious Religions*. It was translated into Dutch, French, and German. Going through ten English editions by 1697, it became a staple of Anglo-Protestant reading on both sides of the Atlantic. It was a bestseller in England, quoted by John Milton, held in the library of Harvard College, and well known to Boston divines such as the Mathers, the Princes, and Jonathan Edwards.[42]

The erstwhile chaplain to Charles I, Ross articulated his perspective as early as 1642, at the beginning of the civil wars. He predicted then that the multiplication of what he called "many sorts of Religions" in England would bring "tumultuous disorders." He provided a peculiar list of such false "Religions,"

chiefly Protestant sectarian and radical movements with unconventional social practices and political views, as well as crypto-Catholicism.[43] He framed
Pansebia accordingly, arguing that traditional, staid Anglicanism—modest
in both ceremony and theology—was essential to England's welfare. Yet
he also commended some of the ideas of magisterial dissenters such as the
Presbyterians, who, by his account, had good Reformed theology even if
they wrongly rejected episcopacy. He never defined the boundaries of true
English Protestantism. He nonetheless asserted that the state should not tolerate "Pluralities of Religion." There ought to be "Publickly One Religion"
only, he insisted, because only a single confession could promote the "Love,
Unity, and Concord" that bound kingdoms together. Right belief sustained
national solidarity.[44]

In light of the disruptions under parliamentary rule at midcentury,
Ross added a critique of separatist Protestantism to the denunciations
of Catholicism that had appeared in Purchas. He did so by comparing the
ecstasies, enthusiasms, falsehoods, intemperance, and deceits of radical
Protestants to the worst forms of paganism. "In reading this Book," Ross
warned, "we shall find, that the whole rabble of vain, phantastical, or profane
opinions, with which at this day, this miserable distracted Nation is pestered,
are not new revelations, but old dreams" of heathens and idolaters.[45]

In no small feat of historical creativity, Ross attempted to expose the errors
of radical Protestantism by projecting them onto the medieval church. He
warned fellow Englishmen that the Roman Church's illegitimate claims to
authority, fabrications, and errors led to confusion on a grand scale. He focused on Catholic doctrines of post-apostolic revelation, which resulted
in sectarian division and heresy. By his account, heretical sects and orders
had multiplied from medieval times. Bethlemites, Montesians, Eremites,
Templars, and Gladiatores, among others, constituted a roll call of misled
Catholic enthusiasts that mirrored the proliferation of Anabaptist separatists
and misfits who also claimed special revelation. The "new revelations"
of Protestant sectarians, he asserted, merely replicated Catholic idolatry.
Furthermore, Ross paraphrased Purchas to argue that Catholic devotional
regimes echoed pagan rituals. Prayers to the saints, adoration of relics, devotion to the clergy, preoccupation with priestly garments, and the glo-
rification of eucharistic vessels—indeed, many of the details of the Mass
itself—represented falsehood, paganism, and misrule.[46]

Ross presented Islam in similar terms: analogous to the confusions of
sectarian Protestantism and to the errors of Catholicism at the same time.

Reflecting the confessional tendency to pair each religion with one or more civil states, he identified "Mahumetanism" chiefly with Ottoman Turkey, which menaced Venice and Austria through the 1660s. It was one of Europe's "two prevalent Religions," with Christianity as its competitor and military nemesis. He shaped his summary of Islam into a contrast with magisterial Protestantism: Protestant Christianity taught its adherents to rely on God's grace for salvation even as they attempted to honor God through moral and spiritual rectitude, while Islam instructed its devotees to save themselves through meritorious works, all the while inculcating hedonism, licentiousness, and violence.[47]

Ross offered what had become a standard summary of Islamic teaching—on, for example, Muhammad, duties to parents, prayer, Ramadan ("their yearly Lent"), almsgiving, and pilgrimage—without any commendation. The whole point of Islamic "Law," Ross contended, was to provide a means for Muslim men to merit a "Paradise" filled with physical pleasure: "silken Carpets, pleasant rivers, fruitful trees, beautiful women, musick, good cheer, and choice wines, store of gold and silver plate" and "other such conceits." According to Ross, then, Muslims tolerated a plurality of beliefs, Jewish and Christian included, because they cared more about a carnal paradise than they did about religious truth. The major schools of Islamic thought—Turkish Sunni and Persian Shiite—had, he claimed, completely different notions of God altogether, each equally absurd.[48]

Without sound theological grounding, Islamic teaching and practice, by Ross's account, fell into irrationality and inconsistency. He claimed that Muslims prohibited images of the divine and took offense at Christian iconography yet recommended worship of the sun and moon. They also, he maintained, allowed polygamy and believed that "the Devils shall be saved." Their "religious Orders," often small fellowships under an imam, were "wicked and irreligious," dens of pederasty, sodomy, and fornication. Sufi dervishes lived "beastly and beggarly" lives, filled with "ignorance and idleness." They scarred themselves with hot irons, robbed innocent travelers, assassinated their enemies, and ingested intoxicating herbs to rouse them into their frenzied dances. Members of other orders paraded through the streets nearly naked, slashing their bodies with knives.[49]

Ross's disparagement of what he maintained was the Islamic emphasis on human works to merit salvation echoed Protestant critiques of Catholicism. His account of competing religious orders, ascetic practices, and mendicancy mirrored Protestant depictions of Catholic orders, lay and religious. He couched his description of Muslim clerics in Roman Catholic terms: a hierarchy of "Priests" under "their Pope" or grand "Mophti" (mufti) who impinged on the powers of the civil monarch, an "Ecclesiasticall" court that adjudicated civil and religious affairs, and their promotion of "superstition"—a frequent Protestant invective against medieval traditions. Ross's report on the annual pilgrimage to Mecca conjured Catholic pilgrimages to holy sites in Italy or in Jerusalem as portrayed by Protestant travelers such as Lithgow: streams of credulous pilgrims who were fleeced by local merchants or robbed by bandits, veneration of sepulchers and "holy Reliques," adoration of sacred objects, and a plethora of rituals the observance of which falsely promised salvation.[50]

Ross's descriptions also called to mind the radical Protestants who, emboldened by Parliament's suspension of statutes enforcing religious conformity, brought disorder to England during the late 1640s and 1650s. According to Ross, Muslim tolerance for religious diversity had allowed the multiplication of sectarian groups whose practices were immoral and antisocial. Some of their adherents "brag of Revelations, Visions, and Enthusiasms," just as did Quakers and civil-war-era millenarians in England. Others were "*Antinomians*, affirming that there is no use of the Law, but that men are saved by Grace." Here Ross replicated the accusation of immorality and spiritual degeneracy with which orthodox Protestants impugned a variety of free-grace advocates in England and New England. Yet again, by Ross's reading, others, much like Baptist or Mennonite sectarians, imposed strict disciplines of prayer, fasting, and "other spiritual exercises" on their members. *Pansebia* concludes with a brief survey of false teachers and imposters, including the Anabaptist radicals Thomas Muntzer, John of Leiden, and Henry Nicholas, as well as "Mahomet," as though they all belonged in the same basket of misrule. Ross fashioned Islam into a nearly anarchistic, often debauched, certainly disorderly religion. His was not so much an account of Islam as it was a comment on post-civil-war England itself: the misrule caused by open-ended toleration and confessional confusion.[51]

The prospect of religious betrayal in England also provided Ross with interpretive keys to the religions of Asia and indigenous traditions on the fringes of Europe. His description of so-called pagan rituals, be they Chinese, Slavic, or Laplander, focused on shamans or religious teachers who misled people through tricks or false prophecies. One ceremony of the Samoyed or Nenet people of Nova Zembla, he explained, rested on "juggling illusions." A priest would pretend to plunge a dismembered deer into boiling water after which the deer emerged whole and alive, all the while blinding the people with smoke that concealed a live, hidden deer as a prop. It paralleled the ritual magic of the Catholic Mass or the ruses of millenarian radicals who during the days of the Rump Parliament beguiled crowds with candlelit orations and false prophecies.[52]

Ross was even more emphatic in his combined political and religious critique of Native American traditions. Unlike contemporary French commentators, who detected signs of ancient wisdom in Native American religiosity, or Harriot, who pondered an instinctive Native American accord with Christian teaching, Ross fathomed nothing but sadistic frenzy. In his caricature, the Algonquian inhabitants of Virginia "worshipped the Devil," as evidenced by their nighttime rituals of dancing around the fire while howling and throwing deer's blood and tobacco on stone altars. They embraced savagery and rejected civility, he argued. More so than did earlier writers such as Purchas, Ross claimed that disorder and violence accompanied all Indigenous practices in America.[53]

Many other observers likewise inflected their accounts with confessional assumptions. John Josselyn's widely cited travelogues were typical. An aspiring naturalist whose family had large landholdings and positions of power in England and Maine, Josselyn visited New England in 1638 and from 1663 to 1671. Josselyn was a staunch Anglican, yet in New England he formed friendships with puritan leaders, whom he regarded as Protestant allies. Unlike Harriot and Purchas, he mentioned nothing of religious intuition among the Native people that he observed. By his account, Narragansetts, Abanakis, and Wampanoags gave credence only to infernal deities who afflicted them with diseases and terrorized them with frightful apparitions. Conflating anti-Catholic, anti-witchcraft, and anti-Native rhetoric, Josselyn maintained that "they live in wretched consternation worshipping the Devil for fear," deceived by "Priests" or "*Powaws*" who were "little better than Witches" and visited by "infernal spirits" who flew above Native villages in the forms of enemy warriors or English soldiers. Josselyn claimed that Native spiritual leaders were devilish in teaching Native peoples to view the English as devils. Such confusion incited unrest and violence, a threat to English landholding and political stability. The people were, in Josselyn's words, "angry," "malicious," revengeful, and "barbarously cruel," as well as "very lecherous," polygamous, and prone to theft and begging.[54]

From 1670 through 1683, other writers shaped the ongoing accumulation of reports on various religions into readable, simplified histories and geographies. One of the more highly placed authors in such terms was John Ogilby. Royal cartographer and geographer for Charles II, Ogilby authored geographical encyclopedias of non-European countries. His 1671 *America*, a folio of 674 pages with fifty-seven engravings and maps, combined depictions of political and economic institutions with descriptions of religious practices.[55]

His tome offered a narrative of the progress of English colonization in America: sound and prosperous when conducted with loyalty to the crown and England's religious traditions, weak and ineffectual when tainted by sectarian dissent. By his reading, Massachusetts Bay puritans sometimes followed their better angels (those who delivered messages from the royal court) but were tempted by separatism. They never grasped the importance of kingdom and confession as interdependent agendas. Their opposition to bishops and "crying up *Liberty of Conscience*" misled them to disregard their duties to the kingdom. Ad hoc, arbitrary rule followed, each New England colony with its own laws, as did incompetent management of relations with Native peoples.[56]

Ogilby's other works, including his 1673 *Asia, the First Part*, a survey of Persia and India dedicated to Charles II, also reflected state-building, confessional norms. India served as a case in point. He included a composite image of a temple in northern India, cobbled together from previously published sources. The image includes a variety of devotional objects and practices: statues of assorted deities and mythical beasts on the walls, devotees at a fire, and, at the front and center, worshippers dressed in Persian garb kneeling before an obelisk that Ogilby identifies with the deity Mahadeva (Shiva) (Figure 1.4).

The text provided information on the Vedas, role of Brahmans, deities, processions, and purification rites: components of what later British observers called Hinduism. According to Ogilby, Indian syncretism and "idolatry" produced a general confusion and ignorance among the people, expressed in factionalism and violence. The only semblance of political order, which was slight, appeared during the Mughal Empire, when Muslims had insisted on religious and political supremacy and suppressed the Brahmans.[57]

In North America, according to Ogilby, non-Protestant religions produced a succession of miseries. Ogilby attacked Aztec culture as a mixture of human sacrifice, ritual cannibalism, and worship of rulers. According to Ross, Spanish settlers who became rich from Aztec gold and Catholic monks who dozed in their cloisters shamelessly tolerated such brutality.

Figure 1.4 Ogilby, Indian temple
Credit: John Ogilby, *Asia, the First Part* (London, 1673), 146.

His depiction of Algonquian peoples in the Tidewater region, drawn from Purchas, highlighted the power of "King Powhatan" and hostilities between Powhatan and English people, culminating in Indian "Treachery and Cruelty to the *English*." One of Ogilby's striking illustrations—a transposition of an earlier image from Mexico into a Virginia setting—featured Powhatan and "his Court" (Figure 1.5)

Ogilby pictured a larger-than-life likeness of Powhatan or an idol representing the sachem on a platform, reverenced by attendants, worshipped by dancers, served by concubines and slaves. At the feet of the idol is an altar of sacrifice with several corpses nearby. The building takes the form of a rough palace. The image of Powhatan as a human ruler and oversized idol at the same time conflates false religion and frightful power. In Virginia, no less than Mexico, inhumane politics and idolatry went together.[58]

Although Ogilby described differences among Native American religious expressions, he linked all of those expressions to disorder and degenerate so-cial behavior. It was nearly impossible for him "to describe to whom" Native people directed their devotions. The Tidewater Algonquians, for example,

Figure 1.5 Ogilby, Powhatan

Credit: John Ogilby, *America: Being the Latest and Most Accurate Description of the New World* (London, 1671), 200.

embraced what Ogilby counted as a confusion of deities and rituals, including a "good God" and an "evil God," "Necromantick Charms" (invoking spirits of the dead for magical powers) and "Conjuration" of their "Powows" or religious leaders. He replicated Ross's description of nighttime ceremonies with wild dances and ecstatic trances around fire, all evidence of "diabolical Worship." The religion of Iroquoian peoples in New York, filled with what he portrayed as silly myths that legitimated the worship of animals, was no better. By Ogilby's account, Mohawks valorized warfare, cruelty, violence, and cannibalism. He described instances of civility among Narragansetts in eastern Massachusetts or what he in English diction called the southeast "Shires." They were friendly among themselves, upheld their promises in matters of trade, and were "industrious" in maintaining their domiciles. Yet Native "Sachems" tolerated murder and violated treaties made with English commissioners.[59]

Acknowledging the conscientiousness of puritan missionaries to New England, Ogilby also commented on the conversion of some Native peoples to Christianity and its political ramifications. They relinquished "their former Fopperies" and acknowledged "the Power of the *English*-man's God, as they call him." Indigenous converts "would say King *James* was good, and his God good, but their [god] *Tanto* nought." Yet Ogilby lamented the infrequency and impermanence of such conversions. Most Natives rejected the moral demands of Christianity in favor of "the libidinous Pleasures of a lazy life" and resisted English dominion. They had not become truly English. Ogilby gave a reading informed less by ethnographic knowledge than by the discourse of political sovereignty and religious confession.[60]

Other writers conveyed confessional perspectives through inexpensive publications—much more accessible and affordable than Ogilby's lengthy and elaborately illustrated works. No author, editor, or publisher matched Crouch in this regard. Cribbing from Purchas, Ross, and Ogilby, he produced cheap, abbreviated surveys with simple lessons, all punctuated by pugnacious commentary. "You have in this Piece," as he introduced his *Strange and Prodigious Religions*, enough "to satisfie thy Curiosity" about "fantastical Ceremonies," "Schisms and Heresies," the "Imposter *Mahomet*," as well as "a Description of the diverse and ridiculous Rites of most Nations." Crouch offered excerpts taken from Ross, including nearly verbatim accounts of Native American dances and the Nova Zembla priests with their deer.[61]

He linked these stories with commentary on England's Protestant confession. "True Religion," he began his survey, had degenerated into paganism and idolatry in other parts of the world, tending to error and social disorder: the violence of Catholicism in Europe, the devilish idolatries of Native Americans, and the "Tautologies, Incoherencies," and "Absurdities" of Islam in Arabia, Turkey, and Persia. He admitted that English people had entertained millenarian and antinomian heresies in the frenzy of the civil wars. Yet the kingdom recovered its religious sanity by a return to its confessional moorings. To be born English was to inherit an authentic, reasonable, and wholesome religion, which is to say magisterial Protestantism.[62]

Unlike Ross, who spared a scant, confused four pages out of *Pansebia*'s 550 for western African traditions, Crouch devoted dozens of pages to the religious practices in "Guinea," a catch-all term for the coast from Senegambia south through the Gulf of Guinea, including Sierra Leone, the Gold Coast (today's Ghana), and the Congo (or Congo-Angola). In his *English Acquisitions in Guinea and East-India*—the "acquisitions" could refer to land and forts, treaties with local kings, commodities, and slaves all at once—he surveyed the "Guinea" territories in which the Royal African Company, chartered in 1660, had established trading posts and forts.[63] Written after the Revolution of 1688 but still reflecting a confessional perspective, Crouch's work introduced his readers to the concept of fetish worship as a type of "Paganism." Crouch used the term "Fetiche," coming from the Latin for "made by hand" and entering English through the Portuguese, to stand for small handmade objects carried in small sacks, hung around necks, or placed on the ground: amulets made of animals' teeth, piles of soil mixed with suet in which feathers were placed, the heads of small animals, woven circles of straw, animal horns stuffed with dung. As Crouch explained, such fetishes were deployed to remedy illness, protect holders against wild animals, and usher the dead into the afterlife.[64]

Crouch described practices akin to western definitions of religion in the middle regions of Guinea, from today's Sierra Leone to Ghana. He claimed that sometimes a local "Priest," whom the people "call Fetissero," received gold in return for which he preached, made grain and oil offerings to the sea on behalf of fishermen, sprinkled children with water from a basin in which swam snakes, and received advice for "the King" from special trees strewn with ashes. Some people danced and roared in adoration of a new moon. In only one area, according to Crouch, did people pray to an "Almighty," who in the afterlife punished misdeeds and rewarded "well-doers."[65]

Crouch and other Protestants in his day thought that the collection of practices from Guinea were arbitrary and disorderly in the extreme: so localized and indiscriminate, so focused on every-day and sometimes repellent things, as to defy common notions of religion. It appeared to them that different people in different Guinean territories used a confusion of mundane objects to ward off evil powers, including amulets, bits and pieces of animals and the heads of enemies killed in battle, dirt and feathers, grain and oil, trees that were oracles, snakes, tuna fish, the sea itself, and new moons. According to Crouch, the people of the western African coast venerated malevolence itself: powers that caused storms, incited attacks by fearsome beasts, and brought sickness yet never appeared as deities who revealed moral codes, devotional obligations, or overarching purposes. It was no wonder, Crouch maintained, that the kingdoms of Guinea suffered civil wars, usurpations, and disturbances. Civil disorder, as Crouch believed, followed from religious confusion.[66]

Furthermore, Crouch intimated that the materiality of Guinean practice reflected a people bereft of reason and spirituality. It was as though the Guineans were mere bodies attending to mere objects. As Crouch wrote about the string of forts that served the Royal African Company and facilitated trade in those bodies—the commodification of the people of Guinea—he expressed no qualms. He put the issue rather starkly: the company exported to Africa iron, arms, and tools, and imported to England "Elephants Teeth" and spices, "besides numbers of Negroes for supplying the American Plantations." That trade served the kingdom for which Crouch held such esteem. The nature of Guinean worship, as Crouch described it, occluded the humanity of enslaved people and the moral dilemmas of slave-trading.[67]

In his 1685 *The English Empire in America*, Crouch presented Indigenous American traditions as more purposeful, more indicative of a cultural and political system, than were the fetish practices he belittled in his account of Guinea.[68] Yet as he assembled his account of European encounters with Native Americans, he reproduced the standard confessional narrative. He decried Native American traditions tout court. He claimed that they were as disordered and illegitimate as was the whole of Catholicism.

He framed *The English Empire in America* with the claim that English Protestantism went hand in hand with orderly rule, Spanish Catholicism and Indigenous traditions with savagery. Early English adventurers such as the Cabot brothers, Martin Frobisher, and Francis Drake, Crouch claimed, served the crown with valor and avoided carnage. By contrast, the Spanish brought barbarism and "cruelty" wherever they went, from Mexico to Peru. Their assaults—again, an evocation of civil-war-torn England—culminated in the regicide of "glorious Monarchs," the desolation of towns, and horrid bloodshed. As for Native peoples, Crouch offered his readers a parade of curiosities from Newfoundland to Virginia: "whimsical" and "ridiculous" myths, "Prayers to the Devil," "Magical Rites," and "howling Devotions." According to Crouch, Native American religion belonged with all non-Protestant religions in its valorization of misrule, violence, and fury. Like his contemporaries and unlike Harriot, Crouch saw Native American religiosity as the antithesis of nearly everything English: ideas of the deity, notions of morality, social practices, and attendant political loyalties.[69]

We can illustrate this with reference to Crouch's visual representations of Native American ceremonies. Recall Figure 1.2 in this chapter: De Bry's engraving after John White's paintings of the Secotan agricultural ceremony. For De Bry and Harriot, the ritual suggested a Native culture compatible with English ideas of society and prepared for Christianization. Not so for Crouch, who in the post-civil-wars milieu presented all non-Protestant traditions as affronts to Christian truth and English identity. He produced a remarkably different image of the Secotan dance, included in his *English Empire* on a page of illustrations with the caption "Strange Creatures in America." Crouch's note under the image directs the reader to a passage in the text clearly cribbed from Harriot, yet Crouch's picture conveys nothing of the complexity of De Bry's images (Figure 1.6).[70]

Crouch offered a simple drawing without the facial expressions, dress, or poses of White's and De Bry's figures. He also jumbled the dancers together, evoking disorder rather than a choreographed ritual. There is no surrounding village to suggest a place of the dance in communal affairs and devotion. The dancers appear in a mosaic of inhuman creatures, alongside strange birds and beastly reptiles. Crouch rendered them alien to English readers.

Crouch's prose deepened the disparagement. Native Americans adored natural forces, such as fire and water, and devoted themselves to "the Devil." They attempted to appease "Infernal Spirits" who appeared as enemies in the

Figure 1.6 Crouch, Secotan dance
Credit: R. B. [Nathaniel Crouch], *The English Empire in America* (London, 1685), after 164.

form of Mohawk warriors or flames in the sky, an image of which Crouch included among his illustrations. Political betrayal followed devilish devotion.
According to his version of the history of New England, puritans had settled
the land under the kind patronage of King James and made reasonable
treaties with the Native inhabitants. All went well until sachems consulted
"with their Priests and Conjurers," who were "little better than Witches" and
advised an uprising. Under King Philip (Metacom) they betrayed English
trust and "with all manner of Barbarity and Cruelty" waged war until God
punished them. The cause of such perfidy could be traced to a debased religion that had rendered them as wild and irrational as were Protestant
dissenters like the Fifth Monarchists.[71]

Confessional readings of the world's religions had become widespread
enough in Restoration England to serve as popular amusement, at least by
the estimation of Henry Winstanley. An engraver, architect, engineer, and
painter, Winstanley returned to London after a tour of the Continent during
the mid-1670s. He used his knowledge of other cultures to take advantage
of a new market for playing cards in the wake of the government's recen-
sion of Commonwealth-era restrictions on gaming devices. Winstanley also
knew that there was a demand for information in the capital about people
outside of England. Using images and prose from geography books alongside his own impressions, he produced a set of cards that featured illustrated
vignettes of the nations and lands of the world.[72]

Winstanley's cards undoubtedly entertained—they sold well—and gave
lessons that blended descriptions of religious practices into political and economic summaries, which enforced the lesson that creed and government
belonged equally to the public order. Each card, from King down to Two,
presented what Winstanley called a "nation," meaning a country, region, or
land. The top half of the cards had arresting images: two figures, dressed in
the presumed costume of the land, with a perspective of a notable town or
city in the background. The bottom half contained a brief description of the
geography, history, and religion of each country. Each of the four suits of the
cards represented a continent—America, Asia, Africa, and Europe—with
Aces introducing the continent in general.

The King of Hearts informed players about the English, with a list, in no
logical sequence, of rivers, cities, universities, monarchs, and bishoprics of
the Church of England. On the Nine of Hearts, Winstanley described the
Spaniards: the consolidation of previously separate kingdoms under the
monarch in Madrid, their pilgrimage site at Compostela, excellent wines,

Figure 1.7 and 1.8 Winstanley, England, Spain
Credit: Henry Winstanley, Geographical Playing Cards, c. 1675, Huntington Library, San Marino, California

and abundant seaports. They had been "in religion Romanists [Catholics]" for a "long" time (Figures 1.7 and 1.8).

For America, Winstanley devoted the King of Clubs to Virginians, with an account of their government and mix of native "Idolaters" and settlers who "Conform to the Episcopal Government and Liturgy of the Church of England" (Figure 1.9). The text on the inhabitants of New England, inscribed on the Queen of Clubs, explains that "Presbyterian" churches—an imprecise term for puritan congregations—belonged to the orderly settlements of the seaboard, while "Fanaticks," meaning separatist Protestants, hid among the western woods along with "Savage Inhabitants" (Figure 1.10). The Nine of Clubs carried a brief on the people of Mexico, or New Spain, with their riches in gold and cattle, "Beautiful" cities, system of colonial government, and a reflection on the irony of their religious history: once suffering under Aztec rulers who built "Magnificent Temples" and sacrificed "Thousands of Children" to "Idols," Indigenous people now were "Sacrificed in the Mines" owned by Spanish Catholics (Figure 1.11).

Figure 1.9, 1.10 and 1.11 Winstanley, Virginia, New England, Mexico
Credit: Henry Winstanley, Geographical Playing Cards, c. 1675, Huntington
Library, San Marino, California

Winstanley's cards also portrayed completely foreign lands and peoples, as two final examples show.[73] The Queen of Spades pictures the people of Morocco, who lived in the recently united kingdoms of Morocco and Fez. According to the description, a mixture of mosques, hospitals, public baths, and royal palaces dominated their architecture. Pirates from their ports plagued English shipping. Their "Religion," as Winstanley succinctly put it, was "Mahometan" (Figure 1.12). The people of India apart from the Moghul Empire, as described on the Four of Diamonds, had large cities, a rich spice trade conducted through Portuguese colonies, a history of political contestation, and distasteful religion. They were a "Barbarous People," with "thousands of Idols," who allegedly honored their deceased friends by eating them (Figure 1.13).

Even with their peculiar customs, however, the people of Morocco and India resembled those of Spain and England. Winstanley's cards informed the attentive gamester that religious traditions and political institutions were interdependent in every land, so that people inherited their religious identity along with their political or civic identity. Outside of mainstream English Protestantism, religion was implicated in villainy and brutality: the savagery of Native Americans, the misanthropy of Protestant separatists hiding in the woods of New England, the horrors of Aztec and Catholic rule alike in Mexico, the piracy of Muslim Morocco, or the cannibalism of what came to

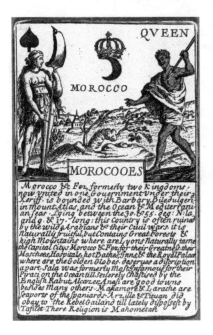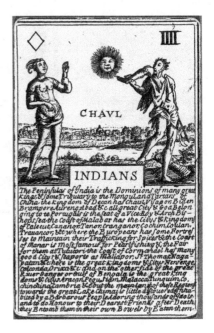

Figure 1.12 and 1.13 Winstanley, Morocco, India
Credit: Henry Winstanley, Geographical Playing Cards, c. 1675, Huntington
Library, San Marino, California

be known as "Hindu" India. Loyal subjects of English rule, by contrast, were
favored with magisterial Protestantism, which produced stability, learning,
and national prosperity. The lesson was as clear on playing cards as it was in
the dictionary of Ross and the geographies of Ogilby and Crouch: all English
people ought to confirm their mutual and common identities as English and
Protestant.

Taking many of their impressions from Purchas and his library of travelers,
writers such as Ross, Ogilby, and Crouch, not to mention the card-maker
Winstanley, articulated a common discourse of the religious "other." They
intermingled creed, church polity, civic government, and national economy.
They placed religion alongside political institutions as part of a national regime, arguing that rulers had a vested interest in promoting a particular
confession as a matter of public discipline. They believed that descriptions
of other religions as idolatrous and devilish—a rubric under which all

non-Protestant religions fell—underpinned political solidarity at home and justified control over settlers and indigenous populations abroad.

Crouch was one of the last commentators who read other religions as reflections of the trials of the Interregnum. His works in fact appeared even as political changes in England had begun to push the distress of midcentury into the background of Protestant memory. The popularity of his work nonetheless indicates the sway that the confessional mode had over Restoration-era observers of religion and the kingdom. Their confessional assumptions originated in various, overlapping political agendas: designs for global empire, critique of factionalism, and support for the state-building projects of the Restoration monarchy. Even Protestant dissenters and critics of the Stuarts contended that English and Protestant identities were inextricably interdependent and that non-Protestant beliefs led to political and social degeneracy.

Those contentions informed Anglo-American Protestants as they pondered the multiple religions with which they were increasingly in contact. Confessional assumptions also raised questions. How were Protestants to think of genuine faith or conversion in a world of inherited religious identities? Could one change one's religion? How? What were their obligations to spread the Protestant message to England's Indigenous subjects (as they viewed them) in America? It is to their answers, reflected in Protestant missions to Native Americans in seventeenth-century New England, that we turn.

2

Praying Indians

Nathaniel Crouch offered vignettes not only of the world's religions but also of the conversion of English men and women to saving faith. One of the more sensational accounts of the latter, included in Crouch's *Mercy Triumphant in the Conversion of Sinners unto God*, concerned an elite woman in London during the 1630s. Although M. K., as the text refers to her, was raised as a Protestant in an England saturated with what Crouch presumed was true religion, she underwent conversion only after an arduous spiritual journey. Her story turned on thoughts of murder, a midnight intervention by the family dog, and the counsel of a famous preacher.[1]

According to her autobiography, as edited by Crouch, M. K. was the daughter of "godly" parents who taught her to read the Bible and the works of spiritual writers. Her parents' deaths when she was a teenager threw her into distress. She wondered whether their demise came as punishment for her sins. Taking counsel from "Godly friends, and reverend Divines," she moved to London (the location of her parents' home is never mentioned), married the son of a preacher, and settled in Westminster.[2] Her husband, alas, fell into dissolute socializing. She then became so filled with "hatred" toward his drinking partners that she had a dream in which she was about to grab a knife and murder one of them. "But God," she exclaimed, intervened. The scripture promise of Deuteronomy 32:35—"vengeance is mine"—came to her mind during sleep. She awoke free of her homicidal intentions, full of "good charity" and trusting God for justice.[3]

Spiritually awakened, M. K. entered a period of self-scrutiny. She meditated on the Ten Commandments and discovered her corruption: her heart as "a sink of sin, a Cage of unclean Birds, and Den of Theeves."[4] She tried but failed to draw near to Christ for mercy, falling into such despair that she could think of "no God, no Jesus" but only of "Hell" filled with "Devils" poised to carry her to destruction. One night during this period of distress, as she slept, something leapt onto the bed. She screamed in terror, thinking that it was the "Devil" coming to take her away. When she awoke to the affections of the family dog instead, she felt such relief that she resolved once again to

The Opening of the Protestant Mind. Mark Valeri, Oxford University Press. © Oxford University Press 2023.
DOI: 10.1093/oso/9780197663677.003.0003

pursue the God who had "preserved" her through her troubles.[5] She did so by using "the meanes" to conversion commonly described in puritan writing. Three or four times a week she attended the sermons of John Dod, a puritan preacher nicknamed "Decalogue Dod" for his expositions of the moral law of the Old Testament. She also took counsel from Dod, an advisor to dissenting families and worthies such as John Cotton. She studied the Bible and prayed. Once again, however, her exertions failed her. She doubted whether she would ever undergo conversion.[6]

When she was at her lowest point, unassured of God's love, she read in John 6 that "No man can come to me, except the Father . . . draw him." That text keyed her spiritual transformation. She pleaded with Christ to do what she could not do by herself: "turn me and I shall be turned; convert me and I shall be converted." She relinquished her will and striving. She confided instead in Christ's work and came to "faith." As she put it, she gained "assurance" and confessed that "I know I do believe and am regenerated by the Holy Ghost." She thereafter related evidence of her conversion: her desire for Christ, joy at the prospect of heaven, love for Christ's people, and contentment at her "Calling" in life.[7]

M. K.'s narrative reflected many of the ideas and practices of England's puritan community. Evidence suggests that Crouch took it from a 1653 book of narratives edited by Vavasor Powell, an eccentric but nonetheless popular preacher who had strong puritan connections.[8] Reformed divines such as Dod and Cotton did not counsel people to rely on dreams or dogs. Yet puritan tropes otherwise shaped M. K.'s narrative: references to "godly" parents and friends, the use of "meanes," and quotations from scripture. The story's emphasis on self-scrutiny and M. K.'s sense of sinfulness, as well as her resolve, Bible reading, attendance on preaching, love for the believing community, and contentment in calling mirrored puritan teaching on the spiritual life. Moreover, its focus on M. K.'s subdued will and total reliance on God's power to "convert" her replicated Reformed ideas about the process of conversion as a divine work in the face of human incapacity.

We can pair the story of M. K. with another report first published in London in 1653—this time from an Indigenous community in New England. It appeared in *Tears of Repentance*, a record of the oral testimonies or relations of faith of fifteen Massachusetts Natives, edited by missionary pastors John Eliot and Thomas Mayhew, Jr. The testimonies were given in the "praying town" of Natick (more on "praying towns" below) to convince neighboring ministers and political leaders to authorize the establishment of an Indian church in the town, which they did some seven years later. One of the more detailed relations came from a man named Monequassun, who eventually learned English and became a schoolteacher in Natick.[9]

Eliot's transcription began with Monequassun's confession of "lusts, thefts," and other sins. When Monequassun encountered Eliot's ministry at Natick, including instruction in Christian prayer and sermons from the Bible, he "hated it" and considered "running away." He nonetheless stayed at Natick and listened to Eliot's teaching. He began to pray in a Christian fashion, "learn the ten Commandments of God," and absorb Protestant doctrine or, as he put it, the "points of Catechisme."[10]

The next stage in Monequassun's story consisted of ambivalence and failed attempts at reform. His resolve was weak. He "fell again to sin" and was "full of evil thoughts." Using puritan terminology, he confessed that he "played the hypocrite," outwardly conforming to Christian teaching yet rebellious in his "heart." Fearing God's "punishment," he craved "wisdom," attended lectures, and "heard the Word." Yet he "thought Christ would not save me, because I repent not." He pondered his sins, such as lusting after women, and pleaded for "mercy." His inability to read and moral lapses equally vexed him, and he began to "pray unto God" for the gift of literacy and a "repentance" that he could not muster in himself.[11]

After a year of praying and studying, Monequassun despaired of conversion. He found that his prayers were "sinful." He wanted only to attend to feeding his family. Then Matthew 6:33 came to his mind—"Seek ye first the kingdom of God . . . and all these things shall be added unto you"— prompting him to continue his studies. When Eliot formed a congregation at Natick, Monequassun prayed for "Christ to open mine eyes," under the impression that he "had to be brought to be willing" to participate. Even as Monequassun came to the point of utter self-denial—he had to be made "willing" if he was to change—he encountered disaster. His wife and one of his children succumbed to a fatal disease. He became "angry at the punishment of God."[12]

After such sorrows, Monequassun surrendered himself to God's will for better or worse. He confessed that he deserved "that God should take away all mercies." In this state of utter helplessness, he relented of his efforts at piety and asked God to "turn" him. This in itself was his turning, his conversion: he "beleeved in Christ for pardon." As a concession to puritan teaching and indication of his faith, he cut his hair. In the rest of his testimony, Monequassun intimated that he understood his conversion according to Reformed doctrine. According to Eliot, Monequassun recounted the basic tenets of puritan Protestantism: original sin, the covenant of grace, Christ's Second Coming, the spiritual disciplines of self-critique and humiliation, and expressions of gratitude for forgiveness.[13]

Although M. K's and Monequassun's accounts emerged from wildly different contexts, they conveyed similar ideas of conversion and its relation to England's confessional order. This is not to say that Massachusetts Natives experienced or thought of conversion to Christianity in the same way as did English Protestants. As several scholars have shown, we can detect differences in the rhetoric, social concerns, and notions of religious adherence between Native American and Anglo-Protestant conversion stories.[14] We also know that Eliot and Mayhew sometimes transposed the language of Native relations to fit Protestant theology and English political agendas.[15] Issus of ethnographic accuracy aside, Eliot portrayed the conversion of Indigenous Americans according to the same pattern in which Crouch presented the conversion of English Protestants.

These two conversion narratives share three confessional assumptions. First, identification with England's confessional order preceded conversion. M. K. inherited her religious identity as an English woman. She was presumably baptized and certainly raised by Protestant parents who taught her to read the Bible and spiritual writers. Nothing in her story indicates that she doubted the truth of Protestant Christianity or chose her fundamental beliefs. She knew the precepts of the Bible and recognized that she had violated the Sixth Commandment when she contemplated murder. She attended Dod's preaching, pondered her corruption, feared hell, and resolved to repent. M. K. was born English and Protestant.

What, then, of Monequassun, born and raised in a Native community? According to *Tears of Repentance*, he became English in mores and Protestant in belief before his conversion. His spiritual transformation began, that is, with his acculturation to England's confessional order. He underwent catechesis, in which he learned the biblical story and Reformed doctrine. He became familiar with Anglo-Protestant morality and rued his violation of the Seventh and Eighth Commandments (prohibitions of adultery and theft). He attended sermons, prayed fervently to the God of the Bible, pondered his moral depravity, feared hell, and resolved to repent. Like M. K., Monequassun used the "means to conversion" provided by Protestant confession and community. As evidence of his identification with English life, he cut his hair, learned to read, and spoke English.

Second, M. K.'s and Monequassun's stories did not pivot on belief per se: a determination for one religion or the other. Those who participated in England's Protestant order such as M. K. and Monequassun acknowledged the truth of Protestant Christianity and falsehood of other religions as a condition for, not the substance of, their conversions. Their conversions, then, consisted of a prolonged struggle to abandon themselves to a Protestant message that they already believed to be true. To use Protestant idioms, they trusted in Christ and turned away from self-will. Such affective transformations could not be freely chosen. God, as it were, had to bring them to submission and change their deepest sentiments. Just as M. K. prayed, "turn me and I shall be turned," so Monequassun "had to be brought to be willing" and therefore asked God to "turn" him.

Third, in presenting the conversion of M. K. and Monequassun in such terms, both accounts featured the language of divine providence rather than of moral liberty. As explained in the following account, "to submit" or "to abandon oneself" conveyed something of moral action on the part of the convert. Yet Crouch, Eliot, and Mayhew used these and related terms to stress the passive nature of human response to divine power. They minimized human choice or, in theological terms, freedom of the will. They maintained that God worked through means or instruments outside the control of M. K. and Monequassun: parental nurture, dreams, the unbidden recollection of key verses of scripture, powerful preaching, or the tragedies of family loss. It was, to recall M.K.'s story, her dream of divine intervention into plans for murder, the antics of her dog, and the power of the words of Jesus in John 6 that pushed M. K. over the threshold into saving faith. Crouch placed the role of moral volition in the background. The same dynamics affected Monequassun: the coming to mind of Matthew 6:33, the sway of preaching, and God "turning" him through the death of his wife and child. Scholarly puritans rarely referred to miracles or dreams, but the conversions of M. K. and Monequassun confirmed Protestant teaching that God drew the unconverted to himself: a conviction given theological phrasing in the lexicon of divine election or predestination.

These accounts are representative of a common response among Anglo-Protestants in the aftermath of England's civil wars: to interpret conversion and evangelization in the context of confessional agendas. Writers such as Ross, Ogilby, and Crouch had asserted that religions outside of moderate English Protestantism were politically dangerous and religiously illegitimate. Confessional Protestants accordingly de-emphasized notions of choosing one's religion or faith. They stressed instead a sincere, heartfelt submission to Christ as presented in a Protestant tradition with which they already identified. Reformed tenets of total depravity, self-abnegation, and divine election confirmed this emphasis on subjection and self-denial.

To put this a bit differently, one had to be brought into England's confessional order, either by birth or by acculturation, prior to soul-saving conversion. Missionaries such as Eliot accordingly began their work among Native Americans with the construction of something akin to an English confessional order in towns such as Natick, replete with infant baptism, catechesis (formal instruction in Christian doctrine, often through recitation of creeds), moral instruction, and an English way of life. These were the means, to use the terminology of puritan spiritual writers, that God used to subdue rebellious human hearts. They reflected state-building and colonial agendas, as well as theological convictions, at the same time.[16]

Conversion Within English Protestant Communities

As the work of anthropologists, literary scholars, and historians of religion has shown, early modern conceptions of conversion may be parsed into several categories: renunciation of one religion and confession of allegiance to a new one; the addition of new beliefs and practices to one's previous religion; a transfer of allegiance from one denomination or tradition within a religion to another, as in from Anglican to Congregationalist; or individuals' sincere adherence to the tradition with which they had long identified—a transformation of the inner self, heart, or soul rather than change of belief or practice.[17] Protestant writers in England and New England focused especially on the first and last of these conceptions, what we can call for short a change of religion and transformation of the soul. The former, however, did not become prominent until the second quarter of the eighteenth century. Before then, confessional agendas led Anglo-American Protestants during the period of the Restoration to emphasize the soul's transformation, or conformity to Protestant teaching.

To describe conversion in this way, post-civil-wars ministers relied on Reformed devotional literature from as far back as the late sixteenth century. Puritans and their admirers, such as Crouch, favored the works of Elizabethan and early-Stuart reformers such as John Knewstub, John Rogers, John Dod, William Perkins, Richard Sibbes, Thomas Shepard, and

Thomas Hooker.[18] Other spiritual writers appealed to Anglicans as well as to puritans: Richard Baxter, Lewis Bayly, Richard Allestree, Joseph Alleine, and John Flavel.[19] These writers elucidated the relationship of human effort to divine grace in sometimes different terms, but they all agreed on the importance of a transformation of soul.[20]

Restoration-era Protestants believed that this literature sustained loyalty to England and England's confession. That was the opinion of Hugh Peter, a vocal dissenter who had served as a chaplain in Cromwell's army. Admittedly, the Restoration government charged Peter with disloyalty, found him complicit in the regicide of Charles I, and executed him. He nonetheless denied the charges and professed his allegiance to England and its confession. In his 1661 *A Dying Fathers Last Legacy to an Onely Child*, written shortly before his execution, Peter surveyed what he deemed to be the best spiritual counsel available for his daughter. His advice, as he put it, demonstrated his devotion to "ENGLAND," and its "Christian Policy." He urged his daughter to avoid Catholic and non-Christian books, which were "the blot of the Nation." She ought instead to read books that nurtured loyalty to "professing *England*" and its "Orthodox" Protestant order.[21]

Which sort of books? Peter endorsed those that presented religious conversion in terms of a compliant will: "a wearisome pilgrimage" of self-denial, or a "*Union with Christ*" that "can never be" until "your Will be so subdued to that Light, that it draw forth" a "Resolution to close with him." Conversion, Peter continued, was "drawn forth" and consisted of mere "consent" to let Christ conform the will in opposition to "Sin, World, Hell" and "Death." Who, then, best to break "an unbroken Heart" and teach an "uncatechised Head"? Peter recommended Thomas Shepard and Thomas Hooker, who wrote of conversion as a lifelong struggle against self-will; or the Westminster Confession, with its affirmation of predestination; or the sage Richard Baxter. Whom to read to be a dutiful subject and "Content" with one's social position? Peter mentioned John Dod, Richard Sibbes, and Jeremiah Burroughs. Religion was "low" and wasted by "Disputes" in other lands. The wisdom of its Protestant writers had made England "famous for Religion" and respected for the loyalty of its subjects.[22]

The texts favored by Peter and his contemporaries, that is, portrayed conversion as a transformation of the soul rather than a choice of one faith over another. To be sure, Protestants celebrated accounts of the conversion of Jews, Muslims, atheists, or Catholics to Protestantism.[23] Yet especially after the civil wars, confessional writers downplayed the usefulness of this paradigm,

with its depictions of individuals who selected their beliefs or decided to adhere to a new doctrine.[24] Protestants often assumed the position taken by
Giovanni Botero, a well-known writer who portrayed proselytization as seduction and religious change as political liability regardless of where it took
place.[25] William Temple conveyed a similar understanding. In his 1673
Observations upon the United Provinces he argued that each country had a
religious culture, expressed through church teaching, official decree, and
popular concurrence. Attempts to convince subjects of any kingdom or republic to change their religion, except under extraordinary, revolutionary
conditions, interfered in the affairs of the state and violated the people's normative assumptions. People in fact could not simply change their religion,
"for Belief is no more in a man's power, than his Stature or his Feature; And
he that tells me, I must change my Opinion for his, because 'tis truer and
the better . . . may as well tell, I must change my gray eyes for others."[26] Even
high-minded rationalist philosophers such as Descartes, Malebranche, and
Leibniz, for all of their speculative innovations, promoted what they held
to be philosophical systems best suited to sustain the dominant religious
traditions—Protestant or Catholic—of their home countries. Within this
agenda, conversion appeared less as a choice for one god or another—or for
no god—than as a sincere adherence to received teaching about God.[27]

The works of Thomas Shepard and Thomas Hooker reinforced the idea
that conversion meant a transformation of the soul for those who already
assented to Protestant belief. Shepard, to be sure, supported missions to
Native peoples and urged atheists or other non-Christians to "make choice"
of the Christian God. He nonetheless warned readers of his 1642 *The Sincere
Convert*—republished through the 1660s—that concerns for the evangelization of non-Christians misled English people to presume that they had
no need of conversion because they were raised Protestant. They deluded
themselves that baptism and assent to the creeds of the Church of England
amounted to genuine, saving faith. "Because they hold fast this opinion," i.e.,
that Christ was the way of salvation, "they think they hold fast [to] *Jesus Christ*
in the hand of faith." Yet they had not necessarily experienced the heartfelt
sense of need, the desperation, and the self-denial—even the "inability to
believe"—that brought them to real faith. In fact, it was "a harder matter to
convert a man in *England* then [*sic*] in the *Indies*; for there they" do not presume to "believe in Christ already, as most amongst us do." Shepard insisted
that English Protestants needed conversion as much as did the Indigenous
residents of Massachusetts.[28]

Other Protestants elevated the transformation of English souls above the proselytization of non-Christians in even stronger terms. One of the most widely published of them, Richard Baxter, introduced his influential 1658 *Directions and Perswasions to a Sound Conversion* by arguing that missions to "the professed Atheist, Heathens, and Infidels" too easily distracted English Protestants from their own spiritual depravity. The pressing issue of the day, he insisted at length, concerned those who had inherited a Protestant identity along with their English one, but who had never experienced the self-denial of conversion: self-deceiving "Hypocrites within the Church" who "must be Converted or Condemned." In his 1667 *The Reasons for the Christian Religion*, Baxter lamented that most of the world was non-Christian. He presented arguments to the effect that natural reason attested to the superiority of Christianity above all other religions. He intended his book, however, not as an apology for Christianity to non-Christians but as an encouragement to English Protestants who were afflicted with doubt and "Melancholy" at the prospect of so many alternatives to Christianity. He intended to bolster their confidence in the truth of their confession.[29]

In his 1672 *An Alarme to Unconverted Sinners*, Joseph Alleine—like Baxter, a favorite among dissenters but also read by Anglicans—included a lengthy statement by Baxter that put the issue in stronger terms. Those who maintained that "Conversion is fitter for Pagans and Infidels" than for "Christians and Protestants" had it completely wrong. It was not just a "Puritane" opinion but a central tenet of all Protestant teaching that born and bred Christians especially needed to attend to their conversion. Conversion was "not the taking on us the profession of Christianity," which English people had done. It was "the thorow change both of heart, and life." The welfare of England's Protestant order, the Presbyterian Jonathan Clapham wrote in 1669, rested not on the idea of a choice of belief but on the extent to which people were taught "to adhere" to their Protestant identity. As usual, Crouch omitted any nuance as he cribbed from his predecessors. In his Introduction to *Mercy Triumphant*, he maintained that the conversion of "Pagans and Infidels" to Christianity was less important than was the conversion of "Christians and Protestants" to genuine faith and a godly life.[30]

Of the many possibilities for their descriptions of conversion, then, Anglo-American Protestants were drawn to images that prompted sincere adherence to the tenets of the kingdom's confession. From the lexicon of practical divinity, they selected idioms of submission, self-denial, and conformity to God's will rather than of self-determination, liberty of choice, or individual decision. A strong sense of the power of divine providence and unreliability of human volition flowed through puritan spiritual counsel.[31]

We can refer, for example, to the works of Shepard, the Cambridge, Massachusetts, minister who deconstructed the notion that the act of conversion was in willfully choosing to believe. Shepard advised his readers to discern whether they had relinquished all claims of the will: claims to Christ, to divine blessings, to the very idea of liberty itself. "Art thou willing," he asked, "to part" not only "with thy sins" but also "with health, wealth, liberty" and "your own life?" Even that willing, he continued, could not be self-willed. "Art thou willing," he continued, "that Christ should make thee willing?" It might have sounded nonsensical, but it made a point: one had to will conversion to undergo it, but such willing required the abandonment of the will. All that the striving sinner could do was to "pitch thee upon a Promise."[32] Protestant ideas of human sinfulness or depravity served such exhortation. The "poore creatures whom the Lord hath humbled," Shepard wrote in *The Sound Beleever*, perceived themselves as "vile," "unworthy of childrens bread as dogs." That being the case, they were to trust nothing in themselves, not even their trust. They were to confide only in Christ.[33]

Jane Stevenson, a member of Shephard's congregation, put such language to her own use when she described her conversion as learning to be "content" with God's will instead of hers, to desire Christ rather than seek the benefits of knowing Christ.[34] Another parishioner of Shepard's, the ferry-keeper John Shepard (no relation to Thomas Shepard), recounted that "the Lord never broke my heart till now" but recently had done just that and "given" Shepard a "heart" to "love" God and hate sin.[35] Thomas Shepard's notebook from his Cambridge parish contains accounts of dozens of men and women who learned to renounce their deliberate choices and, instead, to trust only in Christ.[36]

As part of England's confessional discourse, the rhetoric of self-denial lent itself to explicitly political application. Like his predecessors, Baxter urged those seeking conversion to "let go of the world," "renounce it," "close with Christ," and fall "in Love with God and Holiness."[37] He contrasted this view with the false teaching that he believed had accompanied the disorders of the civil wars. Separatist radicals, he maintained, had twisted the idea of religious adherence into personal preference and mere belief. They adopted and discarded their "Opinions" at a whim. Promulgating outrageous ideas under the guise of liberty of conscience, they spread "censuring, reviling, and divisions" through the land, deepening England's crisis. Such "Meer

Opinionists" ought instead to have pursued real conversion: the mortification of "their carnal, selfish inclinations." This would have enhanced order
and solidarity in a disunited England.[38]

Less rigorously Reformed divines such as Allestree, sometime chaplain to
Charles II, were equally wary of antinomian excesses and therefore drew on
the idioms of self-mortification rather than exertion of the will. As Allestree
put in his widely consulted 1659 *The Whole Duty of Man*, the "lowly and
unfeigned submission" to God—"to his Will" and "Wisdom"—marked the
center of conversion. So too with Alleine, who characterized conversion as
complete self-renunciation: to "resign up," as he put it, "all thy powers and
faculties, and thy whole interest." Alleine ended his book with exemplary
prayers for the would-be convert, one of which evoked the dangers of political sedition: "Save, Lord, or else I perish. I come to thee, with the rope about
my neck."[39]

Several Protestants relied on the allegory of a pilgrimage to convey a lifelong struggle for self-denial. The turnings or transformations mentioned
in books such as Crouch's *Mercy Triumphant*, they often claimed, merely
initiated a long process of conformity to holiness.[40] Writers such as Shepard,
Hooker, and Baxter insisted that confidence in a single "choice" or act of faith
often misled people into a false sense of assurance: trust in one's experience
rather than in Christ.[41] John Bunyan's 1678 *The Pilgrim's Progress* presented
the allegory of pilgrimage so vividly that the book quickly entered the canon
of spiritual writing. It became one of England's most popular works of
prose fiction by the end of the century, inspiring many imitators. The pilgrimage trope conveyed the message that conformity of the soul to Christian
virtues—and the confessional order—was more important than moments of
human choice, which often misled the pilgrim.[42]

Pastors and practical divines sometimes elucidated the theological rationale for submission in terms of the Reformed doctrines of divine election, predestination, or the eternal decree: the power of divine will over
human willing. Among spiritual writers, the Hartford, Connecticut, minister
Hooker most explicitly stressed the absoluteness of divine power over human
volition. God by "physical determination," he claimed in a formulation that
many eighteenth-century divines would reject, made people to detest their
sins, desire holiness, and cleave to Christ. He explained that one had to "have
a will to receive Christ" and the "grace" to "lay hold of God," but that only
"the Lord by a holy kind of violence" could draw "a sinner from corruption to
himself." He declared in more simple terms that "I do not do it but [it is] only

donne in me." Or, as he put it in a remarkable turn of phrase, "God makes of an unwilling will a willing will."[43]

Philosophical coherence aside—one could question whether Hooker's language obscured the very meaning of "will"—he provided a formulation of conversion nearly empty of the notion, and certainly absent the language, of deliberation and willful choice. Other New Englanders did the same. Shepard informed his conversion-seeking flock that they "cannot, nor ought not" exercise their "own strength" to "receive Christ." They were to wait on the Lord to instill his "strength."[44] Daniel Gookin, a military captain, member of Shepard's congregation, and overseer of Native villages, put his conversion account in these very terms: "The Lord made me lie down at his feet" and "made me contented" to "be disposed of as God would."[45] The New Haven minister John Davenport was even less delicate: "God is able, by his Absolute Power to convert whom he will, and by what means he will."[46] Protestants in England too drew on Calvinist tenets to critique human willfulness. As Hugh Peter counseled his daughter, any "Resolution" that she had to "close with Christ" would "never" come to pass until her "Will" was "so subdued to that Light, that it draw forth" her "choice, and consent" to that end. Christ himself, he wrote, "will set the Will to work" and "make the Will delight" in conversion.[47] In 1676 the English Presbyterian Christopher Nesse attributed the power of self-abnegation itself to divine intervention. The "ability" to "bow yourself with all of your might" and "welcome Christ into your heart," he contended in a perplexing diction, "is his." Or, as he put it yet again, divine "love is the cause" of faith.[48]

Other Protestants moderated the language of predestination. The irenic Baxter wished to make room for Anglican teaching that the very idea of faith implied some measure of moral volition. Conversion, he wrote in his treatise by that name, "is sometimes taken *Actively*," meaning that the convert is "an Agent in the actual turning of his own soul," and "sometimes *Passively*, for that change that is hereby wrought." In sum, "God and Man are both Agents in this work." Baxter nonetheless favored the passive definition because it better captured the mandate for submission and hedged the idea of human willfulness. We ought simply to confirm, as he wrote, that the Holy Spirit "causeth man to Believe."[49] Giles Firmin, a sometime Presbyterian preacher and physician who had spent fifteen years in New England before his return to England, argued that the doctrine of election ought to be moderated by directions to pursue divine assurance.[50] Yet, for Firmin and Baxter, as well as for Hooker, Shepard, and Nesse, or Gookin and Peter, the doctrine of divine election validated their insistence that the Lord subdued the human will in the process of conversion.

God did so most commonly, they contended, through the "means of conversion," i.e., the ordinances and practices of England's and New England's churches. As the inheritance of English subjects, conveyed through families and churches, these means were conferred automatically on English children. They were, in other words, unbidden and unchosen, all the work of providence rather than the effects of individuals' decisions. Spiritual writers after the civil wars thus stressed inherited religious identity—the precepts of England's confession—as the typical means to conversion. They did so particularly in their emphasis on baptism, family piety and nurture, catechesis and preaching, and the discipline of the church or local Christian community.

We can take, for example, the works of John Flavel, an English Presbyterian whose treatises on the spiritual life were respected across the Protestant spectrum. In his 1678 *Divine Conduct, or the Mysterie of Providence*, Flavel argued that providence shaped people's souls through their place and time of upbringing. His explication reinforced assumptions about the superiority of English Protestantism and the illegitimacy of other religions. Citing Brerewood's account of the world's cultural differences, Flavel asked his readers to ponder "how deplorable" it would have been to have been born "worshipping *Devils*" and "full speed in the direct road to Damnation." "Suppose," Flavel continued, "your Mothers had brought you forth" in different lands. What then? In "*America* among the *Salvage* [sic] *Indians*," one would have been "destitute and defenceless," without "civility." Had it been in Russia, Mexico, or Peru, one would have been "wretchedly poor" or "enslaved and oppressed." Had it been in an Islamic or Catholic land, one would have been subject to "mad and wild dreams" and "Antichristian delusions." Even if it had been in England before its Christianization, one would have been raised in the darkness of Druid paganism.[51]

His readers, however, had the "singular mercy to be born" in Protestant England, "the fortunate Island" and "Garden of God." In contrast to Russia or Mexico, England boasted a wholesome political-religious order. In England, "a public confession among the people" and laws protecting the "true Religion" provided widespread prosperity and "the ordinary means of salvation": ordinances of the church, godly counsel, preaching, catechesis, and family piety. Flavel emphasized the importance of the family and especially motherly nurture as providential instruments. God gave English Protestants "education" in the "principles of Christianity" as "Mothers milk." Had they been fed instead with "soul-destroying prejudices" and raised by "cruel and ungodly Parents" they would have been "drawn headlong to Hell."[52]

For Flavel, the Calvinist idioms of predestination and the divine "Decree" for salvation captured the strength of such unchosen influences on one's conversion. The "hand of Providence," as Flavel put it, began the "blessed work of Conversion upon" English "souls" through their birthplace and upbringing. God's "performance" of "Conversion," therefore, called for English people to submit to the providential mercy that came through the religion of the nation. The power of national origin overshadowed the possibility of selecting or changing one's faith.[53]

As Protestants in England and New England embraced confessional assumptions, they increasingly depended on baptism and other inherited traditions as prompts to conversion.[54] For many Anglicans, infant baptism especially signified this work: a conferral of divine favor before individuals had the power of choice. For dissenters such as puritans, the sacraments did not so much confer favor or grace as represent a covenant that bound adherents to divine law and offers of redemption. The covenant alerted individuals to their sinful state as they failed to meet its obligations. Baxter, to illustrate, taught his parishioners that the invocation of the Holy Spirit in baptism alerted them to the sin of drunkenness (Ephesians 5:18: "be not drunk with wine . . . but be filled with the Spirit"), and the "Communion of Saints" proclaimed in the Apostles' Creed and recited at confirmation highlighted the iniquity of carousing or having communion with bad company. In this sense, baptism and confirmation provoked the sense of guilt that began the process of conversion. Cotton twisted the meaning of baptism away from guilt, contending that parents ought to baptize their children because the rite indicated the covenant of grace passed down from one's ancestors to one's offspring. English children, Cotton explained, did not come to faith by hearing the "gospel" as strange and disconcerting news, as did "heathens." Rather, the "conversion" of English children was "much more kindly, and as it were, more easie and natural." Conversion, that is, was a ratification of Christian identity conveyed through baptism.[55]

Protestant laypeople in New England, especially women, often related their conversions in these terms. Dorcas Downey of Cambridge, for example, claimed that Christ had begun her conversion through the "ordinances" she had observed as a young girl in England. The Haverhill, Massachusetts, laywoman Sarah Eastman attributed her conversion to her birth "in a land of light" and upbringing under the "ordenances of baptism and lords supper." One earnest mother inscribed her copy of Baxter's *Directions and Perswasions to a Sound Conversion* with a prayer that presumed the transmission of Christian identity, and therefore the means of conversion, through the family. "Shall Solomon my son," wrote Elizabeth Rogers, "serve him Thou the God of my father, with a perfect heart and with a willing mind." Solomon, she continued, could not voluntarily or willfully choose his faith. If he were to be converted, it had to be by God's work: "if you [God] seek him he will be found of thee."[56]

Hundreds of other "godly parents," by the accounts of divines such as Shepard or writers such as Crouch, conveyed Protestant identities and the means of conversion through the dissemination of Protestant teaching. As did M. K.'s parents, they provided godly books and instruction in the household, often relying on printed catechisms. They also brought their children to the parish church, where children received instruction, heard preaching, and were subject to the counsel of elders who, among other tasks, helped people to discern their progress in conversion and correct self-deception. William Perkins, one of the canonical divines, maintained that preaching excited otherwise blasé spirits, convicted easy consciences, and sparked sleepy minds in the unregenerate before they had even the slightest will to change. The story of Elizabeth Oaks, a single woman adopted by a family of Cambridge (Massachusetts) merchants and parishioner of Shepard's, turned completely on catechesis and preaching. Orphaned while in England, sickly, and tired of pursuing her spiritual life, she began "Reading catechize"—a reference to Shepard's catechetical sermons that circulated in manuscript among his congregation. Shepard taught her that fatigue and despair were aspects of evangelical humiliation and in themselves indications of the Lord's work, even signs of divine election. In addition, Shepard's sermons from Romans illumined the evangelical tenet that "before a person chose" Christ, "the Lord gave the soul a heart to choose Christ." The desire for union with Christ, in other words, was a divine gift. It could not be attained by human devotion. Oaks took such consolation from this instruction that Christ became her "peace and life and light," the real cause of her conversion.[57]

Missions to Algonquian Communities in New England

Even though English Protestants emphasized the transformation-of-soul pattern of conversion, with all of its stress on divine providence, they confronted a diverse world in which religious choice appeared, as William James put it, as a "*forced* option."[58] They encountered a growing scholarship on the world's religions, travelers' descriptions of pluralistic cities such as Amsterdam, accounts of Catholic missions in Asia, Mexico, and South America, and Protestant manifestoes for missions to non-Christians in colonized lands. Along with such literature, day-to-day exchanges between New England's Protestants and Indigenous inhabitants raised questions about how best to promote conversion among a people who were strangers to England's confessional order yet resided in territory claimed by England. In this context, Protestant observers pondered how to bring Native Americans into the confessional order as preparation for their conversion.[59]

Those means included Protestant missions established during the early 1640s by John Eliot and Thomas Mayhew, Jr. in southern New England. New England's missionaries received occasional support from Parliament and the crown but operated under the auspices of their local churches, the Commissioners of the United Colonies (a New England confederation for the oversight of affairs with Native peoples and promotion of confessional orthodoxy), and, after 1649, the New England Company (a London-based missionary society sanctioned by Parliament). Missionaries such as Eliot and Mayhew also corresponded with advisors such as Baxter, supporters in London like the scientist Robert Boyle, and commissioners throughout New England.[60]

Eliot became the most prominent transatlantic spokesman for New England's missionaries. He preached his first "Indian" sermon at Neponset, near Roxbury, in 1646. In 1650, he established the first of fourteen "praying towns" in the Bay Colony: villages of Algonquian residents who had come to identify as Christian. From 1646 to 1671, Eliot, Mayhew, and other missionary preachers produced a series of eleven progress reports, known today as the "Eliot Tracts."[61] Eliot translated key devotional texts into the Massachusett dialect of the Algonquian language: Baxter's *Call to the Unconverted*, Shepard's *The Sincere Convert*, and Bayly's *Practice of Piety*. He also completed a translation of the Bible into Massachusett in 1663. Support for missions and publicity on their behalf had begun to wane by that time, though, and the work came to a violent stop with King Philip's War in 1675 and 1676.[62]

Leaders of the Bay Colony and their patrons in England often defended missionary activity as an instrument of national expansion and security. The evangelization of Indians, so their argument went, would enhance England's international reputation, offset the advance of Catholic regimes, pacify Native inhabitants of America, expand opportunities for trade, and encourage interest in New England. In addition, divines in Boston and London combined scholarship on the ancient origins of the American "Indians" with interpretations of biblical prophecy to gauge the millennial and geopolitical significance of the conversions that they hoped might ensue from missionary work. Their speculations conflated the ethnic, religious, and political identities of Native Americans, who were pictured either as originating in central Asia, irredeemably pagan, and destined to be the apocalyptic enemies of England, or as descendants of the lost tribes of Israel, who would be converted and serve in the armies of light against England's foes. As Edward Winslow, an agent of the colony to London and fundraiser for the New England Company, informed Parliament, missions had to do with more than the conversion of individuals. Missions concerned the fate of "Nations" around the globe and England's relationship to the "Family, Tribe, Kindred, or people" who "filled the vast and long unknown Countrey of America."[63]

Colonization and missionary activity appeared to English Protestants, then, as interdependent agendas shaped by international political contests. From their perspective, England's leaders had three options in response to the European contest for North America. (This is to set aside a fourth option, namely, the complete eradication of Native populations or genocide: a strategy sometimes contemplated by early advocates of colonization but eschewed by English missionaries.) First, they could refrain from colonization. This policy, according to proponents of colonization, would have exposed Native people to the depredations of the Spanish and French, in contrast with which English rule was humane. Second, they could colonize but not evangelize Native peoples. In their view, this policy would have eventuated in disorder and discord—just as England had experienced during the civil wars. Third, they could evangelize along with colonization. This, according to confessional Protestants, was the best option. They claimed that it offered the possibility of the protection of Native peoples and establishment of a prosperous and cohesive order in English America—a claim that occluded the social and political realities that followed English colonization, including warfare, enslavement of Indians, and the destruction of Native patterns of life.[64] The violence of English colonization erupted quite visibly with the outbreak of King Philip's, or Metacom's, War in 1675. This widespread conflict between Indigenous peoples and English settlers diminished expectations for evangelistic success. It led observers such as Increase

Mather, who had supported evangelization before the war, to claim that Indians were for the most part irredeemably savage, traitorous, and resistant to civilizing.[65]

Three decades prior to Metacom's War, however, New England's missionaries set out to transmit English Protestant identities to Indigenous inhabitants along with the gospel. Advocates advertised New England missions in such terms even before the establishment of Eliot's praying towns. The first of the Eliot Tracts, *New Englands First Fruits*, included reports from the first third of the seventeenth century that several "Indian" people embraced the idea of being English and Protestant as nearly synonymous. By one account, a man called "Sagamore John" in Plymouth was drawn to the English language, to English "behavior" and clothing, and thereafter "would much commend English-men and their God." Another "*Indian*" in Salem reportedly had such "love to the *English* and their ways" that "he labored to transform himself into the *English* manners and practices, as if he had been an English man indeed." He changed his name to William. Wequash, a Pequot from Connecticut, put the issue simply: he desired "the English mans God." He learned Christian doctrine, repented of his hostility toward the English, separated himself from all but the first of his wives, and on his deathbed requested that his children be raised and educated as English.[66]

We can take Eliot's "praying towns" as the most widely publicized mission in which evangelization included the full scope of England's confessional order: inculcation of English identities and patterns of life, Protestant catechesis, moral reform, and occasional conversions—followed by the organization of churches.[67] All of this implied the interdependence of political and spiritual practices. When Eliot began the organization of praying towns, the General Court of Massachusetts purchased land, created local law courts, appointed constables from the Native community, and organized elections. The Court enacted special codes that mandated English hygienic habits and prohibited spousal abuse, drunkenness, gambling, and fighting—all thought to be vices prevalent among Native Americans. To be sure, Eliot recognized sachems as tribal leaders and countenanced several Indigenous practices: traditional medicine, music, bodily ornamentation, and burial customs, as well as seasonal sojourns for hunting and fishing. Yet Eliot's codes proscribed many Native traditions. They required all able-bodied males to work, barred public nudity, and included prohibitions against powwowing, i.e., attending feasts with Native spiritual leaders, ceremonial dancing, and healing rites.

In addition, Eliot encouraged English-style grooming and clothing, farming, and European-style dwellings.[68]

For Eliot, Shepard, and their contemporaries, such disciplines were the means not merely of political domination but also of the potential salvation of Indian souls. Missionaries relied on the idiom of "civility" to bridge the two domains.[69] Eliot claimed that he found "it absolutely necessary to carry on civility with Religion" because "civility" meant literacy and a settled pattern of life—both of which were integral to Native attendance on the Bible, preaching, and the ordinances of the church. Where "religion" was "extremely degenerate," Shepard observed of Native Americans, the people "must be brought to some civility before religion can prosper," a characterization that other puritans made of the rural poor in Ireland, Wales, Maine, and Virginia alike. Even Roger Williams, the Rhode Island maverick who rejected other aspects of a confessional order as coercive and therefore religiously suspect, opined to officials in 1654 that Native Americans had to be brought from "Barbarisme to Civilitie" before their conversion. The leaders of the New England Company agreed. Throughout their founding deliberations, they described the cultivation of civility as the initial phase of their mission.[70]

What did the civilizing process have to do with conversion? Various proponents of Native American missions from William Crashaw in 1610 to Solomon Stoddard in 1723 contended that the Christianization of ancient Britain helped to explain. By their account, Britons were a barbaric and savage people, unprepared for the gospel, until the Romans brought concepts of civility or moral law that incited a desire for the knowledge of God. Missionaries likewise viewed the institution of codes of behavior, accompanied by admonishment for Native people to establish a regimen of labor, residence, and marital fidelity, as, in part, a prompt to moral conscience. According to Protestant conceptions of conversion, English social ideals introduced Indians to the precepts of natural law and the moral rules given in the Bible, and an awareness of the moral law in turn led to the recognition of guilt, a dread of punishment, and a longing for forgiveness. The Eliot Tracts contained numerous reports of Natives, such as Monequassun, who eagerly sought teaching on the Christian doctrine of salvation as a remedy for their fear of divine retribution.[71]

Missionaries understood their ministry, then, as the transmission of knowledge that inculcated civility. Only then might their Algonquian interlocutors pursue salvation. As Richard Mather wrote in *Tears of Repentance*, sermons and lessons were works of "preparation" that revealed individuals' need for grace.[72] Belief in essential Christian doctrine—the law of God, human sinfulness, the nature of Christ as divine redeemer, the procurement of forgiveness at the cross, and the promise of eternal life—did not amount to conversion, as Shepard instructed Massachusett attendees at his preaching.[73] It was, however, a condition for conversion. As Monequassun put it, "I now desire to beleeve in Jesus Christ" so "that I may be converted."[74] Shepard urged preachers to deliver sermons that prompted Natives to recognize "plaine and familiar truths," such as Christ's death for sinners, as a preparation for the soul-demanding task of "repentance" from sin and the work of supernatural grace that effected their union with Christ.[75]

Along these lines, Eliot informed his supervisors and supporters that his teaching had moved many Native people to believe in Christ and undergo a genuine reformation of behavior—and that some of those had evidenced real conversion, i.e., a transformation of the soul. The teaching was crucial. Eliot's favorite guides to conversion, such as Shepard, Baxter, and Bayly, presumed that their English readers knew and believed in Christian tenets and much of the Bible. Their spiritual advice was unintelligible apart from such knowledge, which they took for granted as an inheritance of England's confessional order. Eliot and his colleagues labored to convey that knowledge to Algonquian people through instruction on the Ten Commandments, the Psalms, central passages from the Gospels (including the Lord's Prayer), and the Apostles' Creed. Missionaries held catechetical sessions in which they answered Natives' questions about original sin, God's apparent neglect of their people before English settlement, and unanswered prayers.[76]

Eliot also pleaded with his sponsors to fund schools and teachers to instruct Algonquian people in the English language—not only to further their identification as English subjects but also to enhance their knowledge of Protestant teaching. In 1671, he expanded his educational agenda to encompass the promotion of humanist learning. Many of the "praying Indians," he contended to patrons in England, were prepared to move beyond simple catechesis. They required further education to think in philosophical ways and become teachers themselves: to learn "the Liberal Arts and Sciences, and the way to analyze."[77]

Translation of texts such as the Bible, rudimentary theological tracts, and devotional literature into Algonquian dialects, as well as the translation of Algonquian speech into English, were crucial to this enterprise. Eliot wrote Massachusett-language primers on Christian belief, modeled after the Westminster Assembly's longer and shorter catechisms and adapted to his audience. Those primers circulated through Natick as manuscripts from 1651 until 1654 when they were published as *A Primer or Catechism, in the Massachusetts Indian Language*. It went through several editions until 1687. The Connecticut missionary Abraham Pierson produced a primer in the Quiripi dialect of Algonquian, which began with reflections on the natural knowledge of God and proceeded to doctrinal affirmation.[78] On Martha's Vineyard, Mayhew translated key concepts and texts into Wampanoag. He was, perhaps, less insistent on English Protestant doctrine than was Eliot but nonetheless relied on catechesis in Algonquian dialects.[79]

Several contemporary scholars have speculated how such projects of translation joined a European-wide, Catholic and Protestant effort to control Indigenous cultures and exercise linguistic power over colonized peoples.[80] From Eliot's perspective, however, translation was too difficult to be characterized as an exercise of power. Algonquian vocabularies did not convey many Protestant theological concepts, such as a distinction between spiritual and material beings. Eliot in fact found no suitable Algonquian word for "God" and left the term in English in his translations.[81] English missionaries continued to lament the resistance of Iroquoian (such as Mohawk) and Algonquian languages to verbal translation through the mid-eighteenth century.[82] The importance of translation for conversion nonetheless compelled Eliot to persist in his attempts to bridge English and Algonquian speech. He intended his 1666 *Indian Grammar* to teach Algonquian to anglophone Protestants who might become evangelists and work for "the salvation of the Souls of those poor People."[83]

Members of Native communities who accepted an English Protestant identity often did so by adopting some Christian practices and repudiating at least some of their inherited religious habits. The act of praying in a Christian manner—addressing petitions, laments, and reverence to the Christian God—often signaled this new identity. Eliot used the name "praying Indians" in this sense. He claimed that they had abandoned veneration of and petition to other beings such as spirits in nature, ancestors, or malevolent powers. According to some accounts, they also refrained from rituals meant to appease those beings. "Praying Indians" often absented themselves from ceremonies led by non-Christian spiritual leaders and attended Sabbath-day services led by Christian pastors. Mayhew designated these changes as repentance from devil worship and from consultation with "Witches."[84] Anglicans used similar idioms. When Church of England divines developed a special service for the baptism of adult non-Christians in 1662, a rite conducted after lengthy catechesis, they encoded in the Book of Common Prayer a vow to renounce "the devil" (or, as the case required, "Mahomet").[85]

The resolution of Native individuals to attend sermons and lectures, pray, and renounce the devil—i.e., forego traditional ceremonies—marked their acceptance of England's confessional order.[86] According to missionaries such as Eliot, however, the practices of "praying Indians" did not necessarily constitute conversion. As the pieties of English Protestants often masked unregenerate souls, so too with the decisions of Natives to become Christians and residents of praying towns. Christian "Indians" who confessed that their prayers were insincere, harbored doubts about the power of God, or lapsed into sin fit the pattern of all pre-conversion Christians—such as M. K. or Monequassun—whose wills were yet to be tamed by grace. For English Protestants, the ambivalence of many Native Christians toward traditional practices also evidenced their pre-conversion state. Some "praying Indians"—especially those who, according to missionaries, had recently accepted a Christian identity—continued to consult Native spiritual leaders for healing and attend powwows. They also retained some traditional beliefs and spoke of wandering souls, demonic visitations, and an afterlife of lavish gardens.[87]

Protestant observers insisted that these remnants of Algonquian cosmologies or ceremonial practices were incompatible with Christianity. Writers such as Purchas and Ross informed their readers that Indian ceremonies were so devilish and disorderly as to be an affront to true faith in all respects. French missionaries in America saw things differently. Jesuits evangelized on behalf of an international church that defined its mission as the propagation of a non-vernacular, universal sacramental system. They promoted a form of doctrinal orthodoxy untethered to a single national confession or language. They were more willing than their English counterparts to tolerate Native rites and customs, including healing ceremonies, the use of tobacco as a sacred object, dreams and visions, and feasts attended by ancestral spirits. For English missionaries, participation in traditional ceremonies indicated the need for further repentance before conversion—and marked the insincerity of the conversions claimed by Jesuits.[88]

As Eliot and Mayhew transposed stories of Native conversions into a Protestant narrative, they maintained that "praying Indians" such as Monequassun, even with their decision to be identified as English and Protestant, had not undergone conversion until they endured the same trials and self-scrutiny, the same despair and terror, and the same abandonment of the self to Christ that attended the conversion of English people raised as Protestants.[89] Relying on Baxter and Shepard for advice on how to counsel Massachusett Christians, Eliot probed for evidence of self-denial. He instructed his parishioners to pray for the subjugation of their wills to an inscrutable and omnipotent providence.[90]

In missionary telling, then, "Indian" converts confessed their sheer incapacity to submit to Christ in a saving manner. The phrasing of the Massachusett man Nishohkou was typical: "I cannot redeem myself, nor deliver myself."[91] Shepard contended that divine providence was so active in the conversion of "Indians" that even when they feigned interest in Protestant teaching "only to please the *English*," the "power of the Word" overcame their resistance and brought them over to Christ despite their intentions.[92] Mayhew recounted "the *Indians* conversion" as a providential act: "the capacities that God" gave Native Christians to pursue Christ, and the gift of "several providences" that restrained the devil, healed them, and brought them to saving faith.[93] Other missionaries testified to the conversion of "Indians" with accounts of weeping and other emotional expressions, all indications of the power of the Holy Spirit to affect Native souls and overcome Native wills.[94] The rigors of this affective model of conversion, as well as the cumbersome task of "civilizing" Native communities, helps to explain the relatively slow pace of Algonquian conversions in New England. Of the some 1,100 Native residents in mainland Massachusetts in 1674, less than 100 gave the evidence of a conversion experience that qualified them for baptism and church membership.[95]

Even with such few conversions, missionaries such as Eliot attempted to institute the ritual and sacramental practices of a confessional order: the means by which Protestant identity was conveyed from adult "praying Indians" to their children. Missionaries anticipated that family pieties and the ordinances of a church in praying towns, no less than in English towns, served to prepare Christian children for conversion. The Native leaders of Natick, for instance, consented to a civil covenant that encoded the language of a corporate, familial Christian identity. It denoted a Massachusett version of the English idea of a national covenant: "we and our forefathers," it began, "have a long time been lost in our sins but now the mercy of God begins to find us out again" and confirm that "the Lord is our king." Shepard informed the Algonquian people in New England that if they were to be as favored by God as were the English, then they would teach their children the truths of Protestant Christianity just as English parents had done with their children.

Wampanoag Christians on Martha's Vineyard conveyed Christian affiliations through family and clan networks throughout the colonial period.[96]

By 1675, there were enough adult converts for the Indigenous communities at Natick and Hassanamesit to begin to form full-fledged churches that offered the sacraments. There is little evidence that the first generation of Native converts underwent adult baptism, but they embraced confessional patterns as they celebrated baptism for their children and offered the Lord's Supper to fellow church members. Christians from other towns were eager enough for these means of conversion that they traveled to Natick and Hassanamesit to observe and participate. It must have struck Eliot as a confounding providence that the outbreak of war subverted all such occasions.[97]

Long before King Philip's War, Eliot and Mayhew had contended that the evangelization of Algonquian peoples extended England's confessional order to its colonies. In 1653, they reported that they had seen a "Reformation" of "disordered lives" among the "praying Indians." These terms reflected many of the desiderata then emerging from political disruptions in London: civic order, reassertion of the authority of the national government, and affirmation of a common confession. Oxford and Cambridge divines endorsed the mission of the New England Company in 1649, with its agendas for a confessional order, as a precedent and perhaps balm for England, which was torn by "the unhappy differences" of the civil war in "these sad and discomposed [sic] times." New England authorities also voiced anxieties about "Indians" who rejected evangelization. According to their account, Native people who formed local alliances against the colonial government, criticized Shepard and Eliot, and contravened civic codes without remorse were as antinomian as radical dissenters such as Levelers and Diggers. Disloyal sachems, with their powwow-conducting accomplices or "priests," were as tyrannical and deceptive as papists. These were the same terms that writers such as Ross or Crouch used to portray the enemies of an orderly England.[98]

England's need for a confessional order to sustain the state, in other words, shaped the ways that authors such as Baxter, Flavel, and Crouch, Eliot and Shepard, described conversion among English Protestants and the Algonquian inhabitants of New England. They wrote not of a free choice of belief among possible options but of a conformity to the truth as propagated in magisterial Protestantism. Conversion was best described as a form of submission, compliance, even surrender—the very dispositions required of English subjects. This post–civil war agenda helps to explain the hesitations of many New Englanders—outside the likes of Eliot, Mayhew, and Shepard—to pursue the evangelization of Native Americans. The very idea of changing religions sounded almost nonsensical.

If, however, the confessional order and its ramifications for missions rested in part on political, national agendas, then changes in those agendas—in perceptions of the kingdom's commonweal—would result in the transformations of the discourse of other religions and religious adherence. Those changes occurred with remarkable force and clarity in 1688.

3

Revolution and Toleration

In 1685 Gilbert Burnet, a scholarly priest known for his opposition to the accession of James II to the throne, embarked on a journey from London to the Continent. Prosecuted in absentia for treason, he spent three years in exile. It was a fortuitous sojourn. He became an advisor and chaplain to William of Orange, returned to England with William's invading forces, preached at William's coronation, and was consecrated bishop of Salisbury in 1689.[1]

Burnet narrated his travels through France, Switzerland, Italy, and Germany in a frequently published account that was read on both sides of the Atlantic. It included extensive commentary on the treatment of religious dissenters in each country he visited.[2] He contrasted, for example, the "bigotry" of Catholic officials in Italy and France, who persecuted Protestants, to the policies of religious and civic leaders in Switzerland and Germany, who tolerated adherents of different traditions: Jewish, Catholic, Reformed, Lutheran, and Anglican.[3]

Geneva, of all places—hardly a bastion of Anglicanism—was his favorite location in such terms, so much so that he remained there several months. "There is an universal civility" there, he remarked. The city council provided him with a sanctuary in which he conducted worship according to the Book of Common Prayer for the dozen or so English residents.[4] He formed a friendship with local theologian Francis Turretin, who displayed, in Burnet's words, "fervent charity" along with an amiable style of "conversation." The townspeople prayed for "the churches of Great Britain" and for political conditions there. According to Burnet, they "shewed all possible esteem for our constitutions; and they spoke of the unhappy divisions among us" with "great regret": a reference to what Burnet told them were Stuart assaults on constitutional precedents and quarrels between High Church and dissenting Protestants. Burnet had a high regard for policies that bypassed confessional differences and national identities—Genevan Calvinist and English Episcopalian—for the sake of social concord.[5]

The Opening of the Protestant Mind. Mark Valeri, Oxford University Press. © Oxford University Press 2023.
DOI: 10.1093/oso/9780197663677.003.0004

The peaceful coexistence of Catholics and Protestants in other cantons amazed him. The Catholic bishop of the Grisons (or Graubünden), as Burnet described him, was overly fond of fables and miraculous claims attached to local sites but nonetheless was "a good natured man." The bishop "did not make use of the great authority that he has over the Papists there, to set them on to live uneasily with their neighbours of another religion." He did not, that is, set Catholics against Protestants. The Grisons were typical of Switzerland, where Protestants and Catholics, as Burnet put it, "live pretty neighbourly together." They enjoyed prosperity because they had an "interest to unite" in civil affairs despite religious differences. The same held for Fribourg and Lausanne, where good citizens "often moderated" the "heat and indiscretion" of religious disputes.[6]

Burnet claimed also that German Protestants had learned to value a "generous largeness of soul" and "liberty of conscience." Lutheran and Calvinist factions in Heidelberg accordingly had set aside confessional jealousies as a matter of true "learning," "prudence" in civil affairs, and a "happy temper of mind."[7] Soo too, Burnet noted that the Prince of Manheim invited Jews to settle there and "resolved" to "suffer the three religions, tolerated by the laws of the empire," i.e., Catholic, Lutheran, and Reformed, "to be professed there." He even "built a church," which "he called the Church of Concord, in which both [sic] Calvinist, Lutheran, and Papists had . . . the exercise of their religion." The prince knew, Burnet surmised, that such "moderation" attracted commerce and people to his state.[8]

Burnet conveyed the impression that most Protestant territories, where leaders upheld liberty of religious affiliation, enjoyed civil liberties, productivity, and cheerfulness. Most Catholic states, where rulers punished religious dissent, suffered despotism, poverty, and wretchedness. He was "amaz'd," as he put it, "to see so much misery" in rural France, the sufferings of French Protestants after the 1685 Revocation of the Edict of Nantes, the ignorance of priests in Venice, and the wealth and "absolute" power of the pope in Rome, who monopolized the grain trade and set oppressive prices. Burnet was so appalled that he refused an audience with Innocent XI. "If one will compare the faith of Rome and Geneva," he sniffed, "he would be forced to prefer the latter" because it was prosperous and just: a type of genuine, tolerant, and Protestant state. Burnet divided Protestant and Catholic regimes not by doctrine but by social and political markers: tolerant and bigoted, learned and ignorant, prosperous and miserable, liberal and oppressive.[9]

Burnet's travel account signaled a shift in the ways that Anglo-American Protestants described the place of religion in England and their attitudes toward non-Protestant religions. From the mid-1650s through the early 1680s, they conceived of the welfare of the kingdom largely in terms of a confessional order. National solidarity, as they argued, rested on the identification of England with a broad-based, magisterial, and moderate Protestantism. As a corollary, they developed an ideology of the religious "other"—Roman Catholic, Islamic, Guinean-African, radical or separatist Protestant, and Native American alike—as deceptive, violent, and malevolent. Writers such as Ross and Crouch described other religions as illegitimate: an inherent contradiction to English identity and unworthy of consideration or protection.

Political affairs leading up to and following the revolution of 1688, or the Glorious Revolution, prompted changes in this discourse. Many observers during this period came to argue that the well-being of the kingdom depended less on creedal uniformity than on the virtues that Burnet highlighted in his tour of Europe: toleration of different religious traditions, protection of freedom of conscience, and regard for reasonableness and learning. Burnet and his cohort frequently extolled "civility" as well, shifting its meaning from English social customs, which is how John Eliot used it, to a moral disposition or sensibility: what Burnet called a "largeness of soul." Toleration, reasonableness, and civility were, by the account of Protestants such as Burnet, the means of concord within a society. As such, they served as criteria by which to judge the worth of different religions.

Anglo-American Protestants did not abandon their identification of England or New England with a version of Protestantism—and anti-Catholicism—that sustained loyalty to the state.[10] Yet they enlarged the boundaries of what they thought of as acceptable Protestantism and drew distinctions between religious confession and political virtue. England's authors of dictionaries or geographies of religion from 1688 through 1720 reflected these changes in their descriptions of the world's religions. So too, many laypeople who encountered different religious traditions in travels outside England and New England assumed that those traditions were legitimate and even admirable to the extent that they promulgated toleration, reasonableness, and civility.

The following account elucidates this transformation from a confessional to a post-confessional, post-1688 discourse of religion. In so doing, it touches but does not dwell on several issues raised by recent criticisms of an older, so-called whiggish narrative, according to which John Locke and other supporters of the revolution of 1688 (many of whom took on the moniker Whigs) initiated a modern, liberal practice of religious toleration. Several critics have argued, for example, that proponents of the whiggish narrative underestimate the extent to which ideals of toleration derived from persecuted Protestant radicals before the Restoration or from Stuart agendas to validate a Catholic monarch. These critics also observe that Whigs such as Burnet demanded the deposition of James II for the very reason that he was not a practicing Protestant—hardly a tolerant position.[11] Other historians have produced an even more thoroughgoing critique of the whiggish account. The discourse of moderation or toleration, they suggest, masked or tacitly legitimated ways in which the kingdom's officials, in an effort to enhance their power, exercised discipline over dissent. On the ground, in social practice, the subjection of colonized peoples and punishment of outsiders from mainstream Anglo-Protestantism belied the liberty of conscience. There were cycles of persecution, ambivalence, and pragmatic accommodation according to the needs of the state.[12]

While assuming the salience of these criticisms of the whiggish narrative, this chapter is focused less on the history of toleration as an ideal, or on its implementation in social or political policy, than it is on differences between pre-1688 and post-1688 approaches to religious description and how those differences reflected changing political mandates. Whiggish writers in England and New England—meaning those who sympathized with the constitutional monarchy and its policies, whether or not they belonged to a Whig faction in parliamentary affairs—absorbed decades-old ideals of toleration and put them to new use. Allied with the crown after 1688, they expanded the meaning of toleration and linked it to what they regarded as other social virtues such as reasonableness and civility. Very little in this story, to be sure, indicates modern, liberal ideas of religious self-determination or of a firm distinction between religious and political expression. None of the writings discussed here represented a wholesale transformation in social practice. Yet the following discussion nonetheless includes evidence that the ideas illustrated in Burnet's travelogue had a practical effect in certain times and places, in incidents and encounters that reflected different approaches to other religions. The Anglo-Protestant discourse of religion and politics and of the religious "other" in 1700 bore slight resemblance to the discourse prior the revolution.

Apologists for the Revolution of 1688

A cursory account of the revolution of 1688 and religious arguments on its behalf helps to explain the political impetus for a post-confessional, purportedly tolerationist approach to different religions. During the last decade of the reign of Charles II (1660–1685) and throughout the brief reign of James II (1685–1688), proponents and critics of the Stuarts debated, adjusted, and questioned the meaning of England's Protestant confessional order. The controversies of the period often combined political and religious matters: the legality of adherence to Catholicism within the realm, the extent of acceptable Protestant dissent from the Church of England, and the relative powers of the crown and Parliament to determine such matters.[13]

In the midst of such disputes, antagonists manipulated the concept of religious toleration to suit their agendas. In 1672, Charles II—James's older brother—promulgated the Declaration of Indulgence, an attempt to suspend several laws against Protestant nonconformity and Catholic forms of worship. Perhaps most controversial, the Declaration would have suspended the Test Act, a 1672 law that required public officeholders to deny Catholic sacramental teaching. By removing such restrictions, the Declaration allowed for a Catholic monarch. Parliament abrogated the Declaration, refusing to pass it into law. In 1687, James, who was known to be a Roman Catholic, re-issued the Declaration of Indulgence—an act that challenged Parliament's authority to decree religious requirements for a monarch's reign. Dissatisfaction with James came to a head when he initiated proceedings to eject or depose members of Parliament, justices, bishops, and university professors who refused to endorse and abide by the Declaration. His apologists claimed, in part as an effort to gain dissenters' support, that James represented a policy of moderation and toleration. His critics, including many Tory Anglicans, charged him with assault on England's constitution, violation of parliamentary prerogative, and intent to create a Catholic dynasty that would eventually abolish Protestantism in England. James's non-Tory opponents, so-called Whigs, supported the right of Parliament to enact and enforce conditions on royal succession, i.e., to require subsequent monarchs to be Protestant.[14]

After the Declaration, Whigs moved to oust James from the throne, and in the process advertised themselves, in heated polemic against the Stuarts, as the party of true toleration. Parliamentary leaders invited William of Orange—a grandson of Charles I, the Protestant husband of James's daughter Mary, and the Dutch stadtholder, chief magistrate, and prince of the United

Provinces (the Dutch Republic)—to assume England's throne. Although he was known to be a champion of Protestant interests on the Continent, and engaged in hostilities against France, William had formed an alliance with Spain, had several Catholic army officers, and supported laws that allowed for a diversity of religious practices in the Netherlands. From this perspective, it was William who challenged the idea of a uniform confessional order.

William and his Dutch forces invaded England in November 1688, meeting with slight resistance from James and Jacobite loyalists. During the next two months, Burnet assisted William in his negotiations with privy counselors and the assembly of Lords. In February 1689, Parliament appointed William and Mary as monarchs and announced a Declaration of Rights that condemned royal encroachment on the constitution, required a Protestant monarchy, and asserted the liberties or prerogatives of Parliament. Aligning itself with William's international campaigns, Parliament declared war on France in May 1689.

There were strategic reasons for William and his supporters to appear as if it were they, rather than the deposed James and his partisans, who advanced liberty of conscience and toleration in England. The success of the revolution depended on the support of different religious factions in the kingdom: Anglicans, Presbyterian and Independent dissenters, Quakers, Baptists, and patriotic Catholics. Liberty for nonconformists secured a majority coalition in Parliament. It expanded connections with, and strengthened loyalties of, overseas colonies such as Massachusetts and Pennsylvania. It abetted alliances with European Protestant regimes, chiefly the Netherlands and Protestant German states. William's promise to give Catholics liberty to worship in private also appealed to his Catholic subjects in the Netherlands and aided his diplomatic overtures to Spain and Austria. Interconfessional alliances at home and abroad strengthened England's military fortunes and overseas commerce, which in part funded defense of the kingdom. Liberty and toleration served the new national order.[15]

Religious and civic leaders in New England celebrated William's accession as a relief from an unsympathetic and crypto-Catholic government installed by James: the so-called Dominion of New England and its Governor Edmund Andros. Angered by James's annulment of their long-cherished charter, the imposition of new navigation acts and hostile officials, and encroachments by Andros on unsettled land claims in Maine, they endorsed the removal of Andros by Boston mobs. Increase Mather, a prominent Boston pastor then in London to plead with James for less onerous policies in New England, immediately began negotiations for a new charter with the Williamite court and government.[16]

Scores of pamphleteers and polemicists limned events in London and Boston as an assertion of English rights, including liberty of conscience. According to Whigs, the Stuart crown by that time had so succeeded in centralizing power—or in making claims to power—that the threat to England's well-being appeared to originate less in faction and disorder, as it had in the days of the civil wars, than in an overly powerful court.[17] Drawing from mid-seventeenth-century republican rhetoric, they championed liberty of conscience and toleration as protections against royal absolutism. They promoted William as a defender of England's constitution who would enact policies that protected the liberties of loyal English subjects whatever their confession. Historians have disagreed about the extent to which Whig and Williamite policies produced religious liberty in practice, yet the turn in argument away from confessional uniformity is clear. All sides in the revolutionary contest claimed that England's welfare depended on indulgence or liberality toward—that is, toleration of—some religious difference within England's public order. The rhetoric of religious freedom, even applied in limited scope, was clearly seen as a political benefit.[18]

Whigs fastened on constitutional arguments in what became something of a mantra: William served England's liberties because he protected liberty of religious conscience. In 1687, Burnet translated a tract by one of William's Dutch supporters, 50,000 copies of which were printed, that claimed that the prince upheld the rights of free conscience, and would give English, Irish, and Scottish Catholics religious freedom. Burnet also produced his own apologia for William, published anonymously in London, in which he argued that James had disqualified himself from the throne by acts that violated the will of the people to live in a Protestant kingdom. It was not anything peculiar to Catholic belief or practice that disqualified James. It was, so Burnet argued, James's disregard for England's constitution and Parliament: his violation of the law in his defiance of the Test Act, deputation of an ambassador to Rome, erection of Catholic chapels, and appointment of a Jesuit to the Privy Council.[19]

We can include also a piece of propaganda issued just before the "Dutch invasion," William's *Declaration . . . Of the Reasons Inducing Him, to Appear in Armes in the Kingdom of England.*[20] It was by all accounts a ubiquitous statement: read from dozens of pulpits, reprinted in dozens of editions within months, posted in public spaces, and distributed throughout the British

Isles. Burnet, who assisted in its composition, had advised William to issue it as an appeal for English support. In it, William maintained that the people of England had embraced Protestantism as a free choice of conscience, over a long period of time and through great distress. Now a Catholic king meant to abolish the liberties of such a choice by sheer fiat, subjecting the people of England "in all things relating to their Consciences, Liberties, and Properties, to Arbitrary Government." William argued that James intended the "Subversion of the *Protestant Religion*" in England through "Plots and Conspiracies" that confused the meaning of toleration, set previously amicable Protestants against each other, and elevated anti-tolerationist Catholics into positions of power.[21]

William's *Declaration* shaped facts into polemics, and the polemics revealed a discursive norm that functioned as public argument on behalf of the new monarchy: political unity rested on a defense of liberty of conscience, or toleration. William accordingly presented himself as an enemy of arbitrary and absolutist Catholic oppression and friend to religious freedom. He promised to protect a Parliament that would pass laws to establish an accord "between the Church of England, and all Protestant Dissenters." He also vowed to leave unmolested all "good Subjects," whatever their creed, Roman Catholic included.[22] William consented to the Test Act but refused to reinstitute harsh penalties for dissent or recusancy (Catholic worship in private). He appointed as bishops men such as Edward Stillingfleet, Richard Kidder, John Tillotson, and Burnet: moderate churchmen who favored cooperation among Anglicans and all other Protestants. They often were called "latitudinarian" for their acceptance of a wide range of liturgical practices and theological doctrines.[23]

The anonymous author of yet another Williamite tract, *King William's Toleration,* reiterated the tolerationist refrain with a few additions. The author explained that William's promise (in his *Declaration*) to eschew "Persecution" confirmed Protestant teaching, according to which "faith" implied an individual's relationship to God by an act of conscience rather than by state or ecclesiastical decree. So too, according to *King William's Toleration,* William brought dissenters and Anglicans together under a capacious definition of Protestantism, assembled as a common front "against the danger of the *Papists* from abroad" and at home. The pamphlet's argument ultimately rested on political criteria. "The Advance of the *Nation,*" the author held, depended on national unity and commercial expansion, and toleration enhanced both. Therefore, "the fullest *Liberty of Conscience* that is but *Tolerable*" was necessary, the very strength of the kingdom that was Protestantism's most powerful defender.[24]

Expressed through the rhetoric of liberty of conscience and loyalty to England's constitutional order, Williamite agendas shaped religious and political discourse in New England as well.[25] Increase and Cotton Mather's justifications for the overthrow of Andros and the new charter closely paralleled the writings of Burnet, Locke, and other apologists for the new government in London. In the 1689 *Declaration, of the Gentlemen, Merchants, and Inhabitants of Boston*, Cotton Mather imported the idioms of William's pre-invasion text—including papal plots to extinguish Protestantism and the arbitrary exercise of power against liberties—to urge resistance to Andros. Mather argued that Andros had, like James, packed the courts with unjust magistrates and jurors. By Mather's account, Andros also relied on Catholic military officers to lead campaigns against French enemies to the north, with poor results, hinting at collusion with the French. Mather paraphrased *King William's Declaration* to link Williamite London to Boston as twin guardians of Protestant and "*English Liberties*": both "signally made up of *Reformed Churches*" that were under assault by a Catholic "Design" for "the extinction of the *Protestant Religion.*" Mather continued to extol William and the ideals of liberty of conscience and to sound the alarm against royal absolutism and Catholic coerciveness nearly a decade after the Glorious Revolution and, yet again, twenty-five years after that, when 1688 still struck Mather as a battle for "an Everlasting *Liberty of Conscience.*"[26]

The discourse of liberty of conscience and toleration became so normative that it served satirical assaults on the old confessional order long after 1688. Daniel Defoe, a favorite of New Englanders, assumed in 1703 that his readers needed no new arguments for William's policies of toleration. They could simply chuckle at the farce of William's critics who claimed that he had wrongly protected dissenters and latitudinarians—"Fanaticks" and "Mungrel Churchmen" with "a slovenly rude way of Worship"—from plunder, murder, and prison. For Defoe, such Tory sentiments were laughable because they were patently disloyal to England.[27]

The new Parliament incorporated this perspective on religion and the state into the Toleration Act of 1689, confirmed six weeks after William's coronation. Locke stood in the background of the Act, advising his fellow Whigs from the Netherlands.[28] Polemicists and legislators in London admittedly did not attend to the most expansive sections of Locke's letters: philosophical arguments that legitimated a nearly total freedom of belief. Those arguments far exceeded the limits of William's toleration. Yet Locke's pronouncements indicated the direction of the discourse in this period.[29]

Much of the argument in Locke's first *Letter on Toleration* proceeded from his differentiation between the purpose of the state and of the church, which set his position apart from the assumptions of the confessional order. The state, he argued, could not compel belief because only those beliefs that were freely chosen could be regarded as genuine, sincere, or honest (a point made in less precise fashion by *King William's Toleration*). In addition, as Locke maintained, to grant civic rulers the power to enforce religious adherence was to provide a precedent for any state—Catholic or Islamic included—to choose which religion to enforce. The duty of the state, he insisted, concerned temporal affairs only, such as life, liberty, health, and property.[30]

Locke thought that this principle of separation excluded the state from any interference in matters of doctrine or creed. He admitted that the government had a duty to settle quarrels over rites and ceremonies when they rose to the level of public disturbance, but in nearly every other matter of worship Locke maintained that the civil government had no authority, not even to forbid idolatry. He illustrated his point with reference to Native Americans. "If they believe that they please God and are saved by the rites of their forefathers," he wrote, "they should be left to themselves." Indeed, any attempt to extirpate Native American "idolatry" by civil punishments or confiscation of property—the very agenda that the confessional writer Alexander Ross had endorsed in 1651—amounted to justification for coercion everywhere.[31]

Locke, however, made two exceptions. The first concerned Catholicism. He thought it intolerable in many forms because it was intolerant. With its reliance on coercive measures such as the Inquisition, the Catholic Church denied the very liberty of conscience on which the English constitution rested. It also took the form of a hostile state with its assertions that papal excommunication of rulers released their subjects from duties to obey them or recognize their reign. England could accept the private devotions of recusant Catholics, Locke maintained, but it could not countenance the public worship or officeholding of Catholics who might claim, for example, that Protestants were damned or that the reign of an enemy to the papacy such as William was illegitimate. Second, Locke contended that the state ought not to provide toleration for atheists because they denied that there was divine sanction for the moral virtues upon which the commonweal rested, such as honesty and regard for the rights of others. Atheists were not necessarily vicious, in Locke's view, but atheism in itself endangered the very notion of a moral appeal beyond individual judgment, preference, or expedience.[32]

The authors of the Toleration Act drew from many of Locke's contentions, but their aims were narrowly political. They intended to bring dissenters into alliance with the monarchy: "some ease to scrupulous Consciences in the Exercise of Religion," the act began, "may be an effectual meanes to unite their Majesties Protestant Subjects." It reinterpreted the Elizabethan Act of Uniformity to authorize all Protestant ministers who affirmed orthodox, Trinitarian theology and gave an oath of allegiance to the crown.[33] It permitted the public worship of dissenting churches, including Presbyterian, Independent, and Baptist—the last by a provision that they were not to be penalized for their refusal to baptize infants. It also permitted Quaker meetings and accommodated Quaker "scruples" by providing an alternative to oath-taking in the form of a simple declaration. The Act excluded atheists, Roman Catholics, and non-Trinitarian Protestants, e.g., Socinians, from legal recognition in such terms, although it did not prohibit private worship by Catholics or other Christians who professed loyalty to the government.[34]

Supporters of William in New England, such as the Mathers, contended that the combination of William's rule and its religious policies had saved Massachusetts. As Increase maintained in 1691, the Toleration Act had put an end to old animosities between dissenters and "churchmen," drawing New England happily into the royal orbit despite the fact that a new royal council refused to restore the original charter of Massachusetts Bay.[35] Increase lauded Williamite bishops, including Archbishop John Tillotson, as "Friends to *New-England*, (as well as to all good Men)" who had convinced the council to issue a new charter that restored the colonial legislature. Neither Increase nor Cotton Mather, nor their colleagues in New England, to be sure, embraced the Arminian theology of Tillotson or other latitudinarians. Yet many New Englanders recognized that an alliance among Church of England bishops, Whig political leaders, and agents of puritan Massachusetts, along with the support of sympathetic Quakers and Catholics, had secured the Massachusetts government. Puritan divines in London agreed that the new charter, including provisions that extended the Toleration Act to Massachusetts, was a godsend. The subordination of confessional jealousies to post-1688 ideals of liberty on both sides of the Atlantic had become a political blessing.[36]

Cotton Mather later reflected on how the revolution of 1688 and the charter of 1691 compelled him, his father Increase, and, by extension, other leading New Englanders to reconsider the place of religion in the civic order.[37] In a 1724 retrospective on the career of Increase, he recalled his father's realization that religious toleration was a virtue. Increase "found himself Obliged" by Whig politics "unto a *change of Sentiments*" concerning "the vile Method of *Enforcing Religion by Persecution*" that had been integral to New England's confessional order before 1688. Previous laws that "Inflicted *Punishments* on the Broachers of *Pernicious Errors*"—the banishment of antinomians, prohibition of Anabaptist meetings, and exclusion of Quakers—appeared by 1691 as horrible mistakes. Increase "greatly" decried "the Nonsense and Folly of *Converting People* with Penalties." Old-fashioned critics of "*Toleration*," who moaned that the Toleration Act violated New England's covenantal identity as Reformed, he concluded, were deluded. Increase's participation in the ordination of a pastor to a congregation of Baptists in 1691 signaled his new frame of mind. Cotton added his own sentiments: "it is a Thousand pitties, that the *Unhappy Laws* made in the Colony" in its early history would "stand upon Record." Indeed, most New Englanders had "Disclaimed" the old laws that enforced a particular brand of Christianity.[38]

Like Locke, whose *Letter*, and voice in the Toleration Act, provided Cotton with the vocabulary he used to describe Increase's change of mind, the Mathers expressed a religious rationale for noncoercive policies. According to Cotton, even the despicable French knew that they could not compel people to believe: it was "*Unreasonable*" to coerce people to worship in any way "not Proceeding from a *Conscience* Perswaded." Liberty of conscience—the freedom to believe as one chose according to one's reason—was a religious mandate that confirmed the revolutionary monarchy in London and the new government in Boston.[39]

Cotton Mather made this clear in his 1702 *Magnalia Christi Americana*, a quirky, capacious history of New England that blended differences among sects and denominations into a pan-Protestant, Anglophilic narrative. At times, he sounded as though the mandate for toleration extended to all religions. "If we think our own *Understanding* to be a *Standard* for all the Rest of Mankind, we do certainly" overestimate "*our selves*," he warned. More often, he extended the idea of cooperation and mutual recognition in Protestant ecumenical terms. "Let the *Table* of the Lord," he wrote in reference to a common communion, "have no *Rails* about it, that shall hinder a Godly *Independent*, and *Presbyterian*, and *Episcopalian*, and *Antipedobaptist*, and *Lutheran*, from sitting down together." Such a sentiment would have been nearly unthinkable among established pastors in Boston in 1670. By 1691 it had become a rhetorical commonplace.[40]

William's policies and the Toleration Act did not mark a complete rejection of older assumptions about England's Protestant order. Historians have interpreted the Act as a progressive decree of religious liberty, a revolutionary declaration of the power of the state to mandate and control religious life, or as a conservative sanction for a massive Anglican establishment with small-scale concessions to respectable Protestant dissent.[41] Parliamentary legislation after the Act in fact denoted contests over the meaning of toleration and its relation to the religious establishment. The Test Acts, which barred those who were not communicant members of the Church of England from most public offices, remained in place until 1828. The new regime met rumors or discoveries of Jacobite plots against the monarchy in 1696, 1700, 1715, and 1722 with harsh anti-Catholic decrees. In 1698 Parliament passed a Blasphemy Act, which prohibited from public office those who claimed to be Christian but denied the Trinity.[42]

For all of that, however, the scope of acceptable or legitimate religious practice did widen in England and its colonies. English Catholicism grew in the wake of the Act, partly as a result of benign neglect on the part of the king and local officials. The number of private chapels, conventicles, and devotional circles rose significantly, and Catholics no longer committed a legal offense by attending a private Mass rather than Anglican worship. Many Catholics prospered economically and were promoted to high office as counselors. The Treason Act of 1695 formally distinguished between Catholic adherence and treason.[43]

Dissenting groups too flourished after the Toleration Act, with thousands of new congregations established before the turn of the eighteenth century. They had recognized ministries with legally licensed ordinations, worshipped in public, built meetinghouses, appealed for members, performed marriages, and baptized children or new converts. The Test Acts were only intermittently enforced, partly because of popular acceptance of dissent among civic officials such as the Lord Mayor of London. In 1695, Parliament let the Licensing Act expire, effectively permitting the publication of nearly any theological opinion, including Catholic catechisms and Bibles, apart from outright blasphemy or sedition. Anti-Trinitarian sects spread. After the Revocation of the Edict of Nantes, Huguenot immigration to England further increased the variety of Protestants, as did an influx of refugees from Belgium, the Palatinate, and Salzburg. Many refugees from the Continent were attached to radical forms of enthusiasm and millenarian ideas but nonetheless were supported by the English Church and exempted from parliamentary stipulations on nonconformity.[44]

Burnet and other latitudinarians fostered an international coalition of Protestants, from Boston to Leipzig and London to Malabar, that confounded any presumed equivalence between being English and being a particular sort of Protestant. For latitudinarians, the "Protestant interest" came to encompass a wide range of different churches, movements, and nationalities.[45] Interconfessional cooperation, especially in proposals for international missions, went hand in hand with a theological literature focused on the defense of Christianity as a simplified set of beliefs and moral imperatives. Doctrinal precision and interconfessional debate—among Lutherans, Calvinists, and various types of Anglicans—yielded to calls for cooperation and union through a rational, affective, and sincere form of Christian belief.[46] Burnet maintained as well that an irenic agenda and support of toleration would define international Protestantism over and against Catholicism. He insisted that Protestant confessional divisions held little meaning in the post-1688 world.[47]

New England Protestants embraced similar agendas. Mather's affirmation of "liberty of conscience" culminated in alliances with a wide array of Protestants.[48] He had a robust correspondence with August Hermann Francke, the head of the Pietist community at Halle, about common denominators among Protestant confessions: belief in Christ, prayer, and works of love. He recounted his exchanges with Johann Ernst Gründler, a leader of the Danish-Pietist mission in Tranquebar (in the southwest coastal region of India), about the possibilities of ecumenical missions abroad. Lay leaders in Massachusetts, such as Samuel Sewall, believed that New Englanders belonged to an international coalition of Protestants of various denominations throughout Europe.[49]

In light of the possibilities of the evangelization of non-European peoples, Mather advised other New Englanders to put an end to "*Controversies of Religion,*" regard all other Protestants as partners, and see the adherents of other religions as interlocutors. He declared that the "true Citizen" thus cherished religious liberty. He also gushed, as was his wont: "there are Hundreds of Thousands of Generous Minds" (the phrase echoed Burnet's description of Heidelberg divines) who would take the day in such a spirit, "and the Mean, Little, Narrow Souls, that know no *Religion*, but that of a *Party*" with political privilege, "will become deserted Objects for the *Disdain* and *Pity*."[50]

Such changes, even if partial, indicated that the new discourse of religion and the state had implications beyond parliamentary acts: a detachment of English identity from any one meaning of Protestant. Locke himself thought that the significance of the Toleration Act exceeded its original legislative limits. As he informed a Dutch correspondent, the Act was not "so wide in scope as might be wished for by you and those like you who are true Christians," but it represented progress and "beginnings," the "foundations" of "that liberty and peace" that "is one day to be established."[51] He may have had in mind something like the conditions set down in his 1669 *Fundamental Constitutions of Carolina*, a provisional instrument adopted by the Lords Proprietors of Carolina (and suspended in 1690). The *Constitutions* gave full toleration to all theists, prohibited any person from molesting the worship of or using abusive language "against any religion," and allowed slaves to choose their own religion. It protected the rights of Native Americans to maintain their modes of worship and barred the confiscation of their property for religious reasons. Although the document had short-lived effects, it revealed the ethos that informed Whig discourse.[52]

To return to the often discordant political and ecclesiastical affairs in London, the language of toleration and pan-Protestant concord was an ideal, not a reality in practice. Contests for power between Whigs and Tories, and disputes among High Church Anglicans and their latitudinarian opponents, became more heated at the turn of the eighteenth century, at least until the consolidation of Whig power after 1714. Admirers of the Williamite monarchy constructed their discourse of toleration, a broad Protestant coalition, and political consensus as a response to the factionalism that shaped public affairs in the decades following 1688. Anglo-American Protestants promoted their post-confessional views to foster unity in light of what appeared to be partisan rage.[53]

Whig tracts, royal declarations, the Toleration Act, and parallel accounts from New England, in sum, suggested that England's welfare ought to be untethered from a confessional order. The Church of England still enjoyed formal establishment. Protestantism still enjoyed widespread support under the banner of the "Protestant Interest." By the terms in the texts discussed here, however, one could be a good Anglican, Baptist, Quaker, sectarian, or even Catholic subject. The very meaning of "good" had taken on

political—we might even say "secular" in the modest sense of excluding theological doctrine—valences: tolerant, reasonable, and loyal to the kingdom.
As Cotton Mather put it, public virtues such as being a "*Good Neighbour*"
and a "*Good Subject*" endowed a person with rights to the "Temporal
Enjoyments" of life and property "before"—meaning whether or not—"he is
a *Christian*." In this sense, one did not necessarily inherit a religious identity
along with one's political identity as English. One freely chose one's religion
as a right of being English.[54]

Religious Comparison and the Idea of Toleration

The political impetus to tolerance and, with it, a non-doctrinaire approach
to different religions in the public sphere occupied major post-confessional
thinkers across Europe during the turn of the eighteenth-century: the German
jurist and natural law philosopher Samuel von Pufendorf, Locke, the French
philosopher and religious scholar Pierre Bayle, and the Prussian philosopher Gottfried Wilhelm Leibniz, among others. They also occupied English
Protestant scholars of the world's religions, who reframed descriptions of the
religious "other." Previous writers such as Ross and Crouch had evaluated
other religions according to their proximity to Protestant creed and deference to the religious establishment. Post-1688 writers analyzed religions
according to moral principles with political import, such as liberty of conscience, reasonableness, and civility.

For Whig sympathizers on both sides of the Atlantic, Bayle (whose works
were rapidly translated into English and greatly influenced Locke) offered
an especially telling new approach to religious comparison. A Huguenot
who spent much of his illustrious career in Amsterdam, Bayle issued several arguments against religious persecution, with French royal policy in
mind. The most learned and admirable Europeans, he announced in 1686,
had forsaken dogmatic wars and religious violence in favor of "Gentleness,"
"Civility," and "Politeness." He used this moral-political agenda to frame
his commentary on different religious figures and movements in his 1692
Historical and Critical Dictionary. Bayle's dictionary, which he claimed to
have designed to correct errors in other dictionaries such as Moréri's (more
on Moréri below), offered learned synopses of religious events and figures and
provided moral and philosophical—chiefly skeptical—arguments for toleration. In a remarkable feat of cross-cultural pairing that must have appealed

to Whigs, Bayle compared England's revolution of 1688 to a 1688 Buddhist coup against a pro-Catholic monarchy in Siam (Thailand).[55]

He also used the entry on "Mahomet" to critique the coercive measures of Catholicism and endorse tolerant traditions within Islam. He began with a description of a traditional Christian argument that the spread of the ancient church in the face of Roman persecution demonstrated the truth of Christianity. Yet, Bayle observed, western critics had denounced Islam by contending that it had spread quickly and become powerful only because it appealed to base, carnal instincts. Then again, Robert Cardinal Bellarmine had insisted that the size, extent, and power of the Roman Church proved that God favored Catholicism over Protestantism, especially over its small and weak Reformed versions. Bayle concluded that all such arguments about the size and power of a religion revealed nothing about its truth, divine status, or moral worth. He argued that Islam, in fact, conveyed moral precepts with which western Christians ought readily to agree, and some that surpassed Christian teaching. While the Church of Rome promoted violent persecution of non-Catholics, Mahomet commanded his followers to speak well of neighbors, provide charity, and renounce vanity. Bayle's dictionary conveyed the message that doctrine—whether Catholic, Protestant, or even Muslim—had little to do with civic virtue. To serve its function in public life, the best religion promoted charity and tolerance. In this respect, Islam was preferable to polemical and coercive versions of Christianity.[56]

From 1690 through 1715, a new generation of English scholars of the world's religions produced popular works reflecting the same moral criteria that framed Bayle's dictionary. Anglo-Protestants did not fully abandon the chauvinistic assumptions of a confessional order. Yet turn-of-the-century writers largely jettisoned previous arguments for confessional uniformity. Their apology for English Protestantism rested instead on claims that Protestantism accorded with the ideals of liberty of conscience, regard for learning, and respect for civility that held together an increasingly diverse kingdom. They accordingly set about to canvass the religions of the world for indications of those same ideals, rarely adding substantive detail to that provided by Purchas and Ross.

Patrick Gordon produced one of England's first religious geographies written from this new perspective, his 1693 *Geography Anatomized*. A naval chaplain and fellow of the Royal Society, Gordon traveled to America as one of the first missionaries of the Society for the Propagation of the Gospel. He intended his work, which was published in nineteen editions through 1749, to inform ordinary clergy and middle-class households about the variety of religious choices in the world and the importance of worldwide evangelism. To that end, he provided a primer on geography, with sections devoted to basic terms such as horizon, latitude, and longitude, and analyses of problems such as measuring the equator, along with basic descriptions of geographical features, economies, political histories, and religious institutions of each land. Gordon's book became a mainstay of commentators and clerics in England and New England. American newspapers cited Gordon frequently as a source of background information to explain faraway events: Protestant alliances in Europe, Ottoman military defeats, reports of miracles in Catholic lands.[57]

Gordon signaled his regard for liberty of conscience and toleration at several points. As a missionary, he had a vested interest in the notion that political regimes ought to allow for the religious debate and change of affiliation implied in evangelism. Moreover, he understood toleration as a boon to England. He dedicated one edition of his work to Thomas Tenison, a Williamite bishop with Whig loyalties and latitudinarian convictions who succeeded Tillotson as Archbishop of Canterbury. As he extolled England's post-1688 mixed constitution, Gordon tied the political virtues of the Williamite monarchy—its regard for the "Industry, Liberty and Happiness of the Subject"—to its tolerance for religious dissent. As Gordon put it, "True *Reformed Religion*" was "publickly profess'd" in William's England without factionalism and fury. Because, Gordon continued, "all Sects and Parties are tolerated," the kingdom enjoyed unity and concord. In this light, Gordon validated religions that worked in public for the common good and critiqued those that legitimated arbitrary power and coercion. His criticism of Catholicism included evidence of intolerance and state coercion. He mentioned the cruelty of the Revocation of the Edict of Nantes in France. From his perspective, only the fear of the Inquisition or sheer ignorance— abetted by laws that prohibited the publication of Protestant material— explained why otherwise cultured Italians adhered to Catholic practice.[58]

Gordon also analyzed non-western traditions according to the standards of liberality and civility that, he claimed, bound together different factions in England. His description of the peoples of North Africa as barbarous and brutish had more to do with what he described as their unsociable practices than with their religious beliefs. He reported that Native Americans in New England were cruel when provoked but otherwise gentle and, moreover, "very Ingenious and quick of Apprehension." He maintained that their intelligence portended well for their receptivity to Christianity, if only New Englanders would set aside their doctrinal quarrels and attend to missionary work.[59]

Toleration also served as a criterion for analysis in William Turner's 1695 *History of All Religions in the World*. A vicar in Sussex, Turner produced an encyclopedic work: 607 pages of geographic facts, summary accounts, definitions, and assorted details about religion throughout the world.[60] According to his account, English Protestantism's suitability for interconfessional cooperation recommended it as both true and excellent. He dedicated his work to yet another of the period's Williamite bishops, Robert Grove, who served as a chaplain in the royal court. As Turner informed Grove, he sought to demonstrate the sublimity of nearly all versions of Protestantism in England, so that "we may have no occasion of Disputing" and reason instead for "Loving like Christians."[61]

He reiterated cross-confessional themes in his Preface "To the Reader." A fair, impartial, and unconstrained examination of the world's religions, he maintained, would lead the reader to three conclusions. First, atheism and skepticism were untenable positions: antisocial and improbable. Second, Christianity appeared to be the most rational and sociable form of religion. Third, Christianity constituted an essentially single religion with a common set of beliefs and practices despite its different "Sects and Branches." That being the case, he urged mutual toleration and interconfessional cooperation, especially among all Protestants and between Protestants and Greek Orthodox believers. "I am my self as Catholick," meaning liberal and cosmopolitan, "as is Lawful," Turner explained, "so I would to God our Western Christians" would learn about other versions of Christianity, work to find common ground in "Creed and Liturgy," and engage in "Charitable Communications and Communion" with other traditions, especially "all the Subdivisions of the Greek Church."[62]

Like Gordon, Turner also contended that toleration would enable cooperation among mission workers from different churches and at the same time display to non-Christians the merits of Christianity. Christianity was appealing, he argued, because true Christians offered salvation without compulsion. Evangelistic activities in this sense rested on a platform of liberty of conscience: the superiority of voluntary faith over inherited identity as the basis of belief. Turner argued that mutual cooperation among confessions would in this regard "enlarge the pale, and promote the Gospel amongst Jews and Mahometans and Pagans." Protestants previously had been known by "the opprobrious Distinctions of Sects and Schisms." It was now time to "Unite," "lay aside" their "Prejudices," and be known by their tolerance and concern for the common good. Such ecumenism, Turner insisted, undergirded not only England's government but also Protestant missionary efforts among unbelievers in Africa (the "Mahometans") and America (the "Pagans"). Turner emphasized his evangelistic intentions with the inclusion of a whole section devoted to stories of conversion from the days of St. Augustine to seventeenth-century New England.[63]

Turner sustained this argument by the very organization of his material. Rather than define the major headings for his subjects in regional or national terms—the religion of England or of New England, for example—he made religious practices themselves the chief categories for his book. Part I covers worship practices, rituals, and creeds. It gives general definitions of subjects such as objects of worship, priests, vestments, feast days, sacrifices, singing, rites of purification, sacraments, weddings, funerals, and ecclesiastical courts. Following each definition, Turner provided cursory descriptions by tradition (so, e.g., the prayer practices of Jewish synagogues, Orthodox, Protestant, and Catholic churches, Islamic mosques, and ancient pagan temples). Part II concerns moral teaching and social practices: notions of divine law, confession and mortification, love to enemies, obedience to civil rulers, domestic duties, industriousness, proper dress, and chastity. Turner's work modeled a new description of religion as an activity that could be defined, categorized, and given (a rather jumbled) taxonomic order apart from (or only coincidently attached to) national identity or political establishment.

The same could be said for the English version of a 1701 book originally authored by a French Jesuit named Louis Moréri. Moréri's *Great Historical, Geographical, Genealogical and Poetical Dictionary* was a favorite of New England divines, including Cotton Mather and Jonathan Edwards. Mather recommended that New England pastors secure a copy because successive editions steadily increased its "*Immense Treasure*" of historical facts. The dictionary appeared not only in his family library but also in the collections of Harvard and Yale. The popular writer John Clarke, upon whom Edwards relied for advice on accumulating a useful library, also urged his readers to consult Moréri.[64]

English Protestants might also have trusted Moréri's work because it had been edited and enlarged by Jeremy Collier, an English clergyman who added some entries, corrected others (Bayle's critique of Moréri undoubtedly came

REVOLUTION AND TOLERATION 87

into play), and provided a strong rationale for such a work. Unlike Gordon and Tuner, Collier hardly revered the revolution of 1688. He refused to give an oath to the new monarchy (making him a "nonjuror") and was briefly imprisoned for denouncing William's accession. He nonetheless contributed to the new style of religious dictionary, all the more resistant to confessional readings perhaps because of his nonjuring status. He argued that the great profusion of dictionaries and geographies published toward the end of the seventeenth century marked a new stage in the advancement of learning. It linked Protestants and Catholics in a common enterprise that required data from all quarters, whatever confessional or religious origin.[65]

Moréri and Collier (hereafter simply Collier) accordingly offered little in the way of opinion about the theology or beliefs of different religions. Their dictionary instead focused on ceremonial practices and the extent to which their subjects displayed tolerance or intolerance. One of its lengthiest entries, on the Roman "Inquisition," provides details about clerical vestments, processions, the use of candles, and the choreography of judges and the accused during the final *auto de fé*. Collier implied that the Inquisition amounted to an unreasonable attempt to impose creedal assent. As a public act, it fell short of what English people understood to be virtue—the virtue of allowing liberty of conscience. So too, the entry on the "Pope" fastened on rituals of adoration of the Pope and the massive, intimidating bureaucracy that constituted the See of Rome.

Works on the world's religions in this period also deployed criteria such as reasonableness, learnedness, or humaneness, as cognates of toleration. Collier characterized the Jesuit controversialist "Robert Bellarmine," for example, as a "great Prelate" and learned historian. His bête noir, John Calvin, stands equally impressive as a "Person of Sense" with "considerable Learning," "a good Memory, and fine Pen." Indeed, Collier crossed all confessional boundaries by suggesting that if Calvin had a fault, it was his "inflexible Severity" and tendency toward "*Roman* Tyranny." Collier was less interested in parsing the doctrinal superiorities of Protestant or Catholic creed than he was in illuminating the political virtues (or vices) of his subjects according to sensibilities that promoted national solidarity: generosity of spirit, toleration of dissent, honest scholarship. In such terms, he also provided terse and largely dispassionate observations on Islam and its founders (entries, e.g., on "Ali" and on "Mahometism"). Collier shifted into a critical mode only when he described Islamic rituals that appeared to elevate bodily gesture or ecstatic experience over learning. Collier's entry on "AMERICA" similarly describes

Native peoples chiefly in terms of the extent to which they could be deemed "civil" or custodians of "Laws" and "Government." They displayed in sum "a Mixture of Civility among some, more than others." Genius and civility functioned for Collier as analytic categories that could apply across religious traditions.

Travel and Religious Encounters

The revolution of 1688 did not completely alter the discourse of the religious other. Protestant dictionaries and geography books from the turn of the century displayed a mixture of antipathy toward non-Protestant religions and sentiments for toleration and mutual respect. Travel narratives written by laypeople from this period similarly reflected a midpoint in the transformation of views of religion: a mixture of inherited conventions and post-confessional innovations. Locke, who compiled one of England's largest libraries of travel books (some 350 titles in Latin, Italian, French, Spanish, and English) noted that accounts from the sixteenth through the mid-seventeenth centuries appeared outdated. He criticized narratives such as John Smith's and compilations such as Hakluyt's and Purchas's as overly polemical. They contained erroneous accounts, he complained, and overlaid empirical description with theological commentary, "excessive full" of "mean quibbling." From Locke's perspective, travelers writing during the first decades of the eighteenth century displayed less theological "quibbling."[66]

To put this a bit differently, Locke thought that recent travelogues properly described other religious practices as more or less tolerant, reasonable, and civil. Those three terms were interrelated in whiggish discourse. Toleration protected liberty of conscience and the freedom of religious choice that sustained political liberty (and, in England, the constitutional monarchy). Such choice was rightly made—genuine and sincere—when it followed the dictates of reason. One was to choose one's religion according to European-wide standards of intelligibility, veracity, and morality. Those standards in turn included civility and amity as the means of society. To illustrate, we can focus on three travel narratives from the period—by John Stoddard, Jonathan Belcher, and Lady Mary Wortley Montagu—with brief mention of related texts from other writers.

Stoddard paid attention especially to the issue of toleration. A son of the well-known Massachusetts preacher Solomon Stoddard, John entered government service as a commissary to French forces in Canada after his 1713 graduation from Harvard. In 1713 and 1714 he traveled to Quebec and Montreal in order to negotiate the terms of release for New Englanders captured during Queen Anne's War (1702–1713). He recounted his journey in an unpublished diplomatic journal.[67]

Throughout his account, Stoddard contrasted people who exhibited tolerance and civility with others who displayed bigotry and incivility. After his trip to Quebec under escort of "friendly Indians," he met with the governor general of Canada, the Marquis de Vaudreuil. Stoddard described Vaudreuil as a polite counterpart, who assured him in perfectly liberal cadences that "all prisoners should have free liberty to return" to New England. Yet, as Stoddard complained to Vaudreuil, Jesuit priests had so intimidated the prisoners that many of them feared to leave. Priests had gone from house to house, threatening New Englanders with hell or loss of family and possessions should they leave Quebec. To "terrify" such poor souls with "the danger of perdition" appeared to Stoddard "as barbarous and inhuman."[68]

From this point on, Stoddard portrayed a contest between the Catholic Vaudreuil, an agent of empire who appreciated civility and eschewed religious coercion, and the resident Jesuits, who "vexed and disquieted" New Englanders "about their religion." Vaudreuil instructed local priests that the King of France himself had decreed that the prisoners were to be given "liberty and freedom" in such matters, so that they could choose their religion with "candor and sincerity"—a nearly Lockean formulation of liberty of conscience. Such was the governor's "honor and justice," in Stoddard's words, that he allowed English Protestants to conduct worship in Quebec: a display by Vaudreuil and his officers of "good character," "reason," and "principles of justice." In this setting, by Stoddard's account, agents of the French monarchy exhibited more public virtue—more toleration of religious difference and concern for liberty—than did zealous Catholic priests.[69]

Further developments complicated the whole matter of the prisoners and their religion. According to Stoddard, Vaudreuil was unable to restrain the Quebecois Jesuits. The governor also had learned, as he informed Stoddard, that Louis XIV had naturalized some of the English prisoners and accordingly prohibited them from returning to New England. During the next three weeks, Stoddard, Vaudreuil, and other officials on both sides engaged in negotiations and arguments about religious liberty and state coercion. When Vaudreuil temporarily left Quebec to settle some affairs in Montreal, the acting lord intendant of Quebec prohibited visitations to prisoners on the Sabbath. Stoddard protested. He argued that Protestant preachers ought to be allowed to appeal to New Englanders who had professed Catholicism under duress. English captives, he observed, might choose to return to their English and Protestant faith. Stoddard contended that "since" Jesuits had used "all possible endeavors" to "persuade them to embrace" Catholicism, "with which they were" merely "infatuated, no man could suppose it reasonable that we should be prohibited liberty to use means to undeceive them." Genuine religious conviction, as Stoddard implied, was a matter of reason, deliberation, and free choice. When the intendent countered that French law forbade Protestantism, Stoddard invoked precepts from international law. The intendant rebuffed Stoddard with a telling admission: French priests had told him that English preaching "undid all that they had done in seven years" of Catholic proselytization.[70]

Similar disagreements plagued Stoddard when he traveled to Kahnawake, near Montreal, to recover English children held in the Mohawk village. Jesuit priests had instructed village elders to refuse to repatriate the children. Stoddard explained to the "chiefs" that such instruction contradicted European-wide mores that children did not have the "discretion" or reason to choose their kinship and ought to be returned to their families. The "chiefs" agreed with Stoddard. They had, as Stoddard later told Vaudreuil, "such principles of justice engraved on their minds, that they account it [the return of children] very reasonable." Mohawk leaders nonetheless refused his request because, as they told him, "the Bishop had been there" and warned them that the release of the children "would thereby be the occasion of their damnation, and Christ would be angry with them." According to Stoddard, English Protestants and French Catholic army officers defended liberty of conscience. Kahnawake Mohawks upheld principles of reason and justice. Jesuit missionaries, on the other hand, deployed hellish intimidation and state power.[71]

Stoddard's journal continued in this vein even as it recounted the arrival of English ships at the Quebec harbor, prepared to take on passengers returning to New England. Priests milled about the crowds at the landing, urging newly released prisoners to stay. Stoddard again encountered what he thought to be Jesuit coercion. "The priests," as he wrote, badgered "many of our young and simple people, and by a sort of force constraining of them to abide in this country." It was "justly resented" by New Englanders as "unworthy, and not one instance can be given of such like practice in New England," or even "in all Europe" in the aftermath of the revolution of 1688. Stoddard portrayed the New England mind as fixed on liberty of conscience. He may well have overgeneralized, but even his exaggeration in such terms revealed the salience of the ideal of toleration.[72]

Stoddard's narrative represents a trend among Protestant travelers: to evaluate different religions (in this case, Catholicism) not as a whole—good or bad, true or false—but as discrete communities that manifested various degrees of toleration. There was politically admirable Catholicism, to put it crudely, and politically dangerous Catholicism. In this sense, Stoddard's perspective mirrored Locke's. During his travels in France during the 1670s and the Netherlands during the 1680s, Locke came to admire Catholic immigrants from Armenia and eastern Europe who professed a doctrine of tolerance for other religions. He regarded as ridiculous but innocent the culture of relics in everyday French Catholicism: bones and teeth, remnants of the Virgin's milk, water pots from the wedding party where Jesus turned water into wine. He merely laughed at attendants who boasted that the basilica church in Toulouse held the entire bodies of six of the apostles and remains of 100 other apostles. Locke presented such claims as neither mean-spirited nor threatening. He deplored, however, French royal officials or papal emissaries who stripped away the rights of Huguenots and eventually pronounced a policy of outright persecution.[73]

Locke's last observation indicates that Protestants rendered a common opinion about the institutional Catholicism of the papacy, or what they characterized as a militant, Jesuit-led, Rome-enforced campaign to compel people to the Church of Rome through threats of perdition or civil punishment. Protestant writers used "popery" to stand for power and tyranny. It had little to do with Catholic theology or devotion proper.[74] Burnet put the issue in historical, highly polemical terms. If one wanted to know the character of Catholicism as directed by the papacy, one only had to tick off some of the signal events of 1685: the attempted subversion of the English monarchy, the Revocation of the Edict of Nantes, the abrogation of toleration for the Waldensians (a Protestant group in Alpine Italy and France), and a Catholic coup against the Protestant ruler of the German Palatinate. It was a tale of political aggression and intolerance.[75]

The young New Englander Jonathan Belcher used the same post-confessional standards to characterize the religious practices of the people he met while traveling. The son of a well-to-do Boston merchant, Belcher took a journey in 1704 to London, through the Netherlands to Hanover (the family seat of the future royal dynasty of England). Although business occupied much of Belcher's itinerary, he filled his diary with observations on the varieties of Christianity he encountered.[76]

Throughout his account, Belcher expressed admiration for religious communities that practiced cross-confessional tolerance along with deliberate and learned piety. He was pleased, for example, by the erudition of people he met in the Netherlands and esteemed the religious diversity of its towns. Quaker, Brownist (Anabaptist), and Jewish merchants, he noted, flourished in Rotterdam. The respect for art and history displayed in the museums of Leiden impressed him. The tolerance and various cultures of Amsterdam delighted him, in part because of the city's attendant prosperity. He was awestruck by the size of its public exchange, the number of windmills, the immensity of the Dutch mercantile fleet, and the prevalence of workhouses, hospitals, and asylums for the city's needy. A culture of science and reason, toleration, and civility went together in the Reformed Netherlands.[77]

From Amsterdam to Hanover, Belcher commended forms of Protestantism that he had never experienced in New England. He marveled at the fact that Catholics and Lutherans in the western Saxon town of Osnabrück shared a common bishop, alternatively appointed by the Lutheran prince and Roman hierarchy. He was hosted in Hanover by the electress Sophia and her son the elector of Hanover, the future George I of Britain (electors were German princes or heads of state who chose the emperor). Belcher cautiously approved of the court's version of Lutheranism. As he described it, worship at the elector's chapel was remarkably formal: a brief sermon, sung liturgies of Psalms and hymns, the use of an orchestra, and kneeling at rail for communion. The chapel featured "alters" with "silver crucifixes and pictures round which are histories of our Saviour and of his passion." Belcher was perplexed by the monasteries and convents maintained by German Lutherans. Religion at the Hanoverian court was hardly Reformed, yet Belcher nonetheless was won over by the piety and kindness of its adherents.[78]

The deeper Belcher traveled into Germany, the more he regarded different religions according to what he regarded as sincere and learned adherence. On his way to Berlin, he visited Jesuit houses and Benedictine monasteries, giving mixed reviews. He was put off by monastic students who roamed the streets begging for alms and taken aback by monks who made a show of their frequent devotions but otherwise "live as much at their ease and take their pleasure," with their gardens, fishponds, good wine, servants, and frequent travel. Their disparagement of neighboring Pietists struck Belcher as hypocritical. Yet the generosity and conviviality of many of his Catholic hosts charmed him, as did the magnificent libraries with thousands of books that marked monasteries as nurseries of learning. He especially appreciated the fact that the monks at the Lamspringe Abbey, which served as a home for displaced English Benedictines, lived amicably with their Lutheran neighbors.[79]

Berlin, however, affected the young New Englander like no place else in Europe. The palace of Frederick I, king of Prussia, captivated him. Belcher might have felt a political affinity with the Prussian court, an inveterate enemy of France and sometimes ally of England. He admired Frederick's massive amount of military armaments. There was more to Belcher's affection, however, than politics and firepower. The gardens, libraries, and chambers of curiosities that held objects from China and Japan bespoke a genuine interest in knowledge. Belcher conversed and dined with the president of Frederick's new Academy of Science, none other than the great Leibniz. Belcher admired Leibniz as a paragon of cosmopolitanism, who urged Europeans to learn from the moral teachings of Islam and from what Leibniz called "the natural theology of the Chinese" (Confucianism). Belcher found the philosopher to be not only erudite but also "civil and obliging." Belcher claimed in addition that a genuine religious "spirit" filled the royal palace, conveyed by a large library that held a handwritten translation of the Bible by Luther and a gallery that held a painting of Christ that "strikes one with an awfull reverence." According to Belcher, the combination of reflection, knowledge, and civility in Berlin made Lutheran devotional practices, which New Englanders might otherwise have dismissed as semi-Catholic formalism, to be sincere and well-informed.[80]

Other Protestant travelers used the rhetoric of reasonableness and sincerity to critique what they perceived as Catholic and Islamic proselytizers who compelled Protestants to convert. Stories circulated in print, especially during the first decades of the eighteenth century, of Catholic missionaries in England and Europe who seduced, cajoled, or intimidated Protestants to convert. As one pamphlet claimed, many papists relied on "Compulsion, Constraint or Fear, or in the hopes of worldly Interest." Such conversions were, by Protestant standards, insincere and therefore counterfeit. By contrast, good Protestant ministers appealed to Catholics to embrace faith deliberately: "voluntarily and freely" and without "Mental Reservation," as the same pamphlet put it.[81]

So too, travelers through the borderlands of New England and Canada accused Jesuit missionaries of appealing to base instincts to gain Native

American converts.[82] Joseph Baxter, for example, a New England missionary to Maine in 1717, presented himself as a judicious evangelist in
competition with Jesuits. In the midst of meeting with the Abenaki near
George-Town and Brunswick, he encountered the Jesuit Sébastian Rale,
who, by Baxter's account, attempted to foil English attempts to form
friendly relationships with the Abenaki. Baxter persisted. His method
was to socialize and "discourse with them," as he put it frequently, on
basic Christian doctrine, empathize with their personal tragedies, and
offer Christianity as consolation and preparation for death. They in turn
"seemed very well pleased" with his message. By Baxter's account, Rale, his
fellow Jesuits, and the local "Penobscot Friar," by contrast, frightened the
Abenaki with prophecies of hellfire and social catastrophe. Baxter inflected
his narrative with an Anglo-Protestant polemic that revealed a discursive
presumption: amicable exchange served religion and social order just as
dogmatism betrayed them.[83]

Accusations of coercion colored Protestant travelers' description of Islam
as well. Scholars on both sides of the Atlantic knew something of Islam from
Christian theological critiques of the Qur'an, reports from the Ottoman
wars, and accounts by merchants in the Levant.[84] More widespread and
popular narratives came from English and New England travelers—chiefly
mariners and merchants—who were captured by Barbary pirates, sold to
North African overseers, and pressured to convert to Islam.[85] Captives often
reported intimidation: threats of civil penalties such as fines and harsh physical punishment for refusal to convert and promises of monetary reward for
those who became, as English Protestants put it, *renegados*. Several of these
writers projected fears of papist coercion onto Islamic subjects. Protestant
tales of Ottoman atrocities toward Christians in the Levant and the Arabian
Peninsula, for example, appended reports of Catholic assaults on French
Protestants, as though they were twin outrages. Likewise, English narratives
of captivity in North Africa, such as the diary of William Oakley, compared
the suffering of slavery in the Barbary coast to the martyrdom of Protestants
in Europe at the hands of papal officials. According to this literature, intolerant Muslims were as contemptible as Jesuit proselytizers and Roman
inquisitors.[86]

In her widely noted travelogue, Lady Mary Wortley Montagu deployed
the standards of tolerance, reasonableness, and civility with mixed results: a
mockery of European Catholics, ambivalent report on German Lutherans,
and appreciation for scholarly Muslims. An aristocratic woman of letters with

ties to Alexander Pope, Horace Walpole, Richard Steele, and Joseph Addison, Montagu traveled with her husband, a commissioner of the Treasury, on a diplomatic mission from England through Europe to Istanbul from 1716 through 1718. Her letters from abroad, published in several versions and editions, exuded disdain for zealotry and irrationality. They also expressed regard for gentility and learning, which by Montagu's account made for cordiality across lines of religious difference.[87]

She objected to the thick, material religiosity of Catholic and Lutheran commoners in Germany as impolite. The relics she saw in the "Jesuit church" in Cologne and, to her consternation, a Lutheran church in Nuremberg, appalled her. Her concern was not that relics—encrusted with precious gems, ornamented in gold, and presented in glass *enchassures*—represented idolatry but, rather, that they exhibited poor taste. She quipped that they wasted good jewelry. Medieval statues, including images of mythical beasts such as griffins, struck her as debased. Like Belcher, she found that the learnedness and sobriety of upper-class Prussian Protestantism accorded with English social norms and political sensibilities. "Perhaps I am partial to" Leipzig, she wrote, because "they profess the Protestant religion" and did so "with quite another air of politeness than I have found in other places."[88]

As she traveled eastward, Montagu came into contact with the very sort of religion she appreciated: learned, intellectual Islam. She delighted in conversations with a Muslim scholar in Belgrade. On hearing from her that English Protestants, unlike European Catholics, "did not worship images," the scholar warmed to Montagu. They compared their "creeds" and found common ground. She realized that "Mahometism" was "divided into as many sects as Christianity" but that learned Muslims, like learned Christians, detected a common belief among their confessional differences.[89]

The moral high-mindedness of Muslim scholars also impressed Montagu.[90] Their iteration of Islam, to be sure, differed from that of the common person on the street in Istanbul. Just as highly cultured teachers kept their wine drinking "from the people," so too they quietly taught a version of "plain deism"—a reference, as Montagu elucidated, to a school of Islamic teaching that stressed rational reflection and the ethical life. Her Muslim conversation partner assured her that "if I understood Arabic, I should be very well pleased with reading the Alcoran, which is so far from the nonsense we charge it with; it is the purest morality." Previous English commentators such as Ross had described the Qur'an as a muddle of deception, false claims to miracles, ridiculous fables, theocratic politics, and carnal fantasies. Montagu's interlocutor introduced her to what she regarded as the commendable moral teaching and reasoned approach to theology in Islam. She spoke with other Muslims who had "no more faith in the inspiration of Mahomet, than in the infallibility of the Pope." They professed "deism among themselves" and asserted the difference between theological creed and civil law—law as a "politic institution." They promoted a non-confessional, tolerant order in a good post-1688 fashion.[91]

On the rest of her travels, Montagu continued to search for sociability among "the diversity of religions I have seen." She did not see it in European Catholicism or Greek Orthodoxy, with their dense creeds and meddling in politics. She found it by contrast in Islam and in liberal English Protestantism. Perhaps, she mused, such commonalities could provide a basis for interreligious engagements. She informed her correspondent in England that if rational theologians such as William Whiston could speak Arabic then they would "persuade the generality" of Muslims to embrace "Christianity." Cultured religion implied, for Montagu, an appeal to reason that made possible conversion across religions without coercion. She also implied that reason disclosed the merits of Protestantism.[92]

After 1688, it was a commonplace among English—and whiggish—Protestants to refrain from making critical judgments about whole religious traditions. Rather, they looked for evidence of toleration, reasonableness, and civility in particular communities from across the religious spectrum, just as they scowled at evidence of intolerance, irrationality, and incivility in whatever tradition they encountered. Dictionary authors such as Gordon and Turner, even the Tory Collier, filled their entries with commentary on the social virtues or vices of particular religious groups and figures rather than with confessional or creedal characterizations of Catholicism, Islam, or Native American traditions per se. Travelers wrote their observations under the same assumptions. The New England merchant Thomas Fayerweather, to offer one final example, expressed this outlook in what he regarded as his own practice of tolerance. He described the Abenakis he met in Maine in 1720 as "civill" and friendly. Fayerweather attended a Native religious ceremony—as he did a Mass led by the local friar—without scruple, and hosted convivial gatherings with Native sachems and Catholic priests aboard his ship.[93]

This is not to say that Protestant critiques were ethnographically objective—they were inflected by their own prejudices—but merely to indicate how the post-1688 discourse shaped Protestant descriptions of other religions. During the transitional decades following the Glorious Revolution, to be sure, confessional and post-confessional discourses overlapped. Some Tory writers adopted customary arguments about the need for a single confession, the falsehood of all other traditions, and conversion as the appropriation of a creed inherited and assumed to be true. Others, such as Locke and his deist contemporaries, suggested non-theological, civic virtues as the bedrock of national order. Many, such as Burnet, the Mathers, and the scholarly authors of dictionaries, along with travelers such as Stoddard, Belcher, and Montagu, moved between discourses, voicing sentiments that we can identify as in-between the old confessional agenda and the various programs of a later, Enlightenment liberalism.

Yet for all of the halfway measures and endurance of the confessional model, the political and religious transformations from the 1680s through the 1710s—the center of which was the revolution of 1688—were a turning point. Earlier attempts at narrowly defined measures of toleration yielded to a widespread acceptance of religious dissent and difference within but not limited to a Protestant consensus. The writers discussed in this chapter separated English political identity from any single confession. The very idea that the kingdom no longer depended on doctrinal conformity for the loyalty and solidarity of its subjects prompted new perspectives on non-Protestant religions.

The implication became clear over the following half century. Later writers would stress, even more so than Gordon or Turner, Belcher or Montagu, that such understandings of the place of religion in the kingdom implied the importance of moral liberty or liberty of conscience. Unlike the commentators discussed in this chapter, they also would claim to have identified the deep, politically dangerous occasions of religious intolerance and coercion: religious ceremony itself.

4

Empire and Whig Moralism

In 1742, London publishers brought out Thomas Broughton's two-volume *An Historical Dictionary of All Religions from the Creation of the World to this Present Time*.[1] It was, at the time, one of the largest dictionaries of the world's religions yet offered to the Anglo-Protestant world by an English author. Broughton was a minor celebrity in his day, a scholarly rector in Huntingtonshire who translated parts of Bayle's *Dictionary* into English, wrote the English-language libretto for Handel's *Hercules*, and authored tracts in defense of orthodox Protestantism against deist critics.[2] Hundreds of English consumers subscribed to his *Dictionary*, many of them undoubtedly eager to add it to their household libraries as a marker of civility.[3] The *Dictionary* had an audience also across the Atlantic. The Massachusetts divine Jonathan Edwards referred to it, the library of Harvard added it to its shelves, Benjamin Franklin acquired a copy for his library in Philadelphia, and the Boston-area woman of letters Hannah Adams used it liberally as she compiled her own dictionary of the world's religions.[4] Amid a flurry of mid-eighteenth-century English books on the world's religions, Broughton's stood out for its respectability and popularity.

A frontispiece by Hubert-François Gravelot precedes the text. A French illustrator, Gravelot had moved to London in 1732, initially to assist in the illustration for the English-language version of an encyclopedia of religious ceremonies produced by the Frenchmen Bernard Picart and Frederic Bernard. (More on Picart and Bernard's work in the next chapter.) Gravelot soon gained the favor of the city's literati and established himself as a teacher to aspiring English artists such as Thomas Gainsborough.[5] His illustration for Broughton's *Dictionary*, informed by years of work on similar projects, offers a striking tableau (Figure 4.1).

In the background are representations of religions gone bad, signaled by a calf on a pedestal, a figure of idolatry. Behind the pedestal are images of ceremonialism, priestly power, and hyper-emotionalism: a western, presumably Catholic, cathedral; a mosque; an Egyptian pyramid; and a classical temple to which votaries bring animals for sacrifice. The kneeling figure at the lower

The Opening of the Protestant Mind. Mark Valeri, Oxford University Press. © Oxford University Press 2023.
DOI: 10.1093/oso/9780197663677.003.0005

Figure 4.1 Gravelot, Broughton frontispiece

Credit: Thomas Broughton, *An Historical Dictionary of All Religions from the Creation of the World to this Present Time*, 2 vols. bound in one (London, 1742), frontispiece to vol. 1.

left margin may represent an ascetic worshipping before a statue of an Indian deity. These images convey Broughton's ideas of devotion corrupted by irrational deference to mystery and priestcraft. Unlike Nathaniel Crouch, the writer/publisher discussed in Chapter 1 who featured an image of the devil on a pedestal in the frontispiece to his survey of religions, Broughton omitted references to devils or malevolent forces from his dictionary. He focused on priestly power and ceremony as the essence of idolatry. As he put it in the Preface, his work allowed readers to discern the "purity and simplicity" of genuine religion and the "present corruptions" of religion alike "in the *Romish Church*," ancient paganism, some forms of Islam, and "the *Heathen world*," e.g., India. His survey, he continued, demonstrated that "*Superstition*" had usurped "true religion" in "most places." The central problem was this: "the essence of true religion" was "almost lost in show and ceremony."[6]

Three central figures dominate the scene. Moses holds the tablets of the Ten Commandments, the summary of the moral law. Mary, at the very center of the image, contemplates a plain cross, the cup of communion at her right hand and images for the power of the Roman papacy (the keys of Peter, incense, ceremonial cross, tiara, and abject devotees of the papacy) under her feet. To the right of Mary stands the turbaned figure of Ali, the son-in-law of Muhammad and figurehead for Shiite Muslims. The sword in his right hand droops into shadow while the copy of the Qur'an in his left hand is fully illuminated. Ali appears as an earnest teacher of scripture. No less than Moses and Mary, he represents a religion uncorrupted and worthy of admiration. Broughton gave a precis of his work in such terms: the "*meridian lustre*" of divine truth shone through "the *Mosaical Law*," the "*Gospel Dispensation*," and even within certain schools of thought among the "inventions" of "*Mohammed*." Moses, Mary, and Ali signify sincere belief, simple piety, and moral virtue.[7]

Gravelot's picture reflected Broughton's focus on moral and social norms—signified by the Commandments held by Moses, the simplicity of Mary's devotion, and the moral instruction in the Qur'an—by which to gauge particular religious rituals, practices, or teachings. Throughout the dictionary, Broughton bracketed out confessional criteria. He did not judge religious traditions according to the truth or falsehood of their theological doctrines. Instead, he pitted the virtues of politeness or sensibility against the vices of ceremonialism, which, from his perspective, bred undue deference to power. He set simplicity and reasonableness against ecstasy and mystery, which, he contended, led to religious coercion and disunity. He also contrasted religious expressions that cultivated honesty and public-spirited industriousness with those that legitimated dishonesty and indolence.

Broughton and his fellow writers on the world's religions drew many of their observations from writers of the Glorious Revolution era such as Collier and Turner. They inflected their accounts with a language of toleration that marked a departure from confessional assumptions. They depended on many of the stories and accounts in Purchas and Ross but eschewed the old confessional paradigm according to which whole countries or nations were identified with a monolithic religious tradition or a set pattern of religious allegiance. They avoided the sweeping generalizations made by Restoration-era writers: Catholicism in whole as idolatrous, Islam tout court as preposterous, or Chinese or Native American religions in every form as devil-ridden superstition.[8] Looking for indications of social virtue and vice among particular communities within religious traditions, they lauded many Catholic groups as humane even as they condemned the coercive power of the papacy or the Spanish Inquisition. They admired Shiite moral teachers while they vilified the Sunni Islam of the Ottomans. They identified a variety of Native American cultural traditions, some of which they deemed amiable and others of which they denigrated. Broughton's exclusion of the rhetoric of devilry or other forms of supernatural malevolence signaled this more nuanced attitude.

Yet Britain's changing political circumstances during the first half of the eighteenth century—challenges to Whig rule by Tory politicians, Jacobite (pro-Stuart) agitation against the royal court, an agenda to extend and consolidate the administration of the transatlantic British Empire, and colonial warfare with France—compelled Broughton and his contemporaries to redefine and reorder their moral vocabulary. Without rejecting Lockean pleas for toleration as a policy of the state, they attempted to diagnose the religious sources of intolerance that, by their accounts, motivated Tories and Jacobites (not to mention French Jesuits) and bred disloyalty to Britain. They minimized Locke's devotion, as it were, to sincere belief as a criterion for true religion and emphasized instead the dangers of religious zealotry.[9] They focused their commentary on the merits of benevolence, reasonableness, and honesty, and attendant qualities such as liberality, politeness, and industriousness. They took these virtues to minimize political faction, endorse loyalty, legitimate Britain's contest with Catholic foes at home and abroad, and abet the administration—and profitableness—of overseas empire.

The scholars, travelers, and pastors discussed in this chapter, to be sure, do not represent the full range of Protestants in England and New England. Many High Church Anglicans, critical of the Hanoverian monarchy, rejected Whig policies of toleration. They argued that leaders in the church and government ought to enforce theological orthodoxy and return England to its confessional moorings. Some deists, alongside religious skeptics, rejected the basic precepts of Christianity. In addition, sectarian Protestants—chiefly Quakers and Anabaptists—often resisted the established political order and endorsed forms of religious enthusiasm that confounded the standards of reasonableness and social responsibility promoted by writers such as Broughton. Some of them lived on the periphery—literally or figuratively— of Britain's Empire. This chapter, in sum, places contested ideas in the background in order to focus on an Anglo-American Protestant consensus that especially shaped popular interpretations of the world's religions. That consensus was formed by observers in England and New England who professed to be loyal subjects of Britain's religious and political establishment, supported the Hanoverian monarchy, and affirmed the rudimentary tenets of Protestantism. Among its advocates were moderate, latitudinarian, and deist-minded Anglicans, liberal and conservative dissenters such as Presbyterians and Congregationalists, and promoters of evangelical revival on both sides of the Atlantic.

One final preliminary matter: many of these observers argued that the Church of Rome opposed Great Britain and defamed the moral, social, and political virtues on which Britain depended. They rarely addressed themselves to historic Catholic doctrines—on the nature of faith, say, or on sacramental piety. They instead claimed that institutional Catholicism centered in the Holy See, as distinct from Catholic movements such as Jansenism or local Catholic communities that flourished, for example, in Poland, relied on ceremonialism and ecclesiastical authoritarianism to compel adherence. They presumed that Rome was a political danger. This chapter refers in brief to such sentiments about Catholicism while the following chapter provides an extended discussion of anti-Catholicism and how it inflected readings of other religions.

It bears noting, however, that Catholic observations about the world's religions also changed in this period. Jesuit missionaries and scholars toward the end of the seventeenth century turned away from earlier disparagements of other religions as devilish and decadent. Just like Protestants, they came to stress commonalities among different religious traditions and to probe for indications of spiritual sensibilities among the Indigenous peoples of New France and among the people of China. British Protestants could hardly bring themselves to admit the point: some of the transformations in discourse traced below took place across Europe and within Catholicism as well as within Britain and its colonies.[10]

Imperial Agendas

Political disputes within Britain and imperial contests abroad shaped Broughton and his contemporaries' interpretations of religions and the public order. They wrote in the aftermath of a Tory and High Church resurgence under the reign of Queen Anne (1702–1714) and the controversial accession to the throne of Anne's cousin, George Louis, prince-elector of Hanover, who reigned as George I (1714–1727). A German Lutheran, George favored designs for religious toleration and intervention into affairs on the Continent on behalf of different Protestant groups. On assuming the throne, he filled his Cabinet with Whigs. In 1715, Whigs won an overwhelming majority in parliamentary elections and purged Tories from national and local offices. Under George I, George II (1727–1760), and the administration of England's first prime minister, Robert Walpole (1722 to 1742), British officials put into place a massive bureaucracy—magistrates, inspectors, and other officials included—that brought the empire closer than ever to subjects from London to Boston.[11] Imperial economic policy shaped commerce through regulations on currency, taxation, and trade that purportedly helped to fund the British military and protect Protestant interests across the globe. Loyalty to Britain, Protestantism, and commercial expansion appeared to most Whig commentators as a single agenda.[12]

The most affecting encounter with imperial power, at least for New Englanders, came in the form of military conflict. Although Walpole pursued a foreign policy of détente—Britain and France were at peace from 1714 through 1742—the threat of hostilities among French forces in Canada, Native American nations, and English settlers rarely abated during this period. Sporadic conflicts gave way to formal declarations of war in King George's War in North America or the War of the Austrian Succession (1744–1748) and the Seven Years' War (1756–1763). War between the British and the French inspired new forms of patriotism among New England's Protestants. In 1745, a force of New Englanders captured Louisbourg, a French fortress on Cape Breton Island, and their success produced widespread proclamation of divine blessings on Britain. Leading evangelical preachers on both sides of the Atlantic, such as George Whitefield and Jonathan Edwards, labored to demonstrate their loyalty to the empire by setting aside their criticisms of Anglicanism. Throughout the period, Britain's contest with France for empire in North America infused patriotism with anti-French, anti-Catholic, and anti-absolutist sentiments. Political virtue in such terms meant loyalty to England's parliamentary, Hanoverian monarchy and its policy of liberty for loyal subjects, in contrast to France's absolutist, Bourbon dynasty with its intolerance for all non-Catholic sects.[13]

In the context of Britain's imperial aims and wartime footing, political disunity appeared to Protestant commentators as treacherous, especially when it developed into factionalism. By this latter term, they did not refer to regular contentions about policy among members of Parliament, municipal officials, colonial governors and their assemblies, and the crown. Even Whigs suffered intra-party disputes. Many Protestants nonetheless came to decry a certain kind of factionalism—sometimes given party designations such as Court versus Country, Tory versus Whig, High Church versus Low Church—that by their account incited disloyalty to the crown and Parliament.[14]

Whiggish observers in England and New England especially denounced High Churchmen and Tories whose opposition to Hanoverian policy supposedly rose to the level of disloyalty, even to Jacobite treason. They referred, for example, to the Sacheverell Affair of 1709–1710, remembered long after in political pamphleteering, memorialized in playing cards that offered images of the main characters, and followed at a distance by New Englanders such as Cotton Mather. A flamboyant and combative priest who held several offices at Oxford, Henry Sacheverell had gained notoriety for sermons that assailed dissenters, their Low Church defenders, and their Whig political patrons as traitors to the Church of England. Appointed to deliver the November 5 sermon to the City Fathers of London, a day customarily devoted to the celebration of Parliament's deliverance from an alleged Catholic conspiracy to blow up Parliament's buildings (the Gunpowder Plot), Sacheverell blasted Whig notions of toleration. He decried the execution of Charles I, linked regicide to fanaticism, equated fanaticism with dissent, denounced latitudinarianism, seared Whig politicians, and deplored the Toleration Act. After a month-long impeachment trial in Commons, he was suspended. His supporters in London rioted. Mobs burned several Presbyterian houses of worship. Tory candidates flourished in the 1710 elections. By some accounts, some fifty of Britain's 350 members of Parliament (MPs) in that year were covert Jacobites. Critics of Whig-allied monarchs, they supported Stuart pretenders to the throne.[15]

The Sacheverell riots and the 1710 elections appeared as the last gasp for Tories before the coronation of George I, but the Sacheverell Affair nonetheless distressed Whigs for decades. It also affected the terms of political debate that followed. Sacheverell had argued that Whigs, latitudinarians, and dissenters were, in his colorful diction, "clamorous . . . malignants," "miscreants begot in rebellion, born in sedition [against James II], and nurs'd up in faction" who "threaten the ruin and downfall of our Church and State." Sacheverell raised salient questions. Who best eschewed faction, rejected sedition, and supported Britain's church and state? Tories? Jacobites? Whigs? Such rhetoric compelled Whig partisans thereafter to reply in similar terms, to announce themselves as imperial patriots, enemies of faction, sedition, and irrational zeal.

A second controversy, as notorious as the Sacheverell Affair, also provoked widespread concern. It was named the Bangorian Controversy after its chief protagonist, Benjamin Hoadly, the bishop of Bangor. It began in 1715, when George Hickes, the bishop of Thetford and leader of nonjuring prelates (priests who refused to give an oath to William III and his successors) published a sermon that reframed Sacheverall's outbursts in theological terms. Hickes implied that Parliament's overthrow of James II amounted to rebellion against God's reign. So too, he denounced the Toleration Act, with its countenance of dissent and nonconformity to Anglican liturgy, as apostasy. Nonjuring Tories such as Hickes colored the reign of George I as illegitimate and Jacobite (pro-Stuart) rebellion as godly. At the request of George I, Hoadly attempted to rebut Hickes. He delivered a sermon in the royal chapel in which he contended that Christ made a distinction between earthly institutions—including dynastic houses and ecclesiastical denominations—and the kingdom of God. According to Hoadly, it was pure cant to claim that James II had an irrevocable divine appointment, that the Church of England was the only true church, and that the Whig revolution betrayed England. Hoadly maintained that it was therefore right for Britons to confess their fealty to George I. It was also proper for them to take advantage of the kingdom's relative leniency toward dissent by forming or participating in churches as their consciences deemed to be most faithful. A pamphlet war among Hickes's and Hoadly's defenders followed Hoadly's sermon. It roiled the ecclesiastical establishment in England and intrigued readers in New England. For Whigs, the Bangorian Controversy anchored patriotic loyalty to the promotion of toleration and, with it, a capacious definition of religious legitimacy.[16]

It especially galled Whig patriots that Tories such as Sacheverell and Hickes validated the misdeeds of Catholic devotees of the deposed James II. These "Jacobites" planned, or were rumored to have planned, several rebellions against the post-Stuart crown: a 1689 uprising, a 1696 assassination plot, conspiracies to abet a French invasion, a 1715 uprising, and another in 1719. Jacobite MPs opposed warfare with France and supposedly consorted to bring French advisors to London. In 1745, Charles Edward, the so-called Young Pretender, a grandson of James II and last of the Stuarts, led a small force from France to Scotland, with ill-fated designs on London, to reclaim the crown. The "Uprising of 1745" failed, but it unnerved Whig loyalists. Although the Young Pretender had little chance of success, many Protestant writers mentioned Jacobite plots as a near-constant threat to Britain. Popular journals published in London and exported to New England, such as the *Flying Post* and the *Weekly Journal*, reported on supposed secret conclaves among papal officials and European officials who conspired to assassinate the king and invade the kingdom. The threat of conspiracy was sometimes real; French, Scottish, and papal agents had in fact concocted several schemes to overturn Hanoverian rule.[17]

To offset Tory and Jacobite factionalism, Whig partisans promoted a robust culture of patriotism, including institutions that fostered English identities and notions of citizenship. These included publishing ventures, missionary societies, and schools that conveyed expressions of civil society—common ideas of education, decorum, and communal responsibility—closely linked to imperial loyalties. Patriotic symbols such as the Union Jack and songs such as "Rule Britannia" came into fashion during the second quarter of the century, along with poetic and prosaic reflections on Britain's pan-Atlantic prowess and the idea of a worldwide British community. Allegiance to the monarchy, enthusiasm for commerce, and regard for religious liberty united Britons into a formidable empire.[18]

In support of this agenda, a remarkable array of Protestants during the reigns of George I and George II, excluding High Church Tories and separatist movements, endorsed a broad coalition of churches that promoted imperial interests: Anglicans, evangelicals, moderate and rationalist Congregationalists in New England, Independents, Presbyterians, and deists who called themselves Christians. They saw themselves as members of a public order—a civic religion, in the most generic sense—that was unbounded by traditional confessional standards. This notion of Britain's public religion, as distinct from the doctrines and practices of particular Protestant churches, helps to explain the fact that Calvinist evangelicals such as George Whitefield or Jonathan Edwards, to cite just two examples, drew from the sermons of the latitudinarian John Tillotson and the essays of deists such as

John Trenchard when it came to matters of public concern and social morality. In the public sphere—in the realm of national politics—the wisdom of such writers appeared useful even if their theology contradicted Reformed teaching. In the absence of confessional standards, Protestants substituted a discourse of what one historian aptly has labelled "Whig moralism." That discourse rested on forms of reasonableness to which, they presumed, all subjects of the kingdom could subscribe. By their account, it prompted toleration and other forms of civility, excluded irrational enthusiasm, and thereby became a means to national unity.[19]

How, then, to regard the church establishment? Dissenters or nonconformists in England and New England accepted some form of establishment as a civil necessity, a protection against gross immorality and Catholicism. This, at least, was the opinion of the evangelical hymn writer Isaac Watts and Calvinist divine Phillip Doddridge, of stalwarts of the New England ministry such as Boston's Benjamin Colman, even of the religious skeptic Benjamin Franklin. As the Independent Philip Nye put it, all good dissenters endorsed the "Publick and National Ministry" of the Church of England. To be sure, they thought it their liberty to operate outside the authority of Anglican bishops and without conformity to Anglican liturgical practices (hence the appellation "nonconformist" as a parallel to "dissenter"). Dissenters such as New England's evangelicals were convinced that the Church of England was not ordered by scriptural principles. Yet they conceded that it sustained the Whig monarchy and the cause of Protestantism.[20]

Dissenters also recognized that, in England—and, increasingly through the 1720s, 1730s, and 1740s, in New England—officials in the Anglican parish often educated, catechized, and dispensed charity to local residents. Despite the resistance of most congregationalist clergy to the idea (never implemented) of an Anglican bishop in America, parish ministries of the Church of England in New England flourished in this period without widespread protest. Membership in the church grew from 1,000 in 1702 to 12,600 in 1760. According to most dissenters in England, it was not a contradiction for Presbyterians and Independents to organize themselves into national or provincial institutions even as they deferred to the crown and recognized the legitimacy of the Church of England. After all, the monarchy and a whiggish episcopacy protected the liberties of all loyal Protestants. Their confidence was rewarded when George I established an annual gift—the Regium Donam—to support nonconformist ministers.[21]

Whig Criteria for Religious Authenticity

Anglo-American Protestant observers transposed Whig-imperial agendas into moral rules and used those rules as criteria for their analyses of other religions.[22] To illustrate, we can focus on one influential serial publication from the period: Thomas Gordon and John Trenchard's *The Independent Whig*.[23] Gordon and Trenchard were Whig partisans and critics of High Church Toryism who harbored skeptical—vaguely deist—religious opinions. They masked their heterodoxy in the *Independent Whig*, writing essays scattered with professions of loyalty to Protestantism, the Hanoverian monarchy, and Britain's battle against papal tyranny. Published in London and Philadelphia, the *Independent Whig* was referenced in dozens of controversial works on religion and politics from the period, acquired by admirers such as the New England evangelical Jonathan Edwards, and sold by American booksellers through the 1740s.[24]

With frequent reference to the Sacheverell Affair, the Bangorian Controversy, and Jacobite uprisings, Gordon and Trenchard described High Church zealotry and anti-Williamite Toryism as fractious and therefore immoral. They dedicated the publication of the 1722 collection of their essays to an ecclesiastical body that reprimanded Sacheverell, the Lower House of Convocation, before his impeachment by the House of Commons. In that dedication, they asserted that churchmen who defamed the Glorious Revolution did so in disregard of "the Sovereignty of England" and "Liberties" of the English people that were secured in 1688. Gordon and Trenchard then offered a moral analysis: such churchmen were neither "good Subjects" nor real "Christians" but were "Patrons of Tyranny and Promoters of Immorality" who had no place "amongst *Men of Virtue*."[25]

Throughout their essays, Gordon and Trenchard, echoing philosophical authorities such as Locke and Bayle, criticized the ceremonialism favored by High Churchmen as a twofold error. In religious terms, it stemmed from a childlike fixation on sensible objects: a fascination with dense rites, mystical or magical performance, and the authority of priests whose gestures and incantations channeled the divine. When elaborated into ritual, such a fixation became idolatry. In political terms, ceremonialism inculcated terror and thereby induced devotees into obeisance: undue deference to priests and the political authorities they represented. It blinded people to the whims and pecuniary schemes of the priestly class, often leading to factional disorder and sedition. For Gordon and Trenchard, Tory and High

Church emphases on elaborate ceremony and episcopal authority went hand in hand with Jacobite designs to re-establish a Catholic Stuart line intent on the subjection of English people to monarchical tyranny. On nearly every page of the *Independent Whig*, ceremonialism appears as duplicitous and fractious: a legitimization of servility to arbitrary power ("slavery" appears often in their prose), zeal for dogma, and hatred of other religions. Gordon and Trenchard, like later Protestants who followed their logic, reanimated an anti-ceremonial critique that had long been wielded, with racial implications, against non-Protestant peoples, including Catholics and Jews. They did so for political reasons, which is to say for their support of the Hanoverian Empire.[26]

Nineteen years later, Gordon dedicated the third volume of essays to Lord Thomas Pagett, a Whig MP and attendant of the Prince of Wales. Gordon claimed to defend "the Quiet and Stability of this Free State" in opposition to the assault on English liberties promoted by power-hungry clergy. According to Gordon, nonjuring clergy could never "be good Subjects" because they proved to be "Sources of Faction and Discord." High Church Anglicans, extreme Tories, and Catholic sympathizers made "ill Neighbours" because their bad religious taste had justified bad moral and political sentiment. "That Religion which does not produce Morality," they wrote, "deserves another Name. Morality is the only Religion" that sustains "Human Society."[27]

What exactly, then, was good, patriotic sentiment; and what religious beliefs and practices produced that sentiment and promoted the kingdom's interests? Gordon and Trenchard did not provide clear definitions or logical precision. They never clarified the relation between holding certain ideas, having the correlate sentiments, and behaving in appropriate ways. We can nonetheless gather the terms of their commentary into three clusters of interrelated qualities. These functioned as the moral criteria by which they and their Whig contemporaries analyzed the political virtues of religious expression in their day.

First, Gordon and Trenchard used regnant standards of benevolence or humaneness and connected them to sensibility, politeness, and tolerance. These were, in eighteenth-century commentary, moral qualities that induced loyalty and reduced faction. As a term for an essential virtue or disposition, "benevolence" had become integral to the analyses of Moral Sense thinkers such as Francis Hutcheson of Glasgow and Protestant divines who drew from Hutcheson, such as Edwards. In the works of whiggish writers, the affection of benevolence—regard for the interests of others—implied humaneness. It linked individuals into a commonwealth as it displaced vicious inclinations toward narrow or factional self-interest.[28]

As idioms for the social expression of benevolence, sensibility and cognates such as politeness and civility signified a willingness to accommodate oneself to others: deference, decorum, sympathy, generosity, sociability, and—especially important for commentary on religion—tolerance for fellow subjects who held different religious opinions. Whig partisans such as Anthony Ashley Cooper, the Third Earl of Shaftesbury, and the essayists who appeared in periodicals such as Joseph Addison and Richard Steele's *The Spectator* and Edward Cave's *The Gentleman's Magazine* described sensibility as a form of self-control. It disciplined people to form social bonds of trust and mutuality even as they pursued commercial interests and asserted political liberty. It also compelled people in positions of power to sympathy, toleration, and moderation.[29]

Whig moral philosophers such as Shaftesbury, and journalists such as Addison and Steele, took such virtues to be marks of laudable forms of religion and the opposing vices to be indications of inferior forms of religion. Without naming any particular church, an essayist for *The Spectator*, for example, claimed that "Religion" could be divided into two sorts: those that bred "ill Humour" or meanness and those that inculcated "Decency" or sensibility. Only the latter "gives its Professors the justest Title to the Beauty of Holiness."[30] Shaftesbury laced his major work, the *Characteristicks of Men, Manners, Opinions, Times*, with similar claims. According to Shaftesbury, the toleration of different religions in Britain (we can set aside for now the issue of the breadth of such toleration) meant that religions had to prove themselves according to the civic virtues they manifested: "love" for "the Publick" and regard for "universal Good." Judgments about the genuineness of religious claims, that is, ought to adhere to public standards of moral virtue.[31]

So too, according to Shaftesbury, people were at liberty in Britain, unlike in Islamic Turkey or Catholic Europe, to select their religion according to the extent to which its followers displayed the "Justness of thought and style, refinement in manners" and "politeness of every kind" that led to prosperity and stability. For Shaftesbury, certain forms of classical paganism, the religions of India, and British Protestantism could be deemed virtuous in such terms, just as institutional-hierarchical Catholicism and Protestant radicalism—separatist, hyper-Calvinist, or Anabaptist—had proved themselves uncivil, bigoted, and therefore vicious.[32]

Gordon and Trenchard indiscriminately drew from Hutcheson, Shaftesbury, and Addison and Steele. "Affection, Meekness, Humanity and Benevolence," they asserted time and again, were the marks of religions that loyal Britons ought to embrace. Traditions such as Catholicism and High Church Toryism ought to be rejected because they rested on a zeal, enforced by powerful ceremony, that valorized bloodshed and destruction of property: the sorts of public disorder inflicted on French Huguenots and on poor Londoners during the Sacheverell riots.[33] Gordon and Trenchard argued that Anglican critics of Hoadly so revered priestly power and dogmatism that they had become more coercive and violent than were Muslims and Catholics. "The Infidels have slain their Thousands," Gordon and Trenchard parodied I Samuel 18:7, "and They their Ten Thousands."[34] Any religion true to virtue, as they put it, led its adherents to a "benevolent Disposition of Heart, which inclines any Man, of any Religion, to think well, and hope well, of every Man, of every Religion."[35]

In the hands of Gordon and Trenchard, such rubrics validated several schools within non-Christian religions just as they discredited Anglo-Catholicism and radical Protestantism. One of Gordon's essays, for example, presented a hypothetical scenario in which a "sensible" and "rational" Chinese observer read the New Testament, after which he visited Rome and England. The scriptural "Gospel" appeared to the hypothetical visitor as politically heartening. It conveyed "the most meek and benevolent System that ever appeared," "contrived to root out" the "Malignity, and Selfishness of human Nature" and to abolish the "Pomp and Tyranny" that afflicted much of humanity. If truly understood, it would "destroy for ever all the Seeds of Strife, Anger, and War." In such terms, the Chinese visitor had the moral sensibility to embrace pristine Christianity. In contrast, the visitor witnessed in Rome, the apex of ceremonial "pomp," little but an unending train of moral and political abominations: "Poisonings, Assassinations, unnatural Lust, Pride, Ambition, Divisions, Tyranny, Poverty, Oppression," and "Fraud and Famine." Similarly, he despaired of the dogmatic quarrels, confessional disputes, and sheer inhumanity among some Lutherans and Calvinists in Europe and Scotland. In England, however, he witnessed the "Wisdom, Gentleness, and christian Spirit" of Parliament, which upheld the Act of Toleration in the face of Tory assaults. Such a policy of religious freedom, the visitor concluded, revealed the goodness of whiggish Protestantism, whose ideas could only come "from the good God." The designs of Tories stemmed from "the worst Passions of the worst Men."[36]

Second, Gordon and Trenchard described a related set of virtues that we can gather under the rubric of reasonableness—such as learning, education, and civility—and linked them to the use of persuasion to promote religious devotion. They set these virtues against the use of power and superstition to coerce adherence. Again, their wording was imprecise. Never defining "reasonableness," they deployed the term to mean honesty, candor, studied reflection, and calmness. Proponents of a reasonable approach to religion relied on "Softness, Perswasion, and [moral] Example" to broach different religious opinions. In so doing, as Gordon and Trenchard argued, reasonable religious people promoted concord through their charity, common understanding through their candor, liberty of conscience through their tolerance, and socioeconomic utility through their concern for the common good.[37]

Gordon and Trenchard mustered such terms into a pell-mell assault on the Catholicism of the papacy, ceremonialism, High Church authoritarianism, episcopal tyranny, and supposed betrayal of British interests to the French. The specter of Sacheverell and the Bangorian Controversy loomed behind Gordon and Trenchard's critique. "Priestcraft," as they put it in one of their more acerbic formulations, "converts all who come within its Influence into Idiots or Lunaticks." Such irrationality was the handmaiden of fanaticism: "Party Rage, an implacable and furious Hatred," and "moral War against all" who differed in the slightest detail of doctrine. The excesses of High Church ritual, including consecrations of mundane objects and buildings, sprinklings of water, and formulaic prayers amounted to a "sort of Incantation or spiritual Jugling."[38]

What did Gordon and Trenchard make of High Church arguments that laxity in the enforcement of confessional standards resulted in apostasy and unbelief? They answered with reference to the evangelistic pull of reasonableness. If British Protestants wanted to bring others into the church, then they ought to eschew dogmatism and ritualism and present a version of Christianity marked by "Truth," "Plainness and Simplicity." These qualities appealed to the moral sentiments and the rational faculties of non-Christian interlocutors. Christianity ought to display itself through "the Reasonableness of its Precepts": its abhorrence of "Violence" and of "Art and Policy" [i.e., deception], "its Intrinsick Beauty," its "divine Lustre," and its inculcation of the "Practice of Piety." How else could British Protestants "make Converts" of Muslims, for example, apart from distinguishing "the Beauty and Truth of the *Gospel*, from the Imposture and Absurdity of the Alcoran?" And how could such a case be made "but by our *Reason*?" According to

Gordon and Trenchard, threats of either temporal or eternal punishments rather than appeals to reasonableness spoiled the case for Christianity.[39]

Gordon and Trenchard applied this standard of reasonableness nowhere more trenchantly than in their critique of violence as a tool for conversion. They contended that High Church Tories who charged proponents of toleration such as Tillotson and Hoadly with apostasy, and who proposed civil penalties for dissent, were akin to the zealots of the most vicious sects of Islam. Gordon and Trenchard recounted the "fakirs," the "bloody Villains," who returned to India from their pilgrimage to Mecca, "drunk with Devotion, and flaming with Zeal." They ran through the streets, "stabbing and killing with a poisoned Dagger, all that are not *Mahometans*." The "Persecutors" in England were "all Faquirs" in such terms. Compelling adherence by force turned "a good Religion" into sheer "Mischief."[40] If Tories had their way, Gordon and Trenchard maintained, then religion in Britain would become state-enforced, censorious, and punitive dogmatism. It would make Britain like Ottoman Turkey, where "Printing is forbid, *Enquiry* is dangerous, and *Free-speaking* is," in all capital letters, a "CAPITAL [crime]." It also would make Britain like Catholic Italy, where crusades against intellectual inquiry and "strictures on the press" produced "deluded Votaries" who were "ignorant," "Slaves," "Idolaters," and "Persecutors" to boot. "Here, in *England*," Gordon and Trenchard asked, "why are we *free*, why *Protestants*"? "Because we are guided by *Reason*" under the freedom of the press and inculcate freedom of thought in churches and public schools.[41]

Gordon and Trenchard's rhetoric reflected a wide spectrum of Protestant sensibilities, even though it excluded Tory Anglicans and separatist or radical dissenters. Liberals or rationalists emphasized "simplicity" and "truth." Pietists or evangelicals favored images of "beauty" and light, as later sermons by Edwards showed. The "practice of piety" evoked the puritan devotional writer John Bayly. In describing reasonableness in such terms, Gordon and Trenchard offered a capacious approach to Protestantism. They in fact claimed that only two theological tenets defined Britain's public religion. One was the authority of scripture alone, and the clarity and reasonableness of scripture, which set limits on the public exercise of ecclesiastical authority and church traditions. The other was liberty of conscience, which minimized the use of power to coerce adherence and thereby promoted genuine faith.[42]

The *Independent Whig* included dozens of essays that replicated the same argument, that nonhierarchical Protestantism promoted liberty of conscience; liberty of conscience allowed reasonableness; and such reasonableness confirmed Britain's rejection of arbitrary power in favor of constitutional principles. Reasonableness implied not only freedom to deliberate and choose one's religion but also the necessity of consent—through parliamentary representation—in political matters.[43] These sentiments were expressed not only by latitudinarian Anglicans but also by English Calvinists such as John Edwards, defenders of evangelical itinerancy in New England such as Elisha Williams, and proto-unitarians such as the Boston firebrand John Mayhew.[44]

It was a common claim among whiggish Protestants: ceremonialism led to superstition, and superstition, fixed as it was on claims to mystery and miracle, belied the reasonableness upon which social exchange, even sociability itself, depended.[45] In political terms, forms of religion that discarded common conventions about knowledge and intelligibility were, as whiggish critics held, fractious. Radical Protestant enthusiasm with its claims to unique and private revelation, High Church authoritarianism with its disregard for liberty of conscience, and Catholic ceremonialism with its appeal to base instincts and superstitions each rent the body politic into private and sectarian factions who barely understood each other. They endangered Britain's imperial order.

The third cluster of criteria by which Gordon and Trenchard evaluated religious expressions concerned economic utility, or what in their terminology was "being useful and beneficent."[46] At a time when Britain relied heavily on trade to fund imperial projects and the military, threats to commerce such as fraudulence, corruption, and avarice, along with incompetence and irrationality, appeared as disloyal. Commentators from the period such as Daniel Defoe and Addison and Steele, among others, made this point often, especially in light of the calamity of the 1711–1720 South Sea bubble, a speculative stock venture that ended in widespread bankruptcy and government intervention. During the 1740s, evangelicals such as George Whitefield labored to prove themselves to be rational, capable, and honest stewards over their affairs. Whitefield presented his charitable accounts for public scrutiny and renounced his previous flirtations with religious enthusiasm. For Gordon and Trenchard, "being useful" served as another gauge for measuring religious devotion.[47]

From an imperial perspective, then, religions that nurtured economic honesty, industriousness, and competence were virtuous, and religions that legitimated dishonesty, carelessness, or greed were vicious. As Gordon and Trenchard accordingly reported, the defenders of Sacheverell proposed the renewal of test acts and oaths of loyalty that would perversely punish Quakers, who had the economic and political virtues that signaled genuine religion. They were "good Subjects"—"Loyal to King GEORGE"—and were honest, frugal, and productive: "Quiet, Temperate, Chaste, Sober, Free from Passion, Industrious," and "true to Liberty and Property."[48] In contrast, by Gordon and Trenchard's measures, Jacobites were "Hellish Frauds." Gordon and Trenchard weighted their explication of such fraudulence with economic meaning. They argued that Tories and Jacobites fashioned themselves after Archbishop William Laud, the infamous, pro-Stuart prelate who sought to oversee, and profit from, government appointments or "Civil Employments," to control the Exchequer and Rolls, and to support the egregious taxation policies of Charles I. Gordon and Trenchard frequently compared High Churchmen to the leaders of the Inquisition, claiming that both groups confiscated property in violation of the liberties of godly people and expressed "Rage against Dissenters" while issuing "Fines, Gaols, and penal Laws" that lined their pockets.[49]

According to Gordon and Trenchard, institutional Catholicism—so admired by the Jacobites—also combined superstition with economic depravity. It ran on "Frauds and Impositions," like "all the forged Religions of the World." Catholic grottos, underground sanctuaries, and secret chapels—some of them in England—were shrouded in darkness in order to provoke dread and elicit donations. Catholic sanctuaries ornamented with gold, rich carpets, and jewel-encrusted images were like the temples of "Heathens," monuments to luxury. Pious monks endured deprivation while prelates lavished themselves with "feast and riot" and rode in "Coaches and Six." Papal ceremony, epitomized in the coronation of the pontiff, had "nothing to do with Christianity," which consisted in "Morality" and "being useful."[50]

Gordon drew another comparison. "The Hierarchy of Rome" was like the priestly class in Japan. Without making distinctions between Shinto and Buddhist devotion, he explained that Japanese priests feigned poverty while demanding "large offerings" to release people from a form of purgatory, defrauded the "simple," engaged in shady financial schemes, and lorded over "a bloody, a murdering Religion" when the emperor turned to the persecution of Christians. No patriot worthy of the name admired either Japanese or Roman priests, who persecuted true believers and cheated their devotees.[51]

The moral and political criteria illustrated in the *Independent Whig*—gathered here under the rubrics of sensibility, reasonableness, and utility—served as a rule by which to measure nearly every form of religion known to eighteenth-century Britons. According to Gordon, the virtues of sensibility stood in contrast to three forms of priest-induced barbarism: devotion to the Dali Lama in Lhasa, which included veneration of his excrement; worship in India of cow urine; and adoration of the "rotten Bones" and "dried Flesh" of relics in Rome.[52] Gordon and Trenchard used the notion of reasonableness to critique the putative irrationality of Muslims who believed in Muhammad's nighttime journey to heaven on a winged horse, the prophecies of Native American spiritual leaders, and the priestly incantations of "Our High Jacobite Clergy" alike.[53] So too with utility: Gordon and Trenchard invoked the "Idleness, Insufficiency, and Debaucheries" of the medieval clergy to ridicule the economic uselessness of contemporary Jacobites.[54] The same criteria could be used also to commend other religions. As illustrated in Broughton's frontispiece, British Protestants admired Shiite Muslims, whom they regarded as the Islamic parallel to persecuted Protestants in Europe, for their benevolence and learning. They also expressed respect for the Jansenists of Catholic France as long-suffering, gentle, and civil.[55]

Various writers with Protestant and patriotic persuasions approached other religions from the same perspective as Gordon and Trenchard. Edward Weston, for example, an under-secretary of state during the reign of George II and editor of the *London Gazette*, wrote a lengthy essay in 1740, reprinted in New England, in which he urged Britons to consider political qualities as they evaluated different religions. Rather than merely accept their given religious identity, Weston argued, persons of sensibility—of "Reason" and "Understanding"—deliberately chose their religious affiliation as an act of moral discernment. According to Weston, "Heathen" religions failed the test of benevolence, with their child sacrifices, obscenities, and tyrannical regimes. Weston also judged much of Islam to have failed tests of civility and patriotism. Muhammad, he claimed, pursued "Rebellion" against "his lawful civil Governors" and initiated a reign of violence and absurdity. Roman Catholicism too manifested political malfeasance, according to Weston. It was commanded by a pope who sought boundless power and control over national governments, and who practiced bigotry and slavery. Weston argued in the end that the Church of England best demonstrated the benevolence, reasonableness, and utility so necessary for England, yet he also accredited other forms of Protestantism as long as they did not inculcate disrespect for the established church and provoke disunity.[56]

Other Whigs were less explicit in such terms but deployed the same criteria. John Edwards, a dissenting Calvinist divine and friend of George Whitefield, extolled the virtues of what he regarded as reasonable and humane interreligious dialogue. He commended Muslim interlocutors who considered the merits of Christianity and reproved fellow Protestants who displayed "bigotry, and every hateful temper."[57] Several writers expressed admiration for what they knew of Confucianism, on the grounds that it offered a benevolent and useful public religion in China.[58] Caleb Fleming, an Independent minister with deist leanings, argued that all religions could be divided into two sorts: those that allowed the "*supremacy*" of individuals to "judge" for themselves in matters of religious "conscience," and those that inculcated priestcraft, persecution, and prejudice. He surveyed most of the known religions of the world and contended that in every instance the former sort of religion led to political stability and prosperity.[59]

Samuel Shuckford, prebendary at Canterbury Cathedral and sometime chaplain to George II, did not share Fleming's theology but did share his whiggish morality. He dedicated his major and frequently republished work, his 1728 *The Sacred and Profane History of the World*, to Charles Townshend, a Whig favorite of George I and scourge of Jacobites. Drawing on the ancient literature of India, Egypt, Babylon, Phoenicia, and Greece, Shuckford argued that all the "sorceries and enchantments" of pagan idolatry were "imposed upon" people through "the political institutions of their rulers," leading to ignorance and disorder. He contended that true religion, by contrast, rested on divine revelation rather than political coercion and fostered civic harmony. Shuckford offered deep historical and philological evidence for Whig ideas of sensibility and Hanoverian policies of toleration.[60]

Just as British Protestants used the criteria of Whig moralism to analyze other religions, so they used them to define common ground among loyal subjects throughout Britain's transatlantic empire. Anglicans such as Broughton, deists such as Toland and Trenchard, proto-Unitarians such as Ebenezer Gay of Massachusetts, and evangelicals such as Whitefield and Edwards all contended that genuine Protestantism promoted the virtues of sensibility, reasonableness, and utility that sustained Britain's commonweal. The latitudinarian Tillotson served as a common authority for them.[61]

We can take as a case in point a letter first printed in the *New York Evening Post* and reprinted in *The Boston Gazette or Weekly Journal* in 1746. The anonymous author, clearly no friend to evangelical preachers, had gone to hear George Whitefield. Expecting to be offended by enthusiastic excess, the writer instead was pleased, especially with Whitefield's declamations against gaming and other prodigality. Following the sermon, the author had a conversation with a "Gentleman" of latitudinarian sentiments. Both men thought that preachers such as Whitefield ought to be judged in public by the "Practice of Virtue" as presented by "heroic" writers such as Tillotson: studiousness, charitableness, affability, "good Sense," and "a polite Taste." They also agreed that by such criteria—sensibility, reasonableness, and utility—Tillotson and Whitefield were of a kind. Other observers of Whitefield after 1745 came to the same conclusion: his doctrine was absurd, but his promotion of tolerance, industriousness, and frugality recommended him as a wholesome influence on Britain's public order.[62]

Attuned to similar virtues, the evangelical pastor of a small Presbyterian congregation in Boston, John Moorhead, advertised the evangelical revivals in which he participated as politically and morally sensible. Moorhead claimed that New Englanders of nearly every religious background—pagan, Catholic, Quaker, Anglican, and Congregationalist included—set aside their "disputable Points," and their "Bigotry and Party Zeal," when they joined in one of Boston's revivals. They embraced "Veracity, Humbleness, Generosity, Temperance and Piety," and became "united in Love, Industry, Attention, and Devotion." What we might surmise were Moorhead's exaggerations revealed the currency of a Whig moralism that elevated ecumenical sentiment over dogmatism in the public sphere.[63]

Broughton's stance toward deists represented a similar liberality. He criticized deists such as Matthew Tindal for their disparagement of scriptural revelation and sacramental devotion. He agreed with Tindal, however, that what mattered for Britain's public religion was "a *compleat* and *uniform System* of *Morality*." As Broughton argued, the traditions of the Church of England, when uncorrupted by Catholic ceremonialism, were as "*civiliz'd*" as any religion of reason. He urged deist critics to appreciate how they and Anglicans shared perceptions of public "Virtue" and promoted religion in "a most rational, and most *excellent*" manner. In Broughton's view, it was Tindal who lacked charity—who failed to recognize that Anglicans and deists alike, despite their theological differences, served Britain through their promotion of reasonableness and moral excellence, the virtues that distinguished publicly legitimate religions from debased and idolatrous religions.[64]

New Studies of the World's Religions

After producing a modest number of works on religions outside of Britain in the wake of the Glorious Revolution, British scholars turned to the world's religions with renewed energies in the flush of the Hanoverian accession and amid designs for transatlantic empire. One English publisher announced that "we have scarce any other Theme" than "Religion" throughout the globe: an indication of the popularity of publications that offered new knowledge about and interpretations of different religions at home and abroad. During the reigns of George I and George II, English publishers found large audiences for works such as Herman Moll's serial geography of the world, Ephraim Chambers's *Cyclopedia*, Broughton's *Dictionary*, Shuckford's *The Sacred and Profane History of the World*, and John Fransham's 1740 *The World in Miniature: Or, the Entertaining Traveller*.[65]

The popularity of this new generation of studies of the world's religions reached New England, where commentators framed their descriptions of Native American cultures and Catholicism within the scope of worldwide religious diversity. At the turn of the eighteenth century, divines such as Cotton Mather had turned their attention to various ancient and Near East religions, looking for traces of theological truth in Persian paganism and Zoroastrianism, Graeco-Roman polytheism, and certain forms of Islam.[66] Mid-eighteenth-century clerics such as Jonathan Edwards, Jonathan Mayhew, and Ezra Stiles set their sights instead on contemporary religious diversity throughout the world. They collected editions of Moll, Chambers, Broughton, Shuckford, Fransham, and other books on religious comparison. Edwards's library included each of these along with dictionaries by Bayle and Collier (both noted in Chapter 3), excerpts by Tillotson and Clarke on other religions, narratives by Jesuit missionaries in China, and Theophilus Gale's *The Court of the Gentiles*, a rambling theological survey of paganism. Stiles, a pastor in Newport, Rhode Island, and future president of Yale, mentioned dozens of publications on the peoples of the Mississippi Valley, Mongolia, and Tartary, among others.[67]

Used by scholars, merchants, political officials, and pastors, dictionaries and encyclopedias were especially influential in shaping popular perceptions of religion in Britain and the world. Their authors often rendered erudite analyses in accessible prose and drew on whiggish political sentiments to shape their observations. The most popular of these encyclopedic dictionaries printed in London were Ephraim Chambers's 1728 *Cyclopedia* and Broughton's 1742 *Dictionary*.

Chambers's two-volume *Cyclopedia* achieved fame nearly from its first appearance. Raised in a Presbyterian home in the northwest of England, Chambers moved to London in 1714, was apprenticed to a bookseller and engraver, and made a name for himself as an essayist for literary magazines. His *Cyclopedia* went through eight editions through 1748, garnered notable publicity, and inspired the producers of the *Encyclopedia Britannica*. Boston booksellers supplied copies to New England clergymen and educators. Translated into French, it was the model for Diderot's *Encyclopedié*. Although the *Cyclopedia* was a general reference work, with entries on scientific, mathematical, and technological subjects, much of its material concerned religion. The subtitle alerts the reader to its scope in such terms: "The Rise, Progress, and State of Things Ecclesiastical, Civil, Military, and Commercial . . . with the several Systems, Sects, Opinions, etc. among Philosophers, Divines, Mathematicians, Physicians, Antiquaries, Critics, etc."[68]

The *Cyclopedia* corroborated Whig politics throughout. In the dedication "To the King," Chambers extolled George II as a patron of learning, friend to commerce, and reformer of "our morals." Describing Britain's mixed or constitutional monarchy as the best form of government in the world, Chambers decried faction as inimical to the commonweal. He studded his entry on "Liberty of Conscience" with hyperbole, claiming that Britain protected the "natural Right or Power of making Profession of any Religion that a Man sees fit," an admirable policy "opposed" by "the Generality of *Romanists*," meaning Roman Catholics. This was pure Whig moralism: sensibility or a concern for moral improvement, reasonableness or devotion to learning and liberty of conscience, and utility or commercial expansion all legitimized loyalty to the crown and hedged against faction.[69]

Chambers announced his approach to religion through a taxonomic chart at the front of his dictionary, a "division of knowledge," as Chambers put it. Later emulated by Diderot in the *Encyclopedié*, the chart conveyed a firm distinction between ethics and theology. Ethics concerned politics and law. Theology concerned divine revelation. Confessional or theological claims, that is, did not belong in the category of public morality that informed political matters. Chambers hewed to this taxonomic division in his subject entries. Unlike observers during the Restoration era, he did not arrange theological schools and liturgical practices by nation. His chart suggested that religious dogma was a species of knowledge different from political ethics. Chambers's taxonomy gave an epistemological rationale, as it were, for a comprehensive and tolerant national order.[70]

Subsequent entries in the *Cyclopedia* on religious topics reflected Chambers's whiggish assumptions. Most of them present figures and school of thought without editorial comment or critique. The entry on "Dissenters," for example, equates the term with "Nonconformists" and defines it as "certain sects, or parties in England, who in matters of religion, church discipline, and ceremonies" dissent "from the Church of England." Chambers provided examples without elaboration: Presbyterians, Independents, and Quakers.

Certain subjects, however, elicited moral commentary. According to the *Cyclopedia*, the papal machinery of doctrinal discipline, from the Inquisition to the detailed prescriptions of canon law, reflected a misuse of power: a form of institutional incivility, as it were. Under the entry of "Acceptance," Chambers explained the practice by which ecclesiastics outside of Rome accepted and enforced papal condemnations of supposed errors or scandals. The issue of Unigenitus, the papal bull of 1713 by Clement XI, exemplified the viciousness of such procedures. The bull condemned as heresy the predestinarian tenets of the French Catholic movement known as Jansenism, even though, by Chambers's account, Jansenists were sincere and devoted to moral reform in France. Rome subsequently condemned related schools of devotion such as Quietism. "Disputes and dissensions" afflicted the church as a result of anti-Jansenist and anti-Quietist injunctions. Wary of these divisive measures, especially where Jansenism and Quietism flourished, Catholic officials in France, Poland, and Germany refused full acceptance of Rome's decrees. According to Chambers, they thereby demonstrated a measure of sensibility.[71]

Throughout, Chambers also identified practices that were irrational and therefore disorderly or coercive. One of the most critical entries in the *Cyclopedia* concerns "Enthusiasm," a catch-all term for claims to immediate divine revelation and miracles, and for ecstatic experience. Chambers characterized it as "rage, or fury, which transports the mind." He named no specific sects but clearly had in mind Catholic mystics, non-Christian shamans or other spiritual leaders, and the radical Protestants of the Interregnum such as Diggers, Levellers, Ranters, and Quakers. Citing Locke, he warned readers that enthusiasm "takes away both reason and revelation, and substitutes in the room of it, the ungrounded fancies of a man's own brain." As a corollary, enthusiasm provoked or legitimated coercion.

"Idolatry," Chambers maintained in another entry, stemmed from such "an inviolable attachment to the senses" that it blinded its adherents to reason. He linked idolatry to "superstition," mindless "scruples," irrational "fears," and persecution of other religions. In his article on "Calvinism," Chambers addressed the absurdity of Catholic writers who censured Calvinism as heretical. One such writer found "an hundred heresies," while another "improves vastly on the list, making the heresies no less than one thousand four hundred." Heresy hunting had no part in Chambers's realm of reasonableness. Rather, attention to reasonable moral duties encouraged people to find common ground with adherents of different creeds. He praised, for example, what he called the religion of "the Siamese," presumably a reference to the Buddhism of Thailand. By his account, the people of Siam "hold the diversity of religions" to "be pleasing" to God, and "the sentiment of these idolaters is doubtless more just than that of our zealots, who hold all but those of their own religion odious to God." By the standards of reasonableness, Thai Buddhists deserved more commendation than did Tory and High Church partisans.

As for the virtue of economic utility, Chambers followed suit with other Whig commentators such as Gordon and Trenchard. In a lengthy article on "Anabaptists," he disparaged the "fanatic zeal" and violent sedition of early Anabaptists such as Thomas Müntzer. Yet Chambers commended eighteenth-century Anabaptists as having developed more "equitable," honest, and socially valuable habits. Quakers, for example, exhibited an "exemplary simplicity," economic productivity, and frugality. Chambers used similar idioms to describe quite distant religious groups. The "Keber," a Zoroastrian sect "among the Persians," were an odd lot by his reading. They attempted to discern by two tests whether the soul of a recently deceased neighbor or loved one would enjoy eternal salvation. They let a rooster roam around the house of the deceased and put it outside, and if a fox captured it, then "the soul of the defunct is saved." Or they placed the corpse in a sitting position against a wall in the cemetery, and if birds came to peck out the right eye, then they "look on him as one of the predestined." Even with such strange practices, however, the Keber were "rich merchants" and a boon to their community because of "the regularity"—the honesty and probity—of their lives.

Whig moral rubrics similarly colored Broughton's *Dictionary*. The whole work was devoted to religious subjects—from the names of deities to the history of religious orders and ceremonial practices—with interspersed commentary on contemporary issues such as the recent history of the Church of England. The church, Broughton insisted, demonstrated the virtues of sensibility and sociability, while its Jacobite and separatist-Protestant adversaries displayed fanaticism and unsociability. When observed with proper Protestant (what we can call "low church") decorum, Church of England "ceremonies" were, Broughton claimed, just as Gordon and Trenchard had recommended: "few, and such as tend only to decency and true devotion." In this respect, the church offered "the true mean between" Roman Catholic "Superstition" and radical Protestant "Fanaticism." According to Broughton, moderate dissenters such as Independents and Presbyterians remained within the bounds of civility and loyalty, despite Independents' radical republicanism during the civil wars. Presbyterians had always demonstrated "at least an outward respect" for the monarch and the kingdom's public religious establishment. These dissenting churches were politically legitimate in such terms.[72]

The fanaticism of "Anabaptists, Quakers, and other sectaries," by contrast, contradicted the very essence of sensibility. Radical Protestants prided themselves on small matters such as plain dress and austere manners. They quoted scripture at every turn. Yet they manifested incivility, zealotry, and factionalism. Broughton criticized the claims to extraordinary revelation by Quakers, no less than the worship of roosters by Mongolian peoples or the mystical ecstasies of Turkish sects, on the grounds that they were irrational and therefore bred unsociability and civil discord. Broughton invoked the dark memories of England's civil wars—the Rump Parliament, Diggers, anti-patriotic screeds, and violence—when sectaries spoke "treason," "schism, and murther" and turned their followers "to madness and rebellion."[73]

Broughton gave mixed reviews in his *Dictionary* to Catholic subjects, avoiding generalizations about "Catholicism" per se. On the one hand, he admired the learning of Jansenists and French Molinists (Catholic theologians who applied the idea of God's foreknowledge to the problem of grace and predestination). He acclaimed tolerant Polish Catholics. On the other hand, he lamented the illiteracy of rural Spanish priests and detected a reprehensible mixture of ceremony, zeal, and state-sponsored coercion among the papacy and Catholics who devoted themselves to Rome.[74]

Broughton also critiqued other religious traditions that, by his account, relied on civic authority to enforce adherence. The leaders or caliphs of "Orthodox Mohammedans," as he called Sunnis, held "supreme authority both in respect to spirituals and temporals." They "stigmatized" and condemned the "*Schiites*" of Persia and provoked "great troubles" as a result. He also identified a confusion of state power and religion in the "Dalai Lama," who reigned as the "sovereign Pontiff of the Tartarian idolaters." Islamic severity and pagan idolatry mirrored the vices of institutional Roman Catholicism.[75]

Broughton also commended some traditions and communities within Islam as compatible with Whig moralism. The "original" Islamic "design" to bring "a knowledge of the one true God" to "the Pagan Arabs," as he put it, was "certainly noble," even though it hardened into an oppressive orthodoxy. In Broughton's opinion, many Muslim communities were led by brilliant and liberal-minded theologians. Many others, he lamented, were led by imams who used their power to impose the most speculative beliefs on people— details about the final judgment, hell, and paradise—and required a precise performance of ceremonial duties such as prayer and pilgrimage. Unlike his confessional predecessors, Broughton stressed diversity within Islam, providing taxonomic divisions and subdivisions among Sunni orthodox and heretical sects, and five Shiite sects, such as Gholaites and Nosairians, for a total of twenty-two varieties of Islam.[76]

Broughton and other encyclopedists from the period, such as Picart and Bernard, however, gave no indication that the practices of the people in Guinea (again, the west coast of Africa from Senegambia to the southern Gulf of Guinea) were anything but inhumane and unreasonable, through and through. They reiterated many of the details and interpretations provided by Crouch with little change. Broughton described the veneration of "Fetiches" or the "Deities of the negroes of Guinea," from amulets to tree oracles, as "ridiculous superstitions." He even resorted to the language of "devotions to Devil," which he did not use in reference to any other indigenous tradition. The usually reserved Bernard, who saved the most severe rhetoric for politically powerful religion, used unmeasured prose to describe Guinean worship: "lame and uncertain, and full of Contradictions," a "Composition of Idolatry," and "magical Knowledge." One surveyor for the Royal African Company, William Smith, claimed in a more straightforward manner that the people of Guinea had "no Religion at all" but rather believed that "some Trifle or other," such as a lion's tail, a pebble, or a bit of cloth could "defend them from all Danger."[77]

This invective against Guinean practice en toto suggests that British Protestants regarded the religion of the people of western Africa as a special case, different from indigenous traditions in other parts of the world and not comparable to any other religion. As the anthropologist William Pietz has argued, the fetish object did not appear to observers like Broughton, Bernard, and Smith as idols in a traditional sense, pointing beyond themselves to transcendent powers. They appeared rather as mere physical objects, confined to their material dimensions, that in themselves had power. From the perspective of British Protestants, the fetish was chosen out of mere caprice in a chance encounter, and represented something especially sinister for its random quality, its complete lack of purpose beyond its immediate charms.[78]

Such critiques were an indication that British notions of religious reasonableness served as a justification for race-based slavery. Eighteenth-century writers implied that darkness of skin and devotion to fetishes signified a people less than human and therefore fit for servitude, without a real religion and therefore justifiably subjects of colonial control. To be sure, the moral discourse of whiggish observers at times compelled them to criticize the slave system. Broughton and Bernard decried slavery as cruel, "barbarous and inhuman." Yet they wrote as if its cruelty, however regrettable, was an unavoidable and essential component of Britain's commercial empire—the very empire that, according to them, relied on religion's economic utility as well as its benevolence and reasonableness. Slaveholding Protestants in the Caribbean dealt with the conundrum by developing, as Katherine Gerbner has put it, notions of White and Protestant supremacy: a justification for the bondage of Black pagans and reason to withhold Christian conversion and baptism from slaves. Whiggish encyclopedists rarely wrote in such explicitly racialized terms—Bayle in fact had described many ancient Roman practices and contemporary Catholic practices as forms of fetish worship—but their distinct approach to the "religion" of Guinea reflected the imperial and colonialist underpinnings of their discourse. To put this a bit differently, the enslavement of Africans led commentators such as Broughton to dismiss the religion of Guinea as incomprehensible, a blanket judgment that they made of no other tradition.[79]

As a reference book, Broughton's *Dictionary* represented an especially thorough account of the world's religions. Other British observers, sometimes drawing from the same sources used by Broughton, scattered moral commentary in a less methodical fashion, through ambassadorial reports, geographies, sermons, and travel accounts. Eying the settlement of French Acadia in the wake of the Seven Years' War, British officials, for example, relied on French ethnographies of Mi'kmaq and Maliseet peoples. The English translation of the most important of these, by Antoine Simon Maillard, highlighted the economic diligence and political candor of Native peoples.[80] Imperial aims and Whig morality also affected geographies from the 1740s and 1750s. Andrew Brice's geography contained glowing accounts of cities, such as Philadelphia and Venice, where religious toleration and economic productivity went hand in hand. In his survey of Virginia and the middle colonies, Lewis Evans contended that many Native Americans eschewed religious coercion and arbitrary power, just as did good Britons.[81]

In his account of the peoples of the Levant—part travel narrative, part report for the use of merchants and diplomats, and part geography—Richard Pococke described an array of cultural and religious diversity.[82] Pococke, who held several clerical positions in Ireland, traveled through Egypt, Palestine, and Syria from 1737 to 1742. Celebrated for his scientific curiosity—he collected antiquities, coins, and fossils—Pococke attended to local customs and social behaviors. He took typical Protestant swipes at sacerdotalism, describing Coptic priests as "irreverent and careless" and bereft of kindness. He complimented the Arab people of upper Egypt for their morally sound version of Islam and honesty in business. The Bedouin people of southern Egypt, by contrast, were, by Pococke's account, unacquainted with civility. Their "Heathen religion" had made them "slothful" and "idle" in their economic lives and "malicious" in their dealings with outsiders. Their politics followed suit: tribal, disorderly, and driven by that most dangerous vice in the eyes of a loyal Briton, "faction." According to Pococke, the "Dervishes" of Damascus, members of mystical Muslim sects, "seem to be a good people" except when they took up mendicancy. Like many of his contemporaries, Pococke judged the variety of religions he encountered according to the economic criteria that sustained Britain's overseas empire.[83]

Taking an interest in world religions especially during the 1736–1742 revivals and during his years as a missionary pastor to Mohicans and Mohawks in Stockbridge, Jonathan Edwards deployed whiggish analyses to the same effect. He asserted that non-Christian traditions exhibited variation in moral and political virtues. He admired the moral inclinations of many Indigenous peoples and agreed with deists and freethinkers who discerned in Confucianism a virtuous civic theology undergirded by basic religious truths. He also critiqued branches of non-Christian religions that exhibited, by his judgment, social or political inhumaneness. He argued, for example, that the Islamic leaders of Arabia conducted "external ceremonies" that encouraged servility. They led a religion bereft of benevolence: revengeful, bloody, and oppressive to women. Muhammad propagated his teachings "not by light and instruction, but by darkness, not by encouraging reasoning and search [sic] but by discouraging knowledge and learning, shutting out these things and forbidding inquiry." Muslims spread their faith either "by armies" or by "hoodwinking mankind and blinding their eyes." It was clear to Edwards that the inheritors of this sort of Islam, the Ottoman Turks, were prefigured in biblical imagery as the eschatological allies of Roman Catholicism and the apocalyptic foes of the godly.[84]

Eighteenth-Century Travelers

We can detect Whig moralism also in the travel accounts of many British Protestants in this period.[85] Not every British traveler, to be sure, employed the same language. Itinerant Quaker missionaries such as Susanna Morris, Elizabeth Hudson, and Ann Moore, for example, described their encounters almost exclusively in terms of hospitable and godly Friends posed against hostile and worldly Protestants outside the circle of Friends.[86] Yet most British Protestant travelers narrated their encounters with religious others in ways that reflected the ideals of Gordon and Trenchard, Chambers and Broughton.

The diary of the surveyor, merchant, and shipmaster William Pote, Jr., demonstrates how the new discourse of the world's religions was transmitted to and affected an ordinary New England layman with an extraordinary story. In May 1745, Pote left his home in Falmouth, Maine, to transport supplies to the English Fort Annapolis Royal in Nova Scotia. Ambushed by French-allied Indians as his ship drew near to shore, Pote was interrogated by French officers and handed over to what he called "a Camp of the hurons," meaning a party of Huron or Wyandot people. Over several harrowing months, his captors marched him through the woods and transported him by canoe to Quebec. He also encountered Mi'kmaq and Maliseet groups along the way.[87]

Pote interpreted his encounters—narrated while he sat in a Quebec prison—through the prism of regnant conceptions of civility, humaneness, and reasonableness. He may well have learned that language in part from his pastor in Falmouth, Thomas Smith, an evangelical Congregationalist who took an interest in other religions. Preaching at the ordination of a neighboring pastor, Smith contended that Protestants cherished freedom of conscience and, unlike Catholics, did not lord their clerical position over people. Echoing the rhetoric of Gordon and Trenchard, he referred to "the *Papal Hierarchy*; and all such imperious *lordly Clergy-men*," including High Church Tories, whose practices reflected false religion throughout history. Smith cited Samuel Clarke's comparisons among pagan, Islamic, and Roman Catholic notions of priestly authority. In another sermon, Smith drew from geographical dictionaries that described the cultural contours of the world. His journal contains frequent references to the religious affiliations of Native Americans and the practices of Spanish and French Catholics. Smith conveyed a Whig understanding of the world's religions to parishioners such as Pote.[88]

Pote's journal reflected that understanding. Unlike English captives from the previous century who described Native peoples as devilish idolaters, such as Mary Rowlandson, he held no monolithic opinion of Indigenous people.[89] He judged his captors in terms of their sociability. He found the Mi'kmaqs and Maliseets to be brutish and uncivil, quick to inflict pain and eager to kill. Their religious ceremonies, especially dances during which they taunted captives, were menacing. He described his Huron captors, by contrast, as civil and reasonable, honest and candid, despite what he regarded as their vile table manners and occasional fits of malice, such as their mirth when Huron women beat him with nettles. As he put it, the Hurons were "the most Civilised Nation of Indians" who "could all," like Pote himself, "talk Exceeding Good french." Their leaders often had "Compassion" for him, giving him moccasins and blankets. He in turn attempted to "Conform my Self to their manners and Customs" to the extent that they were amiable.[90]

Pote's moral distinctions among Indigenous peoples carried imperial and racial meanings—the laudable Native community as civil in Anglo-Protestant terms—yet nonetheless rested on notions of virtue and humaneness that in whiggish use often crossed lines of ethnicity, creed, and imperial allegiance. Even the Hurons' Catholic practices, including their nightly and morning prayers and attendance at various masses conducted in small villages or at impromptu chapels set up in the forest by visiting priests, evoked Pote's admiration. According to Pote, their chants expressed genuine happiness. He attempted to show civility as a measure of esteem. He even determined to attend Mass with his captors. On one such occasion, he fretted that wearing his ragged shirt might appear impolite. Failing to use the proffered holy water, partake of the consecrated bread, and cross himself, he was, as he put it tongue in cheek, "Intirely Excommunicated" and disallowed from entering "their church afterwards." He in fact lauded his captors for their respect of his moral scruples. On this and other occasions, they teased him but, unlike visiting Jesuits, never compelled him through force or threats of punishment. Pote's journal gives hints, in anecdotal form, of a reordering of the categories by which Britons made their observations of non-Protestant traditions.[91]

Whig desiderata for an ecumenical Protestant public religion, defined according to Shaftesbury-esque notions of sensibility and reasonableness, informed the travelogue of another mid-century Protestant, the Scottish-born physician and resident of Annapolis, Maryland, Alexander Hamilton (unrelated to the future secretary of the treasury). Raised a son of a Presbyterian theologian at Edinburgh, Hamilton attended an Anglican church when at Annapolis, professed deist principles, and was the founder of the Tuesday Club, a salon devoted to polite manners, literary conversation, and philosophical debate. As he recounted the rituals and proceedings of the club, he included dozens of comments about the world's religions, including parallels between Native American ceremonies and those of the club, the dangers of sacerdotalism and Catholic ritual, and the fraudulence of Muhammad. In 1744, he traveled from Maryland to Maine and back. Along the way, he had dozens of interactions with talkative people: rustic skeptics at wayside stops who denounced all clergy as avaricious charlatans, Presbyterians who collared him on a ferry to hold forth on election and regeneration, and Anglican priests who bemoaned the dissipation of their flocks even as they drunk themselves silly at late-night social gatherings.[92]

Hamilton professed to stand above sectarian partisanship and make judgments based on reason, moral practicality, and especially polite sentiment. The ecclesiastical identity and theological tenets of his interlocutors mattered little to him. He lavished praise on some Anglicans for their learning while condemning others as snooty and avaricious. He affiliated with freethinkers yet chastised an especially dogmatic skeptic who failed to appreciate the moral meaning of religious worship for the commoner. He scorned Moravians for their practice of communal living and suggested that they were cheats, without any description of their beliefs. He criticized Quakers for their pacifism but complimented their reticence to debate doctrine. He excoriated evangelical fanaticism and described some Presbyterians as dour to the point of being unsociable yet admired the evangelical Presbyterian preacher in New York Ebenezer Pemberton because Pemberton's preaching was smart. Hamilton became enamored of Boston's West Church, where the Presbyterian William Hooper delivered what Hamilton heard as morally satisfying sermons with proper literary flair. Hamilton described Hooper's "discourse" as "being sollid sense, strong connected reason, and good language." He even liked a Baptist meeting in Newport, where the preacher "gave us a pritty good tho trite discourse upon morality."[93]

Hamilton judged religious congregations and individual acquaintances according to "rules of modesty and good manners." If his encounters evinced what he determined to be sociability, intellectual generosity, and cheerfulness—virtues right out of Shaftesbury—then he admired and recommended the people involved. If they exhibited selfishness, dogmatism, and somberness, then he disapproved. He derided religious services in which priests or pastors ordered their audience to believe handed-down doctrine without rational deliberation. He frowned on theological disputation of all sorts, whether conducted by itinerant evangelicals or skeptical would-be philosophes, as inherently divisive as well as oppressive.[94]

Hamilton's observations were complicated by his finicky tastes yet consistent in their application of Whig principles. He claimed that he derived his moral rules from an abhorrence of "all tyrannicall and arbitrary notions" as betrayals of Britain's constitutional and imperial order.[95]

These two travelers, Pote and Hamilton, represented the influence of whiggish moralism on Anglo-American Protestants of different social and religious backgrounds. Pote was a merchant mariner with evangelical sentiments nurtured by his Congregational church. Hamilton was a physician with deist sentiments who identified loosely with an Anglican parish. Despite their theological differences, they shared the same standards for the evaluation of the religious other: the virtues of benevolence or civility and reasonableness, and the vices of inhumaneness or incivility and dogmatism or coercion. They learned that discourse from other loyal subjects of Britain—Pote's pastor, Smith, and Hamilton's fellow members of the Tuesday Club—who transmitted the interpretations of commentators such as Gordon and Trenchard, Broughton and Chambers, Shafesbury and Tillotson.[96]

The diffusion of this discourse throughout Anglo-American Protestantism signaled the importance of Britain's political agendas for common understandings of religion. Those agendas often reflected the imperial aims of the Hanoverian monarchy and the Whig Parliament. Deists, evangelicals, mainstream dissenters, and latitudinarian Anglicans alike were convinced that they belonged to a public religious order that served Britain through the promotion of benevolence, reasonableness, and utility. They judged other religions according to those virtues rather than by confessional standards. They condemned ceremonialism, priestcraft, dogmatism, and intolerance as factional and corrupt, whether in London, Quebec, Constantinople, Algonquian villages, or Chinese cities.

New methods for the study of religion, that is, confirmed the ascendency of the Whig government after the Glorious Revolution in England and, several decades later, legitimized Britain's political and commercial empire—an order resting not on received religious tradition but on a decided separation between revealed religion and public, civil discourse. In this sense, the chief effect of the eighteenth-century turn in comparative religion, with all of its claims to rationality and objectivity, was not unbelief. It was, rather, the assumption that religions ought to be separate from the political and social institutions upon which the commonweal rested but nonetheless ought to validate the moral sensibilities that sustained it. For these observers, no religious tradition violated that axiom more than the institutional Catholicism of the papacy. To further understand the eighteenth-century transformation in religious comparison, we must attend to the Church of Rome in some detail.

5

Power, Ceremony, and Roman Catholicism

In 1733, London publishers released the first volume of the English version of *The Ceremonies and Religious Customs of the Various Nations of the Known World*, the period's most ambitious work on the world's religions. It was the product of two French Protestants, the engraver Bernard Picart and the writer and editor Jean Frederic Bernard. The sheer size of Picart and Bernard's masterpiece set it apart from previous dictionaries and encyclopedias. The first edition, in French, appeared in seven folio volumes between 1723 and 1737. Organized by religious tradition rather than by nation, it consisted of volumes dedicated to Judaism; Catholicism; the religions of America and India; the traditions of Asia and Africa; Greek Orthodoxy and the magisterial Protestantism of Calvinism and Lutheranism; other Protestant traditions, including Anglicanism, Quakerism, and deism; and a final volume on Islam.[1]

Ceremonies and Religious Customs achieved fame especially for Picart's detailed illustrations. Beside hundreds of head-pieces and tail-pieces (decorative images at the beginning and end of chapters), it featured 263 plates of engravings, from nine smallish images on a single page to several folio fold-outs. Picart and his assistants relied on various sources for their engravings: previously published images of ceremonies in distant lands, first-hand descriptions by travelers, instructions for ceremonies in Rome along with Catholic histories of notable processions or rituals, and the paintings and engravings of predecessors such as DeBry.[2]

Bernard drew on hundreds of sources for the text, including travel and discovery narratives, scientific studies, the ethnographies of Lafitau and other Catholic missionaries, literary and political histories, linguistic and philological essays, and travel compilations such as Purchas's *Pilgrimes*. He also used accounts of papal processions, descriptions of street festivals, and stories of people who had observed the rituals of separatist conventicles and secret societies. He interspersed brief descriptions and excurses on religious practices with lengthy essays on general topics such as the nature of religious ceremony, the culture of the Americas, and the history of Lutheranism.[3]

The Opening of the Protestant Mind. Mark Valeri, Oxford University Press. © Oxford University Press 2023.
DOI: 10.1093/oso/9780197663677.003.0006

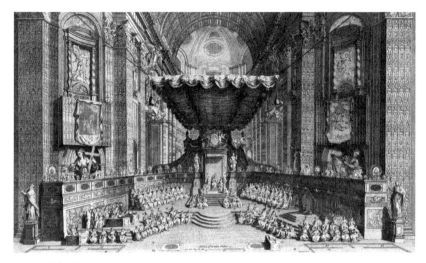

Figure 5.1 Picart, canonization ceremony
Credit: Bernard Picart and Frederic Bernard, *The Ceremonies and Religious Customs of the Various Nations of the Known World*, 7 vols. (London, 1733–1737), 1: after 392.

Two of Picart's elaborate engravings capture the perspective of the work: one of a papal ceremony in Rome, and the other of a Buddhist rite in Japan. In the first, Picart attempted to convey the ceremonial excess and public power of the Roman Catholic Church through an image of the 1712 service for the canonization of four new saints, which took place in the Basilica of Saint Peter. His illustration, after etchings by Federico Mastrozzi and Antonio Valerio, demonstrates the vastness of the basilica (Figure 5.1).[4]

On the sides are 150 bishops, cardinals, and other ecclesiastical officials. In the center of the picture Pope Clement XI officiates and is revered as though nearly divine. Bernard noted that a previous pope had claimed to be God.[5] Strung horizontally across the space, an elaborate drapery forms a dropped ceiling, making for a temporary theater, as Picart calls it. Oversized statues, tapestries, and paintings of saints line the high walls, reaching to a vaulted ceiling. Few Protestants would have missed the hints of idolatry, and no one could have missed the sense of awe evoked by the powerful scene.

Picart's engraving of a Buddhist temple in Japan (Figure 5.2) bore a close likeness to the portrait of papal majesty. One encounters in it the same perspective as in the canonization scene, in a building not unlike Saint Peter's.[6]

There too, a horizontal curtain makes for a dropped ceiling, underneath which sits the object of devotion, the Buddha. Statues of mythic beings line

Figure 5.2 Picart, Japanese temple

Credit: Bernard Picart and Frederic Bernard, *The Ceremonies and Religious Customs of the Various Nations of the Known World*, 7 vols. (London, 1733–1737), 4: after 410.

the sides. The walls rise to a vaulted ceiling. Dozens of worshippers observe. In the Japanese temple, unlike in Saint Peter's, there are ceremonial fires: always a sign for Bernard of irrational ecstasy. Otherwise, the Japanese temple of "a thousand idols," as Picart labelled his illustration, looked very much like Saint Peter's during a canonization ceremony.

These engravings reflect two developments in the Protestant discourse of anti-Catholicism and, by extension, of the world's religions. First, Picart and Bernard contended that powerful ceremonies—often dense with material objects—legitimated an alliance between priests and secular rulers who persecuted religious dissenters. The Church of Rome stood out as the stereotype of such intolerance. Previous writers had made this observation on and off. Picart and Bernard made it relentlessly, through each of their volumes. As Bernard noted, the central figure in the canonization ceremony, Clement XI, had issued Unigenitus, a bull that condemned Jansenism for its deviance from papal teaching on grace. Clement depended on Louis XIV to enforce the bull in France and compelled the king to oppose Jansenist defenders within the church. Among those made saints in the 1712 ceremony was Pope Pius V, an inquisitor and scourge of Huguenots. By Bernard's account, chief priests in Japan followed the same script, learning to use state power from their encounters with Catholic priests. The "established Religion supports itself" and inhibits new sects, he contended, through "their Inquisition." They relied on the emperor to persecute religious rivals, including Christian missionaries.[7] Picart and Bernard's depiction of Catholic and Buddhist worship disclosed a nexus between ritual and coercion.

Ceremonies and Religious Customs used striking visual representation to convey the scope and intensity of ceremony. It was one thing to read prose about the awe-inspiring pomp of a papal coronation or the fearsome force of an Aztec ritual, which Londoners and Bostonians did. It was quite another to see them as detailed images. To enhance the visceral sense of ceremony, Picart and Bernard drew attention to architectural space, ritual choreography, and sacred costume. They also included images of and digressions on physical objects: rosaries, talismans, medallions, tobacco pipes. They compared Catholic, Islamic, and East Indian prayer beads, and priestly garments across traditions. Images of such objects demonstrated the extent to which different religious performances appealed to the physical senses rather than to abstract thought. In *Ceremonies and Religious Customs*, readers were meant to feel the pull of ceremony into the depths of zealotry.[8]

As a related contribution to the literature on the world's religions, Picart and Bernard described the institutional Catholicism of the Roman See as the archetype of all religions in which priests or other religious leaders used public rites and rituals to accrue power. Picart fashioned his image of a Buddhist temple in Japan to conform to his conception of Roman Catholic grandeur. Buddhism, as Picart and Bernard imagined it, was intelligible as an analog to Catholicism in Saint Peter's: awe-inspiring ceremony evoked obeisance to a priestly class who aspired to monopolize religious authority. Gordon and Trenchard had made a similar point in the *Independent Whig*, asserting that Buddhist priests who demanded money for salvation and asked the state to persecute their religious competitors were just like Roman Catholics.[9]

Drawing on Picart and Bernard and several of their British contemporaries, the following account offers an alternative to historical and literary interpretations that explain anti-Catholicism as a fixed ideology of theological, racial, and nationalistic sentiments through the seventeenth and eighteenth centuries.[10] Such interpretations rightly observe that Protestants relied on a vocabulary that stemmed from Reformation-era polemics: terms such as idolatry, superstition, and antichrist. Yet mid-eighteenth-century Protestants such as Picart and Bernard gave a different meaning to those terms than did their predecessors. They rarely aimed their critiques at theological targets, as had seventeenth-century Protestant polemicists. They made few accusations of supernatural evil. Instead, they focused on a long tradition of papal ritual and ceremony that bespoke imperial ambition and competition in the Atlantic theater—a competition that British Protestants especially framed as a contest between papal tyranny and English liberty.

Protestants such as Picart and Bernard also commended some forms of Catholicism. Because Whig commentators were concerned mainly with the political and social ramifications of religious teaching, they validated forms of Catholic piety that disdained political power. To be sure, Protestants warned potential converts to Catholicism by criticizing Catholic doctrine in matters of personal faith. Yet the public discourse about Catholicism changed during the 1730s and 1740s. Whig observers made distinctions among Catholic institutions and communities that shared the same creeds yet differed in social agendas, some of which they described as uncivil, unreasonable, and coercive, and others as humane, reasonable, and tolerant.[11]

The following elucidation of the Protestant discourse around other religions begins with Picart and Bernard, their popularity among Hanoverian Whigs, and their explanations of religious ceremony and political power. It then turns to the ways in which Whig views of the dangers of Catholic ceremonialism inflected their descriptions of other religious traditions. It concludes with illustrations of how laypeople in Britain and New England explained their encounters with Catholics through the lenses provided by Picart and Bernard.

French Whigs and the Critique of Ceremonialism

By the time the first English edition of *Ceremonies and Religious Customs* was published, Picart and Bernard had become well known among British intellectuals as fellow Protestants and Whig sympathizers. Raised by a Catholic family in Paris, Picart was trained in book illustration. He became attracted to Jansenism, converted to Protestantism while on a trip to the Netherlands, and joined a circle of expatriate English Protestants in France. Incited by Unigenitus, he turned his art against the Jesuits, Louis XIV, and their policies of religious coercion. He moved to Amsterdam in 1711, where he fell under the influence of Huguenot apologists who attacked Catholic sacramentalism and ceremonialism. Bernard, his collaborator, was born into a Protestant family, his father a Calvinist pastor. He gained firsthand knowledge of Catholic coercion when his relatives were compelled to "convert" to Catholicism and register their change of confession before a local notary. Driven into exile, the Bernard family landed in Geneva, where Jean Frederic learned the bookselling trade, hobnobbed with Bayle, and may well have met Gilbert Burnet. Moving to Amsterdam, Bernard presented himself as a conventional Protestant liberal and associated with a broad range of Protestants. He agreed with much of deist thought, which he attempted to fit into an orthodox Protestant framework. He also admired the work of the English theologian Samuel Clarke, who attempted to harmonize Trinitarianism with Newtonian science. Bernard was so taken with Clarke that he published a French translation of Clarke's major treatise, a *Demonstration of the Being and Attributes of God*.[12]

Among the array of religious refugees in Amsterdam—defrocked French priests, Italian freethinkers, Jews, Moravians, and Socinians (anti-Trinitarians) included—Picart and Bernard sympathized especially with whiggish English Protestants. They shared a long-standing reverence for William III. Bernard's cousin had been a chaplain to Mary Stuart, William's wife, and Picart produced a series of celebratory engravings of the king. In Amsterdam and the Hague, Picart and Bernard entered a circle of Huguenot and English Protestant refugees, many of whom had ties to America, defined by antipathy to Catholic, Bourbon, and Jacobite powers.[13]

Ceremonies and Religious Customs was as much a dictionary for an English Whig audience as it was for a European audience, even though it contained no explicit references to contemporary British disputes such as the Bangorian Controversy. Picart and Bernard were well known in England. As a leading member of a literary society in the Hague, Picart rubbed shoulders with English notables. Members of the society corresponded with whiggish luminaries in Rotterdam, such as Locke, Shaftesbury, Algernon Sidney, and William Penn. Bernard was reputed in London to be an exemplar of a distressed yet virtuous Protestant, particularly because he valorized the Hanoverian crown, idealized Locke, and published the sermons of Tillotson. He worked on a journal that featured the works of English authors and by some accounts formed a close friendship with John Toland, the Whig deist who had taken an interest in religions around the world. The initial translation into English of the French version of *Ceremonies* was made by John Lockman, a proponent of toleration who also translated Bayle and recommended Picart and Bernard's masterpiece in the fashionable *Gentleman's Magazine*.[14] Had Picart and Bernard ever made their way to London, they would have been greeted as honorary Whigs.

English writers on religion acclaimed the English version of *Ceremonies and Religious Customs* as a near epochal publication. Bernard had labored over this version, rewriting some of the introductory essays. He removed original material that might have confounded English Protestants, such as admiring descriptions of Spinoza, libertine skeptics, and assorted European Catholics. It was this edition, that is, rather than the full range of Picart and Bernard's writings, that grabbed the attention of English readers. London newspapers advertised *Ceremonies and Religious Customs* three years before its completion, anticipated its appeal to people of taste, announced its printing, and extolled Picart as the "most celebrated engraver of this or any other age." Widely advertised and originally printed in 800 copies, *Ceremonies* sold rapidly and was reprinted in a one-volume abridgement in 1741. Artisans, plainspoken moral observers, and persecuted Protestants, Picart and Bernard appealed to a wide range of readers. Benjamin Franklin's library in Philadelphia held a copy of *Ceremonies and Religious Customs*. New Englanders learned of it through the advice manual by the English scholar John Clarke, who lauded it as one of the best books on religious geography. They also encountered Picart and Bernard through Broughton's *Dictionary*, parts of which were modeled after and contained citations to *Ceremonies and Religious Customs*.[15]

In his extended essay on "Religious Worship" at the beginning of *Ceremonies and Religious Customs*, Bernard introduced readers to the interpretive core of the work. "The very Essence of Religion itself," he contended, was for believers "to address themselves to God without Formality, and to pray to him without Ceremony."[16] His critique of ceremony rested on the version of public moral reason as recommended by Shaftesbury and Gordon and Trenchard: the conviction that genuine religion was humane, polite, and modest; that it eschewed coercive measures and especially political power; that it was, in a word, sensible. "Men of Taste," Bernard opined, preferred rational, "elevated Thoughts on Religious Matters" focused on beauty and virtue, rather than "the external Acts of Religion."[17] According to Bernard, it was a common mistake for people to devote themselves to "external Acts" that, in a phrase appropriate to the artist Picart, tended to "dazzle the Eyes."

The splendor of ceremony drew unenlightened people to "mystical and magnificent" power rather than to sublime truth.[18] In its worst forms, religious worship devolved into sheer "Ignorance" and "Barbarity," exemplified by Aztec and Incan rites of sacrifice, the frenzies of Turkish dervishes, East Indian asceticism, and what Bernard imagined to be Quaker ecstasies. Such worship misled adherents to submit to the three cardinal vices described by Whig moralists: unsociability or disregard for "agreeable Conversation," unreasonableness or "ignorance," and economic incompetence or "indolence."[19]

How did corrupt worship affect political sentiments? As Bernard explained, ceremony often induced terror and a loss of self-control. It fostered a denial of rational conscience and an abandonment of the self to mystery. It thereby served to control the minds and bodies of participants.[20] Eliciting fear of divine and temporal punishment, it led devotees to capitulate to a small class of rulers and to consent to the persecution of any religion other than that of the priests and their secular patrons. It legitimized collusion between zealots and sovereigns. As Bernard explained elsewhere in *Ceremonies and Religious Customs*, wherever priests or other spiritual leaders held sway, they used "Cunning and Artifice" to "persuade the credulous Vulgar" to set aside common morality and follow them. They thereby gained "Influence on civil Affairs" and "no little Authority in State-Affairs."[21] Nowhere did a sacerdotal class fall in league with kings and princes more powerfully, in their view, than in Catholic Europe.

Other Protestants agreed that the materiality of Catholic ceremony aroused a persecuting spirit. British travelers to Catholic Europe during the 1720s and 1730s, such as George Parker and Andrew Mitchell, described European streets and public squares seemingly filled with reliquaries and priests who threatened lapsed Catholics or converts to Protestantism with eternal and civil punishment.[22] The rationalist Anglican priest Conyers Middleton reported as much after visiting Rome in 1724 and 1725. Like Picart and Bernard, and like Whitefield some three decades later, Middleton attempted to convey the sensory power of Catholic ceremony. He recounted the smells of incense, otherworldly sounds of chanting, sights of thousands of candles, and crowds of "Romanists" who prostrated themselves before images made of wood or stone. Retreating to the ruins of ancient Rome for relief, he discovered, as he maintained, the source of such "idolatrous and extravagant" ceremony. The "conviction, which I immediately received from my senses"—a telling admission of the persuasiveness of empirical experience—led him to realize that the "full pomp and display" of the Roman Church derived from "the Popish and Pagan Religion" of the Caesars. He surveyed the evidence: ancient sculptures, reliefs and inscriptions that described the sprinkling of water as divine blessing, candles and votive offerings, prayers for healing, young boys in surplices, and shrines to memorialize sites of divine intervention. The Church of Rome, Middleton concluded, took its cues from classical paganism. The papacy, that is, relied on the physical intensity of ceremony to sustain imperial ambitions and abet imperial projects, just as had Roman emperors.[23]

When Boston's Jonathan Mayhew delivered the well-known Dudleian lecture at Harvard in 1765, he drew on Middleton's observations to argue that the physicality of Catholic worship abetted the political agendas of the Church of Rome. Mayhew focused his comments on devotion to relics and the sacramental host. As he illustrated the matter, those in Catholic lands who refused to kneel at the procession of the host through public spaces "run the risque of the inquisition or of being knocked on the head by the devout rabble that attend it." The violence that attended the host revealed a vicious concatenation of materiality, ceremony, and intolerance.[24]

Protestants' fascination with what struck them as the materiality of Catholic worship and its connection to political oppression reframed their descriptions of other religions. The rhetoric of idolatry and superstition came to denote political ambition rather than worship of false deities or malevolent supernatural forces. As Picart and Bernard, along with their British contemporaries, pursued their critiques, they deviated from a previous generation of Protestant commentators such as John Locke and William Turner, who, at the turn of the century, stressed the importance of sincerity as a criterion for genuine religion. Deriving many of their arguments from critics such as Bayle and Toland, Picart and Bernard contended that all religions demanded sincere observance. The problem with corrupt, which is to say dazzling, ceremonies was not a lack of sincerity but a lack of sensibility toward one's fellow subjects. The sense of awe fostered by physical display, so the Whig analysis went, produced a zealotry that exacerbated faction and justified inhumane policies. It thereby incited disloyalty especially to a semi-republican, religiously plural kingdom, like the Whig establishment of Great Britain.

By such accounts, the mélange of unreason and power in Catholic ceremony made the most institutionally powerful form of Catholicism—the Catholicism emanating from the papacy—to appear as especially hostile to imperial Britain. As a result, British Whigs fashioned what Peter Lake and others have described as "anti-popery," a rhetoric related to but distinct from the anti-Catholicism of post-Reformation England.[25] Anti-popery was focused on the perceived military and political aggressions of the Church of Rome: papal critiques of the Hanoverian crown, Jacobite rebellion, and the bellicosity of France and Spain. Owen Stanwood and Carla Pestana have shown in different ways that this politicized version of anti-Catholicism demarcated Britain's external foes. Loyal Britons identified their empire as a Protestant state existing in an Atlantic world of Catholic adversaries directed by Rome.[26]

Whig critiques of institutional Catholicism also concerned internal matters, or the stability, solidarity, and prosperity of the kingdom apart from external threats. Whigs contended that if papal religion gained a foothold in Britain and its colonies, then it would undermine the British constitution. "Popery" in this sense stood for an assault on British liberties, including liberty of conscience.[27] It meant the misuse of temporal power to enforce religious adherence, a perversion evidenced in the Inquisition, the pope's pressure on the French monarchy to persecute Huguenots and suppress Jansenists, and the deference of the Spanish and Portuguese courts to the pontiff's officials. It invested Catholic monarchs with an aura of absolute authority. By Whig accounts, it threatened to divide the kingdom into factions that competed for patronage from the state. "Popery" also supposedly undermined the republican virtues that sustained a constitutional monarchy, such as modesty, civility, reasonableness, and utility. The sheer physicality of papal ceremony appeared to such critics to legitimize carnality, incivility, bigotry, and aggression.

The term "papist" accordingly served as a trope for someone of any creed who disregarded the moral standards and notions of reasonableness that, according to Whigs, held together British society and its empire. From this perspective, the machinations of any anti-Hanoverian party—Tory, Jacobite, and Protestant millenarian—were papist in spirit. Accusations of "popery" flew back and forth between hostile Protestant groups. Religious rationalists ridiculed Methodist claims to special revelation as papist. Itinerant preachers vilified Tory demands for conformity as papist. Evangelicals censured the materialism of Anglicans as *Romanist*." Such barbs revealed how "papist" stood for political sentiment rather than doctrinal confession.[28]

During the second quarter of the eighteenth century, an upsurge of interest in conversion across Europe and America further shaped the politics of anti-popery. London and Boston newspapers reported on Protestant conversions to Catholicism in Europe, and Protestant writers worried that the Anglo-French alliance following the 1713 Treaty of Utrecht encouraged Catholic efforts to proselytize Britons.[29] Informed by descriptions of the pernicious effects of ceremonialism, Protestant writers charged that the evangelistic efforts of Catholic priests and friars devolved into coercion. Romish ceremony, they argued, seduced unwary participants to abandon their rational consciences and attach themselves to priests who terrorized unbelievers with hellish scenarios. Officials in Catholic states threatened civil penalties for adherence to Protestantism. Worst, armies of Catholic princes in Europe oversaw the re-Catholicization of Protestant territories. Cotton Mather predicted a European-wide campaign of fiery persecution, signaled by the renewed aggression of "Popish Princes" in Germany, the anti-Huguenot "Edicts" of the "King in France," the hostilities of "the Emperour" in Bohemia, and the changing "Political View" of the leadership in once-tolerant Hungary. Jonathan Mayhew explained that the Church of Rome was antichrist to the effect that it relied on sheer physical force to compel conversion, an exercise of militancy that contradicted true Christianity. This became a common assertion among New Englanders: papists sought converts through threats of civil punishment or bodily pain in the afterlife while British Protestants appealed to individuals' reason and moral consciences. As one newspaper editorialist put it, Protestant regimes gave "Man the Right of *private Judgment* in Matters of Religion," while "*Popery*" replaced private conscience with ecclesiastical and civil intimidation, which removed all incentive for candor and moral choice.[30]

Protestants claimed that this was as true in America as it was in Europe. British missionaries, officials, and army officers who hoped to gain allies through the conversion of Native people on the frontier with Canada complained that French Jesuits usurped secular authority or guaranteed earthly riches to gain Iroquoian converts. Jesuits, by one colonial agent's account, promised that devotion to the Virgin Mary would bring bountiful hunts. According to Cotton Mather, a captured sachem reported that French missionaries taught that "the Lord Jesus Christ was of the French Nation," that it was "the English who had Murdered him," and that true Catholics "must Revenge His Quarrel upon the English." A British army officer grumbled that "Papist Indians"—or "Jesuited Indians"—had so absorbed the "persecuting and intolerant Spirit of Popery" that they conducted warfare in a bloody and gruesome manner, incited by "the infernal Applause of their Priests."[31] Such critics neglected to mention that British missionaries also used threats of hell, preened about British Protestantism, and sometimes urged British soldiers to conduct warfare without mercy. The rhetoric often belied the reality. Yet it was nonetheless telling that Protestants assumed that readers would approve of reasonableness and toleration and disapprove of coercion as means to conversion.

The Weymouth, Massachusetts, minister Thomas Paine framed the issue in terms of a competition for unconverted souls. He contended that the plain truthfulness of Protestant Christianity, presented with a gentle appeal to reason, persuaded nonbelievers and produced genuine conversions. Catholics, he asserted, could make no appeal to the truthfulness of their tradition because it was packed with fables, illogicalities, and licentiousness. They therefore resorted to compulsion, just as did Muslims. Islamic rulers used the "dreadful Engines of Cruelty and War," the specter of "Convulsion and Agony," to gain converts. Catholic magistrates and ecclesiastics issued lurid warnings of hell's torments and if those failed, then brandished "Whips, Racks, and Gibbets." Catholic ceremonialism and proselytization alike channeled religious zeal into physical expression: pomp and procession, miraculous cure and curse, whip and gibbet.[32]

It was no wonder, Paine mused, that atheists found Christianity incredible. Only non-ceremonial Protestantism could counter unbelief. Broughton made the same point in his *Dictionary*. After providing detail about papal ceremonies, much of it taken from Picart and Bernard, Broughton reflected on the irony that modern European "atheism" originated in Italy and France.[33] Drawing at length from Locke and Tillotson, he attributed the "absurd and unreasonable" tenets of modern atheism to revulsion against papal violations of common morality. Modern unbelief and skepticism, by this account, arose in Italy and spread to France in reaction to "the gross superstitions and corrupt manners of the Romish church and court." Roman zealotry was an extreme that led to its opposite, "like the vibrations of a *pendulum*." The institutional Catholicism of the papacy, that is, had quite remarkably produced both political tyranny and religious doubt.[34]

Descriptions of Ceremonial Power

As Picart and Bernard surveyed the religions of the world, they attempted to convey the disparities between corrupt and pure religion in terms of power and ceremony. How best to give readers a sense of the pernicious effects of ceremony throughout the world? They offered visible evidence. This was more than a concession to a scientific epistemology, a duty to give empirical demonstration. Elaborately portrayed scenes of worship and of clerical vestments and sacred objects, often tied to ritual violence such as Aztec sacrifice or the *auto da fé* in the Portuguese Inquisition, exposed the reader to the power of ceremony. In effect, Picart and Bernard attempted to turn the visceral force of ceremony against itself. Just as papal processions or rites could inspire zealotry, so they could—so they ought—provoke revulsion. A papist might see the canonization ceremony in Rome and exclaim, "Ah, how majestic! Here is God!" A person of sense and reason—a good British Whig—would snarl, "Ha, how depraved! Here is tyranny!" Picart and Bernard wanted their readers to be morally provoked, to *see* what went on in Saint Peter's or in the temples of Japan. Only then could readers sense how politically dangerous was the debasement of religion into priestly materialism.

Other Protestants also sought to communicate the full sense of papal ceremony. We can take, for example, one of the travel accounts of the evangelist and imperial patriot George Whitefield. In 1754, the New York–bound ship on which Whitefield was traveling from London stopped at Lisbon for several weeks, including Holy Week. Staying at the house of an acquaintance in the city, Whitefield took the occasion to experience the sounds, sights, and smells of Portuguese Catholic ceremony at its most intense. He narrated his experience in four letters, which he introduced by declaring his goal "to excite" in his "Fellow Protestants and Dear Countrymen" a sense of the threat of "Papal Power" to the "Civil and Religious Liberties" of all Britons. According to his account, Whitefield witnessed how Catholic ceremony prompted acquiescence to the wretched combination of "Church and State" in Portugal. He hoped that his story would lead patriots to reaffirm their love for "Britain! Britain!" and to embrace "the Simplicity" of Protestant "Worship" that reinforced the religious liberties protected by the English constitution. He hoped that they also would thank God that they had been delivered from rebellious Jacobites, who aimed to bring the Roman combination of high ceremony, papal authority, and arbitrary power to Great Britain.[35]

Whitefield, that is, believed that a moving account of religious life in Lisbon would arouse disapproval in his audience: what moral philosophers of the day explained as a judgment based on a confluence of empirical observation, the mental impressions or affections evoked by observation, and a rational reflection on those impressions. He attempted to stir up—to "excite," as he put it—sensations of Catholic ceremonialism by providing descriptions of sights and sounds. He was "affected to see," he wrote, thousands of ordinary people from Lisbon marching through the town, with nearly every day of Holy Week devoted to a different festival or procession. People stopped at every house to bow before, sing hymns to, and kiss crucifixes and images of Mary affixed to doors. Parish priests and over 300 Franciscan friars also paraded, collecting food for the local prison. As Lent drew to a close, another procession featured Carmelite friars who carried huge wax tapers in one hand while the other supported a platform with a large statue of the Virgin, "glittering" with precious stones. Crowds thronged around the statue, singing Marian hymns. It was followed by a life-sized statue of Jesus carrying his cross, which was placed in the cathedral church, to be venerated by "thousands of Spectators." At the end of three days, the cathedral preacher delivered a stirring sermon and led worshippers in extemporaneous prayer. They beat their breasts, clapped their cheeks, and wept "heartily." It sounded like one of Whitefield's evangelistic meetings from the early 1740s, before he turned against such excessive emotionalism.[36]

Throughout his account, Whitefield reminded his readers of the collusion of political and religious authority in Lisbon. Members of the royal court and Portugal's aristocracy attended the ceremonies. They lauded penitents who whipped their flesh with ropes to which iron bits were attached. Whitefield saw nothing but fanaticism. He recoiled in "Horror" when he saw on one of the cathedral's walls a painting of hundreds of Jews condemned by the Inquisition and "carried out from the Church to be burnt." Picart had included an engraving of such burnings in Lisbon. Whitefield looked on Lisbon's Lenten rituals as enacting a "Bigotry" that was "as cruel as the Grave." For Whitefield, forced conversions and corporeal punishments indicated a "Species of Antichrist," a curious formulation that implied that the term "Antichrist" meant all forms of religion that used violence and state power to enforce adherence.[37]

Whitefield reiterated his intent: if Britons vicariously experienced the thick, bloody rituals of Lisbon's Franciscans, the royal court, and their devotees, then they would be alerted to the coercive force of Catholic ceremony. They would perceive the "Sight," sound, and feel of statues painted to portray effusions of blood, of penitents chanting as they flagellated themselves, of the "dismal rattling" of chains around the feet of white-hooded marchers, of doleful songs, shouted sermons, and trumpeted announcement. Whitefield admitted that a "bare Narrative" could not fully communicate the experience. "A Person must be capable of seeing, hearing, and touching such things" to have the complete sense. Yet something of the "whole Scene," "horrible" and affecting as it was, could be conveyed through the report of an eyewitness. Thick description was, Whitefield went on, at least better than mere "metaphysical Distinctions" and "abstract ideas." Images, detailed and colorful narratives, and recollections of sounds could affect Britons with the sheer intensity, the violence, of the religious-political potency of such Catholicism.[38]

The newly founded Ashmolean Museum in Oxford and the British Museum in London offered Britons even more tangible encounters with distant ceremonies. During the eighteenth century, missionaries, army officers, and merchants provided British collectors and curators with, among other curiosities, fetishes from Africa, portable shrines from Japan, amulets with verses of the Qu'ran from Persia, a ceremonial drum from northern Scandinavia, a decorative deer hide with shell beadwork from Virginia, calumets from Canada, a statue of a Hindu deity, a vase with curative elixir from China, and a model of an Indian processional wagon or juggernaut that carried a statue of Vishnu. Encountered in a museum space, many such "idols" appeared as lifelike objects that stared back at curious observers.[39]

Hans Sloane, whose personal collection served as the foundation for the British Museum, was a fixture in the Whig establishment, patronized by William III, knighted by George I, befriended by Locke, and admired by Benjamin Franklin. He shared Picart and Bernard's perspective that such objects revealed the power—which is to say seductions—of religion-made-physical. After Sloane's death in 1753, Whig Prime Minister Henry Pelham raised funds to found the museum. The trustees, many of whom were establishment Anglicans, wanted visitors to the museum to perceive how irrational and dangerous were ceremonial and magical forms of religion. The 1761 catalogue for the museum, meant to guide visitors through the collections, includes criticism of priestly religion, superstition, and ceremonial sacrifice. A mélange of materiality, ritual, irrational emotionalism, collusion with civic authorities, coercion, and political faction—power, in other words—could be felt in ceremonial objects, just as they could be seen in Picart's images.[40]

Images of the World's Religions

For Picart and Bernard, Roman Catholicism epitomized ceremonial and political religion. Five hundred out of 3,500 pages of text and fifty-five out of 263 total plates in *Customs and Religious Ceremonies* were devoted to Catholic subjects.[41] As for the Catholic penchant for ceremony, they noted 165 feast days in the Roman Catholic calendar and described dozens of other ceremonial occasions: celebration of each of the seven sacraments, papal coronations, papal processions, the canonization of saints, trials for the authentication of relics, the Inquisition, benedictions of chapels and churches, special and regular processions, funerals, and dispositions of corpses, among others. Picart provided illustrations of the rituals of the Inquisition (with special attention to its operation in Portugal), the internment of a deceased pope, and the judicial proceedings in which the clergy determined which of the hundreds of body parts exhumed from the Roman catacombs qualified for "translation" into relic status.[42]

By Bernard's account, such ritual devotion to the body served the church's quest for power. *Ceremonies and Religious Customs* portrayed the Catholic hierarchy itself as a highly visible political institution, legitimated by ceremonial display. In his digression on the early history of the Reformation, Bernard described Luther's opposition to Pope Leo X in such terms. According to Bernard, Luther argued that Leo lavished obscene amounts of money on "Acts of Grandeur and Magnificence," a reference to the construction of Saint Peter's Basilica among other projects, in order to "monopolize, and ingross" the gospel, and in so doing acted like "temporal Princes" who asserted their authority through public displays of might. Ostentation, Bernard claimed elsewhere, along with fiery sermons by priests and the church's claim to perform miracles, awed its followers and led them to persecute Christians who dissented from Rome. Bernard reprinted the plaintive works of Jansenists to prove the point.[43]

According to Bernard, the papacy used elaborate ritual to sanctify a bureaucracy that rivaled British and European empires for complexity and legal rigor. Bernard described departments, regulations, revenues, and a remarkable cadre of officials, including, as one study has put it, "chancellors, regents, auditors, prefects, lieutenants, registrars, scribes, secretaries of state, masters of the palace, chamberlains, major-domos, and librarians." When popes issued bulls such as Unigenitus, the decrees were ceremoniously carried through fifteen offices and passed through the hands of some 1,000 officials before being codified. No civil ruler could match such officiousness.[44]

Picart and Bernard gave extended attention to the election and enthronement of a pope, a ceremony that explicitly marked the Roman pontiff as a competitor to secular sovereigns. They devoted twenty-five pages to the organization and procedure of a papal conclave, replete with images of the ballots used by cardinals. *Ceremonies and Religious Customs* described in striking detail the massive post-election procession to the Lateran cathedral to "take possession" of the papal throne, and Picart provided a four-page fold-out image to capture the size and political dimensions of the event: a lengthy train of ecclesiastics, civic officials, and soldiers, with the pope at the center in a coach, winding its way up the Lateran hill.[45]

Picart also included an image of the new pontiff's enthronement, most likely an evocation of the 1724 ceremony for Benedict XIII.[46] British Protestants had read of the affair. Boston newspapers such as the *New England Courant* had described and derided Benedict's enthronement in detail.[47] Picart offered visual evidence that the ceremony appeared for all the world as the coronation of a secular monarch (Figure 5.3).

Even with their portrayal of ceremonial excess in Catholicism, Picart and Bernard did not abandon their conviction that each religious tradition

Figure 5.3 Picart, papal coronation

Credit: Bernard Picart and Frederic Bernard, *The Ceremonies and Religious Customs of the Various Nations of the Known World*, 7 vols. (London, 1733–1737), 1: facing 296.

included different schools, congregations, or local communities, some of which were laudable by Whig standards, and others of which were illegitimate. The very criteria by which the institutional Catholicism of the papacy appeared as irrational and inhumane might well illumine the civility of other traditions within Catholicism or, for that matter, within any religion.

Picart and Bernard—again, as represented by the English edition of their work—accordingly portrayed versions of Catholicism untainted, in their view, by irrationality and zealotry. They lauded Jansenists and Jansenist advocates in the Gallican Church as morally minded and intellectually credible. As a persecuted minority, the Jansenists, like France's Huguenots, Bernard claimed, had not colluded with civic authority. According to Bernard, Catholics in Venice had "put a brake on the ambitious tyranny" of the republic's priests and tolerated other religious traditions.[48] In Picart and Bernard's evaluation, the teaching of learned scholars, or religious services conducted in private, without pretension, could be civil and admirable in any tradition. For Picart, the regular, parish-based celebration of the Mass often appeared as an affair of simplicity and gentility. In his illustration of one such Mass, the priest, attended by two acolytes, faces his people with a modest gesture of blessing as he says the liturgy (Figure 5.4).[49]

The Eucharist is celebrated in front of paintings of the Passion, in which the High Priest Annas condemns Christ. Bernard remarked that the artwork conveyed Christ's rejection of worldly power. Simplicity and regular devotion—the weekly Mass—appeared as humane, while high priestly power appeared as an assault on the Savior.

As Picart and Bernard surveyed non-Catholic religions, they identified two sorts of practices: those that paralleled Roman Catholicism in the misuse of ceremony, and those that paralleled right-minded Protestantism or dissenting groups within Catholicism by the promotion of simple, noncoercive devotion. Issuing criticisms of their own tradition, they portrayed the history of Protestantism as marred by controversies, factionalism, and dogmatic jealousies. They decried the French Prophets (Protestant millenarians) for subjecting their followers to irrational and ecstatic worship, as they did the French Convulsionaries (an offshoot of Jansenists) for their visions, ecstasies, and antisocial fanaticism. They dismissed the Rosicrucians (an esoteric sect) as frauds who conducted mysterious rites and demanded absolute credence.[50]

They nonetheless commended the members of Protestant groups who avoided priests, celebrated simple rituals, fostered tolerance, and lived quiet

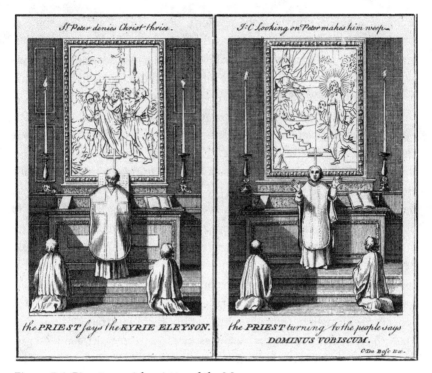

Figure 5.4 Picart, a parish priest and the Mass

Credit: Bernard Picart and Frederic Bernard, *The Ceremonies and Religious Customs of the Various Nations of the Known World*, 7 vols. (London, 1733–1737), 1: facing 325.

lives. Bernard acclaimed English Protestants, Waldensians, and Huguenots because they eschewed dogmatic polemics and testified to their religion through "Compassion and Charity for those who dissent" from them "in Points of Religion."[51] He also extolled magisterial Protestants for their deference to scripture, which implied the authority of reason (an individual's intelligent reading of the Bible) over the authority of church leaders and traditions. The scripture principle, from Picart and Bernard's perspective, validated liberty of conscience or the right of private judgment and delegitimated ecclesiastical authoritarianism.[52]

By such standards, eastern orthodox Christianity appeared to Picart and Bernard as disreputable. They derided Greek Orthodox rituals such as the Holy Fire Ceremony, during which the devout supposedly witnessed the miracle of fire descending from heaven to Jerusalem on Holy Saturday. For Picart and Bernard, ceremonial fires signaled zealotry. With its richly vested priests and the Patriarch, and the chaotic crowds and outbursts of violence, the ceremony merely offered an occasion for local priests to abscond with the money of pilgrims. It scandalized devout Muslim onlookers and appeared as nothing less than a "pious Fraud." The riots, money-grabbing priests, and rampant fraudulence that accompanied the Holy Fire Ceremony hardly complied with Whig standards of public utility.[53]

Ceremonies and Religious Customs also reflected what had become in the mid-eighteenth century a well-published curiosity about variations within Islam, stemming in part from changing relations between Islamic regimes and the west. The defeat of Ottoman forces in Europe at the end of the seventeenth century and a respite from Algerian piracy eased fears of Islam among British and European commentators. New attitudes also followed from a growth in scholarship on the theology of different Islamic sects and on parallels between Islamic doctrine—rigorously monotheistic and moralistic—and deism. Observers dismissed Restoration-era caricatures that presented Islam as inescapably fraudulent, degenerate, and violent. Bernard had collected a small library of the latest books on Islam, many published in London, which challenged common misperceptions that Muslims worshipped Venus, for example, or taught that God was corporeal or had created evil.[54]

Most of Bernard's books on Islam concerned the Safavid, or Persian, Empire, which had become important to Britain's overseas commerce. The Safavids served as a buffer against Ottoman power and as trading partners when British trade with Ottoman merchants collapsed during the 1710s and 1720s. The majority of Persians were Shiite Muslims, who reflected Britain's imperial interests and, according to Bernard's sources, stood as a counterpart to European Protestants persecuted by Catholics. Often harassed by Ottoman and Arab Sunnis, they were by reputation minority voices in the Islamic world who promoted a morally sound and philosophically reasonable version of Islam. Several whiggish writers invoked monotheistic and tolerant schools within Islam as an example for Britain. We can recall the image of Ali in the frontispiece to Broughton. Bernard also read studies of Arabic Hermeticism or academies in medieval Baghdad and Syria that blended Greco-Roman (especially Neo-Pythagorean) ideas with arcane scientific knowledge and spiritualist wisdom. Sometimes blended with Sufi philosophies, Arabic Hermeticism was revived in private, semi-secret schools in Istanbul during the eighteenth century.[55]

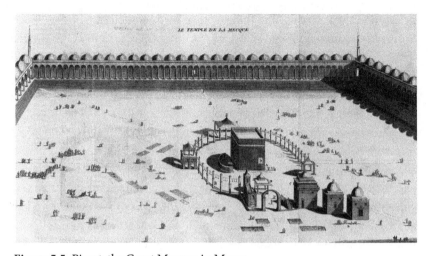

Figure 5.5 Picart, the Great Mosque in Mecca

Credit: Bernard Picart and Frederic Bernard, *The Ceremonies and Religious Customs of the Various Nations of the Known World*, 7 vols. (London, 1733–1737), 7: following 32.

Picart accordingly depicted some Islamic ceremonies as virtuous in Whig terms and others as vicious. His images of Ramadan celebrations and street scenes of Bairam festivals (at the end of Ramadan) in Sunni Istanbul feature ominous ceremonial fires, frenzied crowds, buffoonish clerics, and hints of debauchery.[56] Or we can view his image of the Great Mosque in Mecca, with the massive, cube-like Ka'ba in the center of a colonnaded portico (Figure 5.5).

Picart presented the reader with Sunni Arab power, displayed in a public site, full of magnificence, like the Vatican.[57]

Yet Picart included many scenes of Islamic teachers and devotees who, in private settings—houses and schools, rather than streets and monumental buildings—manifested sobriety, earnestness, and learning. Take, for example, Picart's image of a mufti, a teacher of the Qur'an and Islamic law.[58] A few listeners sit behind him as he expounds the text and gestures toward heaven, eyes uplifted (Figure 5.6).

This became one of Picart's more well-known images, in part because it conveyed respect for unadorned devotion and for deference to a canonical text—the very virtues claimed by Whig Protestants. Picart may have been inspired by his books on Islam, several of which described notable Shiite muftis or neo-Hermetic philosophers. He commended the reasonableness and amiableness of quiet and scholarly versions of Islam just as he derided

Figure 5.6 Picart, a mufti

Credit: Bernard Picart and Frederic Bernard, *The Ceremonies and Religious Customs of the Various Nations of the Known World*, 7 vols. (London, 1733–1737), 7: following 122.

the coercive and irrational forces of public Islamic ceremony. Bernard took such Islamic teaching to be a "mild and gentle" counterexample not only to institutional Catholicism but also to Protestants who in "the Heat of their Zeal, and Pride of their Ambition" aspired to political power.[59]

Even when it came to Native American traditions, in which rituals on the surface bore little semblance to western religious practices, Picart and Bernard conformed their observations to the same pattern that they had constructed for Catholicism: ceremonies that prompted ecstatic experience and subservience to political leaders were vicious; ceremonies that fostered reflection and moral dedication were virtuous. In crafting their account, they relied heavily on the 1705 *History and Present State of Virginia* by Robert Beverly.[60] An owner of large estates near Jamestown and member of the House of Burgesses, Beverly designed his "history" in part as an argument against royal intervention into Virginia's government. Because it conveyed an anti-absolutist and anti-Catholic message, the French translation of the *History*, which was most likely used by Picart and Bernard, found a receptive audience especially among French Protestants.[61]

Beverly's description of the Tidewater Algonquians served Picart and Bernard in two respects. First, it reinforced the message that priests and their irrational ceremonies corrupted natural, moral religion. In making this case, Beverly lauded the non-sacerdotal aspects of Algonquian religion. He dismissed rumors of child sacrifice as ugly nonsense. According to the *History*, he had a "free" and open conversation with Natives who explained to him that they did not worship "the Devil," as Beverly had been told. They in fact "believ'd" in a personal and "universally beneficent" God who was eternal, spiritual, and perfect, who bestowed on humanity the goodness of creation, and who did not coerce belief but rather left people "to make the most of their Free Will" as they made their way through life. As Beverly recalled his conversations, they did attempt to pacify lesser spirits or "the Evil Spirit" that inflicted people through war and natural disasters such as disease, famine, and drought. This was a far cry from the devil worship conjured by seventeenth-century English observers. True to the precepts of the "Law of Nature," they held to simple rules of equity and expected their leaders to be impartial and fair in their administration of justice.[62]

Drawing generalizations from Beverly, other firsthand accounts, and excerpts in Purchas, Picart and Bernard claimed that Native Americans had instincts for a simple and moral religion. Bernard described those fundamental instincts: the "Necessity they are under, of adoring one Supreme Being," of confession of sin, of "Prayer and Repentance, in order to obtain the Favour of Heaven" and "the Immortality of the Soul." Apart from priestly religion, that is, according to Bernard, Native Americans adhered to a form of deism, an iteration of the very same ideas promoted by Lord Herbert of Cherbury. From Picart and Bernard's perspective, the Indigenous inhabitants of America quite reasonably held to the dictates of a universal and natural religion.[63]

Picart and Bernard provided illustrations of Native American rituals that suggested simplicity and compassion—and an aversion to civic power. Picart included one engraving, for example, after De Bry's image, of a graceful mourning ceremony of Timucuan (Floridian) widows who sprinkle locks of hair around a sacred site, and several engravings of what he called "public rejoicings": circles of female and male dancers with serene countenances.[64] He portrayed a Native American people whose religious sentiments could be correlated to a Whig discourse of noncoercion and humaneness—even if that discourse also validated the subjection of those same people to an empire centered in London.

If Picart and Bernard, relying on Beverly, made some aspects of Algonquian theology sound like whiggish Protestantism, then they also drew parallels to debased Catholicism. They described Algonquian priests, for example, who constantly deceived, befuddled, or intimidated people into a form of devotion that contradicted natural morality. Beverly told of coming upon an unattended religious site—a small hut-like structure—where he and his companions found human bones, engraved tomahawks, and a life-size puppet-like figure hanging on a wall, what Beverly learned was the "Idol" Kiwasa. Beverly surmised that the "chief Conjurer" would set up the figure in the dark recesses of the hut and manipulate it with ropes to awe worshippers who thought that it was a living being. It was for Beverly a prime example of how "the Priests and Conjurers have a great sway in every Nation." In Virginia, the "Simplicity" of the people in a "state of Nature" gave "the cunning Priest a greater advantage over them." Priests had debased Native spirituality and deceived "the common people" in order to gain power and offerings such as food.[65]

Picart used this anecdote from Beverly to portray an ambiguity in Algonquian religion. He so insisted on the superiority of private devotion over public ceremony that he redid the image of the Virginian Algonquian figure that John Ogilby had identified with the sachem Powhatan, as discussed in Chapter 1. Recall that Ogilby had used a 1671 illustration of the figure that gave it a massive size and placed it on a large platform in the middle of a palace-like structure, attended by dancing devotees and serving as a site for ritual sacrifice. Following one of De Bry's 1590 engravings, Picart stripped the scene of all palatial, ecstatic, and violent imagery. He presented the "idol," holding talismans, as a gentle figure inside a small, plain thatched tent (Figure 5.7).[66]

Figure 5.7 Picart, Algonquian idol

Credit: Bernard Picart and Frederic Bernard, *The Ceremonies and Religious Customs of the Various Nations of the Known World*, 7 vols. (London, 1733–1737), 3: facing 112.

Nothing in the image suggests political power or human sacrifice. Picart turned the "idol" into an object of private devotion with a pacific title, "The God of the Winds." In such a form, the Algonquian figure represented noncoercive religion, not quite a primal and natural piety but at the same time not the fearsome deity conjured by Ogilby.

Second, Beverly repeatedly used comparisons with Roman Catholicism to explain Algonquian religion, giving Picart and Bernard yet another illustration of how the world's religions were sometimes intelligible as cognates of the Church of Rome. How ought one account for Algonquian spiritual leaders who performed their "Adorations and Conjurations" in a dialect unknown by most worshippers, thereby claiming to be "Oracles" who had secret knowledge and who could foresee the future, asserting after the fact that they had predicted important events such as enemy attacks? They were like European prelates who said the "Mass in *Latin*," all the while holding the mysteries of grace. How to understand a Native devotee who fell under the influence of sacred rituals to the point of ecstasy, trance, and red-hot zeal? They were, according to Beverly, just like fervent papists at sacred shrines.

No "bigotted [sic] Pilgrim," i.e., devout Catholic at a pilgrimage site, "appears more zealous, or strains the Devotion more at the Shrine, than these believing *Indians* so, in their Idolatrous Adorations."[67]

Algonquian people, according to such accounts, displayed the universal misfortunes of sacerdotal religion. According to Bernard, Indigenous priests used ceremonies to pervert primitive religious instincts into violent fanaticism across America. Bernard perceived the depredations of priests throughout what he called "American" ceremonies in Canada, the Mississippi Valley, Florida, the Caribbean, Mexico, Peru, and Virginia (he made no reference to New England). Even though Picart and Bernard depicted variation, they focused on how priests and sachems in most regions had taken advantage of the Americans' "wild and crazy Imaginations, and an habitual Ignorance." The misuse of ritual had obscured Native people's knowledge "of the Supreme Being."[68]

Simple practices of natural piety or deism twisted by priestly ceremony into religious-political bigotry: Bernard made it sound like the history of Christianity in Catholic Europe. As he put it, his countrymen had "been guilty of the same Fault" when they "sullied these pure, these plain Principles" with "the most ridiculous Notions."[69] Bernard used the trope "idolatry" as one characterization of such corrupt religion. By that term, he did not mean the worship of false gods or the devil, or the disorder evoked by Restoration-era commentators. He meant deference to priests who misled people into unreasonable and irrational devotions—ceremonies that induced servility to religious and civic rulers. In this framework, the real idols were absolutism and religious persecution, the vices that fired the indignation of British Whigs.

The most monumental example of such corruption was, for Picart and Bernard, the ritual human sacrifices of the Aztecs, conducted on top of the towering "Temple" for the deity "Vitsliputsli" in the central square of the Aztec capital Tenochtitlan. Picart's image of Tenochtitlan, with an open square around the temple, resembled his image of the Grand Mosque in Mecca with the Ka'ba in the middle (Figure 5.8).[70] In both instances, awe-inducing events occurred in majestic public settings, led by priests in the service of potentates.

According to Bernard, the great square of Tenochtitlan, with its "Cathedral," encompassed scenes of idolatry, priestly brutality, and political oppression. "Idolatry" in Tenochtitlan included "Sacrifices so barbarous and inhuman" as to be called "execrable Worship," conducted by "priests" who donned "pontifical Vestments." Picart's close-up representation of

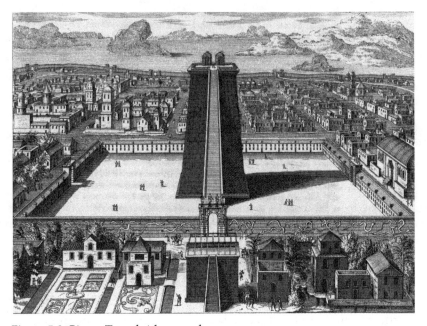

Figure 5.8 Picart, Tenochtitlan temple

Credit: Bernard Picart and Frederic Bernard, *The Ceremonies and Religious Customs of the Various Nations of the Known World*, 7 vols. (London, 1733–1737), 3: facing 150.

what occurred at the top of the "cathedral" illustrated such inhumaneness (Figure 5.9).[71]

These same priests "crowned the King" and received favors in return. Picart and Bernard's rhetoric clearly evoked the Catholicism of the papacy: priests who operated in cathedrals, wearing pontifical vestments and crowning kings who enforced the priests' authority. In Mexico, as in Portugal and Spain—where officials of the Inquisition conducted the burning of heretics also in large public squares—priests and emperors enacted violence as an expression of sacerdotal-magisterial alliance.[72]

Religious Diversity and Roman Catholicism

Picart and Bernard construed the religious diversity of the world as an extension of the contrast between papal ceremonialism and Protestant moralism. In the frontispiece to *Ceremonies and Religious Customs*, Picart presented a

Figure 5.9 Picart, Aztec sacrifice

Credit: Bernard Picart and Frederic Bernard, *The Ceremonies and Religious Customs of the Various Nations of the Known World*, 7 vols. (London, 1733–1737), 3: facing 152.

remarkable "Tableau of the Principle Religions of the World" that gave visual expression to this contrast (Figure 5.10).[73]

The tableau consists of three horizontal layers. The uppermost grouping, in the background, features images for non-western, non-monotheistic religions, framed by foreboding mountains. On the viewer's left are Peruvians at worship before a relief of the sun in a stone housing—a reference to Incan, state-sponsored religion. Above them are "Lapps," as Picart called the Sámi people of northern Scandinavia, with arms raised in veneration of a deer on a pole. Behind them on a plain in the distance is the central square of Tenochtitlan with its tower for sacrifice. On the right side are illustrations for East Asian religions: Indian ascetics and deities, an obelisk from a northern Indian temple, the ever-menacing fire and elaborate pagodas associated with Buddhism. The people of Guinea are conspicuous by their absence—yet another indication of their dehumanization by imperial apologists.

The bottom grouping presents Islamic figures. On the left side a mufti teaches from the Qur'an, surrounded by men dressed as Sufis, Janissaries,

Figure 5.10 Picart, frontispiece

Credit: Bernard Picart and Frederic Bernard, *The Ceremonies and Religious Customs of the Various Nations of the Known World*, 7 vols. (London, 1733–1737), 1: frontispiece.

and princes. On the right kneels a person in Persian dress, presumably a Shiite teacher, with a display of the eight cardinal points of Islam. These images represented socially admirable forms of Islam, scholarly and moral. Other images at the bottom signify ritualistic and cruel versions of Islam. The camel, Picart tells us, is garlanded for sacrifice. The pit on the lower right represents infidels burning in everlasting punishment. Picart posed reasonable, moral, and scriptural Islam against sacrificial, ceremonial, and dogmatic Islam.[74]

The center grouping, showing the conflict between Protestantism and Catholicism, dominates the tableau. On the reader's left, a woman in white, whom Picart calls "TRUE RELIGION," holds a copy of the Bible with German and English translations of the title, an indication that it is the vernacular scripture. She stands, with a gentle countenance, beneath the tree of religion as Protestant heroes prune it of unnecessary branches or accretions. She is circled by those heroes: Menno Simons performing a baptism, John Calvin (above Menno to the left), Martin Luther, Philip Melanchthon (just behind Luther) and, on the other side of the tree, Jan Hus and an Anglican bishop—perfectly poised between Protestant and Catholic sentiments. It is an ecumenical Protestant pantheon.

On the reader's right of TRUE RELIGION, a Franciscan monk attempts to close the Bible, pointing with his left hand to a large book titled the "traditions and conciliar [decrees]" of the Church of Rome, including the tenets of indulgences and priestly absolution. A female figure, named by Picart as the ROMAN CHURCH, wearing the papal tiara, dominates the right side of the scene. In her right hand she offers an olive branch to Protestants and in her left hand she holds a monstrance, a vessel for display of the consecrated bread of the sacrament. Just behind her right hand is the official banner of the Inquisition. The message is clear: the Church of Rome offers reconciliation only to those who convert to Catholicism. Over the left shoulder of the ROMAN CHURCH is a black-hatted Jesuit, waving Unigentitas in the face of an affronted French bishop, behind whom stand Jansenist and Quietist leaders. The ROMAN CHURCH presses under her feet two supine figures: under the right foot, a Jewish teacher grasping a scroll of the Torah and, under the left foot, a figure for the Holy Roman Emperor or secular rule, who relinquishes an orb, a symbol of sovereignty, to the woman. The center of the tableau conveys the heritage of scriptural truth and toleration on the left, and an ecclesiastical force that crushes scripture, persecutes dissent, and aspires to civil authority on the right.

The central focus of this frontispiece is the conflict between Protestant virtue and Catholic vice, scripture and reason as opposed to ritual and coercion. The images of non-Christian religions and of Islam sit in the background and foreground, reflections of this central dynamic. Seen in this way, Picart and Bernard, like Broughton and Chambers, crafted their descriptions of other religions as images of struggles in France between papists and pro-toleration parties and in England between Whigs and Jacobites. In France, ceremonial religion had turned Jansenists into heretics and Huguenots into exiles; in England, it had turned latitudinarians into apostates, dissenters into traitors, and Hanoverians into pretenders. From this perspective, Islamic, Native American, or Buddhist zealotry, including ceremonies that glorified priests and their political accomplices, reflected ceremonial Catholicism. They appeared as corruptions of pure religion not because they deviated from Christian creeds or were conducted by an unfamiliar people but because they combined ecstasy with state power. Shiite teaching, peaceful Algonquian rituals, and Confucian learning, by contrast, could be described as analogues to moderate Protestantism: sensible, uncoercive, and decent. The moral qualities that, for English readers and associates of Picart and Bernard, sustained the Whig-imperial project constituted the standard by which to judge any religious expression.

From this perspective, however, no major religion or cultural tradition appeared as an unchanging monolith, shaped by a theological creed. Ceremonial and political agendas varied from one community to another. As Whig Protestants adopted these assumptions, they followed Picart and Bernard in their interpretations, most poignantly in their descriptions of Catholicism. Their descriptions defied caricature. Increasing contact between British colonists and French Acadians before the Seven Years' War, for example, produced accounts of mutual interests and sympathies, including polite exchanges among Protestants and Catholics in North America. Commentators noted that some prominent Catholics in America advocated for religious toleration and rejected papal supremacy over the kingdom's secular affairs. Newspaper editorialists in America applauded the rise of tolerant ideals within Catholic communities in Germany, France, and Italy. Changes within the papacy itself and its relationship to what Protestants regarded as the most intolerant papists, the Jesuits, produced expressions of admiration. From 1740 to 1758 Pope Benedict XIV gained a reputation for being less bellicose than his predecessors: more reformist, scholarly, and irenic. Increasing tensions between the papacy and the Jesuits, signaled by their expulsion from Portugal in 1758, France in 1764, and Spain in 1767, and culminating in their suppression in 1773, heartened Protestants who looked for forms of Catholicism that were compatible with the ideals of Whig Britain.[75]

Anglo-French warfare during the late 1740s and 1750s, by contrast, led Anglo-American Protestants to excoriate what they deemed to be the militant consequence of hierarchical Catholic ceremonialism. Jonathan Mayhew sounded an alarm in 1750: the re-Catholicization of many parts of Europe had erupted into war between "Liberty, the BIBLE and Common Sense," in opposition to "Tyranny, PRIEST-CRAFT and Non-sense." For Mayhew, "popish idolatry" did not refer to the sentiments of ordinary priests or followers but to the imperial aspirations of the papacy, which sought to be a real "kingdom" in "Italy" and, from there, to crush the "Liberty" of civilized people throughout the western world. "Popish power," as other preachers claimed time and again, meant a political assault on the "Ends of Government" and spread of "Popery, Slavery, and Destruction."[76]

In the midst of the Seven Years' War, Protestant accusations of papal intolerance, absolutism, and deception hardened into apocalyptic invective. For the evangelical Calvinist Jonathan Edwards, the armies of France and Spain evoked the figure of antichrist. He referred to neither a supernatural chiliastic monster nor to Tridentine teaching, but rather to what he called "the pretenses of the Romish clergy to apostolical power" by which the church "claims the whole power of Christ" to rule the world. The Church of Rome was, Edwards observed, an immense, international institution, not merely an intolerant bishop here or there or a malicious pope, as in Calvin's day. Edwards wrote of treasuries of gold, battalions of troops, diplomatic machinations. This drive toward pure power, Edwards maintained, eventually—eschatologically—would conjoin Catholicism to Sunni Islam, an alliance that revealed the political rather than theological threat of the papacy. "Antichrist" expressed imperial might.[77]

Edwards drew on the materiality of Catholic ceremony, including the same details mentioned by Bernard and Picart, to sustain his interpretation. As Edwards put it, the ringing of bells to frighten evil spirits, choreographed rites of exorcism, claims to the healing power of holy vestments, "holy ground," and "holy oil," along with veneration of the eucharistic elements, relics, and "innumerable such like charms" all bespoke sorcery and deception, the very instruments used by the beast of Revelation to gather adherents. The physical dimensions of Catholic rite and ritual clued Edwards and other exegetes such as Cotton Mather to the identity of the "beast" of Revelation 13 and the mysterious number 666, associated with the beast's followers. These figures, by their account, referred to the Church of Rome and her chief minion, the King of France.[78]

Whig standards for judging Catholic communities, however, produced variable readings, among lay and non-scholarly Protestants as much as among divines and encyclopedists. To understand their encounters, Protestant travelers to Catholic lands in this period often drew on the discourse described above: the ills of ceremonial power and coercion, and the benefits of ritual simplicity and toleration.

New England soldiers who served in Canada gave mixed reviews of the French Catholics they met in the aftermath of hostilities. Dudley Bradstreet, an evangelical son of the pastor in Groton, Massachusetts, and a non-commissioned officer, wrote about the piety of the citizens of Louisbourg after it was taken by New England forces in 1745. He admired the strength of devotion among commoners, many of them frightened and despairing. Bradstreet was also taken aback by a severely wounded officer who offered a friar some 10,000 pounds to forgive his sins—leading Bradstreet to quip that he would have gladly performed the same service for half the amount. A fellow soldier in Bradstreet's regiment attended a Mass in the Louisbourg hospital. The apparent contradiction between the citizens' learnedness and their worship perplexed him. Their devotion to "images" and their ritual genuflections signified ceremonial excess in the midst of rubble. Yet he extolled the British terms of surrender that allowed the "Inhabitants of the town" to "enjoy the exercise of their Religion": a practice of tolerance even among papists. On entering Fort Carillon (the English renamed it Ticonderoga) in 1757, Eli Forbush viewed with astonishment the "many monuments of Superstition," particularly a huge red cross with a lead plaque that was inscribed with Constantine's motto, "Hoc Signum [sic] Vincit" ("in this sign, you will conquer"). The superstition, by Forbush's account, was the papal presumption of an ecclesiastical-imperial alliance.[79]

Or, returning to the captive New England mariner discussed in the previous chapter, William Pote commended a Franciscan priest, Chevaleze, for his work among English prisoners in Quebec. According to Pote, this man of "Cevility," who cared for the sick prisoners, attempted to proselytize the English but did so in an amiable manner. He put "his Reasons . . . why the Roman Catholic faith was preferable to the Protestant" in writing and presented them to a Protestant minister for debate and discussion. Chevaleze issued no threats of either temporal or eternal punishment. He respected the prisoners' liberty of conscience. Throughout such accounts, British Protestants judged their Catholic adversaries according to Whig criteria. Simple devotion, learnedness, civility, toleration, and reasoned exchange evoked admiration. Lordly priests, material ceremony, coerciveness, and religious-political collusion evoked censure.[80]

These were widespread interpretations of Catholicism, shared by other travelers. Anglo-American Protestants who journeyed to Europe during this period often made distinctions between the practices of ordinary Catholics and the Church of Rome as an imperial power. The Quaker merchant Isaac Norris (the second) traveled from Philadelphia to the Netherlands and Flanders in 1734. In his account he contrasted the dutiful religiosity of Catholic laity in Antwerp, many of whom suffered poverty, to the excessive riches of churches, with their marble altars and elaborate artwork. So too, Richard Warburton, an aristocrat with estates in Ireland, found an unseemly jumble of wealth, political power, and resplendence in Rome in 1735. Warburton offered plainspoken prose to the same effect as Picart's engravings of Saint Peter's: the basilica was "too much in the stile of a Palace" to be a real church, the Vatican palace—with its 12,522 rooms and 1,200 chimneys—too grand to be a real rectory, and "the Pope" too much of "an absolute Prince" to be a real pastor.[81]

An anonymous traveler to Flanders in 1761 reported along the same lines. Friendly nuns received him with courtesy and spoke "in a familiar manner answering any civil questions" without rancor. Scholarly Irish priests shared meals with him. Yet this traveler also reported on corrupt religiosity. Incited by ritual fervor, unruly crowds threatened to beat him about the head when he declined to kneel at the altar during a service in Antwerp. The splendor of a Mass performed by the archbishop in Brussels stunned him. The sight of people in Bruges kissing a vial supposedly filled with Christ's blood and encased in gold appalled him. The sheer physicality of monks dismayed him: their lengthy processions with tapers, the ascetic garb of Capuchins, and the "miserable manner" in which "they confine and torment their Bodies." These travelers each placed their experiences in whiggish frameworks that distinguished plain and sociable piety from material and vicious ceremony.[82]

Picart and Bernard's focus on ceremony suggested that their readers ought to appreciate diversity within religious traditions: how local practices often belied generalizations about this or that "religion" and its cosmology or theology. The celebration of baptism among a handful of worshippers in a Catholic parish appeared quite different from a papal procession. So

too, the mourning rites of Timucuans in Florida differed from human sacrifice in Aztec Mexico, the meditations of Shiite teachers from Sunni street
festivals in Constantinople, the lectures of Buddhist or Confucian scholars
from prayers in massive temples. *Ceremonies and Religious Customs* showed
that it was misleading to characterize whole traditions without nuance. The
sensible observer, therefore, according to Picart and Bernard, evaluated
the rituals and habits of particular communities according to the criteria
of sensibility, reasonableness, and utility. Like their contemporaries, Picart
and Bernard compiled the existing and ever-expanding knowledge of the
world's traditions into a display of variation that confounded confessional
caricatures. It was no wonder, then, that New England travelers to French
Canada or Catholic Europe, even during times of war, formed friendly
associations with individual friars, monks, and priests, along with Catholic
laity, even as they recoiled at the thought of the Roman pontiff. Protestants
could admire some Catholic communities even as they fought against the antichrist because the papacy affronted reason and endangered free conscience.

The critiques of Picart and Bernard, Mayhew and Middleton and
Edwards, to be sure, served as British polemical devices rather than unbi-
ased observations. They not only masked Catholic narratives that defended
the papacy but also obscured the intolerance of much of Anglo-American
Protestant rhetoric and policy. The authors and illustrators discussed here
had little patience for forms of devotion, in any tradition, that appeared as
threats to Britain's growing empire. They imposed their own taxonomic
uniformity—divisions of religion into reasonable and unreasonable—on a
diverse landscape of religions.

That observation does not belie the importance of the ways in which the
discourse of Whig moralism affected Protestant descriptions of the world's
religions. The single most pervasive theme that ran throughout the literature of comparative religions during the middle decades of the eighteenth
century was this: religious ceremonies or evangelistic practices that mirrored institutional Catholicism in the use of force to compel adherence
were politically dangerous. Politically sound or useful religion, in contrast,
relied on persuasion—on the moral reasonableness of its claims. The new
study of religions, given resplendent expression in *Ceremonies and Religious
Customs* and reflected in common accounts of religious encounter, fastened
on the uncoerced choice of one's religion as a political and moral necessity.
That conviction shaped subsequent encounters between Anglo-American
Protestants and adherents of different religions.

It also raised questions. How best to describe, then, the nature of religious choices and the criteria by which they were to be made? How ought Anglo-American Protestants explain the role of individuals' moral judgments in conversion? To answer, we must turn to the evangelical revivals and the missions to Native Americans that occupied New England's Protestants who thought of themselves as loyal subjects of Britain's Whig-inspired monarchy.

6

Indian Conversions

In 1748, Jonathan Edwards edited the diary of David Brainerd, a missionary among the Lenape (Delaware) who spent his last months in Edwards's home before succumbing to tuberculosis. Edwards's edition of Brainerd's diary was one of America's bestselling religious publications through the early nineteenth century. Edwards presented Brainerd as an ideal evangelist, who engaged different religious traditions and promoted conversion in reasonable and morally appealing ways, or what the text often conveys in the terms "rational and just." At issue is what Edwards—or Brainerd through Edwards's editorial voice—meant by "rational and just."[1]

One incident in the diary illustrates a possible set of meanings. In May 1745, Brainerd traveled from his mission at the Forks of the Delaware in New Jersey to Juniata Island on the Susquehanna River. He initially noted how the language, ritual dances, and burial ceremonies of the Indigenous people there—likely a Susquehannock group—differed from the practices of the Lenape at the Forks of the Delaware.[2] He then had an especially remarkable encounter. A Native spiritual "reformer," dressed in bearskins and a painted mask, emerged from the woods gyrating and shaking his tortoise-shell rattle. Startled at first, Brainerd settled himself and fell into conversation with the man he characterized as "a devout and zealous" non-Christian. "I discoursed with him about Christianity," Brainerd recorded, and the Indian reformer "seemed to like" some aspects of Brainerd's message.[3]

The more Brainerd conversed the more he discovered uncanny parallels between his sense of religion and the reformer's. The man informed Brainerd that "God has taught him his religion" and called him to travel around, find "some good people," spread a message of spiritual revitalization, and discourage dissolute habits such as drinking. A divine spirit, the man said, had touched his affections, so that "his heart was very much distressed" at the state of the Delaware people, just as Brainerd's was. Since being so touched, the man claimed, "he had known God," who had "comforted his heart" while many of his people derided his zealotry. Brainerd noted that the man held "a set of religious notions that he had looked into for himself, and not taken on

The Opening of the Protestant Mind. Mark Valeri, Oxford University Press. © Oxford University Press 2023.
DOI: 10.1093/oso/9780197663677.003.0007

bare tradition." A traveling reformer motivated by a new sense of truth and affection: he was an Indigenous analogue to an evangelical missionary.[4]

According to his own account, Brainerd conducted himself politely and commended his interlocutor. He applauded the man's curiosity, lack of "prejudice," and "uncommon courtesy" as signs of reasonableness. The missionary recognized that the reformer was "sincere, honest and conscientious." Brainerd pressed the case for Christianity, to which the man "would sometimes say, 'Now that [part of Brainerd's message] I like: so God as taught me.' " The reformer rejected Christian beliefs such as the existence of the devil and heaven. He refused conversion. He nonetheless appeared to Brainerd to be a person of genuine religious sentiment. "There was something in his temper and disposition"—here Brainerd used the vocabulary common to Edwards and contemporary moral philosophy—"that looked more like true religion than anything I ever observed amongst other heathens."

The published version of Brainerd's diary presents the missionary as "rational and just" in at least three ways. First, he adopted the view of mid-eighteenth-century Protestant observers who evaluated different religions according to regnant standards of sociability and humaneness.[5] Brainerd, that is, was wise in his commendation of the Native reformer for his efforts to revitalize his people, his humane sentiments, and his "courtesy." At other places in the diary, Brainerd also was candid about the failures of his fellow Englishmen to adhere to the same standards. He complained that "white people" at his own services acted "indecently" and "abusive[ly]" while Native peoples comported themselves "in a public and solemn manner." By this account, Brainerd rightly took decency to be a more important cultural marker than ethnic and geographical identities.[6]

Second, Brainerd's observations in his diary and in *Mirabilia Dei inter Indicos*, an early report on his mission, suggested that he regarded the unevangelized Lenape and Susquehannock as imbued with the same powers of moral reason as Britons. He recognized the reformer's knowledge of fundamental moral and religious principles apart from Christian teaching. Reflecting on his experience, Brainerd urged other missionaries to do the same as he had: find common ground in what was "written in [the] heart" of all people, whatever their culture. Brainerd claimed that effective evangelists began their exchange with Native Americans by affirming that "God" made every person to "feel what [they] should do."[7] As a corollary, Brainerd maintained that previous missionaries who thought that it was necessary to civilize Native Americans before leading them to conversion were mistaken.

Living among the Lenape, he refrained from critique of traditional social practices, affirmed economic pursuits such as hunting, and informed them that English literacy and social custom had little to do with true religion. The English, Lenape, and Susquehannock, according to Brainerd, shared dictates of moral conscience that transcended English ways of life.[8]

Third, according to accounts of his mission, Brainerd appealed to the moral consciences of the Delaware, urging them to choose Christianity voluntarily. He asked the reformer to ponder Christianity as an amiable religion, in a give-and-take conversation, just as he attempted to persuade others about the "merits" of Christianity. By speaking of the Christian message in the cadences of mercy, benevolence, and sympathy, he intended to "engage them, as far as I could[,] to be friendly to Christianity." He claimed that he eschewed hellfire preaching, refusing to terrorize his audiences as he set aside coercion for conversation.[9]

Brainerd maintained that he wanted all nonbelievers to embrace Christianity in ways that were "considerably enlightened and much freed" from all social "prejudices."[10] He urged the Lenape and other Delaware peoples—along with the Catholics, Baptists, Quakers, Presbyterians, Lutherans, Moravians, and anti-religious scoffers who jostled together on the frontier of the Delaware River and occasionally attended his preaching services—to ponder the same choice: to set aside their familial, tribal, or political identities and embrace the gospel as unencumbered, reasoning individuals.[11] He used various idioms to suggest personal volition, inviting his hearers "to come," "receive," or "give up their heart." In Brainerd's view, for the Susquehannock and Lenape, no less than for the unconverted White settlers, conversion meant a conscious decision about the moral merits of Christianity.[12]

Edwards had conformed Brainerd's diary to the discourse of the world's religions developed by post-1688 Protestants such as Gordon and Trenchard, Broughton and Collier, and Picart and Bernard, who placed Native American traditions within a context of global religious diversity.[13] Brainerd, Edwards, and many of their missionary colleagues aligned themselves with that discourse when they discerned the virtues of benevolence, reasonableness, and utility among the variety of Indigenous practices. They made no wholesale judgments on Algonquian or Iroquoian traditions as legitimate or illegitimate. They expressed ambivalence about the reasonableness of Indigenous cultures, to be sure. During periods of violent conflict, or Native hostility to Christian instruction, they criticized Native people as ignorant and savage.

They assumed nonetheless that they would find expressions of religious consciousness, chiefly in the form of moral sentiments, along with the corruption of that consciousness in the form of priestcraft, ceremonialism, and intolerance. From their perspective, such contradictions marked religion from Juniata Island to London, Constantinople to Paris.

Whiggish discourse likewise led New England missionaries to contend that Native people and Britons experienced conversion in the same manner—as a voluntary affiliation based on moral judgment. The old confessional tropes of submission to the power of divine providence, while never discarded, receded in Protestant missionary discourse. Conversion came to be framed as an act of deliberation and willful choice. Missionaries under sway of this new approach to the world's religions accordingly adjusted their evangelistic strategies. They renounced many of the Anglicizing-civilizing agendas of predecessors, such as Eliot, and emphasized the virtues of moral persuasion. They presented Christianity as a remedy for the afflictions that beset Algonquian and Iroquoian people, from disease and death to the predations of colonial powers. They claimed to promote evangelization as an exchange of ideas about sin and salvation among reasonable interlocutors rather than as an exercise of Anglocentric prejudice and power.

To elucidate such claims, this chapter attends to Experience Mayhew's ministry among the Wampanoag of Martha's Vineyard, Brainerd's work among the Lenape Delaware, Jonathan Edwards's preaching to the Stockbridge Mohicans, and Charles Jeffrey Smith's itineration among the Mohawk and Oneida in the Mohawk River Valley. Focused on missionary discourse, the following discussion admittedly offers only a brief consideration of how Native Americans experienced Christianization, which varied by location and attendant political issues such as the dispossession of lands and imperial warfare. It attends less to the voices of Indigenous people than to the voices of Anglo-American Protestants. There is a large and contested literature on the meaning of Indigenous conversions to Christianity in such terms. The following discussion concerns the ways Protestant missionaries, influenced by study of the world's religions, presumed that British and Indigenous people faced the same types of moral dilemmas as they chose their religious identities. That in itself was a remarkable development in Protestant perceptions of the world's religions.[14]

As many scholars have pointed out, the story of Protestant missionary discourse is complicated by the imperial power, settler colonialism, and racialization that shadowed Anglo-Indigenous interactions at nearly every turn. Mid-eighteenth-century Protestant missions cannot be isolated from a history of violence and the dispossession of Indigenous lands, along with racialized readings of Indigenous peoples, that accompanied Christianization. Missionaries such as Brainerd and his contemporaries rarely, if ever, pondered that history in such terms. This chapter broaches such matters along the way, especially after an account of missionaries' ideas about religious liberty, conversion, and missions. It focuses on one part of the longer history: a mid-eighteenth-century moment, among whiggish Anglo-American Protestants, that differed in some ways from the confessional missions of the seventeenth century and the racialized, civilizing missions of the nineteenth century.[15] As historians of missions in the British Empire recently have maintained, the political effects of evangelization differed from one locale to another, from one period to another, despite the overall pattern of colonization. In some instances, the Christianization of indigenous peoples contradicted imperial strategies.[16] Missionaries such as Brainerd and his contemporaries at least thought that their moral and religious discourse ought to be decoupled from some forms of Anglocentric imperialism. The reasons for this conviction are the central subjects of this chapter, and they allow us to detect variation in the complex story of Anglo-Indigenous interactions.

The Great Awakening and Moral Freedom

Protestant interest in missions to Indigenous Americans grew from the 1720s through the 1760s. This reflected a widespread concern for conversion, a matter of intense debate especially during the 1736–1742 revivals known as the Great Awakening. The revivals led to factions among the ministry and splits in churches, marked by controversies about itinerant preaching, ecstatic experiences, and indecorous behavior. Yet such controversies also reflected a common agenda. Pro- and anti-revivalists agreed that New Englanders ought to focus on conversion—their own and others'.[17]

During this period, Anglo-American Protestants across the theological spectrum began to speak about conversion in terms of moral liberty: the uncoerced choice of one's religion. The evangelical preacher and politician Elisha Williams, for example, or the deist mason Jeremiah Gridley, the Anglican lexicographer Samuel Johnson, and the dissenting polemicist Caleb Fleming confirmed the importance of moral liberty.[18] In 1749,

Boston's Jonathan Mayhew spoke for the bulk of New England's clergy when he contended that the "choice of our religion," be it "Trinitarian," "Unitarian," "Papist," "Protestant," "Mahometan" or "Heathen," was a matter of personal and individual responsibility rather than state decree or inherited identity. Reason "obliged" every person—it was a "*duty*," he reiterated—to "think and judge" for themselves about the "truth and falsehood," and the prospect for "happiness," offered by different religious communities. Like his contemporaries, Mayhew used a jumble of verbs to convey the willfulness of these choices, such as "embrace," "assent," and "yield."[19]

This consensus, often informed by whiggish political sentiments, drove Protestants to reconsider their theological language. They realized that puritan teaching on the divine decrees, election, or predestination, which emphasized divine control over conversion, appeared to contradict notions of self-determination. The political implications of predestination appeared ominous to loyal Whigs. That, at least, was the opinion of John Locke, who confided to a friend that he was hard pressed to "make freedom in man consistent with omnipotence and omniscience in God."[20] The question nagged at New England divines such as Cotton Mather and Solomon Stoddard during the 1710s and 1720s. In their descriptions of conversion, they touted human freedom and choice as moral necessities yet defended predestination as theological doctrine—without sustained or coherent explanation.[21]

The experiences of New Englanders during the revivals, moreover, surfaced dilemmas about the relative powers of emotional transformation—often portrayed as a work of providence—and deliberate choice in matters of conversion.[22] Recounting a succession of sensations, from despair and mistrust of God to joy and love toward Christ, spiritual diaries written by New Englanders affected by the revivals focused on divine causation rather than rational moral freedom, despite the language of choice that sometimes entered the script. Critics charged revivalists with violation of the common standards of moral reasonableness. Evangelical apologists on both sides of the Atlantic responded to criticism by insisting that divine outpourings of grace—the ultimate means of revival—cohered with human moral deliberation.[23]

The conundrums of providence and affections, moral reason and volition, beset common New Englanders as much as they did Protestant divines. The memoir of the Newport, Rhode Island, schoolteacher Sarah Osborn illustrates the point. Osborn underwent conversion in 1737, when she was twenty-three years old. By that time, she already had suffered through the death of her husband, impoverishment, and a debilitating illness. The physical and economic pains of life in Newport, as she recalled, were matched by intense spiritual discomfort. The sermons of the local Congregationalist pastor, Thomas Clap, had gotten her thinking about her unwillingness to trust Christ. She saw that she "resisted all the kind invitations of a compassionate Saviour." She reiterated such observations: how "it was now strongly impressed on my mind" that she had rejected God's mercy, much to her "distress." She was "alarmed with these thoughts" even as there "seemed to be conveyed" to her "mind" the possibility that she "may yet obtain mercy."[24]

Osborn continued to use the image of "seeing" or perceiving her own mind at work as she narrated her eventual conversion. Although she could not fathom how God was "willing to receive so vile a wretch," she felt "those powerful influences of the spirit of God" when she read 1 Corinthians 10:13 ("God is faithful, who will not suffer you to be tempted above that you are able; but will . . . make a way for your escape"). This "excited" in her "a sense of the excellence[,] glory and truth of God," and she "had a pleasing confidence and rest in the divine faithfulness." She then did what she had been unable to do before this moment: she chose Christ. She "embraced the promises," and in her words "could freely trust my soul in his hands." It had been "impossible," she explained, for "me of myself to believe" before this experience. In this sense, she demurred about her ability to make a godly choice: "whatever others may boast of a free will, I have none of my own." Yet her conversion culminated in a series of quite willful choices: to "plead," "embrace," "own the covenant," and "give" herself "up." She was "brought to lay down" her "arms of rebellion," a willful act even if she claimed to have had no free will.[25]

Writing an account of her experience rather than a theological treatise, Osborn, like many of her contemporaries, did not clarify the relationship among her affections, the intrusion of divine grace, and her choices in conversion. Influenced by Calvinist teaching, she admitted her inability to convert through her own effort, her complete lack of free will, and the overwhelming power of God to "excite" in her a "sense" of divine things beyond her control. Yet she also described her experience as a sequence of active choices: she resisted and rejected, then embraced and "freely" trusted the promises of God in Christ. After her conversion, Osborn queried pastor Samuel Hopkins about the perplexity of sensations. "Doth" the new believer "not, in flying" to Christ, she asked Hopkins, "choose Christ" and "receive Christ"? "I believe," she countered herself in a Calvinist vein, that "the soul is chiefly taken up" by the pull of divine glory. "Yet," she puzzled out loud to Hopkins, "I think they will make application to the Redeemer, for them-selves" because they "have a consciousness and even assurance, that Christ is offered freely." Osborn's memoir gave expression to the changing—and sometimes tangled—meanings of conversion among New Englanders.[26] The Great Awakening produced dozens of such accounts of conversions in what we might think of as a confusion of causes, divine and human: over-whelming affections, divine visitations, outpourings of grace, and willful, self-conscience acts of faith.[27]

The relationship between providence and human volition concerned missionaries, who attributed to Indigenous people at least some power of moral agency: the ability to choose a religious identity that differed from their inherited tradition. Writing from his vantage as a missionary on Martha's Vineyard, Experience Mayhew contended that the tension had not been resolved by the mid-1740s. In a seventy-page unpublished "Discourse Concerning Human Liberty" he claimed that freedom of religious choice had become an evangelistic and patriotic mandate. Yet it was not quite clear to him how to fit the primary requirement for such liberty—the idea of "Free-Will"—into Protestant teaching on conversion. He nearly threw up his hands: "That Man is a Free-Agent, or that he has a Free-Will is, I think, gen-erally acknowledged to be a Truth; But wherein Man's Liberty does consist, or what the nature and extent of it is, are questions that have been disputed" without resolution "among learned Men of several Denominations." There was no simple answer to the question: Was conversion a matter of self-conscious and willful choice or a matter of divine grace transforming the affections of incompetent and corrupt souls?[28]

During the mid-1750s, another missionary pastor, Jonathan Edwards, attempted yet again to give some order to this jumble of impressions and to do so in a way that accounted for contemporary demands to valorize moral and political liberty more thoroughly than had previous Calvinists. His major writing on the topic, written while he attempted to convince Stockbridge Mohicans and visiting Mohawks to choose Christianity, proved to be an es-pecially enduring example of how evangelical missionaries conformed the tenets of divine sovereignty to the mandates of moral choice. He signaled his approach in the title to his treatise. In contrast to the classic Protestant as-sault on free will, Martin Luther's 1525 *On the Bondage of the Will*, Edwards published his work under a title that sounded more nuanced: *A Careful and Strict Enquiry into . . . Freedom of the Will*. This was not an uncompromising denial of moral liberty. It displayed a missionary's confidence, or at least hope, that people could choose to affiliate with Christianity whatever their social and cultural backgrounds.[29]

Edwards's treatise merits scrutiny because it revealed some of the complexities of Protestant attempts to configure whiggish notions of reasonableness, sensibility, and liberty in a way that accorded with Protestant teaching about conversion as a divine work. Much of the initial argument of *Freedom of the Will* gives the impression that Edwards was determined to validate Calvinist teaching by focusing on the guidance of the will by sensations outside of individuals' control. Edwards relied on contemporary moral philosophers such as Locke and Francis Hutcheson to contend that the term "will" referred to the "principle of mind by which it is capable of choosing." Such "choosing," however, depended on one's perceptions of the goodness or agreeableness of some things and the badness or disagreeableness of others. The will was moved by such perceptions and could even be said to be the same thing as those perceptions. Furthermore, those perceptions were in themselves affections: sensations of like and dislike, love or hate, attraction or repulsion. Now, Edwards reasoned, we cannot say that we freely choose those perceptions or sensations—the deep reasons for our choices—because that would lead us into a circular argument about the source of *that* choice. It would be unreasonable to claim, then, that we have "free will" in the sense of choosing things out of complete indifference or lack of perception. We are always being influenced or shaped by our affections—what we find likeable or unlikeable. For Christians, the ultimate source of that influence was God. Outpourings of Christ's mercy and infusions of the Holy Spirit changed people's dispositions or tastes, transformed their affections, and moved their wills. In such terms, the "cause" of conversion, whether the conversion of Sarah Osborn or of a Mohican sachem, was divine grace.[30]

Yet, Edwards insisted repeatedly throughout his treatise that there was nothing in the above argument that contradicted common notions of freedom. By his account, the will still could be said to be free—to love or hate and therefore to dictate people's choices. There was no physical constraint to or coercion of the will. One was free to "do as one willed," or act according to one's choice. Most people spoke of free will in just such terms. No one thought that free will meant a disconnection with "habitual bias," "the stronger motive," or other such terms for moral tastes over which a person had no control. In common parlance such as in the accounts of evangelical converts or "Indian" proselytes, "the man is fully and perfectly free," and at "liberty" to "do and conduct as he will, or according to his choice." Edwards here gave a

full endorsement of the moral, philosophical, and political mandates to assert the moral competence and freedom of all people.[31]

In the most spirited, and sometimes humorous, parts of his treatise,
Edwards even claimed that evangelical Calvinists better sustained the idea
of moral liberty than did Arminian (anti-Calvinist) critics of the revival.
In order to be called truly free, they argued, the will had to be seen as indifferent: unmoved by previous affections and dispositions. This, Edwards
scoffed, amounted to the absurd claim that someone who made a choice
for no good reason, out of no sense of right and wrong, under the sway of
blind chance or in a state of insensitivity and obliviousness, ought to receive
more praise than someone who chose the good out of deep moral conviction and inclination. Edwards's critique rose to the level of sarcasm. By the
Arminian logic, leaders ought not to induce or motivate people to resist evil
or pursue the good because to do so would take away their freedom and
therefore rob them of their moral agency. This perverse notion of liberty implied that preaching, moral education and training, efforts to reform, and
political persuasion—even whiggish political campaigns—were all immoral.
Edwards again observed that no common person thought this way. They
thought more highly of a deed motivated by a sense of virtue than of a deed
motivated by arbitrary and amoral choice.[32]

Edwards provided a rather powerful example of how the language of
freedom and choice inflected an evangelical conception of conversion. "All
that men do in religion," he wrote in *Freedom of the Will*, "is their own act"
or "an exertion of their own power" according to "the ordinary use of language." He did not deny the validity of that language. He inscribed it onto
the evangelical narrative. It took some fairly clever arguments—and some
that were vulnerable to further critique—for Edwards to make that point. Yet
he insisted. However one came by one's will, he concluded, "man is fully and
perfectly free, according to the primary and common notion of freedom."[33]
As Edwards informed his Scottish correspondent John Erskine, he wanted to
demonstrate that a robust conception of conversion as a divine work accorded
perfectly with political ideas of moral liberty: with the "freedom of moral
agents" that made them "proper subjects of moral governments," agents of
right and wrong, liable to "persuasions, promises and threatenings."[34]

This meant that the accounts of conversion by people such as Osborn
could indeed be considered reasonable in whiggish terms. Many evangelical
converts did not put it as logically or precisely as did Edwards, but they could
rest assured. It was true that they were overcome with divine affections and

at the same time freely chose Christ. That was how the will worked. They could deny that they were free in an Arminian sense, as did Osborn, and also, like Osborn, reflect on their "liberty" to choose. As Edwards said, they could "do and conduct" as they "will."[35] There was no need to choose, as it were, between grace and freedom, no either-or. Edwards modeled a grammar of freedom with which to describe the most important issue of the day: conversion entailed a choice according to a bundle of affections or moral judgments that constituted the will. When he made such claims, Edwards may well have had in mind the Stockbridge Mohicans, who were, by his account, affected by a clash of loves and revulsions and yet at liberty to embrace or reject the Christian message as they willed.

That description of conversion reflected a tenet with which most Anglo-American Protestants—excluding radical New Lights who eschewed the language of reasoned choice—agreed. Transformed affections *and* free choice became the regnant discourse of conversion from cosmopolitan London to the liberal precincts of Boston and the Calvinist outposts of rural Connecticut.[36] In order to promote the conversions so needed in New England, Jonathan Mayhew contended in 1755, "the perplexing question concerning *human liberty*" had to be answered "by those, who can *fully* reconcile our freedom" with divine sovereignty. It was no longer possible to "answer the difficulty, by *denying* human freedom" on one side or "providence" on the other. "God's counsel and providence govern the world," he reiterated, "but yet men are free!"[37] Speaking for much of New England's religious establishment, Ezra Stiles told a clerical convention in 1760 that old disputes between "*calvinism* and *arminianism,*" providence and liberty, were but a dying echo. All New England ministers, he hoped, affirmed both divine grace and "the moral liberty and free agency of man" as essentials.[38]

Protestants were convinced that this emerging orthodoxy ought to inform the conversion of non-westerners as well as of Englishmen. The English Calvinist John Edwards hoped that Muslim visitors to London would respond to evangelical preaching by accepting Christ and realizing that their faith was both a divine work and a human decision. As the English Edwards imagined it in a fictionalized account of one such conversion, a Turkish visitor would rely on the concepts legitimated by New England's Jonathan Edwards in *Freedom of the Will*. The convert would claim that he was not "forced to believe against his inclination." He would instead discover that "the soul is first drawn to Jesus as if it would not come; and then it comes as if it were not drawn."[39]

Native American Moral Conscience

In order to apply the consensus on providence and liberty to the evangelization of Native Americans, Protestants during the mid-eighteenth century rejected many of the strategies used by missionary predecessors such as Thomas Bray. An Anglican priest who had served in Maryland, Bray organized the Society for the Propagation of the Gospel in Foreign Parts (SPG) in 1701 to strengthen Anglican practice in British colonies and support missions to non-Christians throughout the empire. England's abandonment of Native American slavery at the turn of the century prompted renewed interest in what SPG records note as the "conversion of the Natives" in its American colonies.[40]

In his major apologia for the SPG, *Missionalia*, Bray insisted that indigenous peoples would be converted only through the adoption of a civilized lifestyle and Christian worldview. The "Barbarians" of America and Africa, he claimed, could not understand basic precepts about God and "Embrace our most Holy Faith" without being "reduced" to a "Civil Life" or, even more strikingly, "to Humanity." Missionaries ought to require Native Americans, for example, to practice husbandry, build houses, plant crops, dress properly, and learn the catechism. Carpenters, farmers, and tailors would serve as the vanguard for missions and "prepare" Natives "for the Reception of the Gospel."[41]

For Bray, the received dichotomy between barbarism and civility served to distinguish nearly every aspect of Native culture from British Protestantism. "Light and Darkness are not more Opposite than two such contrary Ways of life," he asserted. Given such a view, Bray urged missionaries to teach Native Americans that all traditional beliefs or practices contradicted true religion. In his closing argument, Bray claimed that such an approach to mission served a political end. Anglicized Natives would be a glory "to the British Nation in General," a boon to the empire, a buffer against the French, and "a good Barrier" to savage enemies to the north and west.[42]

Bray's agendas for the SPG hearkened back to older missionary ideas, in stark contrast to the new approaches of Anglo-American Protestants during the 1720s and 1730s. A long-standing missionary society, the New England Company (NEC) jettisoned the civilizing and highly sectarian agendas of previous missionaries such as John Eliot and formed a partnership with the Society in Scotland for Propagating Christian Knowledge (SSPCK). Founded by Anglicans and Presbyterians, the SSPCK endorsed pan-Protestant, ecumenical cooperation in missions. It was directed in New England by a theologically diverse group of commissioners who depended on George I and the General Court of Massachusetts for funding.[43]

Focusing their work on the evangelization of Indigenous people in New England, SSPCK leaders drew on the literature of religious comparison to stress the importance of moral persuasion and a sympathetic approach to Native American cultural and social practices. They associated the agendas of predecessors such as Bray with political intimidation, dangerously close to the strategies of Catholic priests and Native spiritual leaders who supposedly browbeat people into submission. The Society dispatched John Sergeant in 1734 to establish a mission in the Housatonic Valley, the future location of Stockbridge, Massachusetts. Stockbridge served as the center of a NEC/SSPCK network through the 1760s, extending south to Long Island and north to the Mohawk River Valley. Unlike SPG missionaries, who often lived in English towns, SSPCK missionaries lived within or beside Native communities and emphasized evangelization apart from "civilizing" or Anglicizing agendas.[44]

These new-style missionaries rarely, if ever, admitted the fact that they functioned as agents of colonial power and might thereby have compelled, or at least intimidated, the religious choices of Indigenous people. As whiggish Protestants, they maintained that they rejected coercive measures, respected the liberty of conscience of Native Americans, and attempted to persuade them freely to choose Christianity among other religious options. They depended on the vocabulary once suggested by Cotton Mather, who urged them to inquire about the faith of potential converts, Native American or African, with the question, "Whom do you now chuse to Serve?" The language of servitude might well have implied subjection to the British Empire, but the language of choice also implied a regard for the agency of Native Americans. Jonathan Edwards was so attached to the notion of moral liberty that, on at least one occasion, he chastised some of his own people who threatened to use force to compel the re-Christianization of English people who had converted to Indigenous ways.[45]

When the matter of conversion was expressed in such terms—freedom of the will, in philosophic parlance—the criteria for that choice became a central question. By what standards ought one to choose one's religion? Writers such as Gordon and Trenchard, along with the eighteenth-century authors of religious geographies, proffered moral qualities such as humaneness, reasonableness, and utility. From this perspective, the missionary appeal for Native

Americans to choose Christianity implied that Native Americans, as much as English people, made judgments about the moral qualities of traditional practices and Christianity.

To make such judgments, so the logic went, Native Americans had to exercise their own moral reason, which is to say that they *had* moral reason. As Mather had argued, it would have been absurd "if the great God" had imbued only some people—Europeans or other *"Whites"*—with a mind to intuit or induce from experience divine and moral realities. Unlike Britons given to ethnic chauvinism, Mather surmised, God did not limit his gifts of moral conscience to those of a particular *"Complexion,"* especially because "the biggest part of Mankind" were not White but were Black or *"Copper-Coloured."* According to this logic, confirmed by contemporary deists such as Matthew Tindal, missionaries ought to assume that all people had subscribed to innate and universal notions of fundamental moral and religious truths.[46]

In his 1740 *Essay Towards an Instruction for the Indians,* Thomas Wilson, the bishop of Sodor and Man, advised missionaries to trust that Native people had such moral reasonableness. Patronized by George I and known for his cordiality toward various Protestants throughout the empire, Wilson was an influential commentator on missions.[47] He contended that Native Americans and White Englishmen were equally capable of a knowledge of divine truths and equally subject to the temptations of unbelief or idolatry. He deemed ethnic or geographic chauvinism to be irrational, given that ancient Britons were ignorant, savage, and brutal, and that contemporary Englishmen for the most part disregarded Christianity. It was a plain fact, Wilson claimed, that "Heathens can reason as well as Christians, in Matters of so natural a Consequence" as their eternal felicity. To confirm the assertion, Wilson claimed that there were no known atheists among Native Americans, unlike among Europeans.[48]

Wilson affirmed the theory, elucidated by the reformer John Calvin, that human beings' religious instincts chiefly concerned their moral status rather than, say, a recognition of the divine origin of the cosmos (as in medieval Thomist theory). Natural conscience consisted of a knowledge of the existence of good and evil, belief in rewards and punishments, and fear of moral judgment: what Calvin termed "anxiety." Calvin also argued that moral anxiety suggested at least the tacit acknowledgment of an absolute judge and moral arbiter, namely God. Reflecting Calvin's analysis, Wilson contended that missionaries ought to concern themselves with the "Fears" that attended Native and English life apart from Christian faith. They were to presume that they spoke with people who shared their sense of the moral universe, their belief in a God, their dread of judgment, and their desire for "Happiness." Evangelization, Wilson insisted, properly began with confidence in the principled reasonableness of Indigenous people in such terms.[49]

New England missionaries such as Experience Mayhew and Jonathan Edwards shared many of Wilson's perspectives. Raised on Martha's Vineyard, the son of missionary pastor John Mayhew and grandson of missionary pastor Thomas Mayhew, Jr., and the father of the well-known Boston pastor Jonathan Mayhew, Experience Mayhew (hereafter simply Mayhew) was fluent in the Wampanoag dialect of Algonquian. He authored a study of Algonquian language and, along with Josiah Cotton of Plymouth, translated several Protestant works into Wampanoag. Native dialects could serve as vehicles for Christian truth, Mayhew believed, because the Wampanoag people had knowledge of divine things despite differences between English and Wampanoag cosmologies.[50]

Mayhew made this point the centerpiece of a 1720 sermon in support of Indian missions, *A Discourse Shewing that God Dealeth with Men as Reasonable Creatures*.[51] According to Mayhew, God gave all people the ability to make free choices, according to their reason, about whom to worship, obey, and trust. It was "especially" the "Case" that "GOD puts Men unto their own free Choice" in such matters. He contended also that God reasoned with all people through their "natural Powers": their capability of "understanding" their "own Duty," their "proper End" or purpose in life, and the means to happiness. For Mayhew, as for Wilson, Edwards, and other advocates for missions, "reason" meant a sense of one's moral situation—purpose and crises—more than it did philosophical abstraction. Every person raised in any part of the world had such inherent moral consciousness.[52]

Mayhew allowed that people often made bad choices. They lapsed into "Folly and Madness in Departing" from God. They took up shameful practices and lusted after "Abominations" such as riches, prestige, and illicit pleasures. According to Mayhew, idolatry or skepticism in any form contradicted moral reason and evoked sensations of guilt and fear. As he maintained, only divine grace—the means of salvation—provided the ultimate recourse to such guilt. The doctrines that reached to the heart of salvation, such as the Trinity, the decrees of God, the Incarnation, and the Atonement were revealed outside of natural conscience, in scripture. The path to scripture, however, was marked by what Mayhew assumed were self-evident operations of moral reason. God regarded all people "as Intelligent and Rational Beings" whose instincts for "the highest Views, and the most Excellent Employments and Enjoyments" led them to at least ponder the reality of God, the depth of sin, and the need for redemption.[53]

Edwards, who, funded by the NEC, became the mission pastor in Stockbridge in 1751, and John Sergeant, Edwards's predecessor, also emphasized human beings' innate conceptions of good and evil and of divine rewards and punishments.[54] Edwards sometimes depicted Native Americans as ignorant and savage, especially before he had settled in Stockbridge. Yet, informed by studies of the world's religions, he nonetheless affirmed the universality of moral and religious instinct. "God," he contended, had "placed in the mind of every man" a "natural conscience" or "disposition" to expect rewards or punishments in the afterlife. Edwards claimed that this was true of Muslims and the "Indians here in America," who, Edwards concluded, "have enough light to believe" in God, affirm (as one friend of Edwards put it) "Rules of Equity and Justice," and crave divine mercy even "before ever they heard of Christians." Edwards did not imagine that such "light" was salvific unless it led to Christ, but he thought nonetheless that it was morally and even spiritually admirable, certainly sufficient for the exercise of virtue in the civic realm.[55]

For Edwards, moreover, many aspects of traditional Native religion conveyed moral and religious truths: metaphors for heaven and other images within Native cosmologies, dreams or visions that prompted spiritual concern, even ancestral practices and traditional rites such as marriage and burial ceremonies, which reinforced social sentiments. When distinguished from devotion to priestly figures or worship of spiritual forces, these traditional practices appeared to Edwards, as they did to Brainerd, as compatible with, even an inducement to, Christian teaching.[56] Edwards argued that previous descriptions of North America as the realm of Satan and of its inhabitants as "devil" worshippers were therefore misleading. "All the inhabitants of this new-discovered world," he surmised, had "an inclination" toward the truth and would be converted and join the vanguard of Christ's kingdom. By this account, spiritually minded non-Christian Natives were more enlightened than were careless Britons.[57]

To be sure, Wilson, Mayhew, and Edwards maintained that Christian faith was, in the end, more "reasonable" than was devotion to any other religion, including adherence to traditional Native American practices, because Christianity uniquely offered salvation along with worldly comfort. This theological argument often fed colonial presumptions that British Protestants

were the messengers of salvation and in that sense culturally superior to—
or at least more knowledgeable than—Indigenous people. Missionaries did
not contend that the moral consciences of Algonquian and Iroquoian people
marked them as either fully civilized in an Anglocentric sense or as redeemed
in a spiritual sense.

Despite this confluence among notions of reasonableness and moral
choice, promises of salvation, and opinions about British superiority, many
missionaries insisted that the most crucial event in the religious life, which
is to say the conversion that led to salvation, was a matter of moral choice
regardless of the extent to which Natives had conformed themselves to
Anglocentric standards of civility. In this sense, the mid-eighteenth-century
Protestant discourse of conversion clashed with civilizing mandates. So too,
the discourse of rational minds challenged a confessional-era presumption
that the way to Native hearts was through control of Native bodies. Edwards
and his cohort had little regard for western techniques, as some scholars
have put, that were fixed on the physical appearances and external habits of
Indigenous people.[58]

Missionaries' Critique of Anglicization

Protestant missionaries' understanding of conversion as a moral choice
pulled them toward persuasion, rather than toward civilizing or Anglicizing
Native Americans, as an evangelistic method. Reflecting the intentions of the
new or revamped missionary societies, they presumed that the reasonableness of Native Americans rendered civilizing agendas unnecessary for faith.
Likewise, they thought that the virtue of liberty of conscience rendered those
agendas illegitimate because they were coercive. To be sure, New England
missionaries such as Sergeant and Edwards, along with their colleague in
Connecticut and New Hampshire, Eleazar Wheelock, ran schools for Native
children and youth, and in those cases taught English literacy and urged
conformity to English standards of civility.[59] Yet, apart from Wheelock,
they, along with Brainerd and Smith, introduced Christianity to Mohican,
Delaware, and Mohawk people without assuming, as did their missionary
predecessors, that Anglicization was a condition for conversion.

Missionaries in fact scripted into their presentation of Christianity a critique of English settlers that implied a moral equivalence between British
and Native cultures. We can illustrate with one of Edwards's early sermons in

Stockbridge. Edwards addressed nearly a hundred Mohawks, among whom were several sachems who had come to meet with representatives of the Massachusetts Assembly in order to discuss the possibility of a Mohawk settlement in Stockbridge. It was a diplomatic and religious occasion, set against the backdrop of high-level British-Mohawk negotiations in Albany. Edwards revered the British Empire, but his evangelistic appeal rested in part on a deconstruction of British claims to moral superiority and political might—a performance, we might surmise, that displeased British diplomats in attendance. He illustrated the sinfulness of all people with the observation that "the white people"— English and Dutch traders in New England and New York— had shamefully swindled the Natives from the very beginning of colonization and made fraudulent claims on their land. As for the grand negotiations "at Albany," Edwards continued, they were "mere childish trifles in comparison" with the spiritual matters at hand: the revivals and conversions that presaged worldwide redemption. That framing made loyalties to Great Britain appear as contingent and merely instrumental means to greater, salvific purposes.[60]

In another sermon, Edwards told his Native listeners that social life in cities such as Boston and Albany consisted of little more than "mirth and Jollity," drinking, and the ostentatious display of ill-gotten wealth such as "Fine Clothes." The cultural marks of empire, he continued, from "stately Buildings" to bustling "Towns and Cities," disguised the impotence of "Great Kingdoms," all of which eventually would suffer demise. Being English and White hardly mattered in such light. Edwards concluded this sermon with a reflection on the "Image of God" stamped on "Indian" souls and the "happiness and joy" that awaited those who chose Christ. He furthermore decried the English conceit that Indian children were "Beasts," claiming instead that they were fit from birth for glory. Given such skepticism about the virtues of British society and culture, Edwards contended that Native people ought to live in their own communities rather than move to English-style villages or towns, and he often opposed powerful colonists, such as the Williams family, who encroached on Native lands.[61]

Edwards derived his critique of British culture from the Augustinian and Reformed doctrine of original sin. The notion that all people were depraved implied that all social undertakings apart from divine grace were prone to corruption. As he explained this doctrine, he alleged a moral equivalence between Mohicans or Mohawks and Anglo settlers in critical terms. The "white people" who "came over the seas and have settled in these parts," he admitted to his Mohawk and Mohican audience, displayed their depravity in their inhumane treatment of Indians, an indication that "we [English] are no better than you [Indians] in no respect." He also informed his English audience that the doctrine of original sin meant that all people, White and Indian, were moral equals, which induced a sense of solidarity. Edwards even contended that the English and Algonquian languages were equally inadequate for the communication of divine realities, as though both Britons and Mohicans shared the linguistic results of the Fall. He eventually inscribed such egalitarian reflections in his dense 1758 treatise *Original Sin*, written while he was in Stockbridge, in which he claimed that "we are *all*, as we are by nature, *companions* in a miserable helpless condition": a recognition that "tends to promote a mutual *compassion*" among different people.[62]

Brainerd delivered a similar message to the Delaware. He often disdained English civility as pompous and irreligious, and criticized urban life. He in fact identified unconverted Delaware people as more discerning in spiritual matters than unconverted "white people." Many of the "careless spectators of the white people" who attended his preaching, Brainerd claimed, only discovered that they "had souls to save or lose" by observing the responses of "the Indians" to the gospel. That being the case, he made no effort at civilizing, catechesis, or Anglicization before overseeing the conversion of over a hundred Delaware at Crossweeksung (east of Trenton at the Forks of the Delaware) in the spring of 1745. He also warned his Delaware listeners against selling their lands to English settlers or investors and, by implication, abandoning many of their traditional ways. For Brainerd, as well as for missionary colleagues such as Azariah Horton on Long Island, Christianization and civilization were different and often incompatible projects.[63]

No missionary, however, rejected the moral presumptions of Anglicization more thoroughly than did Charles Jeffrey Smith. A native of Long Island, graduate of Yale, and ordained Presbyterian, Smith worked in several missionary posts from 1760 to 1765, funded by private donations (rather than by the NEC or SSPCK). He itinerated through New Jersey, spent several months with Eleazar Wheelock at Moore's Charity School in Connecticut, and went to German Flatts in the Mohawk River Valley (eighty miles northwest of Albany) to evangelize among the Five (Iroquois/Haudenosaunee) Nations, where he gained a hearing especially among the Mohawks and Oneidas. The outbreak of Pontiac's Rebellion in 1763 forced him to leave New York. He then itinerated in western Connecticut, southern New Jersey, Maryland, and Virginia before his return to Long Island.[64]

Like Edwards and Brainerd, Smith distinguished the conversion of Natives from catechesis, conformity to English lifestyles, and participation in imperial society. He criticized the "froth and vanity" of high culture in Albany, which made him "quite sick." British officers in that town appeared to him as "infidel."[65] He frequently used the appellation "white heathen" to refer to British settlers, especially urbane elites, confounding customary uses of "heathen" to refer to non-European people or uncivilized rustics. At the end of his mission among the Oneidas and Mohawks, for example, he determined that "the necessity of Conversion" among the "White Heathen in the southern provinces" (Maryland, Virginia, and North Carolina) was as urgent as it was among the Haudenosaunee.[66]

Other missionaries, such as Smith's successor in the Mohawk River Valley, Samuel Kirkland, thought that Indian cultural practices displayed a type of moral wisdom that belied the cultural assumptions of Anglicization advocates. A Presbyterian who had worked with Wheelock in Connecticut, Kirkland began his mission in 1765, and eventually organized a church of twenty-two members in Canajoharie, a Mohawk village in between German Flatts and Albany. He worked among the Mohawks, Senecas, and Oneidas, and he learned to speak the Mohawk dialect of the Iroquoian language.[67]

As Kirkland recalled in his journal, he admired the moral sensibilities of the Indigenous people of the Mohawk River region. William Johnson, British superintendent of Indian Affairs in the Northern District, and Kirkland frequently spoke of local sachems as virtuous in civic terms, informed by "good sense, humanity, and integrity." Kirkland trusted that he could engage the Mohawk "on rational grounds." At the Oneida village of Onondaga, he attended an elaborate ceremony that included the lighting of tobacco pipes, an oral reading of a message from Johnson, speeches by several sachems, and embraces with kisses. He praised the speakers, one of whom read Johnson's dispatch "with a good grace" and another who "spoke like a Demosthenes." When a "Chief" drew Kirkland by the hand, hugged him, kissed him on both cheeks, and gave him "many blessings," Kirkland received the gestures warmly and returned the kisses—struck, as he later described it, by the feel on his cheek of the chief's face paint.[68]

After Kirkland established himself in the region, he expressed admiration for Iroquoian religious practices. At the ceremony for his adoption into the family of a Seneca sachem, he spoke in what he presumed were Iroquoian idioms, asking that "the Great Spirit might make me a blessing to his family." Kirkland welcomed the consolations of the sachem who spoke of the afterlife in Mohawk images when Kirkland's host (not his adopted father) died. The singing and somber decorum of the mourning service equally moved the missionary. As a Protestant, Kirkland hardly thought that such ceremonies comported with Christian theology or offered salvation. As a new-style missionary, however, he recognized that many traditional rites and rituals reflected a universal and laudable religious consciousness. For Kirkland, Mohawk communal ceremonies exhibited civic virtue and moral sincerity even though they differed from English practice.[69]

Charles Chauncy, a Boston pastor, claimed in 1762 that this distinction between conversion and Anglicization had become axiomatic for New England Protestants. In a sermon for the ordination of Joseph Bowman, a missionary among the Mohawks, Chauncy defended this change from seventeenth-century missionary agendas.[70] He allowed that John Eliot and the first two generations of Mayhews on Martha's Vineyard had overseen many Indian conversions. Yet, he maintained, the praying towns established by Eliot had declined in population and fervor in the decades following their initial successes. The cause of their distress, and of the alienation from Christianity of Indigenous people throughout New England, could be traced to agendas "to change their simple plain way of living for our's [sic]." Chauncy contended that in order to promote the evangelization of "the Indian nations, we should not think ourselves obliged . . . to effect an alteration in that way of civil life they have been used to for ages immemorial." Their housing, clothing, "modes of civility"—by which he meant manners—hunting, fishing: none of these hindered them from "the Gospel." In fact, Chauncy asserted, "I am persuaded, should they change" their way of life "for that CIVILIZED ONE, which some are ready to think so highly necessary," they would turn away from the gospel and succumb to the temptations that had beset impious Englishmen.[71]

According to his sermon for Bowman, Chauncy's ideal missionary was Eli Forbes, who lived among the Oneidas at Oquaga, taught in the local dialect, never established an English-language school, and engaged in amicable conversations "upon the things of religion" with willing and cordial residents. Chauncy began this sermon with an exposition of Genesis 22:18, which relayed a divine promise that the offer of salvation would be made to individuals from all nations. He concluded with a prediction that "the Indian tribe, in our western parts," including Mohawks who were uncorrupted by Jesuit priests, would embrace Christianity when western missionaries put an end to ill-conceived agendas for "civlizing" and spoke with them in the cadences of what Protestants understood as a shared moral conscience.[72]

The Moral Appeal of Christianity

New England missionaries thought that moral reasoning would convince at least some Wampanoag, Delaware, Mohican, and Mohawk people of the appeal of Christianity. These missionaries claimed that the message of divine mercy addressed the problem of suffering and the pain of stricken consciences: miseries as acute for Indigenous people as they were for Englishmen. In this sense, they aimed to make evident a compatibility between Christianity and Native moral experience despite Native suspicions of the incompatibility of Protestantism with traditional religious practice. Unlike their predecessors, Mayhew, Brainerd, Edwards, and Smith placed claims for the humaneness or amiability of Christianity at the center of their conversion discourse rather than speaking of the incontestable truth of Christianity or the severity of the punishments—divine and mundane—for failing to convert.[73]

Thomas Wilson's *Essay* illustrated several ways in which evangelists might make such claims. It included fifteen ideal dialogues as models of persuasion. The dialogue form, popular in mid-eighteenth-century philosophical discourse and recommended by other commentators on religion, such as Frederic Bernard, suggested exchange among equals.[74] In the dialogues, Wilson's ideal missionary does not impose his views on his fictionalized Native interlocutor with an air of authority. Instead, he gives reasons one might choose to become Christian. On hearing the missionary's account of a God who has compassion for those who repent from wickedness, the "Indian" replies that "this Account of the great God is most agreeable to [his own] Reason." In response to the man's query about Christian teaching on the afterlife, the missionary contends that reason tells us that there must be an afterlife in which justice is dispensed and redemption completed. The man acknowledges that his people believe that "the Souls of all good People do go [to] a Place of Rest, and Peace and Happiness."[75]

What, then, the Indian asks, is the cause of so much misery in the world? According to the missionary, the man's "own Reason and Experience must own" that there is "something within us, which opposeth our Reason," a "strong Inclination to Evil," which "we very sensibly feel in ourselves."

"Reason," as Wilson used it here and elsewhere in his *Essay*, referred to a sense of right and wrong rather than to abstract reflection. The evidence was "plain," according to the missionary, in tragic detail: the "Cruelty, the Oppression, the Pride, the Injustice" of British settlers who take Indian lands and conduct unfair trade, the "Murders" and "Drunkenness" that afflict Indians, and—perhaps as an evocation of smallpox—the ways people become "a Plague to others." The missionary persuades the man of every person's need for redemption, not with reference to the dangers of hell but with an appeal to the everyday experience of self-contradiction, cruelty, and anxiety. It is Calvin all over again, presented as a moral dilemma that the man recognizes.[76]

Following a discussion of the Atonement as the provision of redemption, the missionary and the Native talk about the act of conversion itself in the final set of dialogues. The moral pull of Christianity, the missionary explains, is communal. It offers people a new form of social identity: membership in a "holy Society" of "God's chosen people" in which mutuality and concord override proclivities to "wicked" behavior.[77] The Indian asks, "how I may be made a member of that Society?" The missionary reframes the question so that the man will "answer it to your own Reason, and to every one who shall ask you—Why you chuse to be a Christian?" The missionary explains that a personal profession of "Faith"—a voluntary choice—is the only requirement for becoming a Christian. Converts, the missionary continues, are "convinced that it is" their "*Interest*" to "make such a Choice." As Wilson imagined it—and we can assume that his imagination strayed far from the actual experiences and conceptions of many Indigenous people—the Native becomes "convinced" of the reasonableness of Christianity, admires its teaching, desires to become a Christian, and chooses accordingly.[78]

We have no accounts of Anglo-Native conversations as elaborate as Wilson's dialogues, and little indication that Wilson's language captured Indigenous voices, but we do have evidence that contemporary missionaries valorized persuasion—back-and-forth, question-answer conversations rather than authoritative declaration—in their work among Native Americans. As Elam Potter, a Yale graduate and missionary to Catawbas in the Carolinas, put it, "my arguments I thought must perswade every rational being." Mayhew urged his fellow missionaries to reason with their listeners and propose that the Christian message offered a solution to the problem of sin. We "ought," he wrote, "to deal thus with one another," not by "force and violence" but by urging others to "use their Reason very freely" in "weighing and examining the things proposed to them, to be considered by them." Offering his accounts of "Indian conversions" as evidence, Mayhew maintained that that method rendered the gospel intelligible to the Wampanoag. Mayhew, like Wilson and Potter, may well have overestimated the suitability of their notion of moral "reason" to Indigenous cultural and linguistic practice, even if by "reason" they meant a felt sense of the human condition rather than western canons of rationality. Their notion of persuasion nonetheless conveyed their intent to rely on mutual exchange rather than dogmatic assertion. For Mayhew and his contemporaries, Christian doctrine did not widen the cultural divide between British and Wampanoag people. It bridged the divide.[79]

Mayhew's evidence for the importance of exchange or dialogue included his transcriptions and translations of oral testimonies—often given in dialogic form—of Wampanoag conversions, published in 1727 as *Indian Converts*.[80] According to Mayhew, Jerusha Ompan, from Tisbury, often peppered Mayhew with "serious Questions in Matters of Religion," such as whether Adam "had Free-will before his Fall" or whether it was reasonable to impute Adam's guilt to his descendants. He claimed that his answers to her inquiries persuaded her to believe, and she thereafter "exhorted her Relations and Visitors to be diligent Seekers of God."[81] When an "Indian" named James Spaniard, a freed slave in Chilmark, consulted with Mayhew, Mayhew sympathized with James, who "appeared to be discontented." Mayhew described the gospel as a salve for such discontent. James "seemed kindly to accept" a message that promised eternal happiness, "separated himself from the Company, and Society" of hard-drinking "wicked Persons," and confessed that he was "desirous to be reconciled to God."[82] James's conversion, by Mayhew's account, came as a voluntary response to his moral dismay.

Mayhew emphasized the same dynamic in other spiritual biographies. Japheth Skuhwhannan, the son of a Chilmark sachem, "professed his Willingness to submit himself" to Christ after "his own Persuasion of the Truth of the Gospel."[83] Elizabeth Uhquat of Christian-Town experienced a "deep and affecting Sight and Sense of her Sins" and professed Christ.[84] So too, Japheth Hannit, a leader in a Wampanoag church, counseled many people through their conversions. Hannit's standard address to non-Christians, according to Mayhew's translation, began with a discussion of the innate longing "certainly to know" about one's eternal state. Hannit proceeded to explain the gospel and its call to repent and affiliate with the church as the fulfillment of that longing. Mayhew's accounts conveyed the Protestant conviction that Native people, like the English settlers caught up in the Great Awakening, contemplated Christianity as an answer to universal moral dilemmas: Jerusha Ompan's curiosity about the source of wickedness, James Spaniard's sense—a term for moral perception in eighteenth-century philosophy—of discontent, Japheth Skuhwhannan's persuasion, Elizabeth Uhquat's sight and sense, Japheth Hannit's appeal to people's innate desires.[85]

Brainerd too understood Native choices as a response to moral appeal and persuasion. As he came to appreciate the sagacity of the Lenape at the Forks of the Delaware, he increasingly reasoned with them about the congruence between their sense of good and evil and the Christian message. At his services, he spoke of the basic tenets of Christianity and entertained questions and objections. He often improvised. When, for example, he found it difficult "to bring them to a rational Conviction that they are Sinners by Nature," he jettisoned abstract accounts of human proclivity to sin and asked them if they had experienced "Corruption" or moral failures—violence, mistreatment of the weak, laziness, for example—in their daily affairs. When his listeners rejected even these overtures, he directed Delaware Christians to "converse with them about religious matters" in an attempt to "have their prejudices and aversion to Christianity removed." In Edwards's parlance, he attempted to affect their wills by persuading them of the loveliness of Christianity.[86]

For Brainerd, such persuasion did not depend on images of divine retribution but rather on images that elicited moral approval, such as divine benevolence. As he maintained in *Mirabilia*, he preached on biblical texts, such as Isaiah 53, that presented God's compassion for outcasts and mercy for the suffering. He followed the advice of Ebenezer Pemberton, the Boston minister who charged Brainerd at his ordination service to avoid the language of terror—threats of eternal damnation—and stress the beauty of divine mercy.[87]

Brainerd accordingly informed his Lenape auditors that he hoped that he could gain "their Attention" and that his preaching "might meet with Satisfaction," meaning that they would find his message to fit their sensibilities. That satisfaction or appeal included what Brainerd presented as a vindication of the Delaware people in light of English predation and ethnic bigotry. He came, he said, to speak of their happiness, and to distinguish Christianity from "the abominable Practices" of "*white* People" who had stolen their land, pushed them from their villages into the wilderness, inflicted alcohol on them, and brought them unhappiness. He wanted to show them a deity who was not "white" but "a kind and compassionate Saviour" who had fashioned them to enjoy their non-English lives under the canopy of grace. As Brainerd summarized his preaching, he intended to lead people to a "most rational and scriptural" response, a voluntary decision to accept the "Gospel invitation" and move toward Christ: "I spoke not a word of terror, but on the contrary, set before them the fullness and all-sufficiency of Christ's merits, and his willingness to save all that came to him, and thereupon pressed them to come without delay."[88]

Edwards's description of the appeal of Christianity deployed a slightly different set of tropes than Mayhew's "sight and sense of sin" and Brainerd's "all-sufficiency of Christ's merits." Attentive to the power of natural objects— "types" in literary parlance—to convey spiritual realities, Edwards fastened less on moral crises and more on physical beauty and suffering as reasons for Mohawks and Mohicans to consider Christianity.[89] He introduced himself to Mohicans and Mohawks, for example, through a sermon on the "rivers of water" from Psalm 1:3, an image for the offer of salvation to thirsty souls.[90] He sought to convince them of the splendor of the Christian message through an extended meditation on the importance of sunlight to plants. "When the sun shines on the earth and trees," he said, "It gives 'em new life, makes the earth look green. It causes flowers to appear and give a good smell." He stretched the metaphor to cover conversion: "if you would be a wise and happy people, put yourselves in the way of receiving" the divine "light" of the "Word of God." He presumed that natural idioms such as refreshing water and fragrant flowers communicated the attractiveness of Christianity.[91]

Edwards devoted many of his so-called Indian sermons also to what he claimed was the benevolent temper of the God of the Bible rather than to the dangers of perdition—the imprecatory or hellfire message that he delivered to his White congregation from the late 1730s through the early 1740s. According to many of his Stockbridge sermons, the gospel addressed Mohicans' desires for happiness in the midst of worldly afflictions. He drew on their experience of disease—worsened by the smallpox transmitted by English settlers—and venomous snake bites to explain the fitness of the Christian doctrine of resurrection, according to which God would put an end to "death or sickness" and "make both Soul and body Happy and Glorious to all Eternity." He frequently lamented the dispossession of Indigenous lands through British deception or force and unjust legal judgments in such matters. He sympathized with those drawn into imperial warfare, which, he claimed, stemmed from the selfish ambitions of earthly monarchs. He included "Persons" who "long for a Change," such as "the Poor—that they may be rich" and "get out of debt," a reference that evoked Mohicans in arrears to English creditors. He consoled "those that are in captivity, in pain, weary with Labour," terms that suggested wartime suffering.[92]

Stockbridge Mohicans, Edwards presumed, might be moved as well by biblical images of justice and redemption. The doctrine of a final judgment conveyed God's promise that "all things shall be set to rights": the innocent vindicated, the impoverished indemnified, and the war-torn relieved. Edwards invoked the mournful ceremonies of Algonquian and Iroquoian peoples to contrast the sadness of mortal loss to the gladness of heaven, a realm of "Joyful singing and no more groaning and weeping." "If any of you are weary seeing so much wickedness in the world," and "weary of contention," he preached, then "cho[o]se heaven as your house." The moral attraction of the gospel, according to Edwards, included its offer of peace and rest in a time of conflict and exhaustion.[93]

Smith likewise informed prospective New York donors to his mission that the way to persuade Mohawks to consider Christianity was to speak to them as "a common honest neighbor": to present "a rational faith upon scriptural grounds." Smith promised to guard against the "least appearance of enthusiasm" and win his audience through a "calm, serene, pleasant, and cheerful" manner. Shaftesbury-esque virtues, rather than excessive zeal, he contended, would appeal to the Mohawks.[94] In one of his first sermons to an Iroquoian audience, a gathering of some 100 Mohawks, Oneidas, and Onondagas at a barn in German Flatts, he preached from Acts 10:34–35 ("God is no respecter of persons: But in every nation that feareth him, and worketh righteousness, is accepted with him"), a text suited to a transnational and transethnic interpretation of the gospel.[95] Smith understood the message of conversion to transcend political agendas and racial identities. His accounts of seared moral consciences, sober prayers, and professions of faith sounded alike, whether describing Mohawk conversions in German Flatts or Protestant conversions in New Jersey.[96]

William Johnson, who was at German Flatts to negotiate a treaty with the Iroquois confederacy, translated for Smith—an indication, for all of Smith's confidence in the transnational nature of evangelization, that imperial diplomatic matters shadowed Smith's mission. Like Mayhew, Edwards, and Brainerd, Smith offered a Protestant interpretation of "Indian" missions that did not fully account for Indigenous responses. Many Native Americans might well have thought the missionaries' conceptions of moral reason and conversion quite alien and merely an instrument of imperial intervention into their lives. Smith and his missionary colleagues nonetheless were confident that their message resonated with at least some of their hearers, and they recounted several ways Indigenous people altered their religious affiliations accordingly.

Disaffiliation and Affiliation

In the 1670s, a Pennacook tribal leader from the Merrimack River Valley of New Hampshire relied on a telling metaphor to convey his understanding of conversion: becoming a Christian was, as he put it, to "leave my old canoe and embark on a new canoe." The metaphor implied that conversion included a voluntary disaffiliation from at least some aspects of traditional practice. In the early 1740s, the Connecticut Mohegan convert and pastor Samson Occom deployed less nuanced language: Native believers "renounced their heathenish idolatry" when they became Christian. Anglo-American missionaries and Christian Indians described conversion as a choice to reject false gods and identify with the Christian community.[97]

What did "idolatry," or its frequent cognates, "superstition" and "heathenism," mean to eighteenth-century Protestants? For many, such terms implied racial inferiority along with religious deception.[98] According to observers of the world's religions such as Broughton, Chambers, and Bernard and Picart, however, they denoted a different set of qualities: dense ceremonialism, heightened emotionalism, and the power of priests who terrorized people into submission and acted in concert with political authorities to coerce adherence. Admirable and politically commendable religion—true religion—minimized ceremony, eschewed political power, and appealed to the moral reason of its adherents. It upheld the freedom of individuals to choose or reject it according to their uncoerced consciences. The regnant whiggish-Protestant consensus was that all people faced a choice between idolatry and true religion, coercive priestcraft and reasonable dedication.

From this perspective, the mandate to forsake idolatry applied as readily to Britons raised in a Protestant milieu as it did to Native Americans. As did Bernard and Picart, Protestant missionaries often turned the discourse of reasonableness against their own traditions. Solomon Stoddard reminded New Englanders that they had inherited a "Brutish" and "heathenish" cultural history, including the worship of "Idols" such as Odin and Thor, whose votaries demanded obeisance on pain of death. He warned his hearers that this was not merely ancient history; Britons' pagan past partly explained their present-day resistance to the gospel. Charles Jeffrey Smith called members of the Anglican establishment in Maryland and Virginia to disaffiliate from their heathenism in equally salient terms. By his account, many of the residents of the southern colonies, taken in by Church of England ceremonies, submitted to Anglican priests who maintained their positions through political favoritism. In Maryland and Virginia, these priests convinced local magistrates and governors to prohibit Smith's preaching in public, in violation of the people's "Liberty of Conscience." As Smith described it, Williamsburg was particularly idolatrous: a modern-day Sodom dominated by prelates who cherished liturgical formality and never mentioned Christ. Disallowed from the pulpit in Williamsburg's Bruton Parish church and prohibited from preaching near the capitol, he claimed that he had encountered only "two Christians" there, "an old Lady" and a kindly gentleman. The rest were "heathen." In order to become "Christians," they had to renounce their vile misuse of state power and associate themselves with Christ.[99]

According to Smith, Mohawk and Oneida Christians appeared reasonable in comparison to Virginian Anglicans. He noted that they used a simple and scriptural worship book for their services: a translation into Mohawk of several litanies, selections from the Bible, and parts of the Book of Common Prayer, published in 1715. He approved of this modest liturgical practice in part because the Mohawks he knew otherwise rejected what they called the "priest-rid[d]en" formalism of High Church missionaries.[100]

New England Protestants often described the "idolatry" and "heathenism" from which Native converts had disaffiliated as Roman Catholic priestcraft. As erstwhile objects of Jesuit missionary activity, some Mohawks— less discerning, in Protestants' view, than the Mohawk critics of Anglican priestcraft—appeared to Edwards and Smith as prone to the materiality of Catholic worship. Edwards advised Mohawk listeners to eschew French-Catholic practices such as "praying to the Virgin Mary and to Saints and Angels," "crossing themselves," and "confessing sins to the Priest and worshipping Images of Christ."[101] During the Seven Years' War, many British observers parsed the religious options before Indigenous people in a mélange of imperial and religious idioms. According to them, Native Americans faced a choice between French-enforced, priestly superstition—barbarous and savage—and British Protestantism, which incorporated reasonable and uncoercive forms of worship.[102]

Beside issuing warnings against Catholicism, missionaries urged their Algonquian and Iroquoian interlocutors to disaffiliate especially from the ceremonies and rituals of Indigenous spiritual leaders, sometimes called powwows.[103] Anglo-American observers often endorsed traditional teachings and practices that appeared to conform to whiggish ideas of reasonableness, such as Native beliefs in the afterlife, moral codes that encouraged generosity, or mourning and burial rituals (we can recall Kirkland's experiences among the Oneida). Yet they denounced public ceremonies led by spiritual specialists who, among other indications of putative idolatry, were adorned with peculiar body art and garments, received offerings of food or useful objects, relayed visions of future raids or battles, promised physical healing, threatened physical injury through curse or incantation, led communal dances and chants, and invoked any number of non-Christian spiritual forces. Such practices, by missionaries' accounts, reflected the hyper-ceremonialism and nexus of priestly and political power that afflicted most religions, especially Catholicism, albeit in a particularly Native American fashion.

Among the missionaries considered here, Brainerd gave the fullest description and critique of what Protestants deemed to be ceremonial idolatry among Natives: the disordering of their innate moral consciences by priestcraft. He observed a multiday feast with all-night dancing around a fire, a sacrifice of ten deer, and rituals led by "powwows (or conjurers)." By his telling, spiritual leaders claimed to remedy a sickness on Juniata Island by "playing their juggling tricks" (an echo of Ross's descriptions of deer rituals on Nova Zembla), "acting their frantic postures," "making all the wild, ridiculous, and distracted motions imaginable," "singing, howling, thrusting their arms into the air with fingers outstretched," "spurting water as fine as a mist" from their mouths, falling onto the ground, "wringing their sides, as if in pain and anguish, twisting their faces, turning up their eyes, grunting," and "puffing." Brainerd offered details as evidence of the physicality and emotional excesses of rituals that were conducted by powwows. In other accounts, he described spiritual leaders' attempts to coerce adherence with threats of "charming, inchanting, or poisoning Persons to Death." As Brainerd argued, the depravity of such tactics was self-evident, as was the foolishness of following "conjurors" who in fact had "no Power to recover the Sick" or to injure their enemies. Brainerd assumed that the rituals he witnessed on Juniata Island were immoral and deceptive, frenzied and irrational. They were an instance of the corruption that Protestants such as Picart and Bernard attributed to ceremonialism from Japan and Turkey to Italy and Mexico.[104]

Missionaries accordingly salted their accounts of Native conversions with stories of people, including spiritual leaders, who, in becoming Christian, divorced themselves from such practices. According to Mayhew, a Wampanoag "Pawwaw, or Wizard" named Lazarus "became a Christian" when he stopped "worshipping the Devil" and began attending Sabbath worship services. Brainerd recounted several run-ins with local "powwows," some of whom underwent conversion under Brainerd's guidance and quit their "inchanting." When an elderly Delaware man, "an obstinate idolater" in Brainerd's words, decided to become a Christian, he handed over "his rattles (which they use for music in their idolatrous feasts and dances)" to some Christian Delaware, "who quickly destroyed them." According to Edwards, the "manner of worshipping" led by Mohican spiritual leaders in the Stockbridge area included devotion to sinister spirits or animals, dances around fire, and "cutting and tormenting themselves." Edwards described it as a "sottish" frenzy. Mohican converts, according to Edwards, followed their moral reason, shunned these "priests," and forsook their idols when they came to know God.[105]

New England Protestants thought that a freely chosen conversion involved an affiliation with the Christian community, which implied devotion to or trust in the God of the Bible. Mayhew's account of the conversion of the Vineyard man Miohqsoo illustrated the point in detail. According to Mayhew, Miohqsoo queried the Wampanoag minister Hiacoomes about the number of "Gods the English worshipped." Hicaoomes's answer, "ONE, and no more," startled Miohqsoo. "Shall I, said he, throw away all" of the thirty-seven gods he now worshipped "for the sake of one only?" It sounded like a rotten deal. Hiacoomes gently reasoned with Miohqsoo. "For my part," Hiacoomes said, "I have thrown away all these" and fared well. Miohqsoo conceded the point. He then claimed that he would "throw away all my Gods too, and serve that one God with you." After instruction in Christian faith by Hiacoomes, Miohqsoo professed that he had come to "greatly reverence" God's "Son, who had suffered Death to satisfy the Wrath of God." Miohqsoo "desired to be redeemed" and then related the choice that constituted his conversion: he renounced "having many Gods, and going after Pawwaws" and "promised" to "worship the true God, and serve him only." Mayhew also related the story of a woman named Alanchchannum, from Edgartown, who realized that her conversion implied "the absolute Necessity of her chusing the one," that is, "the Lord to be her God," and "flying from the other," that is, from traditional Native powers.[106]

The theological dimension of conversion, which is to say the decision to renounce previously revered spirits for the Christian God, inflected most of these missionaries' accounts of Native conversions. It expressed their conviction that conversion was not chiefly, as in older Protestant paradigms, a soulful conformity to the Christian tradition in which one already believed, but was, rather, a choice to adhere to Christianity as a choice among religious options. It was a voluntary act of allegiance based on moral persuasion. John Sergeant recorded the 1734 profession of faith of his Mohican interpreter Poohpoonue along these lines. According to Sergeant, Poohpoonue confessed that he became "convinc'd of the Truth of the Christian Religion," that is, that "it is the only Way that leads to Salvation and Happiness." Being so convinced, Poohpoonue continued, "I therefore freely, and heartily forsake Heathenish Darkness" and "do now," as a public profession, "seriously and solemnly take the Lord Jehovah, to be my God." In 1745, the Mohegan sachem Benjamin Uncas II accounted "the Christian Religion" as the "Religion I Choose above all others." One of the few records of Mohican or Mohawk conversions left by Edwards, the profession of Cornelius and Mary Munneweaunummic, also reiterated the language of religious choice: "I do now appear" in order "to give my self to God" because "I know my own Heart [has] chosen Him for my Portion."[107]

Protestant efforts to evangelize Indigenous Americans can be measured within the context of colonization as heavy with racial and imperial implications: White Protestants intent on persuading Indigenous subjects to forsake traditional spiritual practices as well as political allegiances. Unlike their predecessors, however, eighteenth-century missionaries envisioned evangelization in ways that had the potential to confound racial and cultural dichotomies. They claimed that every person, from the likes of Sarah Osborn to Poohpoonue and Cornelius and Mary Munneweaunummic, was at liberty to choose to reject or trust Christ for salvation. They likewise held that a choice for Christ implied a renunciation of old patterns—the "heathenism" of worldly skepticism, formalistic Anglicanism, or Algonquian powwows.

According to missionary accounts, Native converts expressed their affiliation with Christianity in social behavior as well: through participation in the public practices of worship and observance of the sacraments. Missionaries celebrated these as collective rituals, attendance at which signaled new loyalties for Native converts. Mayhew informed Wampanoag believers that participation in the Lord's Supper was a distinguishing mark of Christian identity. Brainerd introduced Delaware converts to baptism and the Lord's

Supper as the communal contexts in which they renounced their old deities. Smith offered the sacraments, and at times the rite of marriage, as occasions for Mohawk believers to enact their choice for Christianity. Even the most ceremonially adverse Protestants, who pitted moral sensibility against ritualistic zeal, recognized that some communal rites allowed converts to give expression to the choices by which they joined themselves to a Christian community.[108]

New discourses of conversion and religious choice, influenced by the study of the world's religions and fashioned in the midst of the Protestant revivals, affected many of the ways in which missionaries made their appeals to Native Americans. They maintained that conversion amounted to a rejection of priest-ridden ceremonialism, whether in an Indigenous or Roman Catholic form, and a consent to the moral reasonableness of Protestant versions of Christianity. That reasonableness appeared to them to form a bond between Protestant and indigenous cultures throughout the empire.

They rarely, if ever, pondered the extent to which they had merely replaced older confessional norms with a discourse, conveyed through the language of reason, that was equally alien to indigenous peoples. They continued to operate with Anglocentric assumptions of the nearly self-evident superiority of western definitions of reasonableness and Protestant terminologies for religious experience. To be sure, they turned Enlightenment moral notions against themselves and their culture in moments of self-critique. Yet they deployed a taxonomy of good and bad, civil and savage, sociable and unsociable that suited the British mind, so to speak, but not necessarily the Native American. They did not fathom how their Lockean and Hutchesonian grammars, including definitions of free will, might have sounded strange to Indigenous Americans, for all of the claims to mutuality. The discourse of conversion in 1750 gave more room than it did in 1660 to moral equivalence and cultural exchange among Indigenous peoples and Anglo-Americans— there is no reason to cast that aside—but it retained an Anglocentric and imperial hubris.[109]

Eighteenth-century Protestants might have protested the implied critique, especially its contention that Native and English people did not share conceptions of moral goodness, justice, and freedom of choice. It was, they might have said, a philosophical or theological question whether the common humanity of Britons and Natives included similar convictions about the very meaning of being human: some accounts of goodness and badness, justice and mercy, liberty and compulsion. They would have admitted in their better moments that an exchange of such convictions across cultural divides required an immense work of translation, both ways, and that translation often failed. Yet they would have insisted nonetheless that it was worth the effort, that it yielded moments such as Brainerd's conversation with the reformer on Juniata Island, Edwards's associations with Mohican sachems, Mayhew's dialogue with inquisitive converts, and the affections shared among Smith and his Mohawk and Oneida neighbors. The only option to such work, they might have added, was a willful neglect that exposed the Indigenous inhabitants of North America to the pernicious designs of French or Spanish aggressors and British land grabbers who had no regard for Indian souls or bodies.

We might ask nonetheless whether Wampanoag, Delaware, Mohican, and Mohawk people had any intention to make the religious choices so valorized by Protestants. It is difficult for a twenty-first-century historian to gauge the extent to which such decisive language as disaffiliation from traditional leaders and affiliation with the Christian community captures the religious experiences of eighteenth-century Native converts. The whole idea of the unencumbered choice of one's religion might have appeared to Edwards's Mohican listeners or Mayhew's Wampanoag parishioners as inattentive to the constraints of familial and communal loyalties, linguistic and cultural differences, social relationships, and imperial interventions. When they "chose" Christ, they might well have experienced that choice as more ambiguous and complex than the accounts given by missionaries. "Freedom" was at best relative, at worst deceptive. It could be used as a vindication of colonialist hegemony over purportedly unfree persons.[110]

Edwards, of course, had given some attention to the role of such constraints or impingements on religious choice. In *Freedom of the Will*, he voiced what he presumed his contemporaries knew from their experience: the affirmation of a free will, including the liberty to choose one's affiliations, included a recognition that education, habit, social and political status, or divine grace—what have you—disposed people to make their choices one way or another. By Edwards's account, Mohicans and English settlers still could be said to choose freely, if by "choose" one meant to act according to one's will, and by one's will, one meant a sense of the amiability of things. In the context of missions, this amounted to Edwards's affirmation of the moral agency of Indigenous people even in the face of imperial power. Edwards's explanation might have appeared unrealistic: too inflected by British moral philosophy to address the needs of Native Americans facing settler colonialism, invading armies, and missionaries backed by colonial powers. Yet again, at least some

Native Americans found Edwards's formulations illuminating. Hendrick Aupaumut, a Stockbridge sachem at the end of the eighteenth century, was so taken with Edwards on conversion and choice that he asked Edwards's son to send him a copy of *Freedom of the Will*. Despite our suspicions to the contrary, conceptions of religious choice might have resonated across cultural boundaries in eighteenth-century New England.[111]

Epilogue

Hannah Adams and the Revolutionary Nation

One year after the Treaty of Paris by which Great Britain recognized the independence of the United States, a scholarly writer from Medfield, Massachusetts, Hannah Adams, completed the first American dictionary of the world's religions. Her 1784 *Alphabetical Compendium of the Various Sects [of Christianity] . . . with . . . a Brief Account of the Different Schemes of Religion* was followed by an enlarged edition in 1791, *A View of Religions, in Two Parts.* Adams's dictionary launched her on a respectable literary career, during which she wrote *Summary History of New England* (1799), *The Truth and Excellence of the Christian Religion* (1804), and her 1832 *Memoir.* Adams, who expressed a tentative "preference," as she put it, for the Unitarian movement, identified herself as a dutiful Protestant. A circle of elite admirers in Boston, including Josiah Quincy III, supported her with an endowment. Quincy might well have taken an interest in the world's religions from his father, whose diary contained quotations from non-Christian authorities such as the Roman poet Horace or, even further afield, Zoroaster. Interest in the world's religions was as lively in early national Boston as it was in Hanoverian London.[1]

Adams's works conveyed the central tenets of Anglo-American Protestant commentary on religion as it developed after 1688: liberty of conscience rather than confessionalism as a political mandate, the inculcation of social virtues such as toleration, and the promotion of conversion as a reasoned and willful choice of one's religious identity. These tenets cohered in a logical fashion. The notions of liberty that sustained a constitutional monarchy or a democratic republic served as criteria for the evaluation of religions, depended on philosophical notions of free will, and informed missionary practices of persuasion.

Adams did not explicate this logic but nonetheless applied it, piecemeal, throughout her books. She devoted the first half of her *Summary History* to

The Opening of the Protestant Mind. Mark Valeri, Oxford University Press. © Oxford University Press 2023.
DOI: 10.1093/oso/9780197663677.003.0008

the "principles" of liberty as they developed in New England from the first English settlements through the American Revolution: the "zealous" assertion "of the cause of liberty" that shaped seventeenth-century politics in England and was inherited by New Englanders, the "flame of liberty" that blazed after the misguided intolerance inflicted on Quakers and antinomians during the first decades, and the zeal for "liberty and independence" that fired revolution against Britain and religious disestablishment during the 1770s. Adams endorsed 1688 and 1776 as twin revolutions in which political liberty converged with freedom of religious choice.[2]

Adams's Americanized whiggish assumptions framed her descriptions of different religions in the dictionary. She relied on British writers of the mid-eighteenth century as she made entry after entry in her dictionary. According to her memoir, Broughton's *Dictionary* sparked her interest in the topic altogether. For many of her entries, especially on early Christian sects and religions outside of North America and Europe, she paraphrased, quoted, and cited Broughton or Collier. Her regard for liberty of religious choice echoed her predecessors.[3]

As she surveyed different churches and movements in Christian history, moreover, she focused especially on the philosophical and theological grounding for such liberty: the development in New England of theories of freedom of the will, by Jonathan Edwards especially, that suggested common ground for Protestants with Calvinist or Arminian leanings. An entry on "Arminianism" provided a lucid account of Samuel Clarke's conception of the "self-determining power to the will" and how Richard Baxter attempted "to reconcile Calvin and Arminius." Adams devoted eight pages, in a dictionary with typically one-to-two-page entries, to a subject she called "Necessarians," a late eighteenth-century neologism for a broad array of thinkers who pondered the relationship between the will and external forces on it. According to Adams, they included physical determinists—on which she wrote a separate entry—and moral necessarians who "consider" the admission of some antecedent causes to "moral actions" to be "consistent with spontaneity and choice" and therefore with ideas of moral "merit." Her central figures were Augustine, Leibniz, Edwards, and the Scottish moral philosopher Henry Home, Lord Kames. She included a careful summary of Edwards and his arguments that the will maintained "its liberty, or moral freedom" despite the force of anterior motives or dispositions that governed the will. Adams also provided a fourteen-page entry on "Hopkinsians," followers of Edwards's student Samuel Hopkins, which afforded further opportunity for Adams to explicate the relationship of moral necessity to free will. For Adams and, we might surmise, her readers, the subject of free will was integral to discussions of religious choice and therefore to the practice of toleration in the new nation. It was not a theoretical abstraction, mere grist for theologizing mills.[4]

Debates about the nature of volition also shaped Adams's understanding of conversion. In *The Truth and Excellence of the Christian Religion*, she offered a rational defense of historic Protestantism through brief biographies of and excerpts from English, French, and American figures whom British Whigs and American patriots regarded as heroes from the early seventeenth century through the eighteenth century: Philip de Mornay and Pascal, Winthrop and Milton, Bacon and Boyle, Locke and Newton, Addison and Cowper, Wilberforce, Boudinot, and James Bowdoin, among others. They were all laymen—soldiers, scientists, physicians, mathematicians, politicians, diplomats, military officers, and men of letters—who, by her account, achieved notoriety for their patriotism and benevolence, and for their contentions that Christianity was the most reasonable religious choice even as it shared many tenets with Judaism and Islam.

Adams wanted her readers to be persuaded by their words and deeds— to be converted, in other words—by their reasoned and "zealous defence of the christian religion," their promotion of "a general freedom of religious inquiry," and their refutations especially of skeptics whom Adams described as "deistical," such as Voltaire, Hume, and Bolingbroke. Her exemplars, as she wrote of Newton, demonstrated that "there is nothing in christianity, but will abide the scrutiny of the soundest and most enlarged understanding." She insisted throughout *Truth and Excellence* that such testimonies confirmed the reasonableness and virtues of Protestantism. For Adams and her colonial predecessors, the promotion of conversion—including missions to non-Christians—represented a regard for all people's capabilities and prerogatives to choose their religious affiliation as they willed, the near opposite of bigotry or coercion.[5]

For all of the reflections of Anglo-whiggish Protestantism in Adams's writings, the politics of American independence inflected her work in distinctly American ways. Her dictionary did not reiterate the anti-papal, pro-imperial politics of Britain's mid-century scholarship. British policy itself had become somewhat lenient toward Catholicism in light of the empire's incorporation of Catholic territories such as Quebec, Dominca, and Senegal in the 1763 Treaty of Paris. Adams, however, went further than modest political concessions. Mindful of the military assistance and loans afforded to the Continental Congress by France and Spain, she omitted Broughton's editorial swipes against Catholicism. Her entry on "Papists" offered a straightforward description of papal history and the theology of the sacraments, with no mention of fearsome ceremonies in Rome. In her article on "Italy," written in the wake of late eighteenth-century liberal and anti-Jesuit leanings in the papacy, Adams expressed admiration for what she described as the near disappearance of the Inquisition, the severance of political authority from the church in Italy and France, and the marvel that "persons of all denominations live" in Italy "unmolested" and enjoy "the liberal sentiments of mildness, forbearance, and moderation" that characterized the pontificate of Clement XIV.[6]

In a different, menacing fashion, Adams also reflected a post-Revolutionary agenda to displace Native American populations, who by her account were ruthless enemies to the Americans during the war. Here she rejected the approaches of mid-eighteenth-century commentators who wrote of moral worlds shared by Indigenous people and British settlers. She devoted only two pages to a summary of the beliefs of the "Aborigines" and noted without comment that Indians were "almost wholly extinct" in New England.[7]

There were other indications that Adams had conformed her accounts to post-Revolutionary politics in New England. She set aside Broughton and Collier's effusive recommendations for British Protestantism and especially for the Church of England as the perfect mean between sacerdotal ceremonialism and populist enthusiasm. She contended that New Englanders, unlike Britons, had codified their love of moral freedom into law by disestablishing their churches. Religion in America, as she described it in her state-by-state survey in her *View of Religions*, rested on a separation between the government and the church, pluralism, and conformity to the principles of, as she put it, liberty of "conscience," "toleration," and "free exercise." She gave evidence for her claims through a reading of state constitutions. She emphasized their toleration of personal beliefs and neglected their empowerment of legislatures to support some version of a Protestant order. According to her fanciful reading, Massachusetts "had a most liberal and tolerant plan" by which all people "may worship God agreeable to the dictates of their own consciences, unmolested."[8] Adams's emphasis on liberty of conscience and moral choice—rather than, say, on British imperial virtues such as sensibility and utility, about which she was silent—suggested an American reading of religions that had begun to diverge from its British origins. Adams valorized the political separation of America from Britain as a corollary to New Englanders' fascination with "liberty" and especially freedom of the will.[9]

In so doing, she may well have drawn from her knowledge of patriot preachers in and near Boston who referred to voluntary religious conversion as a precedent for political revolution. John Cleaveland, a separatist evangelical from nearby Ipswich who denounced British rule as servitude, argued in 1771 newspaper editorials that one's political identities were no more fixed by geographical and familial origins than one's religious faith. Just as converts to Christianity renounced their previous affiliations and embraced a new spiritual identity, so too patriotic colonists rejected British rule and defined themselves as Americans. John Allen, preacher for a Baptist congregation in Boston, made the same correlation in 1772. In New Haven, Connecticut, Jonathan Edwards, Jr. exhorted his parishioners in 1774 to abandon their received identities as English and associate themselves with the Continental Congress. In 1775, Samuel Langdon, the president of Harvard, parsed imperial rule as seductive and deceptive servitude: a political analogue to the idolatry from which sinners repented as they trusted in Christ. The spiritual liberty enjoyed by the convert implied in such terms the political liberty of the patriot. Samuel West of Dartmouth, Massachusetts, who knew of Adams, promoted rebellion in 1776 in a provocative sermon to the council of the province. Ruminating on freedom of the will (he attempted an improvement on Edwards's *Freedom of the Will*), he claimed that New Englanders had as much right to change their political loyalties from Britain to the Continental Congress as they had to change their religious loyalties. Scrutiny of inherited religious obligations and the liberty to affiliate with a new community had political implications. For Adams and her patriot-preachers—most of whom tellingly had been involved in missionary activity—the new discourse of conversion culminated in American independence.[10]

Conclusion: Limits and Paradoxes

This study has demonstrated how that discourse, along with transformations in Protestant descriptions of the world's religions, developed in response to political change, from the Restoration to 1688, the establishment of the Hanoverian Empire, and, in the case of Adams, the American Revolution. To recapitulate, the political chaos of the Interregnum prompted writers such as

Ross and Crouch and other Restoration-era observers to take a confessional approach, according to which religions outside mainstream Protestantism appeared malevolent and illegitimate—threats to the unity of the kingdom. Those writers and their contemporaries accordingly described conversion as the soul's subjugation to a God known through Protestant teaching. Credence in that teaching was presumed to be a condition of conversion, which had little to do with a willful choice of one's religion. Within this confessional framework the evangelization of Indigenous people necessitated Anglicization, a civilizing mission, and catechesis as a preparation for conversion.

The crisis of the restored Stuart monarchy and the revolution of 1688 compelled Protestants on both sides of the Atlantic, apart from Tory Anglicans, to reject confessional assumptions and envision religious toleration for most Protestants and even some Catholics as the means of unity in the Williamite kingdom. Although such toleration was limited in scope, it indicated a new mandate to separate political legitimacy from religious creed and to vindicate a non-theological criterion—regard for liberty of conscience—as a rule by which to measure the public acceptability of different religions. Commentators on the world's religions distinguished the ways in which different communities or sects within religious traditions met this test of legitimacy.

The consolidation of Whig power under the Hanoverian crown and the attendant expansion of the British Empire convinced whiggish observers to reformulate further the discourse of religion and the state. As whiggish Protestants conceived of the relationship between national political mandates and religious adherence, they developed a self-justifying logic. The vindication of the republican principles underlying the constitutional monarchy depended in part on the affirmation of moral liberty as a universal principle. In the proper, or patriotic, exercise of that liberty, subjects aligned themselves with the virtues that sustained the empire and Britain's civic society, such as sensibility, reasonableness, and utility. This moral discourse shaped descriptions of different religions into a critique of priestly ceremonialism as tyrannical and unreasonable, and a valorization of religious communities that endorsed free will and moral reasonableness. Evangelists among Native American communities during the mid-eighteenth century adopted such criteria. By their account, they promoted conversion as a choice of one's religious identity according to universal moral principles and in the process dismissed the Anglicizing agendas of Restoration-era missionaries. They instead focused their efforts on what they deemed to be a form of persuasion that crossed ethnic and geographical borders.

Neither Adams nor her whiggish predecessors admitted to the many contradictions of their discourses. They promoted liberty of choice on behalf of a social order fettered by unfreedom for enslaved Africans, Native Americans, and the indigent. They presumed that they had parsed "liberty" and reasonable moral choice as unbounded by ethnic and social identities. They did so, by their accounts, in order to overcome the religious conflicts of the seventeenth century and to provide a reasoned defense of Christianity in an age of rising skepticism. They did not dwell on the fact that British and American contemporaries often deployed those terms to legitimate the inequalities of power and property that attended imperial conquest on the South Asian subcontinent and in North America. Liberty, as it turned out, had little to do with social equality. Reason was defined in quite provincial terms, to suit the social conventions of imperial patriots in London, Glasgow, and Boston. The work of Adams reveals the direction in which that discourse pointed in post-Revolutionary America. She vindicated the Revolutionary generation, curtly dismissed the religions of Guinea as a jumble of fetish worship and strange ideas about the afterlife, and nearly erased American Indians from her dictionary and history. In such terms, Adams anticipated nineteenth-century cultural developments. Many Americans came to construe Enlightenment notions of civility and reasonableness, and the discourse of liberty, to justify a racialized subjugation of the continent.[11]

Some historians have taken cues from these contradictions to posit a nearly inherent and certainly inescapable connection among Protestant views of other religions, missions, imperial agendas, and racialized interpretations of colonized people in the modern West.[12] That line of interpretation discloses the strength of such connections yet potentially obscures the ambiguities in the discourse. It downplays shifting perceptions, as though Protestant views of race, empire, and religion were unchanged from the Restoration through the American Revolution. It minimizes the contingencies—the variation in political conditions—that prompted contestation and transformation in conceptions of religion and ethnicity. It reads nineteenth-century taxonomies of race and religion, which became popular in America when its leaders embraced the prospect of continental conquest, back onto the eighteenth century, when racial taxonomies were only partially developed and not yet invested with notions of scientific authority.[13]

This study suggests that it is possible to recover from whiggish and Enlightened conceptions of religion and conversion alternative meanings—meanings that stand in opposition, rather than as prelude, to nineteenth-century discourses of race and empire. The observers described in this book often set their descriptions of Native Americans, for example, within a world-wide dichotomy, with coercive religious practices on one side and tolerant practices on the other. That dichotomy, rather than a fixation on the religious identities of nations or ethnic groups, often controlled their discussions of Indigenous Americans and other non-Anglo people. Protestants' preoccupation with liberty of conscience in turn led them to voice respect for Native intellectual worlds: their cosmologies and existential dilemmas.[14] It informed missionaries who subordinated Anglicizing agendas to persuasion and to ideals of moral community that crossed Anglo-Indigenous divides. Anglo-American Protestants did not eliminate racialized readings, but they did complicate and sometimes confound them. Their story resists both a tale of inexorable progress toward liberty and a narrative of changeless continuity of Anglocentric racism.

What of related matters such as toleration, interreligious exchange, and the rise of secularity? *The Opening of the Protestant Mind* suggests yet again an ambiguous reading. All of the dictionary makers and travelers invoked in this study—from Turner and Burnet to Collier and Montagu, Broughton and Hamilton—assented to some form of Protestant teaching. Yet they marginalized theological confession from public and political spheres. Along with Protestant missionaries and other observers discussed in this study, they reflected and even helped to create a discourse that valorized an individual's free choice of religious loyalties. In this sense, their story closely aligns with Charles Taylor's account of secularity: the displacement of a culture in which Christian beliefs were presumed to be non-debatable realities, and the emergence of a culture in which reasonable people deliberated and chose their religious beliefs (or non-beliefs) according to non-theological criteria such as the common good. Taylor's definition of secularity—including the formulation of conversion as the selection of one's religion—does not denote a loss of belief but, rather, a change in the description of how belief came about. This helps to explain how Anglicans such as the missionary advisor Wilson, deists such as the journalists Gordon and Trenchard, liberal Calvinists such as Chauncy, and evangelicals such as Edwards spoke of themselves as pursuing a common cause. Their mutual justifications for uncoerced religious choice according to western canons of moral reason accommodated thick religious belief.[15]

Recent critics of a Whig narrative—a story of increasing personal freedoms and political liberties from the Reformation through the 1689 Toleration Act and the latitudinarian policies under George I and II—have contended that the ideas of toleration, which followed from affirmations of religious choice, enhanced the power of the secular state. As these historians argue, the rhetoric abetted the hegemony of loyalist, establishment Protestants, who favored a privatized and rationalized version of religion as belief and excluded competing religious expressions such as Catholicism. In the midst of debates with Tories, Jacobites, and Anabaptist separatists, Whig Protestants, so this counter-whiggish interpretation goes, claimed the high ground of liberty of conscience but nonetheless presumed that they were presiding over a largely Protestant society whose critics were irrational and unpatriotic. They also insisted that "heathen" cultures in their colonies were inferior to "civilized" and Protestant regimes. Postcolonial social theorists also have maintained that western colonial powers asserted their superiority to and rights over colonized, subaltern, or other indigenous subjects through demands for secularization and religious toleration.[16]

Postcolonial analyses and other criticisms of the whiggish story of toleration illumine the implications of toleration and secularization for state power but can also mask the multiple and changing meanings of the discourse of liberty and moral choice. The shift from the confessional mindset of the Restoration era to the Whig moralism of post-1688 England and America introduced nuanced descriptions of different religions, attuned to variety within religious traditions, and sympathetic to the moral assumptions of non-westerners. It allowed for moments of cultural exchange—or opened up spaces for, as Richard White has called it, a "middle ground"—among Anglo settlers and Native Americans.[17] Religious exchange in 1750 did not approximate what we might regard as a capacious cultural pluralism, but it nonetheless looked very different than it did in 1650 on several fronts: less totalizing in critique, more tolerant in at least some respects.

Furthermore, the whiggish discourse of religious choice carried meanings that transcended the political uses to which it was put by eighteenth-century Britons. Notions of liberty of conscience and toleration, of freedom of the will and moral reasonableness, served Anglo-American Protestants as moral standards by which to measure their own religious and social practices as well as those of Catholics, Muslims, and Native Americans. We can recall Brainerd's, Edwards's, and Smith's insistent critiques of British settlers and colonizers. Cultural historians of early modern Europe such as

Carlo Ginzburg and Giovanni Tarantino have argued that writers such as Broughton, and Picart and Bernard, sometimes followed their comparative method to a point of stunning self-critique. For all of their provincialism, their rhetoric of humaneness and candor compelled them at times to expose the monstrousness of empire and slavery, and the duplicity—the hubris—of Eurocentric critiques of non-western religions.[18]

As the South Asian historian Dipesh Chakrabarty has contended in a more expansive comment on modernity, the self-contradictions of Enlightenment humanism, or what I have called here Whig moralism, do not necessarily invalidate its central tenets. Postcolonial criticism and activism, Chakrabarty argues, depend on the discourse of liberty and rationality even if that discourse must be translated and contextualized through concerted effort. We might add that historians too echo some of the tenets of that discourse when they expose the coerciveness and therefore inhumaneness of colonial regimes. The ideas themselves are worth investigation and consideration, even if they were proposed—perhaps because they were proposed—in a context of imperial conquest and racial presumptions.[19]

With its focus on changes in Protestant notions of religious liberty, this study prompts us to appreciate the contingency of ideas about different religions, conversion, and missions. There was no fixed and singular Anglo-Protestant ideology from the Restoration to the American Revolution and beyond—not even of anti-Catholicism. There were moments of contestation and ambiguity, certainly of reformulation. Such alterations belie, or at least complicate, wholesale generalizations about Anglo-American Protestants and their approach to other religions, including their evangelistic missions. Protestant discourses had the potential to create space for mutuality with other peoples and to open exchange with other traditions, just as they had the potential to constrict such spaces and close such exchange. It is the "both and" rather than the "either or" that ought to shape our understanding of, and interest in, that history.

Notes

Introduction

1. Benjamin Webb, Jr., Journal 1748–1769, Massachusetts Historical Society, Boston.
2. Jacob Baily, notes on geography, Volume (reel) 96, document 2, c. 1752, Jacob Baily Papers, Nova Scotia Archives, Halifax, Nova Scotia. For Bailey's biography: James S. Leamon, *The Reverend Jacob Bailey, Maine Loyalist: For God, King, Country, and for Self* (Amherst, MA, 2012). When I leave "indigenous" uncapitalized, it refers to more than North American peoples.
3. John Leland, *The Writings of the Late Elder John Leland*, ed. L. F. Greene (New York, 1845), 410–411; for Hutchinson: Frederick Clifton Pierce, *History of Grafton, Worcester County, Massachusetts* (Worcester, MA, 1879), 179–180.
4. Several London and provincial newspapers circulated the same accounts of such conversions. For one set of references, with the incidents mentioned here, see the following from the *Boston News-Letter*: June 18, 1724, p. 1 (hereafter cited as 6/18/24, p. 1); 11/19/24, p. 1; 3/4/24 [new (calendar) style 25], p. 1; 7/15/31, p. 1; 4/27/32, p. 1; 5/5/33, p. 2; 4/10/55, p. 2.
5. [Thomas Gordon], *A True Account of a Revelation Lately Discover'd to Jeremiah van Husen* (London, 1719), 13–16. The essay was reprinted in 1751 under Gordon's name, in Thomas Gordon and John Trenchard, *A Collection of Tracts by the John Trenchard, Esq; and Thomas Gordon, Esq*, 2 vols. (London, 1751), 1:216–220.
6. "Magisterial" is a Reformation-era term that denotes endorsement of the office of a civil magistrate or ruler, that is, an appreciation for the importance of civil government, public order, political stability, and citizenship apart from specifically ecclesiastical agendas. This excluded radical or sectarian Protestants who either rejected the authority of a secular government or attempted to take the place of the state.
7. Protestant scholars especially during the seventeenth century also devoted much attention to the relationship between Christianity and Judaism. That issue, however, was defined by perceptions that set Judaism apart from other non-Protestant religions: the Christian inheritance from Judaism, a shared scripture, and a long tradition of theological scholarship, from biblical studies to investigations of the apocalyptic role of Israel. One recent study of Protestant descriptions of Judaism during the seventeenth and eighteenth centuries, however, tracks changes similar to the ones narrated in this book: Yaacov Deutsch, *Judaism in Christian Eyes: Ethnographic Descriptions of Jews and Judaism in Early Modern Europe* (New York, 2012).
8. The terminology for the study of the world's religions, or comparative religions, largely refers to post-eighteenth-century academic disciplines and does not quite fit seventeenth- and eighteenth-century approaches. I use them advisedly, without

better terms at hand, to capture the task of describing and analyzing different religions and spiritual traditions in different parts of the world.

9. Peter Harrison, *"Religion" and the religions in the English Enlightenment* (New York, 1990); and Guy Stroumsa, *A New Science: The Discovery of Religion in the Age of Reason* (Cambridge, MA, 2010). For the best comprehensive study of seventeenth-century scholars and political secularization: Mark Somos, *Secularisation and the Leiden Circle* (Boston, 2011). For a history of the field of anthropology that places seventeenth-century developments within the context of the Scientific Revolution and early Enlightenment: Margaret T. Hodgen, *Early Anthropology in the Sixteenth and Seventeenth Centuries* (Philadelphia, 1964).

10. Lynn Hunt, Margaret C. Jacob, and Wijnand Mijnhardt, *The Book that Changed Europe: Picart and Bernard's Religious Ceremonies of the World* (Cambridge, MA, 2010), quotation from 27; and Frank E. Manuel, *The Eighteenth Century Confronts the Gods* (Cambridge, MA, 1959). David A. Pailin, *Attitudes to Other Religions: Comparative Religion in Seventeenth- and Eighteenth-Century Britain* (Dover, NH, 1984) suggests a similar seventeenth-to-eighteenth-century development. For the geographies: P. J. Marshall and Glyndwr Williams, *The Great Map of Mankind: British Perceptions of the World in the Age of Enlightenment* (London, 1982).

11. For a parallel account of the importance of political context, see Ralph Bauer, *The Cultural Geography of Colonial American Literatures: Empire, Travel, Modernity* (New York, 2003), which interprets the literature of early Anglo-Indigenous contact in America in the context of metropolitan attempts to control colonists. Several histories of the British Empire during the seventeenth and eighteenth centuries frame Protestant views of Catholicism and of Native American traditions within the context of colonial and anti-French political agendas, but they pay scant attention to studies of the world's religions or of conversion or, for that matter, to differences between seventeenth- and eighteenth-century concerns for England's internal affairs and the changes that resulted from those differences. They posit a rather unchanging religious landscape in such terms. For a recapitulation of this line of scholarship, see Carla Gardina Pestana, *Protestant Empire: Religion and the Making of the British Atlantic World* (Philadelphia, 2009).

12. In "Enlightenment, Religion, and the Enigma of Secularization: A Review Essay," *American Historical Review* 108 (2003): 1061–1080, Jonathan Sheehan reviews much of the relevant literature and demonstrates that late seventeenth- and eighteenth-century observers such as Pierre Bayle disseminated new approaches by compiling observations of religions without ordering them into a system or logic of religious polemic. By Sheehan's account, they thereby conveyed less an anti-religious mindset than a modern religious mindset attuned to cultural and political context.

13. Tomoko Masuzawa, *The Invention of World Religions: Or, How European Universalism Was Preserved in the Language of Pluralism* (Chicago, 2005); Daniel Dubuisson, *The Western Construction of Religion: Myths, Knowledge, and Ideology*, trans. William Sayers (Baltimore, 2003); and Brent Nongbri, *Before Religion: A History of a Modern Concept* (New Haven, 2013). These accounts follow the example set by Louis Henry Jordan, the University of Chicago scholar whose *Comparative Religion: Its Genesis*

and Growth (Edinburgh, 1905) initiated the history of the discipline. Writing about Protestant commentary on Native Americans, Laura M. Stevens maintains that there was "rhetorical uniformity" and a "stable approach" throughout the whole period of English colonization in America: *The Poor Indians: British Missionaries, Native Americans, and Colonial Sensibility* (Philadelphia, 2004), 28. Other studies that posit a premodern, theologically informed continuity between the seventeenth and eighteenth centuries are Eric J. Sharpe, *Comparative Religion: A History*, 2nd ed. (LaSalle, IL, 1986); Catherine Bell, "Paradigms Behind (and Before) the Modern Concept of Religion," *History and Theory* 45, no. 4 (December 2006): 27–46; and Robert A. Orsi, ed., "Introduction" to *The Cambridge Companion to Religious Studies* (New York, 2012), 1–13.

14. For a concise statement of Smith's position: Jonathan Z. Smith, "Religion, Religions, Religious," in Mark C. Taylor, ed., *Critical Terms for Religious Studies* (Chicago, 1998), 269–284. For reflections on another critic of the category of "religion," Wilfred Cantwell Smith, see Talal Asad, "Reading a Modern Classic: W. C. Smith's *The Meaning and End of Religion*," *History of Religions* 40 (2001): 205–222. For further statements in this line of interpretation, see Orsi, "Introduction" to *The Cambridge Companion to Religious Studies*; and, with an extended focus on anti-Catholicism, Robert A. Orsi, *History and Presence* (Cambridge, MA, 2016).

15. The key text here is Talal Asad, *Formations of the Secular: Christianity, Islam, Modernity* (Stanford, CA, 2003). A parallel account, with a helpful summary of the literature, is given in Nongbri, *Before Religion*. See also Timothy Fitzgerald, *Discourse on Civility and Barbarity: A Critical History of Religion and Related Categories* (New York, 2007). For a helpful reading of Asad in the context of eighteenth-century approaches to religious comparison, see Sanjay Subrahmanyam, "Monsieur Picart and the Gentiles of India," in Lynn Hunt, Margaret Jacob, and Wijnand Mijnardt, eds., *Bernard Picart and the Vision of Religion* (Los Angeles, 2010), 197–214. In *The Invention of World Religions*, Masuzawa contends that the intellectual story of the whole period from the eighteenth through the nineteenth century can be told in terms of European self-consciousness: attempts to trace the origins of Christianity and western identity to Hellenic (rather than Hebraic) modes of thought and to parse non-western religions in terms that validated Europeans' sense of racial and political superiority.

16. Kathryn Gin Lum, *Heathen: Religion and Race in American History* (Cambridge, MA, 2022).

17. David Chidester, *Savage Systems: Colonialism and Comparative Religion in Southern Africa* (Charlottesville, VA, 1996); Jennifer Graber, *The Gods of Indian Country: Religion and the Struggle for the American West* (New York, 2018). For an incisive study of eighteenth-century Protestant missions and slavery in related terms: Katherine Gerbner, *Christian Slavery: Conversion and Race in the Protestant Atlantic World* (Philadelphia, 2018). Gin Lum shows how the concept of the "heathen"—uncivilized, unhealthy, and damned—was a term of comparison that justified White supremacy even as it legitimated missions to enslaved Blacks, Hawaiians, and Indigenous Americans, along with the exclusion of the Chinese in nineteenth- and twentieth-century America: Gin Lum, *Heathen*.

18. Webb Keane shows the contradictions in the language of moral liberty or agency in his anthropological study of Calvinist missions in Indonesia: *Christian Moderns: Freedom and Fetish in the Mission Encounter* (Berkeley, 2007). For a helpful overview of the recent literature on race, nationalism, and culture in early America, see Eran Zelnik, "Self-Evident Walls: Reckoning with Recent Histories of Race," *Journal of the Early Republic* 41 (2021): 1–38.

19. See, e.g., Gin Lum, *Heathen*.

20. Carlo Ginzburg, "Provincializing the World: Europeans, Indians, Jews (1704)," *Postcolonial Studies* 14 (2011): 135–150. Ginzburg draws on the South Asian historian and postcolonial critic Dipesh Chakrabarty, who is discussed briefly in the Epilogue of my study.

Chapter 1

1. R. D. [Nathaniel Crouch], *The Strange and Prodigious Religious Customs, and Manners of Sundry Nations* (London, 1683). For his popularity, see Robert Mayer, "Nathaniel Crouch, Bookseller and Historian: Popular Historiography and Cultural Power in Late Seventeenth-Century England," *Eighteenth-Century Studies* 27 (1994): 391–419. The extent of Franklin's collection is evident by the catalogue of the Library Company of Philadelphia with the relevant information on provenance of rare books. For puritans and Crouch: David D. Hall, *Worlds of Wonder, Days of Judgment: Popular Religious Belief in Early New England* (Cambridge, MA, 1990), 52–55, 112–114.

2. Crouch, *Strange and Prodigious Religions*, image facing A3 in "To the Reader"; quotation from 20.

3. Crouch, *Strange and Prodigious Religions*, 1, 10–11.

4. Crouch, *Strange and Prodigious Religions*, 1–3, 21.

5. On the terms used here and later: in general, we can say that there were violent hostilities between parliamentary and royal factions intermittently from 1642 to 1651, what we can call the "civil wars." Historians who focus on the monarchical nature of England's constitution typically use the name "Interregnum" for the period from the execution of Charles I in 1649 to the Restoration of the Stuart monarchy in 1660. Historians who wish to highlight the rule of Parliament call the period from 1649 to 1660 the "Commonwealth" or "Republic," within which the years of the rule of Oliver Cromwell, 1653 to 1659, are called the "Protectorate."

6. Richard Burton [Nathaniel Crouch], *The Wars in England, Scotland, and Ireland* (London, 1681), A3v, 185, 204–205, 210. For Crouch's sympathies with the parliamentary party but abhorrence of extremism, religious enthusiasm, and regicide during the Civil War, see Matthew Neufeld, *The Civil Wars After 1660: Public Remembering in Late Stuart England* (Woodbridge and Suffolk, U.K., 2013), 108–111, 132.

7. Crouch, *Strange and Prodigious Religions*, 4. For Crouch's judgments on Native American treachery and violence, especially in the Pequot War and King Philip's War: R. B. [Nathaniel Crouch], *The English Empire in America* (London, 1685), 70–73.

8. In technical terms, nonconformists were baptized members of the Church of England who refused to conform to Anglican liturgical practice and ecclesiastical polity. Dissenters were not members of the Church of England and rejected not only the liturgy and polity of the Church of England but also much of Anglican theological tradition: "dissenter" and "nonconformist," *Oxford English Dictionary* (online). Seventeenth- and eighteenth-century writers often used the terms imprecisely and interchangeably.

9. On the trend toward strict or highly polarized definitions of true religion and their political import, see Jonathan Sheehan, "Sacred and Profane: Idolatry, Antiquarianism and the Polemics of Distinction in the Seventeenth Century," *Past and Present* 192 (2006): 35–66.

10. For a summary statement on religion and the colonial project, see Carla Gardina Pestana, *Protestant Empire: Religion and the Making of the British Atlantic World* (Philadelphia, 2009), which summarizes an abundant literature in this vein. For the term "Protestant interest," see Thomas Kidd, *The Protestant Interest: New England After Puritanism* (New Haven, 2004). To sample strong assertions of interconnections among colonialism, religious chauvinism, and empire, see David Chidester, *Empire of Religion: Imperialism and Comparative Religion* (Chicago, 2014); Ralph Bauer, *The Cultural Geography of Colonial American Literatures: Empire, Travel, Modernity* (New York, 2003); and the volume of essays edited by Linda Gregerson and Susan Juster, eds., *Empires of God: Religious Encounters in the Early Modern Atlantic* (Philadelphia, 2011). For challenges to a singular focus on imperial-colonial dynamics, see Barbara Fuchs, "Religion and National Distinction in the Early Modern Atlantic," in Gregerson and Juster, eds., *Empires of God*, 58–69; and Alexander B. Haskell, *For God, King, & People: Forging Commonwealth Bonds in Renaissance Virginia* (Chapel Hill, 2017).

11. English Protestants used "idolatry" in various ways. Puritans often deployed the idiom to critique remnants of medieval ritual in English churches and Anglican practices in America: David D. Hall, *The Puritans: A Transatlantic History* (Princeton, 2019); and Susan Juster, "Iconoclasm Without Icons? The Destruction of Sacred Objects in Colonial America," in Gregerson and Juster, eds., *Empires of God*, 216–237. They also, as argued here, conflated idolatry and political disorder. For "idolatry" and political authority: Jonathan Sheehan, "The Altars of the Idols: Religion, Sacrifice, and the Early Modern Polity," *Journal of the History of Ideas* 67 (2006): 649–673. For a review of early modern uses of "idolatry" with attention to Protestant-Catholic differences: Joan-Pau Rubiés, "Theology, Ethnography, and the Historicization of Idolatry," *Journal of the History of Ideas*, 67 (2006): 571–596.

12. It pays scant attention to the theologians and philosophers discussed in Peter Harrison, *"Religion" and the religions in the English Enlightenment* (New York, 1990).

13. For the nature of eyewitness accounts and narratives of first encounters, see Stephen Greenblatt, *Marvelous Possessions: The Wonder of the New World* (Chicago, 1991); and the essays in Jaś Elsner and Joan-Pau Rubiés, eds., *Voyages and Visions: Towards a Cultural History of Travel* (London, 1999). A helpful survey of these accounts as

anthropological works is given in Margaret T. Hodgen, *Early Anthropology in the Sixteenth and Seventeenth Centuries* (Philadelphia, 1964).

14. Samuel Purchas, *Purchas His Pilgrimage: Or, Relations of the World and Their Religions* (London, 1613); and *Purchas His Pilgrimes*, 5 vols. (London, 1625). Second and third editions of *Purchas His Pilgrimage* (1614, 1617) have additional material, so I will at times cite these later editions. The fifth volume of *Purchas His Pilgrimes* includes appendices and list of books (it has a publication date of 1626 but is cited as 1625). I cite *Pilgrimage* to refer to the one-volume 1614 version, unless otherwise noted; *Pilgrimes* to refer to the five-volume 1625–1626 work. In subsequent editions, *Pilgrimes* was slightly modified and entitled *Hakluytus Posthumus: or Purchas His Pilgrimes*, because much of the material came from Hakluyt. I cite this as *Hakluytus Posthumus*, with reference to a modern reprint: *Hakluytus Posthumus: Or Purchas His Pilgrimes*, 20 vols. (Glasgow, 1905–1907). For an introduction to Purchas, see David Armitage, "Purchas, Samuel," *Oxford Dictionary of National Biography*, 60 vols. (New York, 2004) (hereafter ODNB), 45: 574–576. For an extensive survey of the circulation of Purchas's works with bibliographies on Purchas, and reference to numerous literary figures: L. E. Pennington, "Samuel Purchas: His Reputation and the Uses of His Works," in L. E. Pennington, ed., *The Purchas Handbook: Studies of the Life, Times and Writings of Samuel Purchas, 1577–1626*, 2 vols. (London, 1997), 1: 3–118, esp. 3–22. Members of New England's clergy such as Cotton Mather and Edward Taylor cited Purchas: Mukhtar Ali Isani, "Cotton Mather and the Orient," *The New England Quarterly* 43 (1970): 46–58; and Mukhtar Ali Isani, "Edward Taylor and the 'Turks," *Early American Literature* 7 (1972): 120–123.

15. Purchas, *Pilgrimage*, "To the Reader," n. p. For examples of Purchas's tendency to view political, social or economic, and religious practice as an ensemble, see Purchas, *Pilgrimes*, I: 147–176; II: 943, 1083–1084, 1149–1150; and IV: 1336–1367.

16. Purchas, *Pilgrimage*, "Epistle Dedicatorie" n.p.; *Pilgrimage*, "To the Reader," n.p; and *Hakluytus Posthumus*, 19: 220.

17. Edward Brerewood, *Enquiries Touching the Diversity of Languages and Religions Through the Chief Parts of the World* (London, 1614), over a hundred pages of which were excerpted in Purchas, *Hakluytus Posthumus*, 1: 235–402. Later divines such as Jonathan Edwards also cited Brerewood: Jonathan Edwards, *The Works of Jonathan Edwards*, Perry Miller and Harry S. Stout, gen eds., 26 vols. (New Haven, 1957–2008) (hereafter *WJE*), vol. 26: *Catalogues of Books*, ed. Peter J. Thuesen (hereafter JEC), 186.

18. Purchas, *Hakluytus Posthumus*, 19: 263. Purchas used Richard Hakluyt, *The Principle Navigations, Voiages, Traffiques and Discoveries of the English Nation*, 3 vols. (London, 1589–1600). For Hakluyt's biography and religious views, see Peter C. Mancall, *Hakluyt's Promise: An Elizabethan's Obsession for an English America* (New Haven, 2007); David A. Bourchoff, "Piety, Patriotism, and Empire: Lessons for England, Spain, and the New World in the Works of Richard Hakluyt," *Renaissance Quarterly* 62 (2009): 809–858; and David Harris Sacks, "Richard Hakluyt's Navigations in Time: History, Epic, and Empire," *Modern Language Quarterly* 67 (2006): 31–62.

19. [Edwin Sandys], *Europe Speculum: A View or Survey of the State of Religion in the Western Parts of the World* (London, 1632), 3–5, 119. *Europe Speculum* was first

published as *A Relation of the State of Religion* (London, 1605). For Purchas's knowledge of Sandys, see *Hakluytus Posthumus*, 19: 121, 134, 149. For Sandy's career and travels: T. K. Rabb, *Jacobean Gentleman: Sir Edwin Sandys, 1561–1629* (Princeton, 1998), 21–46.

20. William Lithgow, *A Most Delectable, and True Discourse of and Admired and Painefull Peregrination* (London, 1614), B2v–C2v; and, from a posthumous reissue of his works, William Lithgow, *Lithgow's Nineteen Years Travels* (London, 1682), "Epistle Dedicatory," n. p. For his biography: Martin Garrett, "Lithgow, William," ODNB 34: 11–14. For Purchas's use of Lithgow, see Linda McJannet, "Purchas His Pruning: Refashioning the Ottomans in Seventeenth-Century Travel Accounts," *Huntington Library Quarterly* 74 (2011): 219–242. Lithgow's works were popular across the political spectrum, frequently reprinted, and held by the libraries at Harvard and Yale: Harvard College, *Catalogus Librorum* (Boston, 1723), 51; and Yale College, *A Catalogue of Books in the Library* (New Haven, 1755), 18.

21. For Purchas's editing techniques and inconsistent presentations, see Matthew Dimmock, "Faith, Form and Faction: Samuel Purchas's *Purchas His Pilgrimage* (1613)," *Renaissance Studies* 28 (2014): 262–278; McJannet, "Purchas His Pruning"; and Carol Urness, "Purchas as Editor," in Pennington, ed., *Purchas Handbook*, 1: 121–144. For enhanced trade between England and Ottoman Turkey: Ralph Davis, "English Imports from the Middle East," in M. A. Cook, ed., *Studies in the Economic History of the Middle East* (London, 1970), 193–206.

22. For Purchas's ambiguous approach to Indigenous Americans and its relation to colonization, see Loren E. Pennington, "*Hakluytus Posthumus*: Samuel Purchas and the Promotion of English Overseas Expansion," *Emporia State Research Studies* 14 (1966): 5–39, esp. 12–13, 36–37. For accounts of cultural critique and colonial agendas, see L. H. Roper, *Advancing Empire: English Interests and Overseas Expansion, 1613–1688* (New York, 2017); and Richard S. Dunn, "Seventeenth-Century Historians of America," in James M. Smith, ed., *Seventeenth-Century America: Essays in Colonial History* (Chapel Hill, 1959), 195–225. For travel narratives, see Peter C. Mancall, "Introduction: What Fynes Moryson Knew," *Journal of Early Modern History* 10 (2006): 1–9, and the attendant articles that comprise the whole of the issue, 11–168. For Purchas and the Virginia Company, see David R. Ransome, "Pocahontas and the Mission to the Indians," *The Virginia Magazine of History and Biography* 99 (1991): 81–94. Hakluyt and many of his generation drew parallels between the Israelite conquest of Canaan—directed by providence—and the English assault on Virginia: Alfred A. Cave, "Canaanites in a Promised Land: The American Indian and the Providential Theory of Empire," *American Indian Quarterly* 12 (1988): 277–297.

23. Thomas Harriot, *A Briefe and True Report of the New Found Land of Virginia* (London, 1588), excerpted in Purchas, *Pilgrimage*, 3rd ed. (1617), 948–950.

24. Harriot, *Briefe and True Report*, B1r, E2v–F2v.

25. Harriot's comments thus reflect what historians of travel have described as a Renaissance deference to empirical description over ideological critique. See Joan-Pau Rubiés, "Travel Writing and Humanistic Culture: A Blunted Impact?," *Journal of Early Modern History* 10 (2006): 131–168; and Nicholas Popper, "An Ocean of

Lies: The Problem of Historical Evidence in the Sixteenth Century," *Huntington Library Quarterly* 74 (2011): 375–400. Popper shows that Elizabethan travelers used empiricist and Baconian methods, including attention to a wide range of evidence, although they sometimes used such methods to Protestant purpose by proposing the need for missions to Native Americans. These interpretations offer an alternative to Anthony Pagden's intellectual history of the concept of barbarism and Indigenous Americans during the sixteenth century: Anthony Pagden, *The Fall of Natural Man: The American Indian and the Origins of Comparative Ethnology* (New York, 1986).

26. See John W. Shirley, *Thomas Harriot: A Biography* (New York, 1983), esp. 113–174. There were several versions of Harriot's work to which De Bry added engravings from White, including Thomas Harriot, *A Briefe and True Report of the New Found Land of Virginia* (Frankfort, 1590). De Bry also included these engravings in his *America*, Part I (Frankfort, 1590).

27. Kim Sloan, with Joyce E. Chaplin, Christian F. Feest, and Ute Kuhlemann, *A New World: England's First View of America* (Chapel Hill, 2007), esp. 116–117 for the agricultural ceremony painting. See also Paul Hulton, *America 1585: The Complete Drawings of John White* (Chapel Hill, 1984). The image is Plate XVIII in Harriot, *A Briefe and True Report*.

28. See the commentary on De Bry's use of White in Michael Gaudio, *Engraving the Savage: The New World and Techniques of Civilization* (Minneapolis, 2008), ix–xxii, 1–126; and, for De Bry's optimism about the potential for the Anglicization of Carolina, Peter C. Mancall, *Nature and Culture in the Early Modern Atlantic* (Philadelphia, 2018), 85–119. The image is Plate XX in Harriot, *A Briefe and True Report*.

29. Purchas, *Hakluytus Posthumus*, 19: 383–385, 388–389. He cribbed from John Smith, *A Description of New England* (London, 1616) and *The Generall Historie of Virginia, New England, and the Summer Isles* (London, 1624). For Purchas's alarm, see Pennington, "*Hakluytus Posthumus.*"

30. Such inconsistence is shown in their perspectives on race. Kathleen Brown argues that racial tropes among English observers of Native Americans were intermittent and only partially developed before 1650: "Native Americans and Early Modern Concepts of Race," in Martin Daunton and Rick Halpern, eds., *Empire and Others: British Encounters with Indigenous Peoples, 1600–1850* (Philadelphia, 1999), 79–100. So too, Joyce E. Chaplin contends that racial ideologies were inchoate before 1650. Chaplin shows as well that English racialization of Native peoples had more to do with scientific technologies and Native susceptibility to disease rather than with religious matters: *Subject Matter: Technology, the Body, and Science on the Anglo-American Frontier, 1500–1676* (Cambridge, MA, 2003), e.g., 160.

31. On the transition from eyewitness travel accounts, with their humanistic bent, to Stuart-era compilations, see David Armitage, "The New World and British Historical Thought: From Richard Hakluyt to William Robertson," in Karen Ordahl Kupperman, ed., *America in European Consciousness, 1493–1750* (Chapel Hill, 1995), 52–75; Mary C. Fuller, *Voyages in Print: English Travel to America, 1576–1624* (New York, 1995); and Mancall, *Nature and Culture.*

32. For a recent summary of this campaign to reverse Cromwell's policies of toleration, see Hall, *The Puritans*, 33, 296–299.
33. The "confessionalization" thesis is associated especially with Heinz Schilling: Heinz Schilling, "Confessionalization: Historical and Scholarly Perspectives of a Comparative and Interdisciplinary Paradigm," in John M. Headly et al., eds., *Confessionalization in Europe, 1555–1700: Essays in Honor of Bodo Nischan* (Aldershot, U.K., 2004), 21–45. See also Ute Lotz-Heumann, "Confessionalization," in David Whitford, ed., *Reformation and Early Modern Europe: A Guide to Research* (Kirksville, MO, 2008), 136–157. For discussion of the Treaty of Westphalia and the ways it addressed the problem of civil war without yielding a permanent solution, see Benjamin J. Kaplan, *Divided by Faith: Religious Conflict and the Practice of Toleration in Early Modern Europe* (Cambridge, MA, 2007), 172–195, 220–230, 336–337.
34. We can use that term without attributing the peculiarities of German confessionalization to English affairs. For various attempts to apply the paradigm of confessionalization to England and New England, see J. C. D. Clark, "England's Ancien Régime as a Confessional State," *Albion* 21 (1989): 450–474; Brent S. Sirota, *The Christian Monitors: The Church of England and the Age of Benevolence, 1680–1730* (New Haven, 2014); and Jan Stievermann, "Early American Protestantism and the Confessionalization Paradigm: A Critical Inquiry," in Jan Stievermann and Randall C. Zachman, eds., *Multiple Reformations? The Many Faces and Legacies of the Reformation* (Tübingen, 2018), 161–188.
35. Jeffrey R. Collins, *The Allegiance of Thomas Hobbes* (New York, 2005); Moyses Amyraldus, *A Treatise Concerning Religions* (London, 1660); Lancelot Addison, *West Barbary, or, a Short Narrative of the Revolutions of the Kingdoms of Fez and Morocco* (Oxford, 1671), "Preface to the Reader," n.p. For Addison, see William J. Bulman, *Anglican Enlightenment: Orientalism, Religion and Politics in England and Its Empire, 1648–1715* (New York, 2015), 41–114.
36. Sir William Temple, *Observations upon the United Provinces of the Netherlands* (London, 1673), 170, 166–168, 165–184 for the whole passage on religion and the state. For Temple's biography, see J. D. Davies, "Temple, Sir William," ODNB, 54: 84–89.
37. Temple, *Observations upon the United Provinces*, 179–180. Temple also thought that a creedal or confessional state allowed for a peaceful pursuit of foreign policy: Steven C. A. Pincus, *Protestantism and Patriotism: Ideologues and the Making of English Foreign Policy, 1650–1668* (New York, 1996), *passim*.
38. Nicholas Tyacke, "The 'Rise of Puritanism' and the Legalizing of Dissent, 1571–1719," in Peter Grell, Jonathan I. Israel, and Nicholas Tyacke, eds. *From Persecution to Toleration: The Glorious Revolution and Religion in England* (Oxford, 1991) (hereafter GIT), 17–49; and Mark Goldie, "The Theory of Religious Intolerance in Restoration England," GIT, 331–368. During the Interregnum, Congregationalists or Independents differed from Anglicans and Presbyterians by refusing to endorse agendas to establish a single ecclesiastical institution throughout the realm or a national church: Matthew C. Bingham, "On the Idea of a National Church: Reassessing

Congregationalism in Revolutionary England," *Church History* 88 (2019): 27–57. The post-civil-wars context compelled them to reconsider.

39. Protestants in New England often iterated a religious identity, chiefly through the idea of a divine covenant with New England, apart from the religious establishment in London. Yet they adopted many of the assumptions of an English confessional order. They too lamented the disruptions that attended the Interregnum. Their leaders preached and wrote frequently of the need for social and political unity under a common set of English Protestant convictions. A helpful summary of such developments is given in Joseph A. Conforti, *Saints and Strangers: New England in British North America* (Baltimore, 2006). For New England and the Restoration: Adrian Chastain Weimer, "The Resistance Petitions of 1664–1665: Confronting the Restoration in Massachusetts Bay," *New England Quarterly* 92 (2019): 221–262. For Puritan attitudes in England toward the Stuarts: Jacqueline Rose, *Godly Kingship in Restoration England: The Politics of Royal Supremacy, 1660–1688* (New York, 2011).

40. For Protestant consensus and the Exclusion Crisis: Henry Horwitz, "Protestant Reconciliation in the Exclusion Crisis," *The Journal of Ecclesiastical History* 15 (1964): 201–217. The Exclusion Crisis led commentators to fashion political monikers that lasted through the eighteenth century: Whig and Tory. Whig, as opposed to Tory, stood for those who supported Exclusion and conditions on dynastic succession, along with parliamentary restraints on absolutism: J. G. A. Pocock, "The Varieties of Whiggism from Exclusion to Reform: A History of Ideology and Discourse," in J. G. A. Pocock, *Virtue, Commerce, and History: Essays on Political Thought and History, Chiefly in the Eighteenth Century* (New York, 1985), 215–310. For ideas of toleration in this period, see Jonathan Koch, "'The Phanaticks Tyring Room': Dryden and the Poetics of Toleration," *Studies in Philology* 116 (2019): 539–567.

41. Alexander Ross, *Pansebia: Or, a View of the Religions of the World* (London, 1653; 5th ed. London, 1673). Pansebia is Greek for "all forms of devotion."

42. For the publication history and Milton: R. J. W. Mills, "Alexander Ross's *Pansebia* (1653), Religious Compendia and the Seventeenth-Century Study of Religious Diversity," *The Seventeenth Century* 31 (2016): 285–310. For the Mather library: http://www.librarything.com/catalog/Mather Family Library; for the Prince library: City of Boston, *The Prince Library: A Catalogue* (Boston, 1870); Edwards, JEC, 425.

43. Alexander Ross, *Religions Lotterie* (London, 1642), title page and last page [n.p.]. See Mills, "Alexander Ross's *Pansebia*," for how such an ideology shaped Ross's *Pansebia* into a comprehensive account of the world's religions.

44. Ross, *Pansebia*, 505, 502, "Dedicatory Epistle" A2v–3r, "The Preface to the Reader" (n.p.). For Reformed theology and Presbyterians: Ross, *Pansebia*, 394–417, esp. the final section, which contains a florid recommendation for the Swiss theologian Wollebius.

45. Ross, *Pansebia*, "The Preface to the Reader" (n.p.).

46. Ross, *Pansebia*, 281–360 (medieval and post-Reformation sects and orders), and 428–477 (contemporary theology and practice).

47. Ross, *Pansebia* (1653), 144.

48. Ross, *Pansebia*, 146, 149.

49. Ross, *Pansebia*, 147–151.

50. Ross, *Pansebia*, 161, 153, 155–157.

51. Ross, *Pansebia*, 161, 152. The appended section on radicals, heretics, and Mahomet, is numbered separately, 1–67.

52. Ross, *Pansebia*, 103, 73–74. For one such story of beguiling preachers, which circulated widely, see Thomas Broughton, *An Historical Dictionary of All Religions* (London, 1742), 361.

53. Ross, *Pansebia*, 4th ed. (London, 1664), 103–104, 113–114. It is noticeable, then, that Ross omitted reference to the claims by previous Spanish and Italian scholars who described religious practices and symbols common to the peoples of North and South America and classical and pre-classical pagans. These claims were widespread and influenced, among others, the well-known French observer of Native Americans in Canada, Joseph François Lafiteau: Sabine MacCormack, "Perceptions of Greco-Roman and Amerindian Paganism in Early Modern Europe," in Karen Ordahl Kupperman, *America in European Consciousness, 1493–1750* (Chapel Hill, 1995), 79–129. For further comparison between English and French observations, see Gordon M. Sayre, *Les Sauvages Américains: Representations of Native Americans in French and English Colonial Literature* (Chapel Hill, 1997).

54. John Josselyn, *Account of Two Voyages to New-England* (London, 1674), reprinted in Paul J. Lindholdt, ed., *John Jossyln, Colonial Traveler: A Critical Edition of Two Voyages to New-England* (Hanover, NH, 1988), 90, 95–96; 88–105 for the whole section on Native New England society and culture. On Josselyn's biography: Lindholdt, editor's "Introduction" to Josselyn, xiii–xxxvii. Crouch republished these sections from Josselyn in *English Empire*, 88–89.

55. John Ogilby, *America: Being the Latest and Most Accurate Description of the New World* (London, 1671).

56. Ogilby, *America*, 162–164.

57. John Ogilby, *Asia, the First Part* (London, 1673), 143–155; 146 for the image of the Hindu temple, which was produced previously in Olfert Dapper and Jacob van Meurs, *Asia, of, Naukeurige beschryving van het rijk des Grooten Mogols . . .* (Amsterdam, 1672). Relying on Dapper and van Meurs, Ogilby undoubtedly meant to convey syncretism, including a mixture of Indian and Zoroastrian (fire) Muslim practice, but did so in a way that did not represent accurately any particular temple. The meaning of the twisted column is obscure. On "Hindu" and "Hinduism" as the late eighteenth-century British nomenclature for the collection of a diverse set of Indian practices and polycentric devotions, see Julius Lipner, "On Hinduism and Hinduisms: The Way of the Banyan," in Sushil Mittal and Gene Thursby, eds., *The Hindu World* (New York, 2004), 9–34.

58. Ogilby, *America*, 198; 200 for the image of Powhatan; 192–205 for the Tidewater; 246–254 for Mexico. The image originated with a Spanish painting of a Native Mexican icon or idol, with no setting around it, published in a 1622 book. In 1671, a European Jesuit redid the image, placing the idol in this elaborate setting: https://www.virginia history.org/collections-and-resources/virginia-history-explorer/early-images-virgi nia-indians/fanciful-figures.

59. Ogilby, *America*, 150 for quotations; 144–155 for the whole on New England Natives; 179 for unnamed New York Native tribes.

60. Ogilby, *America*, 155, 162.

61. Crouch, *Strange and Prodigious Religions*, A2r-v [italics reversed], 7 (the Nova Zembla story), and 20 (dances, cf. Ross, *Pansebia*, 103).

62. Crouch, *Strange and Prodigious Religions*, 1, 55.

63. R. B. [Nathaniel Crouch], *The English Acquisitions in Guinea and East-India* (London, 1700); Ross, *Pansebia*, 97–101. Ross and Crouch had at their disposal Purchas, who had included descriptions of Guinea from Portuguese Jesuit narratives and letters, the travelogue of the Dutch merchant Pieter de Marees, and the recollections of several English merchants: P. E. H. Hair, "Material on Africa (Other than the Mediterranean and the Red Sea Lands) and on the Atlantic Islands, in the Publications of Samuel Purchas, 1613–1626," *History in Africa* 13 (1986): 117–159. Crouch also drew from the accounts of the Royal African Company.

64. Crouch, *English Acquisitions*, 6, 10, 14–17.

65. Crouch, *English Acquisitions*, 13–14, 22.

66. Crouch, *English Acquisitions*, 23–30.

67. Crouch, *English Acquisitions*, 8. Much of this paragraph is informed by Oliver Lindner, "'Savage' Violence and the Colonial Body in Nathaniel Crouch's *The English Acquisitions in Guinea and East India* (1708) and in Edward Cooke's *A Voyage to the South Sea* (1712)," in Rainer Emig and Oliver Lindner, eds., *Othering, Reification, Commodification and the New Literatures and Cultures in English*, ASNEL Papers 127/16 (New York, 2010), 21–40. For analyses of the relations among the study of religions, colonialism, racial tropes, and descriptions of African "fetishism," see David Chidester, *Savage Systems: Colonialism and Comparative Religion in Southern Africa* (Charlottesville, VA, 1996).

68. Crouch, *English Empire*.

69. Crouch, *English Empire*, 33, 165, 62–63, 66–67.

70. Crouch, *English Empire*, 189; after 164 for the image.

71. Crouch, *English Empire*, 67, 69, 74, 88; 70–84 for New England history; 84–91 for priests and spirits. The image is on 189.

72. Henry Winstanley, Geographical Playing Cards, c. 1675, Huntington Library, San Marino, CA. For information on Winstanley, see H. W. Lewer, "Henry Winstanley, Engraver," *Essex Review* 27 (1918): 161–171; and Virginia Wayland, *The Winstanley Geographical Cards* (Pasadena, CA: privately published, 1967, and held in the collections of the Huntington Library), esp. 1–7. For changes in the laws and the popularity of cards: Edward S. Taylor, *The History of Playing Cards* (London, 1865; repr. Rutland, VT, 1973), 162–172, 389–438; and Roger Tilley, *A History of Playing Cards* (New York, 1973), 72–79. Charles Cotton's *The Compleat Gamester* (London, 1674) reflected a reinvigorated interest in card games. Winstanley did not cite his sources. For an essay on a set of playing cards that feature the "Popish Plots" and an interpretation that stresses the ways different "hands" or selections of cards could convey different narratives: Andrew R. Murphy, Gregory Samuelwicz-Zuker, and Susan P. Liebell, "Shuffling Tyranny: Popish Plots, Playing Cards, and Political Theory," in

Evan Haefeli, *Against Popery: Britain, Empire, and Anti-Catholicism* (Charlottesville, VA, 2020), 133–155.

73. Winstanley's cards on western Africa—"Guinea" and "Negro country"—make no mention of religion.

Chapter 2

1. W. D. [Nathaniel Crouch], *Mercy Triumphant in the Conversion of Sinners unto God* (London, 1696), 41–54. See note 6 for dating.

2. Crouch, *Mercy Triumphant*, 41–43. One such spiritual writer for M. K. was Erasmus, favored by puritans for his critique of spiritual laxity and moral corruption within the Catholic Church: Margo Todd, *Christian Humanism and the Puritan Social Order* (New York, 1987), 87–95.

3. Crouch, *Mercy Triumphant*, 44–45.

4. The images are from Revelation 17 and 18, and Matthew 21.

5. Crouch, *Mercy Triumphant*, 47–48.

6. Crouch, *Mercy Triumphant*, 48–50. Dod preached in and around London during the early 1630s, evidence for the dating of M. K.'s story given earlier. In 1632 he advised Cotton about New England: J. Fielding, "Dod, John," *Oxford Dictionary of National Biography*, 60 vols. (New York, 2004) (hereafter ODNB), 16: 384–385.

7. Crouch, *Mercy Triumphant*, 52–54.

8. The earliest printed version of this story that I have been able to find is in Vavasor Powell, *Spiritual Experiences, of Sundry Beleevers* (London, 1653), 160–216. Puritan divines in London accepted Powell as a part of their cohort until he began to express heterodox ideas as a Fifth Monarchist during the late 1650s. For Powell: Stephen K. Roberts, "Powell, Vavasor," ODNB, 45: 121–124.

9. John Eliot and Thomas Mayhew, Jr., *Tears of Repentance* (London, 1653), 12–20. The numbered pages of *Tears*, with the confession of faith, follow thirty unnumbered pages of prefatory material that constitutes a description of the mission and appeal for support. The whole text of *Tears* is included among the so-called Eliot Tracts, a modern edition of which is Michael P. Clark, ed., *The Eliot Tracts: With Letters from John Eliot to Thomas Thorowgood and Richard Baxter* (Westport, CT, 2003).

10. Eliot and Mayhew, *Tears of Repentance*, 16.

11. Eliot and Mayhew, *Tears of Repentance*, 16–17.

12. Eliot and Mayhew, *Tears of Repentance*, 17–18.

13. Eliot and Mayhew, *Tears of Repentance*, 18–20.

14. Daniel K. Richter, *Facing East From Indian Country: A Native History of Early America* (Cambridge, MA, 2001), 110–150; and Charles Cohen, "Conversion Among Puritans and Amerindians: A Theological and Cultural Perspective," in Francis Bremer, ed., *Puritanism: Transatlantic Perspectives on a Seventeenth-Century Anglo-American Faith* (Boston, 1993), 233–256. For a review of much of the literature on differences between Native American and English accounts of conversion, see Linford D. Fisher,

"Native Americans, Conversion, and Christian Practice in Colonial New England, 1640–1730," *Harvard Theological Review* 102 (2009): 101–124.

15. Kristina Bross, *Dry Bones and Indian Sermons: Praying Indians in Colonial America* (Ithaca, NY, 2004); and Jacqueline M. Henkel, "Represented Authenticity: Native Voices in Seventeenth-Century Conversion Narratives," *The New England Quarterly* 87 (2014): 5–45.

16. There are also other interpretations of the political meanings of conversion, such as in Patricia Caldwell, *The Puritan Conversion Narrative: The Beginnings of American Expression* (New York, 1983). Caldwell argues that differences between English and Anglo-American accounts reflect different political situations in part because conversion experiences gave meaning to political trials and dislocations.

17. Lincoln A. Mullen, *The Chance of Salvation: A History of Conversion in America* (Cambridge, MA, 2017), 1–22, helpfully distills the literature on conversion into a similar taxonomy. Mullen relies in part on the current social science literature about the nature of conversion across different traditions as presented in Lewis R. Rambo and Charles E. Farhadian, eds., *The Oxford Handbook of Religious Conversion* (New York, 2014). For a similar taxonomy to Mullen's, see also David A. Snow and Richard Machalek, "The Sociology of Conversion," *Annual Review of Sociology* 10 (1984): 167–190. Although Protestantism and Catholicism are traditions within the religion of Christianity, seventeenth-century polemicists typically treated them as different religions.

18. Charles Lloyd Cohen, *God's Caress: The Psychology of Puritan Religious Experience* (New York, 1986) examines the psychology of the mysterious experience of grace. Caldwell, *Puritan Conversion Narrative* compares conversion accounts from New England and England and identifies the importance of different political contexts for their formulations. Abram Van Engen, *Sympathetic Puritans: Calvinist Fellow Feeling in Early New England* (New York, 2015) shows the theological variety within this paradigm and places the notion of affection at the center of a widespread English and Protestant culture. Unlike much of the contemporary literature, this chapter is devoted to Protestant discourses of conversion rather than to the psychology of the conversion experience. In *Mercy Triumphant*, Crouch includes Knewstub, Rogers, and Dod as counselors and preachers.

19. For one example of the import of these later writers, see Increase Mather, "To the Reader," a preface to Solomon Stoddard, *A Guide to Christ: Or, the Way of Directing Souls that Are Under the Work of Conversion* (Boston, 1714), i–xii. David D. Hall directed me to the Increase Mather text mentioned here, the Hugh Peter text mentioned later, and suggested the nomenclature of a "canon" of practical divinity. For writers such as Bayly and Allestree, and their popularity with Anglicans and dissenters, see especially Charles Hambrick-Stowe, *The Practice of Piety: Puritan Devotional Disciplines in Seventeenth-Century New England* (Chapel Hill, 1982).

20. For confirmation of this point, see Norman Pettit, *The Hear Prepared: Grace and Conversion in Puritan Spiritual Life*, 2nd ed., intro. David D. Hall (Middletown, CT, 1989).

21. Hugh Peter, *A Dying Fathers Last Legacy to an Onely Child: Or, Mr. Hugh Peters Advice to His Daughter* (London, 1661), 120, 38, 3, 31.

22. Peter, *Last Legacy*, 2–3, 5, 10, 31. On Hooker, see Baird Tipson, *Hartford Puritanism: Thomas Hooker, Samuel Stone, and Their Terrifying God* (New York, 2015).

23. Catholic converts to Protestantism such as Neal Carolan and Anthony Egan contended that the absurdities and scandals of the Church of Rome convinced them to abandon the church of their birth and choose the truth of Protestantism. Yet even when relating such tales, authors and editors were wary of the language of liberty of choice. They often interposed details of providential intervention. See Neal Carolan, *Motives of Conversion to the Catholick Faith* [i.e., a critique of such motives] (Dublin, 1688), "Preface," n. p.; and Anthony Egan, *The Franciscan Convert: Or, a Recantation-Sermon of Anthony Egan* (London, 1673), 5. Ever focused on strange events, Crouch included in *Mercy Triumphant* the story of an atheist member of the court of Charles II who was converted through an intolerable urinary pain: Crouch, *Mercy Triumphant*, 155. As Molly Murray has shown with reference to literary figures such as John Donne, the idea of a soulful, affective change rather than a change of beliefs dominated discussions of Catholic to Protestant conversions (and vice versa) during the Restoration: Molly Murray, *The Poetics of Conversion in Early Modern English Literature: Verse and Change from Donne to Dryden* (New York, 2009). For background to the issue of conversion between Catholicism and Protestantism, see Michael C. Questier, *Conversion, Politics and Religion in England, 1580–1625* (New York, 1966). For Elizabethan-era and early Stuart-era descriptions of conversion from one religion to another, see Peter Mazur and Abigail Shinn, eds., "Introduction: Conversion Narratives in the Early Modern World," *Journal of Early Modern History* 17 (2013): 427–436, which introduces a University of York, Centre for Renaissance and Early Modern Studies, project on "Conversion Narratives in the Early Modern World."

24. For a seminal essay on puritan ideas of conversion as important for the English state, see Jearald C. Brauer, "From Puritanism to Revivalism," *The Journal of Religion* 58 (1978): 227–243. For conversion as an issue of moral standing—of guilt and forgiveness—rather than of belief, see D. Bruce Hindmarsh, *The Evangelical Conversion Narrative; Spiritual Autobiography in Early Modern England* (New York, 2005), 33–60.

25. Giovanni Botero, *Commonweales Throughout the World* (London, 1616), 22–23, 62.

26. Sir William Temple, *Observations upon the United Provinces of the Netherlands* (London, 1673), 168.

27. For confirmation of these points, see Steven Nadler, *The Best of All Possible Worlds: A Story of Philosophers, God, and Evil in the Age of Reason* (Princeton, 2010); and Peter Harrison, *"Religion" and the religions in the English Enlightenment* (New York, 1990), 19–60.

28. The first edition of Shepard's *Sincere Convert* was published in London in 1642. Citations here are to Thomas Shepard, *The Sincere Convert* with *The Saint's Jewel* and *The Soul's Invitation* (London, 1669), 10, 182–184.

29. Richard Baxter, *Directions and Perswasions to a Sound Conversion* (London, 1658), A2r; and Richard Baxter, *The Reasons for the Christian Religion* (London, 1667), 198, and "To the Christian Reader," n. p.

30. Joseph Alleine, *An Alarme to Unconverted Sinners* (London, 1672), "An Epistle to the Unconverted Reader," n.p.; 8, 19; Jonathan Clapham, *A Guide to the True Religion: Or a Discourse Directing to Make a Wise Choice of that Religion Men Venture Their Salvation Upon* (Edinburgh, 1669), A2v, 16; Crouch, *Mercy Triumphant*, A3r–A3v.

31. Ample evidence for this is provided in David D. Hall, *The Puritans: A Transatlantic History* (Princeton, 2019).

32. Shepard, *The Sincere Convert*, 196. The term "liberty" here undoubtedly refers to customary civil privileges rather than to political ideas of self-determination or to philosophical notions of freedom of conscience.

33. Thomas Shepard, *The Sound Beleever: A Treatise of Evangelical Conversion* (London, 1653), 169, 260.

34. Goodwife Jane Stevenson, relation of faith, in Mary Rhinelander McCarl, "Thomas Shepard's Record of Relations of Religious Experience, 1648–1649," *William and Mary Quarterly*, 3rd ser., 48 (1991): 432–466, quotation from 443.

35. John Shepard, relation of faith, in McCarl, "Thomas Shepard's Record of Relations," 444–445.

36. George Selement and Bruce C. Woolley, eds., *Thomas Shepard's Confessions*, vol. 58 of the Publications of the Colonial Society of Massachusetts (Boston, 1981).

37. Richard Baxter, *A Treatise of Conversion* (London, 1657), 262 ("let go" and "renounce"); and *Directions and Perswasions*, 287, 504 ("close with Christ" and falling in love).

38. Baxter, *Directions and Perswasions*, A3r–v.

39. [Richard Allestree], *The Whole Duty of Man* (London, 1659), 34; Alleine, *Alarme to Unconverted Sinners*, 158, 183. For Allestree, his mentor Henry Hammond, and their ideas on sin and self-mortification, see Neil Lettinga, "Covenant Theology Turned Upside Down: Henry Hammond and Caroline Anglican Moralism, 1643–1660," *Sixteenth Century Journal* 24 (1993): 653–669.

40. Hambrick-Stowe, *Practice of Piety*, 199.

41. Michael McGiffert, ed., *God's Plot: The Paradoxes of Puritan Piety, Being the Autobiography and Journal of Thomas Shepard* (Amherst, MA, 1972); Tipson, *Hartford Puritanism*; and Baxter, *Conversion*.

42. John Bunyan, *The Pilgrim's Progress* (London 1678 [the first part] and 1684 [the second part]). For the issue of conversion in Bunyan, see Zachary McLeod Hutchins, *Inventing Eden: Primitivism, Millennialism, and the Making of New England* (New York, 2014), 178–208.

43. Thomas Hooker, *The Unbelievers Preparing for Christ* (London, 1638), 41; and *The Souls Preparation for Christ* (London, 1638), 62 ("holy violence"); the other quotations from Hooker, unpublished sermon and miscellaneous reflections, quoted and cited in Tipson, *Hartford Puritanism*, 288.

44. Quoted in Hambrick-Stowe, *Practice of Piety*, 80.

45. Daniel Gookin, relation of faith, in McCarl, "Thomas Shepard's Record of Relations," 454.

46. John Davenport, *God's Call to His People to Turn unto Him; Together with His Promise to Turn unto Them* (Cambridge, MA, 1669), 6.

47. Peter, *Last Legacy*, 2–3.

48. [Christopher Nesse], *The Crown and Glory of a Christian . . . in a Sound Conversion* (London, 1676), 9–11, 22.

49. Baxter, *Conversion*, 10–11.

50. Giles Firmin, *The Real Christian, or a Treatise on Effectual Calling* (London, 1670); see Jonathan Edward Warren, "Polity, Piety, and Polemics: Giles Firmin and the Transatlantic Puritan Tradition," Ph.D. diss., Vanderbilt University, 2014, esp. 132–184.

51. John Flavel, *Divine Conduct, or the Mysterie of Providence* (London, 1678), 32–35.

52. Flavel, *Divine Conduct*, 36–37, 42.

53. Flavel, *Divine Conduct*, 46, 59.

54. For the importance of baptism, family piety, and conformity to the religious order in New England after 1670, see Hambrick-Stowe, *Practice of Piety*, 242–277; and Douglas L. Winiarski, *Darkness Falls on the Land of Light: Experiencing Religious Awakenings in Eighteenth-Century New England* (Chapel Hill, 2017), 25–130.

55. Baxter, *Conversion*, "Epistle Dedicatory," (a)r; and John Cotton, *The Covenant of Gods free Grace* (London, 1645), cited and quoted in C. J. Sommerville, "Conversion Versus the Early Puritan Covenant of Grace," *Journal of Presbyterian History* 44 (1966): 178–197, 193. Sommerville points out that Cotton also criticized what he described as Anglican presumptions that the ritual of baptism, rather than conversion in light of baptism, conferred salvation.

56. Downey's relation of faith, in McCarl, "Thomas Shepard's Record of Relations," 461; Sarah Eastman, relation of faith in the Haverhill, MS, First Congregational Church records, quoted in Winiarski, *Darkness Falls on the Land of Light*, 30; Baxter, *Directions and Perswasions*, inscription on endpaper in a copy held at the Huntington Library, San Marino, CA. McCarl's "Thomas Shepard's Record of Relations of Religious Experience" offers further evidence from Cambridge, MA.

57. Elizabeth Oaks, relation of faith, in McCarl, "Thomas Shepard's Record of Relations," 441–442. For Perkins, see Tipson, *Hartford Puritanism*, 274–286. For the spiritual counsel of the church as a source of communal knowledge of individual's spiritual states, see Brauer, "From Puritanism to Revivalism"; and Sarah Rivett, *The Science of the Soul in Colonial New England* (Chapel Hill, 2011), 23–69.

58. William James, "The Will to Believe," quoted and cited in Mullen, *Chance of Salvation*, 277.

59. For surveys of the abundance of literature on conversion, see Mazur and Shinn, "Introduction: Conversion Narratives in the Early Modern World," 427–436, and subsequent articles. See also Lieke Stelling, "Recent Studies in Religious Conversion," *English Literary Renaissance* 47 (2017): 164–192.

60. For the narrative of missions summarized in this and the following paragraph, see Richard Cogley, *John Eliot's Mission to the Indians Before King Philip's War* (Cambridge, MA, 1999), 1–51; and Bross, *Dry Bones*, 1–27. For the United Colonies, see Neal T. Dugre, "Repairing the Breach: Puritan Expansion, Commonwealth Formation, and

the Origins of the United Colonies of New England, 1630–1643," *The New England Quarterly* 91 (2018): 382–417.

61. I cite later portions of the Eliot Tracts as republished in Clark, ed., *Eliot Tracts*. Clark provides a general introduction to the publications in the "Introduction" to the *Eliot Tracts*, 1–53.

62. Linda Gregerson, "The Commonwealth of the Word: New England, Old England, and the Praying Indians," in Linda Gregerson and Susan Juster, eds. *Empires of God: Religious Encounters in the Early Modern Atlantic* (Philadelphia, 2011), 70–83; 73 for the devotional works. For the importance of Eliot and his translations: Bross, *Dry Bones*, 34, 69–94.

63. Edward Winslow, ed., *The Glorious Progress of the Gospel* (London, 1649), 145–146. The primary and secondary literature on politics, missions, and eschatology is immense and is evaluated in depth in Cogley, *John Eliot's Mission*. For Catholic parallels to this line of thought, see Nicholas Griffith and Fernando Cervantes, eds., *Spiritual Encounters: Interactions Between Christianity and Native American Religions in Colonial America* (Lincoln, NE, 1999). See Michael Leroy Oberg, *Dominion and Civility: English Imperialism and Native America, 1585–1685* (Ithaca, NY, 1999) for the development of ethnocentric imperialism during this period.

64. There are isolated passages in the literature that anticipate outright extermination, but none of the missionaries discussed in this chapter advocated Native genocide. Most of the English observers described non-defensive violence against Native Americans as the tactic of Spanish colonizers in contrast to English. For a discussion of recent literature on many of the issues, including a pointed debate about the Native American experience rather than, as I have summarized here, Protestant discourse, see the essays by David J. Silverman, Christine M. DeLucia, Alyssa Mt. Pleasant, Philip J. Deloria, and Jean M. O'Brien, in *AHR* Exchange: "Historians and Native American and Indigenous Studies," *American Historical Review*, 125 (2020): 517–551.

65. Bross, *Dry Bones*, 112–145; Cogley, *John Eliot's Mission*, 247. To sample Increase Mather's turn of mind, see Increase Mather, *A Relation of the Troubles which Have Hapned in New England* (Boston, 1677). Cotton Mather criticized Mayhew, under whom the Wampanoags of Martha's Vineyard had come to profess Christianity, for being overconfident that the Wampanoags had undergone conversion. In his *India Christiana* (Boston, 1721), Cotton Mather reiterated his critique of Mayhew. For post–King Philip's War debates about the English-ness of "praying Indians," see Louise A. Breen, "Praying with the Enemy: Daniel Gookin, King Philip's War, and the Dangers of Intercultural Mediatorship," in Martin Daunton and Rick Halpern, eds. *Empire and Others: British Encounters with Indigenous Peoples, 1600–1850* (Philadelphia, 1999), 101–122. Papal support for Catholic missions to the Americas similarly declined as hostilities among France, Spain, and England rose during the last quarter of the seventeenth century: Luca Codignola, "The Holy See and the Conversion of the Indians in French and British North America, 1486–1760," in Karen Ordahl Kupperman, ed., *America in European Consciousness, 1493–1750* (Chapel Hill, 1995), 195–242.

66. [Thomas Weld, Hugh Peter, and Henry Dunster (?)], *New Englands First Fruits. In Respect, First of the Conversion of Some, Conviction of Divers, Preparation of Sundry of the Indians* (London, 1643), 2, 4, 5–7.

67. Cogley, *John Eliot's Mission*, 5–9 provides a summary of the stages of evangelization from the establishment of a civil order through catechesis, moral improvement, conversion, and the establishment of churches.

68. Cogley, *John Eliot's Mission*, 41–58, 240–241. Lisa Brooks, *Our Beloved Kin: A New History of King Philip's War* (New Haven, 2018), describes such codes as an assault on a whole way of life and not merely piecemeal behavioral restrictions. The establishment of a colonial regime in itself—including the purchase of lands, adjudication of disputes between tribal groups, and negotiations of treaties between English and Native occupants—assumed the authority of English law over all residents of the Bay Colony. The government of Massachusetts decreed boundaries between townships, legislated the fencing of fields, and established law courts.

69. There is a long-standing debate about the relationship of political, cultural-racial, and religious intentions. For the cultural-racial reading: Neal Salisbury, "Red Puritans: The 'Praying Indians' of Massachusetts Bay and John Eliot," *William and Mary Quarterly*, 3rd ser. 31 (1974): 27–54; for the political reading: Bross, *Dry Bones*; and for a critique of nationalistic readings: Gregerson, "The Commonwealth of the Word." An important study of conversion and Jesuit missions among the Ottawa and Illinois offers insights by way of comparison: French-speaking Jesuits insisted much less on French national identities than English missionaries did on English identities. In addition, Jesuits minimized the agenda of civilizing Native Americans. They emphasized participation in the sacraments, which were celebrated as international and eternal in scope. See Tracy Neal Leavelle, *The Catholic Calumet: Colonial Conversions in French and Indian North America* (Philadelphia, 2012).

70. Eliot in Winslow, ed., *Glorious Progress of the Gospel*, C4v, quoted in Gregerson, "The Commonwealth of the Word," 80; [Thomas Shepard], *The Day-Breaking, If Not the Sun-Rising of the Gospell with the Indians in New England* (London, 1647), 15, quoted in Cogley, *John Eliot's Mission*, 7; and Roger Williams, quoted in Linford D. Fisher and Lucas Mason-Brown, "By 'Treachery and Seduction': Indian Baptism and Conversion in the Roger Williams Code," *William and Mary Quarterly*, 3rd ser. 71 (2014): 175–202, quote from 191. For the New England Company leaders: William Kellaway, *The New England Company, 1649–1776: Missionary Society to the American Indians* (New York, 1961), 81–121.

71. See, e.g. William Crashaw, *A Sermon Preached . . . Before . . . the Lord La Ware* (London, 1610), C4v; and Solomon Stoddard, *Question: Whether God Is Not Angry with the Country for Doing So Little Towards the Conversion of the Indians?* (Boston, 1723), 9. See further evidence in Alden T. Vaughan, *Roots of American Racism: Essays on the Colonial Experience* (New York, 1995), 44–49.

72. Richard Mather in Eliot and Mayhew, *Tears of Repentance*, in Clark, ed., *The Eliot Tracts*, 264.

73. [Thomas Shepard], *The Day-Breaking*, in Clark, ed., *Eliot Tracts*, 86.

74. Richard Mather in Eliot and Mayhew, *Tears of Repentance*, in Clark, ed., *The Eliot Tracts*, 264; Monequassun's relation of faith in *Tears of Repentance*, in Clark, ed., *The Eliot Tracts*, 276.

75. Shepard, *The Day-Breaking* in Clark, ed., *Eliot Tracts*, 84, 92–93. For one example of a convert who, as the central tenet of her faith, believed in Christ's death for her: Winslow, ed., *Glorious Progress*, in Clark, ed., *Eliot Tracts*, 151.

76. Eliot reiterated many of these and other such questions in dialogue form, clearly invented in detail but taken from experience. He intended these to teach Christian Indians how to respond to the questions of their people: John Eliot, *Indian Dialogues for Their Instruction in that Great Service of Christ* (London, 1671). The questions of Eliot's interlocutors suggest to James Ronda a form of Indian resistance to Protestant indoctrination, just as Huron criticisms of Jesuit teaching displayed resistance to Catholic indoctrination: James P. Ronda, "'We Are Well as We Are': An Indian Critique of Seventeenth-Century Christian Missions," *The William and Mary Quarterly*, 3rd ser. 34 (1977): 66–82.

77. John Elliot [Eliot], *A Brief Narrative of the Progress of the Gospel Among the Indians in New England* (London, 1671), 5.

78. John Eliot, *A Primer or Catechism, in the Massachusetts Indian Language* (Cambridge, MA, 1654), known as *The Indian Primer*; and Abraham Pierson, *Some Helps for the Indians Shewing Them How to Improve Their Natural Reason, to Know the True God, and the True Christian Religion* (Cambridge, MA, [1659], misdated as 1658). For these catechisms, see Cogley, *John Eliot's Mission*, 119–120, 185.

79. David J. Silverman, "Indians, Missionaries, and Religious Translation: Creating Wampanoag Christianity in Seventeenth-Century Martha's Vineyard," *William and Mary Quarterly*, 3rd ser. 62 (2005): 141–174; Bross, *Dry Bones*, 81. For a full study of Mayhew's mission on Martha's Vineyard: David J. Silverman, *Faith and Boundaries: Colonists, Christianity, and Community Among the Wampanoag Indians of Martha's Vineyard, 1600–1871* (New York, 2005).

80. Allison Margaret Bigelow, "Imperial Translations: New World Missionary Linguistics, Indigenous Interpreters, and Universal Languages in the Early Modern Era," in Bryce Traister, ed., *American Literature and the New Puritan Studies* (New York, 2017), 93–110.

81. Sarah Rivett, "Learning to Write Algonquian Letters: The Indigenous Place of Language Philosophy in the Seventeenth-Century Atlantic World," *William and Mary Quarterly*, 3rd ser. 71 (2014): 549–588.

82. French Jesuit missionaries used visual and mnemonic systems to convey western Christian concepts and overcame such resistance more readily than did their English counterparts: Sarah Rivett, *Unscripted America: Indigenous Languages and the Origins of a Literary Nation* (New York, 2017).

83. John Eliot, *The Indian Grammar Begun* (London, 1666), A2v.

84. Mayhew letters in Henry Whitfield, ed., *Strength out of Weaknesse* (London 1652), in Clark, ed., *The Eliot Tracts*, 238–241; and Winslow, ed., *Glorious Progress*, in Clark, ed., *Eliot Tracts*, 149.

85. Matthew Dimmock, "Converting and Not Converting 'Strangers' in Early Modern England," *Journal of Early Modern History* 17 (2013): 457–478, quote from 473.

86. There is some ambiguity about the role of voluntary "choice" in this resolution. It might seem at first glance that English rule allowed for no option outside of conformity. The General Court of Massachusetts Bay enacted laws against blasphemy and idolatry in 1646, which theoretically prohibited traditional religious practices and voided the concept of voluntary choice. New England's magistrates, however, understood the legislation to proscribe explicit assaults on the Christian God from within English communities and not to apply to traditional Native practices. The laws were never enforced until a few isolated cases came to trial in the late 1660s: Cogley, *John Eliot's Mission*, 41–43.

87. This interpretation of the issue of insincerity differs from the reading given by Bross, *Dry Bones*, 79–83. For Christianized Indians who retained traditional practices: Douglas L. Winiarski, "Native American Popular Religion in New England's Old Colony, 1670–1770," *Religion and American Culture* 15 (2005): 147–186.

88. Protestant consternation at Natives who held on to traditional practices lasted into the eighteenth century: Daniel K. Richter, "'Some of Them . . . Would Always Have a Minister with Them': Mohawk Protestantism, 1683–1719," *American Indian Quarterly* 16 (1992): 471–484. For Jesuit tolerance of Native ceremony: Leavelle, *The Catholic Calumet*, 1–18, 126–153.

89. For an overview of issues of translation and conversion accounts: Alison Stanley, "The Reformation of Their Disordered Lives: Portraying Cultural Adaptation in the Seventeenth-Century Praying Indian Towns," in Robin Peel and Daniel Maudlin, eds., *Transatlantic Traffic and (Mis)Translations* (Durham, NH, 2013), 87–111. See also Cogley, *John Eliot's Mission*, 135; and Cohen, "Conversion Among Puritans and Amerindians."

90. For Eliot's reliance on Baxter and Shepard: Cogley, *John Eliot's Mission*, 136; Gregerson, "The Commonwealth of the Word," 73; and Bross, *Dry Bones*, 94. For confirmation of the view of conversion presented here: Annie Parker, "Conversion in Theory and Practice: John Eliot's Mission to the Indians," in James Muldoon, ed., *The Spiritual Conversion of the Americas* (Gainesville, FL, 2004), 78–98.

91. Quote from Cogley, *John Eliot's Mission*, 129. Alison Stanley, "The Reformation of Their Disordered Lives," 105–108, rehearses the story of Nishohkou.

92. Thomas Shepard, *The Clear Sun-Shine of the Gospel Breaking Forth upon the Indians in New England* (London, 1648), in Clark, ed., *The Eliot Tracts*, 138.

93. Winslow, ed., *Glorious Progress*, 148.

94. Winiarski, "Native American Popular Religion in New England's Old Colony."

95. For a helpful discussion of the existential trials of conversion, see Robert James Naeher, "John Eliot and the Indian Exploration of Puritanism as a Source of Meaning," *The New England Quarterly* 62 (1989): 346–368. For the numbers of residents and converts, Cogley, *John Eliot's Mission*, 137, 142–143. There were an additional 250 converts on Martha's Vineyard.

96. The covenant is quoted in Cogley, *John Eliot's Mission*, 112; Shepard, *The Day-Breaking*, in Clark, ed., *Eliot Tracts*, 89–90l; and, for family and clan: Winiarski, "Native American Popular Religion in New England's Old Colony."

97. Cogley, *John Eliot's Mission* 168–169. During the war, the General Court of Massachusetts disbanded most of the praying towns and took direct control over the remaining ones. It took nearly half a century before Protestants resumed missionary activities on a large scale in New England: Bross, *Dry Bones*, 146–185.

98. Eliot and Mayhew, *Tears of Repentance*, 223, quoted in Bross, *Dry Bones*, 23; the quotation from the English divines is cited in Gregerson, "The Commonwealth of the Word," 78. For other evidence, see Bross, *Dry Bones*, 104, 126–129; and Kristina Bross, "From London to Nonantum: Mission Literature in the Transatlantic English World," in Gregerson and Juster, eds., *Empires of God*, 123–142.

Chapter 3

1. Burnet had preached before James's brother, Charles II, and had been appointed chaplain of Rolls Chapel but had fallen out of favor with the Court. James's antipathy was predictable: Martin Greig, "Burnet, Gilbert," *Oxford Dictionary of National Biography*, 60 vols. (New York, 2004) 8: 908–923; and Tony Claydon, *William III and the Godly Revolution* (Cambridge, U.K., 1996).

2. Gilbert Burnet, *Some Letters, Containing an Account of What Seemed Most Remarkable in Traveling Through Switzerland, Italy, etc.* (Rotterdam, 1686). I have cited the following edition, which was popular in mid-eighteenth-century New England: Gilbert Burnet, *Dr. Burnet's Travels* (London, 1737). For the popularity of Burnet's *Travels*, see Jonathan Edwards, *The Works of Jonathan Edwards*, Perry Miller and Harry S. Stout, gen eds., 26 vols. (New Haven, 1957–2008), vol. 26: *Catalogues of Books*, ed. Peter J. Thuesen, 357.

3. Burnet, *Travels*, v. For Burnet and Catholicism, see Tony Claydon, "Latitudinarianism and Apocalyptic History in the Worldview of Gilbert Burnet, 1643–1715," *The Historical Journal* 51 (2008): 577–597.

4. The council did so without deliberation, a pleasant surprise for Burnet. There is evidence that the leaders of Geneva increasingly tolerated religious dissent soon before and after the Revocation of the Edict of Nantes in 1685: Jennifer Powell McNutt, *Calvin Meets Voltaire: The Clergy of Geneva in the Age of Enlightenment, 1685–1798* (Burlington, Vermont, 2013), 25–67.

5. Burnet, *Travels*, 7, 212–213.

6. Burnet, *Travels*, 53–55, 35–36.

7. Burnet, *Travels*, 229–231.

8. Burnet, *Travels*, 231.

9. Burnet, *Travels*, 2, iv, xv, 39, 5.

10. See esp. Owen Stanwood, *The Empire Reformed: English America in the Age of the Glorious Revolution* (Philadelphia, 2011).

11. E.g. Scott Sowerby, *Making Toleration: The Repealers and the Glorious Revolution* (Cambridge, MA, 2013). For an account of literature on the rise of tolerationist ideas during the early 1680s, see Jonathan Koch, "'The Phanaticks Tyring Room': Dryden and the Poetics of Toleration," *Studies in Philology* 116 (2019): 539–567.

12. Steve Pincus, *1688: The First Modern Revolution* (New Haven, 2009), for state-building agendas; Alexandra Walsham, *Charitable Hatred: Tolerance and Intolerance in England, 1500–1700* (New York, 2006) for cyclical patterns; and Ethan H. Shagan, *The Rule of Moderation: Violence, Religion and the Politics of Restraint in Early Modern England* (New York, 2011) for the legitimization of hegemonic power through the rhetoric of moderation.

13. This and the following three paragraphs are based on the essays in Ole Peter Grell, Jonathan I. Israel, and Nicholas Tyacke, eds., *From Persecution to Toleration: The Glorious Revolution in Religion in England* (Oxford, 1991) (hereafter GIT); J. G. A. Pocock, "The Varieties of Whiggism from Exclusion to Reform: A History of Ideology and Discourse," in J. G. A. Pocock, *Virtue, Commerce, and History: Essays on Political Thought and History, Chiefly in the Eighteenth Century* (New York, 1985), 215–310; and Sowerby, *Making Toleration*.

14. "Whig" originated as a term for those who supported the exclusion of Catholics from the throne and conditions on dynastic succession, along with parliamentary restraints on absolutism. "Tory" referred to those who opposed "Exclusion" as an absolute law and favored what they thought of as the ancient privilege of dynastic succession and a court with power over Parliament, even though they opposed James. See also the brief discussion of the Exclusion Crisis in Chapter 1.

15. Jonathan I. Israel, "William III and Toleration," in GIT, 129–170; and Pincus, *1688*, 404–411.

16. For events in New England, see Richard S. Dunn, "The Glorious Revolution in America," in Nicholas Canny, ed., Alaine Low, asst. ed., *The Oxford History of the British Empire*, vol. 1: *The Origins of Empire: British Overseas Enterprise to the Close of the Seventeenth Century* (New York, 1998): 445–466.

17. Jacobite critics of the invasion in turn raised the specter of anarchy—a return to the sort of misrule that characterized the Interregnum—even as they too deployed the rhetoric of English liberty: Tony Claydon, "William III's Declaration of Reasons and the Glorious Revolution," *The Historical Journal* 39 (1996): 87–108.

18. For the extent and language of political pamphleteering or propaganda, see Lois G. Schwoerer, "Propaganda in the Revolution of 1688–89," *The American Historical Review* 82 (1977): 843–874; and Claydon, "William III's Declaration." For different perspectives on the extent of toleration actually implemented, see the essays in GIT.

19. Israel, "William III and Toleration," 138–139 (for the Dutch tract); and [Gilbert Burnet], *An Inquiry into the Measures of Submission to the Supream Authority* (London, 1688).

20. William III, *The Declaration of His Highness William Henry . . . Prince of Orange, Etc. Of the Reasons Inducing Him, to Appear in Armes in the Kingdom of England, for Preserving of the Protestant Religion, and for Restoring the Lawes and Liberties of England . . .* (The Hague, 1688).

21. William III, *Declaration*, 4–5. For its ubiquity, see Schwoerer, "Propaganda in the Revolution." Claydon, "William III's Declaration," admits that the tract was widespread but argues that it was not particularly effective as a propaganda tool.

22. William III, *Declaration*, 7.

23. Israel, "William III and Toleration."

24. [Anon.], *King William's Toleration: Being an Examination of that Liberty of Religion, Which May be Expected from His Majesty's Declaration, with a Bill for Comprehension and Indulgence* (London, 1689), 3, 9. A similar tract is [T. Long], *Reflections upon a Late Book, Entitled the Case of Allegiance Consider'd* (London, 1689).

25. See Michael P. Winship, "Godly Republicanism and the Origins of the Massachusetts Polity," *WMQ* 3rd ser. 63 (2006): 427–462.

26. [Cotton Mather], *The Declaration, of the Gentlemen, Merchants, and Inhabitants of Boston . . . April 18th, 1689* (Boston, 1689), n.p.; Cotton Mather, *Parentator* (Boston, 1724), 112. The most extensive statement of Mather in this regard was his *Eleutheria* (Boston, 1698). See Rick Kennedy, "*Eleutheria* (1698): Cotton Mather's History of the Idea of Liberty That Links the Reformation to the Glorious Revolution and the American Revolution," in Peter C. Messer and William Harrison Taylor, eds., *Revolution as Reformation: Protestant Faith in the Age of Revolutions, 1688-1832* (Tuscaloosa, AL, 2021), 28–39.

27. [Daniel Defoe], *King William's Affection to the Church of England Examin'd* (London, 1703), 3, 17, 23.

28. For Locke's influence, see John Marshall, *John Locke, Toleration, and Early Enlightenment Culture* (New York, 2006); and Sowerby, *Making Toleration*, 10, 256–259.

29. John Locke, *Epistola de Tolerantia* (Gouda, 1689); and *A Letter on Toleration* (London, 1689). I have used an edition with paired Latin and English versions, published under the title *Epistola de Tolerantia: A Letter on Toleration*, the Latin edition edited, with a "Preface," by Raymond Kilbansky, and the English edition translated with an "Introduction" by J. W. Gough (Oxford, 1969). Kilbansky's "Preface," vii–xliv, provides the information about the dates and circumstances of the letter. (For the letter itself, I will cite it as follows: Locke, *Letter*.)

30. Locke, *Letter*, 65–77.

31. Locke, *Letter*, 113, 115.

32. Gough, "Introduction," 3–10; and Sowerby, *Making Toleration*, 256–259.

33. It did so by waving the requirement for clergy to subscribe to Articles Twenty and Thirty-Four through Thirty-Six of the Thirty-Nine Articles, which dealt with church traditions, rituals and ceremonies, and episcopal polity and authority.

34. William and Mary, "An Act for Exempting their Majestyes Protestant Subjects dissenting from the Church of England from the Penalties of certaine Lawes" [Chapter XVIII.Rot.Parl. pt. 5. nu 15], accessed online at http://www.british-history.ac.uk/report.aspx?compid=46304. For background, Nicholas Tyacke, "The 'Rise of Puritanism' and the Legalizing of Dissent, 1571-1719," in GIT, 17–49, esp. 19.

35. [Increase Mather], *A Brief Account Concerning Several of the Agents of New-England . . . with Some Remarks on the New Charter* (London, 1691), 5, 8.

36. Increase Mather, *Brief Account*, 14, with "An Extract of a Letter . . . by some of the most Eminent *Nonconformist Divines in London*," 24.

37. Much of the material on Cotton Mather in this and following paragraphs takes its cues from an unpublished paper by Jan Stievermann, "Cotton Mather's Biblical Politics of Religious Toleration," given at the March 2018 conference on "Religion and Politics in Early America," Society of Early Americanists, St. Louis, MO.

38. Cotton Mather, *Parentator*, 57–58, 61. For debates about toleration in Massachusetts: Kenneth Silverman, *The Life and Times of Cotton Mather* (New York, 1984), 55–82 and 138–156; and Adrian Chastain Weimer, "Elizabeth Hooton and the Lived Politics of Toleration in Massachusetts Bay," *WMQ* 74 (2017): 43–76. For evidence of the diversification of religious life in New England at the close of the seventeenth century, along with changing perceptions in New England of affairs in London, see Joseph A. Conforti, *Saints and Strangers: New England in British North America* (Baltimore, 2006).

39. Cotton Mather, *Parentator*, 58–59. Mather's reference to the French is somewhat oblique but it is quite plausible that he referred to official royal statements from Paris, which admitted the point about belief. For one of Mather's most extensive discussions of Locke and toleration, see his *Eleutheria*.

40. Quotes in Silverman, *Cotton Mather*, 141; and [Cotton Mather], *Manuductio ad Ministerium: Directions for a Candidate for the Ministry* (Boston, 1726), 127.

41. For the progressive reading, see Tyacke, "The 'Rise of Puritanism'"; for the revolutionary and statist reading, Pincus, *1688*; and Elizabeth A. Prichard, *Religion in Public: Locke's Political Theology* (Stanford, CA, 2014); and for the conservative reading, John Spurr, "The Church of England, Comprehension and the Toleration Act of 1689," *English Historical Review* 104 (1989): 927–946; and Shagan, *The Rule of Moderation*. Many recent works have stressed the limits placed on toleration or even the hegemonic agendas hidden by the discourse of moderation, perhaps more so than is warranted: Ethan H. Shagan, ed., "Introduction" to *Catholics and the Protestant Nation: Religious Politics and Identity in Early Modern England* (Manchester, U.K., 2005), 1–21; Walsham, *Charitable Hatred*; Benjamin J. Kaplan, *Divided by Faith: Religious Conflict and the Practice of Toleration in Early Modern Europe* (Cambridge, MA, 2007); and the "Critical Forum" on Stuart B. Schwartz, *All Can Be Saved: Religious Tolerance and Salvation in the Iberian Atlantic World* (New Haven, 2008), with comments by Lu Ann Hozma, David D. Hall, Marcy Norton, Andrew R. Murphey, and Stuart B. Schwartz, *William and Mary Quarterly*, 3rd ser. 66 (2009): 409–433.

42. Tyacke, "The 'Rise of Puritanism.'"

43. John Bossy, "English Catholics After 1688," in GIT, 369–387. Bossy also shows that Catholics were adept at maneuvering around occasional acts, such as the Land Tax, that encumbered Catholic landholding. For the general history of toleration in post-1688 America: Evan Haefeli, "Toleration and Empire: The Origins of

American Religious Pluralism," in Stephen Foster, ed., *Oxford History of the British Empire: British North America in the Seventeenth and Eighteenth Centuries* (Oxford, 2003), 103–135.

44. Tyacke, "The 'Rise of Puritanism,'" 41–43 for the growth of dissent and Lord Mayor; Grell, Israel, and Tyacke, editors' "Introduction" to GIT for post-1689 legislation. For radical enthusiasm, see Lionel Laborie, "Radical Tolerance in Early Enlightenment Europe," *History of European Ideas* 43 (2017): DOI: 10.1080/01916599.2016.1203600. For confirmation of the argument here about the breakdown of the confessional order and alliance between Whig politics and religious liberty, see Hugh Trevor-Roper, "Toleration and Religion After 1688," in GIT, 389–408; Katherine Engel, "Connecting Protestants in Britain's Eighteenth-Century Atlantic Empire," *WMQ* 75 (2018): 37–70; and Pincus, *1688*, 407–425.

45. Pestana, *Protestant Empire*, discusses the "Protestant interest" but ties it more closely to peculiarly English and imperial identities than I suggest here.

46. Sirota, *The Christian Monitors*, for cooperation; for the defense of Christian belief in ecumenical, theological terms; see Dewey D. Wallace, Jr., *Shapers of English Calvinism, 1660-1714* (New York, 2011).

47. Israel, "William III and Toleration," 164–165; Claydon, "Latitudinarianism and Apocalyptic History in the Worldview of Gilbert Burnet," esp. 595; Richard H. Popkin, "The Deist Challenge," in GIT, 195–215; Laborie, "Radical Tolerance in Early Enlightenment Europe" (for toleration of radical groups); and Andrew Pettegree, "The French and Waloon Communities in London, 1550-1688," in GIT, 77–96.

48. Mather, *Parentator*, 141.

49. Cotton Mather, *India Christiana* (Boston, 1721), 66 (for Gründler); Oliver Scheiding, "The World as Parish: Cotton Mather, August Hermann Francke, and Transatlantic Religious Networks," in Reiner Smolinski and Jan Stievermann, eds., *Cotton Mather and Biblia Americana—America's First Bible Commentary: Essays in Reappraisal* (Tübingen, Germany, 2010; repr. Grand Rapids, MI, 2011), 131–166. See also Jan Stievermann, *Prophecy, Piety, and the Problem of Historicity: Interpreting the Hebrew Scriptures in Cotton Mather's Biblia Americana* (Tübingen, Germany, 2016), 92–95. For Sewall and international Protestantism: Mark Peterson, *The City-State of Boston: The Rise and Fall of an Atlantic Power* (Princeton, 2019), 205–206.

50. [Cotton Mather], *Manuductio ad Ministerium*, (Boston, 1726), 119, 125, 129.

51. Locke to Philippus van Limborch, 6 June 1689, in E. S. DeBeer, ed., *The Correspondence of John Locke*, 8 vols. (Oxford, 1976–1989), 3: 633.

52. "The Fundamental Constitutions of Carolina: March 1, 1669," online version http://avalon.law.yale.edu/17th_century/nc05.asp#3. David Armitage has argued that Locke's version of English colonization and empire pointedly excluded claims over religious practice: "John Locke: Theorist of Empire?," in Sankar Muthu, ed., *Empire and Modern Political Thought* (Cambridge, MA, 2012), 84–111, online version http://nrs.harvard.edu/urn-3:HUL.InstRepos:10718367.

53. For an effective and well-annotated summary of party politics in the period: Tony Claydon, *Europe and the Making of England, 1660-1760* (New York, 2007), 220–353.

54. Cotton Mather, *Parentator*, 58–59.

55. The quote about new European mores appeared in English in Pierry Bayle, *A Philosophical Commentary on . . . Luke XIV.23*, 2 vols. (London, 1708), 1: 7, quoted in Kaplan, *Divided by Faith*, 333. Bayle's comments on Moréri come from Pierre Bayle, *An Historical and Critical Dictionary. By Monsieur Bayle*, 4 vols. (London, 1710), "Preface to the First French Edition," n. p. For Bayle and Moréri and how Bayle would have been read by his contemporaries as a Protestant despite his skepticism: Paul Burrell, "Pierre Bayle's Dictionnaire historique et critique," in Frank A. Kafker, ed., *Notable Encyclopedias of the Seventeenth and Eighteenths Centuries: Nine Predecessors of the Encyclopédie*, no. 194 of Studies on Voltaire and the Eighteenth Century (Oxford, 1981), 83–103. Nearly every catalogue of books from this period that I have searched, from Locke's personal listing to those of clerical libraries (including the Mathers and, later, Jonathan Edwards) and colonial colleges, includes Bayle. Locke respected Bayle but criticized Bayle's epistemological skepticism and promotion of toleration for atheism: Alex Schulman, "The Twilight of Probability: Locke, Bayle, and the Toleration of Atheism," *The Journal of Religion* 89 (2009): 328–360. For Bayle and the 1688 revolutions: Byran A. Banks, "Pierre Bayle's Revolutionary Script: Protestant Apologetics and the 1688 Revolutions in England and Thailand," in Peter C. Messer and William Harrison Taylor, eds., *Revolution as Reformation: Protestant Faith in the Age of Revolutions, 1688–1832* (Tuscaloosa, AL, 2021), 13–27.

56. Bayle, *Historical and Critical Dictionary*, 3: 2095, 2097 ("Mahomet").

57. Patrick Gordon, *Geography Anatomized: Or, a Compleat Geographical Grammer* (London, 1693). I have used and hereafter cite the sixth edition: Patrick Gordon, *Geography Anatomiz'd: Or, the Geographical Grammar*, 6th ed. (London, 1711). For Gordon's biography: W. K. Lowther Clarke, *Eighteenth Century Piety* (London, 1944), 91–95; for American newspapers and Gordon: Thomas S. Kidd, "'Let Hell and Rome Do Their Worst': World News, Anti-Catholicism, and International Protestantism in Early-Eighteenth-Century Boston," *New England Quarterly* 76 (2003): 265–290.

58. Gordon, *Geography Anatomiz'd*, A3r–A4v, 217, 219–220, 85–101, 173.

59. Gordon, *Geography Anatomiz'd*, 324, 366.

60. William Turner, *The History of All Religions in the World* (London, 1695), italics reduced.

61. Turner, "Epistle Dedicatory," in *History of Religions*, A3r.

62. Turner, "To the Reader," in *History of Religions*, n.p.

63. Turner, "To the Reader," in *History of Religions*, n.p.; and 504–589 (for the conversions and encounters).

64. Cotton Mather, *Manuductio ad Ministerium*, 70. Moréri began the dictionary in Paris in 1670; it was first published in Lyon in 1674 as a single-volume work. For a general discussion of Moréri: Arnold Miller, "Louis Moréri's Grand dictionnaire historique," in Kafker, ed., *Notable Encyclopedias of the Seventeenth and Eighteenths Centuries*, 13–52. Edwards consulted the following edition, which I have used here: Lewis Morery [Louis Moréri], *The Great Historical, Geographical, Genealogical and Poetical Dictionary*, 2nd ed., revised by Jeremy Collier (London, 1701) (hereafter Moréri). Edwards referred to it as "Collier's Dictionary." Collier's revision of Moréri

was expanded to 4 vols. (London, 1705). For references to Mather, Clarke, Moréri, and Edwards, see Jonathan Edwards, *The Works of Jonathan Edwards* (New Haven, 2008), vol. 26: *Catalogues of Books*, ed. Peter J. Thuesen 67, 77, 177–178, 253. Clarke in fact urged would-be scholars such as Edwards to read authors not of their own "Sect" and "Papists and Protestants" to reach each others: John Clarke, *An Essay upon Study* (London, 1737), 48, 52. For evidence of Protestant use of Catholic biblical scholarship and ancient history, see Jonathan Sheehan, *The Enlightenment Bible* (Princeton, 2005); and Reiner Smolinski, ed., "Introduction" to *Cotton Mather and Biblia Americana*, 10 vols. (Tübingen, Germany, 2010–2022), vol. 1: *Genesis*, ed. Reiner Smolinski (2010), 3–210, esp. 77–174. For the college libraries mentioned here, see Harvard College, *Catalogus Librorum Bibliotechae Collegii Havardini* (Boston, 1723), 11; and Yale College, *A Catalogue of Books in the Library of Yale-College* (New Haven, 1755), 13.

65. Collier, in "The Preface" to Moréri, n.p. There is no pagination in Moréri; all subsequent references to Moréri may be located under the word entry of the dictionary. Collier, a nonjuring priest (i.e., he refused to take an oath of allegiance to William of Orange) known as an irascible pedant and critic of the stage, nearly doubled the size of Moréri's original work, making it two volumes.

66. John Locke, "A Catalogue and Character of Most Books of Voyages and Travels," in *The Works of John Locke*, 9 vols. (London, 1824), 9: 522–564 for Locke's bibliography and commentary as a whole; 546 for the quote (see also 552). For the relative size of the library, see Armitage, "John Locke: Theorist of Empire?," 6, 11, 19 (pagination in the online version).

67. John Stoddard, "Stoddard's Journal," *New England Historical and Genealogical Register* 5 (1851): 21–42.

68. Stoddard, "Journal," 26, 28.

69. Stoddard, "Journal," 28–30.

70. Stoddard, "Journal," 29–30, 33.

71. Stoddard, "Journal," 34–35.

72. Stoddard, "Journal," 36.

73. For France, I have used John Lough, ed., *Locke's Travels in France, 1675–1679* (New York, 1953), which includes Locke's journal from two separate journeys (hereafter, *Locke's Travels*). For the Netherlands and Locke's other comments in this section, I have used transcriptions of Locke's manuscript journals from 1684 and 1686 at the Bodleian Library, Oxford University, Oxford, U.K., transcriptions by Daniel K. Richter and kindly shared with me (hereafter "Locke's Journals"). Locke also visited the house churches of Labadists—a small Reformed sect known for its communal living and radical primitivism—who promoted toleration. For the Armenian Catholics and Labadists, see "Locke's Journals," MS. Locke, f. 8, 100–103, 114–121. For observations on relics, *Locke's Travels*, 138, 221–222; for anti-Huguenot persecution, *Locke's Travels*, 41, 89–90.

74. Peter Lake, "Anti-Popery: The Structure of a Prejudice," in Richard Cust and Ann Hughes, eds., *Conflict in Early Stuart England: Studies in Religion and Politics, 1601–1642* (New York, 1989): 72–106; Owen Stanwood, "The Protestant

Moment: Antipopery, the Revolution of 1688–1689, and the Making of an Anglo-American Empire," *Journal of British Studies* 46 (2007): 481–508. Stanwood maintains in addition that English proponents of empire contrasted Whig, constitutional, and commercial agendas with French, Catholic, and absolutist imperial agendas. The best essay from a large literature on English and New England anti-Catholicism is Owen Stanwood, "Catholics, Protestants, and the Clash of Civilizations in Early America," in Chris Beneke and Christopher S. Grenda, eds., *The First Prejudice: Religious Tolerance and Intolerance in Early America* (Philadelphia, 2011): 218–240.

75. Gilbert Burnet, *Bishop Burnet's History of His Own Time*, 3 vols. (London, 1725), 3: 1120, quoted in Kaplan, *Divided by Faith*, 337.

76. Jonathan Belcher, "A Journal of My Intended Voyage and Journey to Holland, Hannover Beginning at London Saturday July 8th: O.S. 1704," manuscript at the Massachusetts Historical Society, Boston. I have used a transcription made and kindly provided by Mark Peterson. Ebenezer Pemberton, Belcher's pastor, preached a sermon clearly intended in part to prepare Belcher for the trip. Known for his ecumenical, latitudinarian spirit, Pemberton regarded long journeys as occasions to demonstrate learning, politeness, and tolerance rather than confessional zeal: Ebenezer Pemberton, *Advice to a Son* (London, 1705). For Belcher's biography: Michael C. Batinski, *Jonathan Belcher, Colonial Governor* (Lexington, KY, 1996); for Belcher's journey: Peterson, *City-State of Boston*, 206–217.

77. Belcher, "Journal," 7–8, 13–21, 29–30, 33 (manuscript pages as noted in Peterson's transcription).

78. Belcher, "Journal," 37, 46–48, 53.

79. Belcher, "Journal," 59–60; 56–61 for the whole Hanover to Berlin portion.

80. Belcher, "Journal," 73–74, 76–78, 82. Leibniz gave his reflections on Islam and Confucianism in his correspondence, selections of which were edited and published in the 1710s. See, e.g., [Anon.], *Four Treatises Concerning the Doctrine, Discipline, and Worship of the Mahometans* [with Leibniz's correspondence included] (London, 1712); and Gottfried Wilhelm Leibniz, *Discourse on the Natural Theology of the Chinese*, trans., intro. Henry Rosemont, Jr. and Daniel J. Cook (Honolulu, HI, 1977).

81. The quote is from a popular tract that purports to recount the nefarious attempts of a priest to convert the daughter of a Protestant aristocrat: [Anon.], *An Account of the Seducing of Ann* (n.p., 1700), 3. For another widely published account in such terms, see [D. Aubon], *The French Convert* (Boston, 1725). For an oft-published account of an Italian convert whose conversion was a matter of being rationally persuaded of the truth of Protestant teaching: [Niccolo Balbani], *The Italian Convert* (London, 1689), with frequent reprintings, including Boston, 1751.

82. For criticism of Jesuit missions: Evan Haefeli and Owen Stanwood, "Jesuits, Huguenots, and the Apocalypse: The Origins of America's First French Book," *Proceedings of the American Antiquarian Society* 116/1 (2006): 59–119; and Laura M. Stevens, *The Poor Indians: British Missionaries, Native Americans, and Colonial Sensibility* (Philadelphia, 2004), 80–81.

83. Joseph Baxter, "Journal of the Rev. Joseph Baxter of Medfield, Missionary to the Eastern Indians in 1717," *New England Historical and Genealogical Register* 21 (1867): 45–60, quotations from 49, 51, 53–54.

84. Humphrey Prideaux's 1697 *The True Nature of Imposture*, which went through eight editions to 1723, served as a primer for Islamic theology and arguments that Islam—with its denial of the divinity of Jesus—was a fraudulent form of deism. New England preachers relied on Hakluyt, Purchas, Sandys, Richard Knolles, Peter Heylyn, and Louis LeComte for their information: Thomas S. Kidd, "'Is It Worse to Follow Mahomet than the Devil?': Early American Uses of Islam," *Church History* 72 (2003): 766-790; Mukhtar Ali Isani, "Cotton Mather and the Orient," *The New England Quarterly* 43 (1970): 46-58; and Mukhtar Ali Isani, "Edward Taylor and the 'Turks,'" *Early American Literature* 7 (1972): 120-123.

85. Twenty-two such accounts were published in London from 1577 to 1704, excerpts and reprints of which appeared in Boston. For a survey of such publications, see Nabil Matar, "Introduction" to *Piracy, Slavery, and Redemption: Barbary Captivity Narratives from Early Modern England*, ed. Daniel J. Vitkus and Nabil Matar (New York, 2001), 1-53. For an account of the extent of the enslavement of English people and the alarm it raised through English society and among architects of empire: Catherine M. Styer, "Barbary Pirates, British Slaves, and the Early Modern Atlantic World, 1570-1800," Ph.D. diss., University of Pennsylvania, 2011.

86. William Oakley's 1676 *Ebenezer* went through several editions through 1764, including several reprints on the eve of the revolution of 1688: William Oakley, *Ebenezer: Or, a Small Monument of Great Mercy* (London, 1676), in Vitkus and Matar, eds., *Piracy, Slavery, and Redemption*, 127-192. Several English writers recognized that the Qur'an never legitimated the use of civil power to compel conversion and observed that different Islamic rulers deployed force in different measure, but most commentators wrote at least of serious intimidation and civil penalties for violation of Qur'anic commands: Robert C. Davis, *Christian Slaves, Muslim Masters: White Slavery in the Mediterranean, the Barbary Coast, and Italy, 1500-1800* (New York, 2003), 105, 125; Nabil Matar, *Islam in Britain, 1558-1685* (New York, 1998): 21-72, esp. 45. On English attitudes toward conversion to Islam, see Jonathan Burton, "English Anxiety and the Muslim Power of Conversion: Five Perspectives on 'Turning Turk' in Early Modern Texts," *Journal for Early Modern Cultural Studies* 2 (2002): 35-67. For one account of Ottoman cruelties with comparison to persecution of Huguenots, see *The Turkish Fast*, broadside (Boston, 1698), taken from *The Monthly Mercury*, December 1697, cited in Nan Goodman, *The Puritan Cosmopolis: The Law of Nations and the Early American Imagination* (New York, 2018), 1.

87. Mary Wortley Montagu, *The Letters and Works of Lady Mary Wortley Montagu*, ed. Lord Wharncliffe, notes by W. Moy Thomas, 2 vols. (London, 1893). A similar discourse controlled the narrative of the New England traveler Sarah Kemble Knight, a widowed businesswoman who, on a journey from Boston to New York in 1704, cast the various people she met into one of two categories: sociable and civil or unsociable and uncivil: Sarah Kemble Knight, *The Journal of Madam Knight* (1825), intro. Malcolm Freiberg (Boston, 1971), e.g., 4, 18, 22-24, 27, 30, 34-35.

88. Montagu, *Letters*, I: 230, 232, 234, 257.

89. Montagu, *Letters*, I: 289.

90. Locke too admired Turkish Muslims with a scholarly bent, who sincerely sought the truth and reasoned their way to their beliefs. They might have rejected Christian

teaching out of sheer prejudice, he admitted, but many Christians were equally prejudiced in their refusal to examine the veracity of the Bible: Marshall, *John Locke*, 614–615.

91. Montagu, *Letters*, I: 290, 372. For a different reading of Montagu, which stresses her encounters with Islam as a vehicle for feminist assertiveness and resistance to imperial aggrandizement, see Humberto Garcia, *Islam and the English Enlightenment, 1670–1840* (Baltimore, 2012), 60–92

92. Montagu, *Letters*, I: 289, 291.

93. Thomas Fayerweather, "Diary, 1720," Fayerweather Family Papers, Massachusetts Historical Society, Boston.

Chapter 4

1. Thomas Broughton, *An Historical Dictionary of All Religions from the Creation of the World to this Present Time*, 2 vols. bound in one (London, 1742), a reissue of *Bibliotheca historico-sacra* (London, 1737–1739).

2. Ruth Smith, "Broughton, Thomas (1704–1774)," *Oxford Dictionary of National Biography*, 60 vols. (New York, 2004), online, https://doi.org/10.1093/ref:odnb/3589.

3. For household libraries of reference works, see Linda C. Mitchell, *Grammar Wars: Language as Cultural Battlefield in 17th and 18th Century England* (Burlington, VT, 2001).

4. The 1742 edition had some 200 subscribers. For Edwards: Jonathan Edwards, *The Works of Jonathan Edwards*, Perry Miller and Harry S. Stout, gen eds., 26 vols. (New Haven, 1957–2008) (hereafter *WJE*), vol. 26: *Catalogues of Books*, ed. Peter J. Thuesen, 213 (hereafter JEC). For Franklin, see the card catalog annotations and copy of the *Dictionary* at the Library Company of Philadelphia. For Adams: Hannah Adams, *An Alphabetical Compendium of the Various Sects* (Boston, 1784), with citations on nearly every page to Broughton.

5. For Gravelot, see Hanns Hammelmann and T. R. S. Boase, *Book Illustrators in Eighteenth-Century England* (New Haven, 1975), 38–46; and Alice Newlin, "The Celebrated Mr. Gravelot," *The Metropolitan Museum of Art Bulletin*, new series, 5 (1946): 61–66.

6. Broughton, *Historical Dictionary*, "Preface," 1: vii.

7. Broughton, *Historical Dictionary*, "Preface," 1: vii.

8. A few throwbacks continued to be published. The London cartographer Herman Moll, e.g., produced, from 1711 to 1717, five volumes of a serial publication on world geography that replicated Alexander Ross's descriptions, nation by nation: Herman Moll, *Atlas Geographus; or a Compleat System of Geography*, 5 vols. (London, 1711–1717).

9. For Locke on sincerity: Paul Bou-Habib, "Locke, Sincerity, and the Rationality of Persecution," *Political Studies* 51 (2003): 611–626.

10. To sample a large literature on Catholicism and the religious other: Arnold H. Rowbotham, "The Jesuit Figuralists and Eighteenth-Century Religious Thought,"

Journal of the History of Ideas 17 (1956): 471–485; and Jeffrey D. Burson, "Introduction: The Culture of Jesuit Erudition in an Age of Enlightenment," *Journal of Jesuit Studies* 6 (2019): 387–415 and attendant essays by Michela Catto, Carolina Armenteros, and Daniel J. Watkins: 416–466, 486–504.

11. John Brewer, *The Sinews of Power: War, Money and the English State, 1688–1783* (Cambridge, MA, 1990).

12. David Hancock, *Citizens of the World: London Merchants and the Integration of the British Atlantic Community, 1735–1785* (New York, 1995). Katherine Carté has aptly termed this collection of imperial interests and pan-Protestant sentiments "imperial protestantism": Katherine Carté, *Religion and the American Revolution: An Imperial History* (Williamsburg, VA, and Chapel Hill, 2021), 23–82 (quotation from 82).

13. For evangelicals: Peter Y. Choi, *George Whitefield: Evangelist for God and Empire* (Grand Rapids, MI, 2018). For the equation of English loyalty to anti-Catholicism: Owen Stanwood, *The Empire Reformed: English America in the Age of the Glorious Revolution* (Philadelphia, 2011). The authoritative account of the Seven Years' War is Fred Anderson, *Crucible of War: The Seven Years' War and the Fate of Empire in British North America, 1754–1766* (New York, 2000).

14. Patriot Whigs, including several ex-Tories and notable writers such as Jonathan Swift and Alexander Pope, opposed Walpole's administration. See, for definitions of terms and parties, Linda Colley, *In Defiance of Oligarchy: The Tory Party, 1714–1760* (New York, 1982); Linda Colley, *Britons: Forging the Nation, 1707–1837* (New Haven, 1992); J. R. Jones, *Country and Court: England, 1658–1714* (Cambridge, MA, 1978); and Caroline Robbins, *The Eighteenth-Century Commonwealthman: Studies in the Transmission, Development and Circumstance of English Liberal Thought from the Restoration of Charles II Until the War with the Thirteen Colonies* (Cambridge, MA, 1959). For Court thinkers, the crown itself, the nobility, and the crown's cadre of officials secured the liberties of loyal subjects through their promotion of the kingdom's security and order. For Country thinkers, whose ideas have been categorized under the rubric "republicanism," the collective will of virtuous subjects and the rule of elected officials secured liberty and defined the constitution. For essential definitions of the empire in this period and its connection to Whig ideas of liberty, see David Armitage, *The Ideological Origins of the British Empire* (New York, 2000).

15. For the affair and fallout: Geoffrey Holmes, *The Trial of Doctor Sacheverell* (London, 1972). Publications relating to the affair, including Sacheverell's offending sermon, appeared in the Mather Family Library held at the American Antiquarian Society. For the playing cards: "Impeachment of Dr. Sacheverell" cards at the Beinecke Library, Yale University, New Haven, CT, discussed in William B. Keller, *A Catalogue of the Cary Collection of Playing Cards in the Yale University Library*, 4 vols., vol. 1: entry "ENG 88" (New Haven, CT, 1981). Eighteenth-century writers often capitalized the term "Dissenters," especially when it referred to non-Anglican Protestants as a legal class to which particular statutes and regulations were addressed. When left uncapitalized, the term has a more general reference.

16. George Hickes [posthumously], *The Constitution of the Catholick Church and the Nature and Consequence of Schism* ([London], 1716); and Benjamin Hoadly, *The*

Nature of the Kingdom, or Church, of Christ (London, 1717), which went through several editions. For background to and the import of Hickes's sermon: William Bradford Gardner, "George Hickes and the Origin of the Bangorian Controversy," *Studies in Philology* 39 (1942): 65–78. For notice of the Bangorian Conroversey in New England, see Edwards, JEC, 61–62.

17. See Jeremy Black, "The Catholic Threat and the British Press in the 1720s and 1730s," *The Journal of Religious History* 12 (1983): 364–381.

18. Armitage, *Ideological Origins of the British Empire*, esp. 170–195; David S. Shields, *Oracles of Empire: Poets, Politics, and Commerce in British America, 1690–1750* (Chicago, 1990).

19. Lawrence E. Klein, "Sociability, Solitude, and Enthusiasm," *Huntington Library Quarterly* 60 (1998): 153–177, quote from 157. For Whitefield on Tillotson in such terms: George Whitefield, *Three Letters from the Reverend Mr. G. Whitefield* (Philadelphia, 1740), esp. 4–5. For a relevant study of how moral categories replaced theological tenets among Protestants, see Thomas Ahnert, *The Moral Culture of the Scottish Enlightenment, 1690–1805* (New Haven, 2014). The term "public sphere" as defined by Jürgen Habermas still merits attention: Habermas, *The Structural Transformation of the Public Sphere: An Inquiry into a Category of Bourgeois Society*, trans. Thomas Burger with Frederick Lawrence (1962; 1989; repr. Cambridge, Massachusetts, 1991); and, for its American deployment, John L. Brooke, "Consent, Civil Society, and the Public Sphere in the Age of Revolution and the Early Republic," in Jeffrey L. Pasley, Andrew W. Robertson, and David Waldstreicher, eds., *Beyond the Founders: New Approaches to the Political History of the Early American Republic* (Chapel Hill, 2004), 207–250. Evangelicals such as Edwards nonetheless offered a severe theological criticism of Quakers and anti-Trinitarians, as in Edwards, *WJE*, vol. 9: *A History of the Work of Redemption*, ed. John F. Wilson (hereafter *HWR*), 431–432.

20. Nye, quoted in J. F. Maclear, "Isaac Watts and the Idea of Public Religion," *Journal of the History of Ideas* 53 (1992): 24–45, 30. Maclear's article, which names the figures mentioned here, informs much of this and the following paragraph.

21. Mark Smith, "The Hanoverian Parish: Towards a New Agenda," *Past and Present* 217 (2012): 79–105; Jeremy Gregory, "Refashioning Puritan New England: The Church of England in British North America, c. 1680–c. 1770," *Transactions of the Royal Historical Society*, 6th ser., 20 (2010): 85–112 (membership figures on 99). For the Regium Donam: Maclear, "Isaac Watts," 30.

22. For political theory and its impact on accounts of other religions, see, John Marshall, *John Locke, Toleration, and Early Enlightenment Culture* (New York, 2006); and the essays in William J. Bulman and Robert C. Ingram, eds., *God in the Enlightenment* (New York, 2016).

23. The following discussion relies on the following versions: Thomas Gordon and John Trenchard, *The Independent Whig*, nos. 1–53, 2nd ed. (London, 1722); and Thomas Gordon, *The Independent Whig*, nos. 55–74, 2nd ed. (London, 1741). Each number refers to a serial essay. These works will be cited by number (i.e., essay) and page, as follows: *IW*, 2:11 refers to the London 1722 edition, essay number 2, page 11; *IW*, 56:63 refers to the London 1741 edition, essay number 56, page 63.

24. On Trenchard and Gordon: Frank E. Manuel, *The Eighteenth Century Confronts the Gods* (Cambridge, MA, 1959), 57–81. For American holdings and the sale of publications: Edwards, JEC, 15; and Benjamin Franklin, *A Catalogue of Choice and Valuable Books* (Philadelphia, 1744), 13.

25. *IW*, "Dedication" to the 1722 edition, x, xxxi.

26. See Manuel, *The Eighteenth Century*, 60–63, 129–148, 168–183, and 211–240. For the long history of anti-ceremonialism and anti-Judaism, see Geraldine Heng, *The Invention of Race in the European Middle Ages* (New York, 2018); for anti-Catholicism, see Robert A. Orsi, *History and Presence* (Cambridge, MA, 2016).

27. *IW*, "Dedication" to the 1722 edition, xiv–xvi.

28. On benevolence: Norman Fiering, *Jonathan Edwards's Moral Thought and Its British Context* (Chapel Hill, 1981).

29. Philip Carter, *Men and the Emergence of Polite Society, Britain 1660–1800* (Harlow, Essex, U.K., 2001), 15–52; Lawrence E. Klein, "Politeness and the Interpretation of the British Eighteenth Century," *The Historical Journal* 45 (2002): 869–898. On sympathy and moderation: Steve Bullock, *Tea Sets and Tyranny: The Politics of Politeness in Early America* (Philadelphia, 2017).

30. *The Spectator*, no. 292, 4 February 1712, quoted in Klein, "Sociability, Solitude, and Enthusiasm," 164.

31. Anthony [Ashley Cooper], Third Earl of Shaftesbury, "Treatise I: A Letter Concerning Enthusiasm," in *Characteristicks of Men, Manners, Opinions, Times*, 3 vols. (London, 1711; rev. ed. London, 1732; repr. with intro. Douglas Den Uyl, Indianapolis, 2001), 1:23.

32. Shaftesbury, *Characteristicks*, 1:7.

33. *IW*, 23:169.

34. *IW*, 40:319.

35. *IW*, 56:16.

36. *IW*, 64:97–102.

37. *IW*, 22:161, 163, 166.

38. *IW*, 22:160–161, 165.

39. *IW*, 63:90–91, 31–32, 229–230; 35:272–273. Jonathan Sheehan has maintained that the eighteenth-century shift away from confessional polemics represented a concern among Christians of several confessions to defend the very concept of religion against atheism: Jonathan Sheehan, "Comparison and Christianity: Sacrifice in the Age of the Encyclopedia," in *Regimes of Comparison: Frameworks of Comparison in History, Religion, and Anthropology*, ed. Renauld Gagné et al. (Leiden, 2018), 177–209.

40. *IW*, 63:83, 85.

41. *IW*, 35:275.

42. *IW*, 6:35–41 and 9:58–67.

43. It is in this sense that Charles Taylor writes of "secularity" not as a rejection of religious ideas but as the modern assumption that we are free to choose our beliefs: Charles Taylor, *A Secular Age* (Cambridge, MA, 2007), esp. 1–19.

44. For the names mentioned here: John Edwards, *The Safe Retreat from Impending Judgments* (London, 1762), esp. 8–9; [Elisha Williams], *The Essential Rights and*

Liberties of Protestants (Boston, 1744); and Jonathan Mayhew, *Popish Idolatry* (Boston, 1765).

45. On superstition and unsociability, see Klein, "Sociability, Solitude, and Enthusiasm," 166.

46. *IW*, 52: 427.

47. For the South Sea bubble: Perry Gauchi, *The Politics of Trade: The Overseas Merchants in State and Society, 1660–1720* (New York, 2001). For Whitefield: Kristen Beales, "Auditing Revival: George Whitefield and Public Accounting in Colonial America," *Church History* 90 (2021): 824–846.

48. *IW*, 21: 159.

49. Thomas Gordon, *The Independent Whig*, vol. 4 (London, 1747), v, vii, ix, xi.

50. *IW*, 52: 420, 423, 425, 427.

51. *IW*, 69: 138, 142.

52. *IW*, 68: 132–136.

53. *IW*, 18: 135.

54. *IW*, 24: 231–232.

55. On Islam: Humberto Garcia, *Islam and the English Enlightenment, 1670–1840* (Baltimore, 2012).

56. [Edward Weston], *The Englishman Directed in the Choice of His Religion* (1729; 2nd ed. London, 1740), 4, 47, 81. The American reprint (Boston, 1748), adds to the title *Reprinted for the Use of English Americans*. For a brief introduction to Weston: Karl W. Schweizer, "Edward Weston (1703–70): The Papers of an Eighteenth-Century Under-Secretary in the Lewis Walpole Library," *Yale University Library Gazette* 71 (1996): 43–48.

57. [John Edwards], *The Conversion of a Mehometan* [alternatively titled *A Christian Indeed*] (London, 1757; repr. New London, 1775); and, for warnings against coercion, Edwards, *Safe Retreat from Impending Judgments*, quotation from 33.

58. See Guy Stroumsa, *A New Science: The Discovery of Religion in the Age of Reason* (Cambridge, MA, 2010), 25, 145–149.

59. [Caleb Fleming], *The Palladium of Great Britain and Ireland* (London, 1762), 24.

60. Samuel Shuckford, *The Sacred and Profane History of the World*, 4 vols. in 2 bindings (London, 1728; revised James Creighton, Philadelphia, 1828), 1: 284.

61. Stephen Foster, "Rereading Liberalism: Omission, Ambiguity and Anomaly in New England Sermonic Literature, 1699–c. 1750," *The New England Quarterly* 92 (2019): 477–516. Whitefield and Edwards criticized Tillotson during the early 1740s but became more accommodating after 1745. Edwards treated Tillotson and deists as legitimately Protestant interlocutors, especially in his commentaries on the Bible, even as he attempted to make an apology for experimental Calvinism from their analyses: Robert E. Brown, *Jonathan Edwards and the Bible* (Bloomington, IN, 2002), 57–87. For the overall point here of Protestant self-awareness and empire: Katherine Carté Engel, "Connecting Protestants in Britain's Eighteenth-Century Atlantic Empire," *WMQ* 75 (2018): 37–70.

62. *The Boston Gazette or Weekly Journal*, no. 1278, September 9, 1746, first page; and letter in the *London Magazine*, 17, November 4, 1745, reprinted in n.a., *Itinerant*

Observations in America: Reprinted from the London Magazine (Savannah, 1878), 552. To be sure, critics such as Charles Chauncy did not come to the same conclusions about Whitefield during the early 1740s. Whitefield had assumed more of a rational and polite style by 1746. The point here, however, concerns the criteria by which such judgments were made, not the judgments themselves.

63. John Moorhead, "An Extract from a Letter," *The Christian Monthly* 2 (Edinburgh, 1743): 11–27, quotations from 22.

64. Thomas Broughton, *Christianity Distinct from the Religion of Nature* (London, 1732), 4, 16, 27, 32. Broughton's piece was a reply to Matthe Tindal, *Christianity as Old as the Creation* (London, 1730).

65. The quote is from A. B., "The Epistle Dedicatory" to Bernard Fontenelle, *The History of Oracles and the Cheats of Pagan Priests*, cited in Manuel, *Eighteenth Century*, 1. Further note is made of Chambers later. Moll, *Atlas Geographus*. Fransham's book, a popular gazetteer of world cities, was published in London.

66. Mather mentions these works in his frequent and scattered notations in his biblical commentaries: Cotton Mather, *Biblia Americana*, gen. ed. Reiner Smolinski, exec. ed. Jan Stievermann, 10 vols. (Tübingen, 2010–2022), vol. 1: *Genesis*, ed. Reiner Smolinski (2010), *passim*; and Mather, *Biblia*, vol. 10: *Hebrews-Revelation*, ed. Jan Stievermann, ed. assistants Michael Dopffel, Ryan P. Hoselton, and Benjamin Pietrenka, esp. the appended essays "Scripturae Nucleus," 889–900, and "Patriarcha, or, the Religion of Noah," 901–907. An especially helpful discussion of Mather and the orientalists, with rich detail on Zoroastrianism, is provided in Stievermann, "Editor's Introduction" to Mather, *Biblia*, 10: 132–143.

67. For Edwards: Gerald R. McDermott, *Jonathan Edwards Confronts the Gods: Christian Theology, Enlightenment Religion, and Non-Christian Faiths* (New York, 2000), esp. 6–7, 12–13, 93; and, for an illustrative reference to Chambers, Edwards, *WJE*, vol. 2: *Religious Affections*, ed. John E. Smith, 233. For Mayhew: John S. Oakes, *Conservative Revolutionaries: Transformation and Tradition in the Religious and Political Thought of Charles Chauncy and Jonathan Mayhew* (Eugene, OR, 2016), 137–139. For Stiles: Ezra Stiles, "Itineraries," vol. 1 (1760–1762), entries from 1761, microfilm at Beinecke Library. Many of the works mentioned here are included in Yale College, *A Catalogue of the Library of Yale College in New-Haven* (New London, 1743), 14–15, 20.

68. Ephraim Chambers, *Cyclopedia, or, an Universal Dictionary of Arts and Sciences*, 2nd ed. (London, 1738). For publication and distribution information, with notes on Chambers's biography and popularity: Lael Ely Bradshaw, "Ephraim Chambers' *Cyclopedia*," in Frank A. Kafker, ed., *Notable Encyclopedias of the Seventeenth and Eighteenths Centuries: Nine Predecessors of the Encyclopédie*, no. 194 of Studies on Voltaire and the Eighteenth Century (Oxford, 1981), 123–140; and Richard Yeo, "Ephraim Chambers's *Cyclopedia* (1728) and the Tradition of Commonplaces," *Journal of the History of Ideas* 57 (1996): 157–175.

69. There is no pagination in the *Cyclopedia*. Reference may be made to the dedication "To the King" and to the appropriate entries, e.g., "Censor," "Monarchy," "King,"

"Liberty of Conscience." Subsequent references to entries in the *Cyclopedia* will be made in the body of my text unless otherwise noted.

70. Chambers's chart comes at the end of the Preface. Some intellectual historians detect secularization here.

71. See also the entries on "Albigenses" and "Inquisition." For the Jansenist controversy and the French monarchy: B. Robert Kreiser, *Miracles, Convulsions and Ecclesiastical Politics in Early Eighteenth-Century France* (Princeton, 1978). For further discussion of Chambers's view of Jansenism and rebuke of Catholic coercion, see Bradshaw, "Ephraim Chambers' *Cyclopedia*"

72. Broughton, *Dictionary*, 1: 326; 1: 528–529.

73. Broughton, *Dictionary*, 1: 361; 1: 328; 1: 400–401.

74. Broughton, *Dictionary*, 2: 324–325.

75. Broughton, *Dictionary*, 1: 527, 1: 33, 1: 301.

76. Broughton, *Dictionary*, 2: 110–111 (the quotation), 110–115 for the whole.

77. Broughton, *Dictionary*, 1: 413, 2: 331; Bernard Picart and Frederic Bernard, *The Ceremonies and Religious Customs of the Various Nations of the Known World*, 7 vols. (London, 1733–1737) (hereafter *CRC*), 4: 433; William Smith, *A New Voyage to Guinea* (London, 1744), 26–27. A full discussion of Picart and Bernard is given in the following chapter.

78. William Pietz, "The Problem of the Fetish, I," *RES: Anthropology and Aesthetics* 9 (1985): 5–17; William Pietz, "The Problem of the Fetish, II: The Origin of the Fetish," *RES: Anthropology and Aesthetics* 13 (1987): 23–45; and William Pietz, "The Problem of the Fetish, IIIa: Bosman's Guinea and the Enlightenment Theory of Fetishism" *RES: Anthropology and Aesthetics* 16 (1988): 105–124. Many discussions of European descriptions of the fetish, and especially of "fetishism" as a category for a type of religious practice, center on the Frenchman Charles de Brosses, an amateur historian and politician who coined the term "fetishism" in 1760: Charles de Brosses, *Du culte des dieux fétiches our Parallèle de l'ancienne religion de l'Egypte avec la religion actuelle de Nigritie* (Genéve, 1760), translated as *On the Worship of Fetish Gods: Or, a Parallel of the Ancient Religion of Egypt with the Present Religion of Nigritia* in Rosalind C. Morris and Daniel H. Leonard, eds., *The Returns of Fetishism: Chalres de Brosses and the Afterlives of an Idea* (Chicago, 2017), 44–132. As Manuel argues, in *The Eighteenth Century*, 184–209, De Brosses intended to show, as a criticism of Christian apologists, that ancient Egyptian hieroglyphs, which portrayed supplication to animals, were not allegorical (prefigures of monotheism) but veneration of material objects plain and simple.

79. Picart and Bernard, *CRC*, 4: 472. Gerbner, *Christian Slavery*. For religious comparison and notions of control: David Chidester, *Savage Systems: Colonialism and Comparative Religion in Southern Africa* (Charlottesville, VA, 1996), 11–16. For Bayle: Manuel, *The Eighteenth Century*, 31–32. For a critique of eighteenth-century ideas of fetishism and its racial implications: J. Lorand Matory, *The Fetish Revisited: Marx, Freud, and the Gods Black People Make* (Durham, NC, 2018). See also Webb Keane, *Christian Moderns: Freedom and Fetish in the Mission Encounter* (Berkeley, 2007), in which

Keane argues that European missionary attempts to assert the primacy of the rational mind and agency over and against the materiality of the fetish failed to convince indigenous Africans because the fetish conveyed the power of communal identities. For criticisms of slavery nonetheless: Carlo Ginzburg, "Provincializing the World: Europeans, Indians, Jews (1704)," *Postcolonial Studies* 14 (2011): 135–150; and Giovanni Tarantino, "From Labelling and Ridicule to Understanding: The Novelty of Bernard and Picart's *Religious Comparison*," in Giovanni Tarantino and Paola Wyss-Giacosa, eds., *Through Your Eyes: Religious Alterity and the Early Modern Western Imagination* (Leiden and Boston, 2011), 235–266.

80. Antoine Simon Maillard, *An Account of the Customs and Manners of the Micmakis and Maricheets Savage Nations* (London, 1758).

81. Andrew Brice, *A Universal Geographic Dictionary*, 2 vols. (London, 1759), 2: 1031–1032, 1336–1339; and Lewis Evans, *Geographical, Historical, Political, Philosophical and Mechanical Essays* (Philadelphia, 1755), e.g., 14–16.

82. For Pococke's biography and influence, see Mohamad Ali Hachicho, "English Travel Books About the Arab Near East in the Eighteenth Century," *Die Welt des Islams*, new ser., 9 (1964): 1–206, esp. 35–38.

83. Richard Pococke, *Description of the East and Some Other Countries*, 2 vols. (London 1743–1745), 1: 176–178.

84. Edwards, *WJE*, vol. 23: *The "Miscellanies" 1153–1360*, ed. Douglas A. Sweeney (hereafter 1153–1360), #1334 (c. 1755), 327–330; #s1350–1351 (c. 1755), 432–486, in which Edwards dealt with the account of the freethinker Chevalier Andrew Michael Ramsay, *The Travels of Cyrus: To Which Is Annexed, a Discourse upon the World and Mythology of the Pagans* (London, 1727). In addition to Whig moral analyses, Edwards also made a theological argument to the effect that non-Christians derived what sound knowledge they had of God not from nature itself, as some deists held, but from the dissemination of ancient Hebrew wisdom. From his perspective, devotion to priests, statues, talismans, the sun, or even to Muhammad, violated such knowledge and incurred divine judgment: McDermott, *Jonathan Edwards Confronts the Gods*, 143; and Edwards, *WJE*, vol. 10: *Sermons and Discourses, 1720–1723*, ed. Wilson H. Kimnach, 537. For an overall perspective, see McDermott, *Jonathan Edwards Confronts the Gods*, 194–206. Further discussion of Edwards is provided in Chapter 6.

85. European presses produced some 3,500 titles in travel accounts during the eighteenth century, over double the number from the previous century: Lynn Hunt, Margaret C. Jacob, and Wijnand Mijnhardt, *The Book that Changed Europe: Picart and Bernard's Religious Ceremonies of the World* (Cambridge, MA, 2010), 5.

86. Margaret Hope Bacon, *Wilt Thou Go on My Errand? Journals of Three 18th Century Quaker Women Ministers* (Wallingford, PA, 1994). A similar account is given by the eminent Quaker physician from London John Fothergill, although Fothergill often used Whig moral categories, rather than the intensely spiritual rhetoric of Quakers. Fothergill in fact allowed that even in spiritually dark New England, a few tolerant souls among non-Friends treated him with "Calmness and Civility.": John Fothergill, *An Account of the Life and Travels, in the Work of the Ministry, of John*

Fothergill (London, 1754; repr. Philadelphia, 1754), 37. Other sectarian groups, such as Moravians, shared even less of the rhetoric of Whig Protestants: see, e.g., "A Journey of Moravians from Bethlehem, Pa., to Bethabara, N.C., 1753," in Newton D. Merreness, ed., *Travels in the American Colonies* (New York, 1916), 325–364.

87. Pote's diary was published as *The Journal of Captain William Pote, Jr. During His Captivity in the French and Indian War*, ed. John Fletcher Hurst with "Historical Introduction" and annotations by Victor H. Paltsits (New York, 1896). Pote's biography is covered by Paltsits in the "Historical Introduction," xi–xxii. The quote is from 14.

88. Thomas Smith, *The Great Duty of Gospel Ministers* (Boston, 1751), 45–46; Thomas Smith, *Extracts from the Journals Kept by the Rev. Thomas Smith*, ed. Samuel Freeman (Portland, ME, 1821), 30, 39; Thomas Smith, *A Practical Discourse to Sea-Faring Men* (Boston, 1771), e.g., 8. Clarke's use of comparative religions may be seen in his *Works*, which Smith cited: *The Works of Samuel Clarke*, 4 vols. (London 1742), e.g., 1: 145, 378, 385, 409–410, 577. For Pote's involvement in Smith's congregation: Portland, Maine, First Parish Church, *Baptism and Admission: from the Records of the First Church in Falmouth*, compiled by Marquis F. King (Portland, ME: Maine Genealogical Society, 1898), 91.

89. Mary Rowlandson, *The Sovereignty and Goodness of God* (Boston, 1682), ed. Neal Salisbury (Boston, 1997).

90. Pote, *Journal*, 26, 16, 23, 20, 57, 14–15, 31.

91. Pote, *Journal*, 16, 34, 54, 29, 23. For ways in which British writers deployed a typology of civilized and good as opposed to savage and bad Natives, with racial and imperial inflections: Peter Way, "The Cutting Edge of Culture: British Soldiers Encounter Native Americans in the French and Indian War," in Martin Daunton and Rick Halpern, eds., *Empire and Others: British Encounters with Indigenous Peoples, 1600–1850* (Philadelphia, 1999), 123–148; and Troy O. Bickham, *Savages Within the Empire: Representations of American Indians in Eighteenth-Century Britain* (Oxford, 2005).

92. Dr. Alexander Hamilton, *Gentleman's Progress: The Itinerarium of Dr. Alexander Hamilton, 1744*, ed. Carl Bridenbaugh (Chapel Hill, 1948); for background and biography, see editor's "Introduction," xi–xxxii. See also Robert Micklus, ed., *The History of the Ancient and Honorable Tuesday Club* by Alexander Hamilton, 3 vols. (Chapel Hill, 1990), esp. "Introduction," 1: xv–xxxiv. For Hamilton's religious views, see J. A. Leo Lemay, *Men of Letters in Colonial Maryland* (Knoxville, TN, 1972), 213–256. For the religious observations mentioned here: Hamilton, *History*, 1: 31–33, 182–183, 212–214; 2: 167–168, 254–255; 3: 135–136. For one example of conversations on a ferry, see Hamilton, *Gentleman's Progress*, 162–163.

93. Hamilton, *Gentleman's Progress*, quotations from 130, 150–151; other details from 26–28, 33, 120, 20–22, 182.

94. Hamilton, *Gentleman's Progress*, quotations from 155, 190, 130; for the skeptics, 144.

95. Hamilton, *Gentleman's Progress*, 19.

96. See, e.g., Hamilton, *History*, 1: 201, 88; 2: 26.

Chapter 5

1. Bernard Picart and Frederic Bernard, *The Ceremonies and Religious Customs of the Various Nations of the Known World*, 7 vols. (London, 1733–1737) (hereafter *CRC*, without mention of the authors). Volumes 6 and 7 of this edition were bound together.

2. Lynn Hunt, Margaret C. Jacob, and Wijnand Mijnhardt, *The Book that Changed Europe: Picart and Bernard's Religious Ceremonies of the World* (Cambridge, MA, 2010), 135–165.

3. Hunt, Jacob, and Mijnhardt, *The Book that Changed Europe*, 105, 112–134.

4. *CRC* 1: after 392. Because Picart's engravings were purchased separately from Bernard's text, different printings of *CRC* sometimes included different engravings and located them in different places in the volumes. The sources for the engraving are discussed in Paola von Wyss-Giacosa, "Visual Provocations: Bernard Picart's illustrative strategies in *Cérémonies et coutumes religieuses de tous les peuples du monde*," in Giovanni Tarantino and Charles Zika, eds., *Feeling Exclusion: Religious Conflict, Exile and Emotions in Early Modern Europe* (New York, 2019), 233–258, esp. 238.

5. Hunt, Jacob, and Mijnhardt, *The Book that Changed Europe*, 206.

6. *CRC* 4: after 410.

7. *CRC* 4: 296–297; Hunt, Jacob, and Mijnhardt, *The Book that Changed Europe*, 656; Wyss-Giacosa, "Visual Provocations," 238; Guillaume Calafat, "The Gallican and Jansenist Roots of Jean Frederic Bernard and Bernard Picart's Vision of the Inquisition," in Lynn Hunt, Margaret Jacob, and Wijnardt Mijnhardt, eds., *Bernard Picart and the First Global Vision of Religion* (Los Angeles, 2010), 291–312, esp. 298–300.

8. For Picart's aims: Wyss-Giacosa, "Visual Provocations."

9. Thomas Gordon, *The Independent Whig*, nos. 55–74, 2nd ed. (London, 1741), no. 69, 138. Thomas Gordon and John Trenchard, *The Independent Whig*, nos. 55–74, 2nd ed. (London, 1741), no. 69, 143–144.

10. Many scholars of New England and Catholicism describe a stable tradition of anti-Catholic rhetoric from Puritan foundations through the Seven Years' War, intensified in periods of warfare into fits of millennial hysteria: Thomas S. Kidd, "'Let Hell and Rome Do Their Worst': World News, Anti-Catholicism, and International Protestantism in Early-Eighteenth-Century Boston," *New England Quarterly* 76 (2003): 265–290, which depends heavily on Jeremy Black, "The Catholic Threat and the British Press in the 1720s and 1730s," *The Journal of Religious History* 12 (1983): 364–381; Francis D. Cogliano, *No King, No Popery: Anti-Catholicism in Revolutionary America* (Westport, CT, 1995); Gayle Kathleen Pluta Brown, "A Controversy Not Merely Religious: The Anti-Catholic Tradition in Colonial New England," PhD diss., University of Iowa, 1990; John Corrigan, "Amalek and the Rhetoric of Extermination," in Chris Beneke and Christopher S. Grenda, eds., *The First Prejudice: Religious Tolerance and Intolerance in Early America* (Philadelphia, 2011), 53–72; Jenny Franchot, *Roads to Rome: The Antebellum Protestant Encounter with Catholicism* (Berkeley, 1994); and, from an Atlantic history perspective, Carla Gardina Pestana, *Protestant Empire: Religion and the Making of the British Atlantic*

World (Philadelphia, 2009). Much of the literature on anti-Catholicism and the history of comparative religions has given scant attention to Picart and Bernard and instead has focused on their seventeenth-century predecessors such as John Spencer and the deists: Hunt, Jacob, and Mijnhardt, *The Book that Changed Europe*, 308; and Guy S. Stroumsa, "John Spencer and the Roots of Idolatry," *History of Religions* 41 (2001): 1–23.

11. For other observations of nuance within anti-Catholic rhetoric, see Evan Haefeli, "Conclusion: History, Polemic, and Analysis," in Evan Haefeli, ed., *Against Popery: Britain, Empire, and Anti-Catholicism* (Charlottesville, VA, 2020), 289–299; and Anthony Milton, "Epilogue: Words, Deeds, and Ambiguities in Early Modern Anti-Catholicism," in Haefeli, ed., *Against Popery*, 301–320.

12. Hunt, Jacob, and Mijnhardt, *The Book that Changed Europe*, 46, 61, 63–69, 92–93, 110–111. For Clarke, see Thomas C. Pfizenmaier, *The Trinitarian Theology of Dr. Samuel Clarke (1675–1729): Context, Sources, Controversy* (New York, 1997).

13. Hunt, Jacob, and Mijnardt, *The Book that Changed Europe*, 30–31, 54, 89–90; and Wijnand Mijnardt, "Jean Frederic Bernard as Author and Publisher," in Hunt, Jacob, and Mijnardt, eds., *Bernard Picart*, 17–34.

14. Hunt, Jacob, and Mijnhardt, *The Book that Changed Europe*, 78, 97–99, 221, 232. For Lockman: Giovanni Tarantino, "From Labelling and Ridicule to Understanding: The Novelty of Bernard and Picart's Religious Comparison," in Giovanni Tarantino and Paola Wyss-Giacosa, eds., *Through Your Eyes: Religious Alterity and the Early Modern Western Imagination* (Leiden and Boston, 2011), 235–266.

15. The quotation is in Frank E. Manuel, *The Eighteenth Century Confronts the Gods* (Cambridge, MA, 1959), 7. For advertising, see, e.g., London's *Daily Gazeteer*, March 22, 1744, advertisement [n.p]. For Bernard's editing: Tarantino, "From Labelling and Ridicule to Understanding"; and Hunt, Jacob, and Mijnhardt, *The Book that Changed Europe*, 29. For the general repute of *Ceremonies* and printing information: Hunt, Jacob, and Mijnhardt, "Introduction" to *Bernard Picart*, 1, 3. For Clarke and Broughton: John Clarke, *An Essay upon Study*, (London, 1737), 300; and Thomas Broughton, *An Historical Dictionary of All Religions from the Creation of the World to this Present Time*, 2 vols. (London, 1742), e.g., 89. On Franklin: a copy of the 1733 volumes in the Library Company of Philadelphia, purchased in 1769, was closely read, as indicated by marginal notations.

16. *CRC* 1: 24, 13; see the whole "Dissertation upon Religious Worship," 1: 1–26.

17. *CRC* 1: 251–252.

18. *CRC* 1:1.

19. *CRC* 1: 1–2, 24.

20. Catholic observers such as Lafitau provided a more optimistic account of ritual yet, like Protestant commentators, described the rituals of different religions, including Native American traditions, as producing comparative effects on minds and bodies: Mary Helen McMurran, "Rethinking Superstition: Pagan Ritual in Lafitau's *Moeurs des sauvages*," in Mary Helen McMurran and Alison Conway, eds., *Mind, Body, Motion, Matter: Eighteenth-Century British and French Literary Perspectives* (Toronto, 2016), 110–135.

21. CRC 3: 17–18.
22. Jeremy Black, "The Catholic Threat and the British Press in the 1720s and 1730s," *The Journal of Religious History* 12 (1983): 364–381.
23. Conyers Middleton, *Letters from Rome, Shewing the Exact Conformity Between Popery and Paganism*, 4th ed. (London, 1741), 131–133.
24. Jonathan Mayhew, *Popish Idolatry* (Boston, 1765), 9. For Dudley: Pauline Maier, "The Pope at Harvard: The Dudleian Lectures, Anti-Catholicism, and the Politics of Protestantism," *Proceedings of the Massachusetts Historical Society*, 3rd ser., 97 (1985): 16–41.
25. Peter Lake, "Anti-Popery: The Structure of a Prejudice," in Richard Cust and Ann Hughes, eds., *Conflict in Early Stuart England: Studies in Religion and Politics, 1601–1642* (New York, 1989), 72–106. For other studies of variation in "anti-popery" from the seventeenth to the eighteenth century and the turn to political issues and patriotic meanings: Evan Haefeli, "Protestant Empire? Anti-Popery and British-American Patriotism, 1558–1776," in Haefeli, ed., *Against Popery*, 203–233; Tim Harris, "Anti-Catholicism and Anti-Popery in Seventeenth-Century England," in Haefeli, ed., *Against Popery*, 25–50; and John Wolffe, "A Comparative Historical Categorisation of Anti-Catholicism," *Journal of Religious History* 39 (2015): 182–202. For a subtle account of the shifting meaning of idolatry and its relation to superstition, across Protestant, Catholic, and deist commentary: Joan-Pau Rubiés, "Theology, Ethnography, and the Historicization of Idolatry," *Journal of the History of Ideas* 67 (2006): 571–596.
26. Owen Stanwood, "Catholics, Protestants, and the Clash of Civilizations in Early America," in Beneke and Grenda, eds., *First Prejudice*, 218–240. See also Pestana, *Protestant Empire*.
27. Clement Fatovic, "The Anti-Catholic Roots of Liberal and Republican Conceptions of Freedom in English Political Thought," *Journal of the History of Ideas* 66 (2005): 37–58.
28. [Cotton Mather], *Suspiria Vinctorum* (Boston, 1726), 19; George Lavington, *The Enthusiasm of Methodists and Papists Compared*, 2 vols. (London, 1749 [parts 1 and 2] and 1751 [part 3]); and Conyers Middleton, *Miscellaneous Tracts* (London, 1752). For discussion and further evidence of "Catholic" as an invective for other Protestants, see Alexandra Walsham, *Church Papists: Catholicism, Conformity and Confessional Polemic in Early Modern England* (Woodbridge, Suffolk, U.K., 1993).
29. Black, "The Catholic Threat and the British Press"; and Raymond D. Tumbleson, *Catholicism in the English Protestant Imagination, 1660–1745* (New York, 1998).
30. Cotton Mather, *Suspiria Vinctorum*, 12–14; Jonathan Mayhew, *Only Compulsion Proper* (Boston, 1739), 133–140, referenced in John S. Oakes, *Conservative Revolutionaries: Transformation and Tradition in the Religious and Political Thought of Charles Chauncy and Jonathan Mayhew* (Eugene, OR, 2016), 137; Anon., "The Difference Between Popery and Protestantism," *The American Magazine* 3 (1746): 10–12, quotation from 11.
31. Catherine Ballériaux, "'Tis nothing but French Poison, all of it': Jesuit and Calvinist Missions on the New World Frontier," in Jorge Cañizares-Esguerra, Robert Alexander

Maryks, and R. P. Hsia, eds., *Encounters Between Jesuits and Protestants in Asia and the Americas* (Leiden and Boston, 2018), 275–301, quotations from 279–282.

32. Thomas Paine, *Of the Evidence of Christ's Death, Burial, and Resurrection* (Boston, 1732), 16.

33. It was common to describe Rabelais and his sixteenth-century contemporary Etienne Dolet, along with Italian freethinkers such as Pietro Pomponazzi, as atheists: Lucien Febvre, *The Problem of Unbelief in the Sixteenth Century: The Religion of Rabelais*, trans. Beatrice Gottleib (Cambridge, MA, 1982), 101–151. For Broughton's descriptions of papal ceremonies: *Dictionary*, 1: 533–535; 2: 258–263.

34. Thomas Broughton, *Dictionary*, 2 vols. (London, 1742), 1: 97–98.

35. George Whitefield, *A Brief Account of Some Lent and Other Extraordinary Processions* (London, 1755), 14, 20. For popular descriptions of moral judgment in the terms used here and the following paragraph: Norman Fiering, *Jonathan Edwards's Moral Thought and Its British Context* (Chapel Hill, 1981).

36. Whitefield, *Extraordinary Processions*, 2–6.

37. Whitefield, *Extraordinary Processions*, 19. For Picart's images: *CRC* 2: after 322, which is included in the midst of Bernard's extensive discussion of the Inquisition across Europe: *CRC* 2: 247–350.

38. Whitefield, *Extraordinary Processions*, 7, 12–13, 29.

39. For the Ashmolean, the decorative deer hide, and the Hindu statue: The Ashmolean Museum University of Oxford, *The Ashmolean Museum: Crossing Cultures, Crossing Time* (Oxford, 2014), 32–33, 84; and J. C. Harle and Andrew Topsfield, *Indian Art in the Ashmolean Museum* (Oxford, 1987). For the British Library, Sloane, and the other objects listed here: James Delbourgo, *Collecting the World: Hans Sloane and the Origins of the British Museum* (Cambridge, MA, 2017), esp. 15, 141, 173, 183–185, 235, 249, 278–287, 292; Alison Walker, Arthur McGregor, and Michael Hunter, eds., *From Books to Bezoars: Sir Hans Sloane and His Collections* (London, 2012); and Jill Cook, "Believing and Belonging," *The British Museum Magazine* 89 (2017): 24–28, image of the juggernaut on the cover. On collections of Native American objects and their eighteenth-century meanings: Christian F. Feest, "The Collection of Native American Indian Artifacts in Europe, 1493–1750," in Karen O. Kupperman, ed., *America in European Consciousness, 1493–1760* (Chapel Hill, 1995), 324–360; and Christian F. Feest, "European Collecting of American Indian Artifacts and Art," *Journal of the History of Collections* 5 (1993): 1–11. For museums and their sensory impact: Constance Classen and David Howes, "The Museum as Sensescape: Western Sensibilities and Indigenous Artifacts," in Elizabeth Edwards, Christ Gosden, and Ruth B. Philips, eds. *Sensible Objects: Colonialism, Museums, and Material Culture* (New York, 2006): 199–222.

40. For Sloane: Delbourgo, *Collecting the World*. For the trustees and whiggish intentions for the museum, Kim Sloan, ed., with Andrew Burnett, *Enlightenment: Discovering the World in the Eighteenth Century* (Washington, DC, 2003); and Troy O. Bickham, *Savages Within the Empire: Representations of American Indians in Eighteenth-Century Britain* (Oxford, 2005), 34–50. The catalogue is by Robert Dodsley, entitled *The General Contents of the British Museum* (London, 1761), esp. 26–35.

41. Hunt, Jacob, and Mijnhardt, *The Book that Changed Europe*, 194.

42. *CRC* 1: 310–379, 446–447; 2: 108–109.

43. *CRC* 5: 326; Hunt, Jacob, and Mijnhardt, *The Book that Changed Europe*, 118–119.

44. Hunt, Jacob, and Mijnhardt, *The Book that Changed Europe*, 206.

45. *CRC* 1: 304 for the quotation, after 304 for the image.

46. *CRC* 1: facing 296.

47. *CRC* 1: 283–309 for the election and coronation, with some eleven pages of images inserted. The image is facing 296. For the newspaper account, just one of many: *The New England Courant*, Jan. 25–Feb. 1, 1725.

48. *CRC* 2: 78.

49. *CRC* 1: facing 325.

50. *CRC* 5: 319–360 for their critical history of Protestantism; Hunt, Jacob, and Mijnhardt, *The Book that Changed Europe*, 274, 279; Anne Vila, "The 'French Convulsionaries' and their Fellow Fanatics in Bernard and Picart's *Cérémonies et coutumes religieuses de tou les peuples du monde*," December 10, 2021 seminar paper, University of Minnesota project on *CRC*, to be published as part of Vila's forthcoming *Convulsive Enlightenment: Lives and Afterlives of the Convulsionaries in French Culture and Theory (18th to 21st Centuries)*.

51. *CRC* 5: 360; Hunt, Jacob, and Mijnhardt, *The Book that Changed Europe*, 114.

52. *CRC* 5: 319–322.

53. *CRC* 5: 161; for further evidence on utility, see Hunt, Jacob, and Mijnhardt, *The Book that Changed Europe*, 28.

54. David Brafman, "Picart, Bernard, Hermes, and Muhammad (Not Necessarily in That Order)," in Hunt, Jacob, and Mijnhardt, eds., *Bernard Picart*, 139–168; and Kiswar Rizvi, "Persian Pictures: Art, Documentation, and Self-Reflection in Jean Frederic Bernard and Bernard Picart's Representations of Islam," in Hunt, Jacob, and Mijnardt, eds., *Bernard Picart*, 169–196. For broad accounts of British politics and changing perceptions of Islam: Alexander Bevilacqua, *The Republic of Arabic Letters: Islam and the European Enlightenment* (Cambridge, MA, 2018); and Humberto Garcia, *Islam and the English Enlightenment, 1670–1840* (Baltimore, 2012). The most influential of the books in Bernard's library, which challenges misperceptions, was [H. Reland], *Four Treatises Concerning the Doctrine, Discipline and Worship of the Mahometans* (London, 1712).

55. Brafman, "Picart, Bernard"; and Rizvi, "Persian Pictures."

56. Rizvi, "Persian Pictures," 187–190. For the Bairam festival image: *CRC* 7: following 128.

57. *CRC* 7: following 34.

58. *CRC* 7: following 122.

59. *CRC* 4: v; Rizvi, "Persian Pictures," 179–182.

60. [Robert Beverly], *The History and Present State of Virginia* (London, 1705).

61. See Susan Scott Parrish, editor's "Introduction" to Robert Beverly, *The History and Present State of Virginia* (Chapel Hill, 2013), xi–xxxviii; and Jeffrey Ruggles, *Dictionary of Virginia Biography*, "Robert Beverly (d. 1722)," *Encyclopedia Virginia* online (http://encyclopediavirginia.org/entries/beverly_robert_d_1772).

62. Beverly, *History*, 37, 33, 42.

63. *CRC* 3: 15.

64. *CRC* 3: facing 132 (the Timucuan widows); and facing 100 and 161 (rejoicing dances). De Bry's engraving of the Timucuan's is reprinted in Theodor De Bry, *Voyages en Virginie et Floride* (Paris, 1927), 265, Plate 19.

65. Beverly, *History*, 31, 44, 33.

66. *CRC* 3: facing 112. De Bry's engraving appears in Harriot, *A Briefe and True Report of the New Found Land of Virginia* (Frankfort, 1590), Plate XXI.

67. Beverly, *History*, 34, 44.

68. Bernard, "A Dissertation on the Religion of the Americans": *CRC* 3: 1–120, quote from 13.

69. *CRC* 3: 15.

70. *CRC* 3: facing 150.

71. *CRC* 3: facing 152.

72. *CRC* 3: 149–150, 160.

73. This frontispiece was not included in every English version.

74. Rizvi, "Persian Picture," 169, 190. Broughton later described a ceremonial camel, festooned with flowers and ornaments, in different terms. By his account, such a camel carried a gold-covered copy of the Qur'an from the sultan of the Ottoman Empire to Mecca, after which the camel enjoyed a life of leisure: Broughton, *Dictionary*, 2: 110.

75. For one example from Acadia: Mark Peterson, *The City-State of Boston: The Rise and Fall of an Atlantic Power* (Princeton, 2019), 255–277. For comment on tolerant American Catholics: Michael D. Breidenbach, *Our Dear-Bought Liberty: Catholics and Religious Toleration in Early America* (Cambridge, MA, 2021), 93–146. For American newspapers and reports on the papacy and other European developments: William Harrison Taylor, "'Conscious of their own Idolatry': American Newspapers, the Suppression of the Jesuits, and American Religious Liberty," in Peter C. Messer and William Harrison Taylor, eds., *Revolution as Reformation: Protestant Faith in the Age of Revolutions, 1688–1832* (Tuscaloosa, AL, 2021), 75–95. For Benedict XIV: Rebecca Messbarger, Christopher M. S. Johns, and Philip Gavett, *The Enlightenment and Benedict XIV: Art, Science and Spirituality* (Toronto, 2016).

76. Jonathan Mayhew, *A Discourse Concerning Unlimited Submission* (Boston, 1750), "Preface" [n.p.], iii; and Thomas Prince, *Sermon Culloden* (Boston, 1746), 8-10, 17.

77. Jonathan Edwards, "Notes on the Apocalypse" and *An Humble Attempt*, in *The Works of Jonathan Edwards*, Perry Miller and Harry S. Stout, gen eds., 26 vols. (New Haven, 1957–2008) (hereafter *WJE*), vol. 5: *Apocalyptic Writings*, ed. Stephen J. Stein, 98, 138; see 117 and 178 for Islam and heathenism. For Edwards's collection of religious geographies: *WJE*, vol. 26: *Catalogues of Books*, ed. Peter J. Thuesen, 77, 177, 188, 206, 217–218, 241, 253, 282, 305.

78. Edwards, "Notes on the Apocalypse," 139–140; see Stephen J. Stein, "Cotton Mather and Jonathan Edwards on the Number of the Beast: Eighteenth-Century Speculation About the Antichrist," *Proceedings of the American Antiquarian Society* 84 (1975), 293–315.

79. Dudley Bradstreet, "Dudley Bradstreet's Diary," *Proceedings of the Massachusetts Historical Society*, 2nd ser., 11 (1896–1897): 416–446 (430 for the wounded officer

and the friar); [Anon.], "Journal from New England to Cape Breton," by a soldier in the 4th Massachusetts regiment, Huntington Library, San Marino, CA, published in Louis Effingham DeForest, ed., *Louisbourg Journals 1745* (New York, 1932): 1–54, quotations from 34; Eli Forbush to Steven Williams, August 4, 1757, *The Bulletin of the Fort Ticonderoga Museum* 1 (1929): 19–23, quotation from 22.

80. William Pote, *The Journal of Captain William Pote, Jr. During His Captivity in the French and Indian War*, ed. John Fletcher Hurst with "Historical Introduction" and annotations by Victor H. Paltsits (New York, 1896), 109, 122–123.

81. Isaac Norris, travel diary included in journals and accounts, 1733–1749, Huntington Library; Richard Warbuton, "Some Notes of a Tour Made in Italy in the Years 1735 and 1736," Huntington Library, ms. pp. 69–71, 74.

82. [Anon.], Diary of a trip to Holland, June 1761, entries from July 17–21, Huntington Library.

Chapter 6

1. Edwards's edition of Brainerd's diary was first published in 1749. This chapter refers to the modern edition that indicates Edwards's editorial interventions: Jonathan Edwards, *The Works of Jonathan Edwards*, Perry Miller and Harry S. Stout, gen eds., 26 vols. (New Haven, 1957–2008) (hereafter *WJE*), vol. 7: *The Life of David Brainerd*, ed. Norman Pettit (hereafter cited as Brainerd, *Life*). For background and composition, see Brainerd, *Life* "Editor's Introduction," esp. 5–16; for the quote, 309. Three other important works on Brainerd, Edwards, and missions inform my comments here and later in the chapter: Rachel Wheeler, *To Live upon Hope: Mohicans and Missionaries in the Eighteenth-Century Northeast* (Ithaca, NY, 2008), esp. 175–222; Rachel M. Wheeler, "Edwards as Missionary," in Stephen J. Stein, ed., *The Cambridge Companion to Jonathan Edwards* (New York, 2007), 196–214; and John A. Grigg, *The Lives of David Brainerd: The Making of an Evangelical Icon* (New York, 2009), 45–146. For the popularity of the diary, see Grigg, 70, 95.

2. Although Brainerd does not name the tribal groups, we can surmise that he encountered the Susquehannock people on Juniata Island, while he lived among the Lenape (Delaware) at the Forks of the Delaware. See Brainerd, *Life*, 333 for further mention of differences between the customs of the Susquehannock and Lenape.

3. Brainerd, *Life*, 329.

4. For this and the next paragraph, Brainerd, *Life*, 329–330.

5. Although there is no evidence that Brainerd studied such literature, his mentor Edwards immersed himself in it, as Chapter 4 demonstrates.

6. Brainerd, *Life*, 351, 355–357, 365–366, 318.

7. David Brainerd, *Mirabilia Dei inter Indicos* (Philadelphia, [1746]), 206–207.

8. Brainerd, *Life*, 301, 314, 317.

9. Brainerd, *Life*, 310, 325, 366. Edwards also intimated that Brainerd surpassed Moravian competitors and deist critics in moral and theological propriety: Brainerd,

Life, 314–317, 346. For criticisms of deism, see also Laura M. Stevens, *The Poor Indians: British Missionaries, Native Americans, and Colonial Sensibility* (Philadelphia, 2004), 118–137.

10. Brainerd, *Life*, 366.

11. Brainerd, *Life*, 316, 324, 346, 351, 365–366.

12. Brainerd, *Life*, 320, 325, 310, 347, 354.

13. Few historians of eighteenth-century missions focus on such issues or on the literature of comparative religions: see, for one example of such omission, David Hempton, *The Church in the Long Eighteenth Century* (New York, 2011), esp. 57–104. For a study of Edwards's familiarity with comparative religions: Gerald R. McDermott, *Jonathan Edwards Confronts the Gods: Christian Theology, Enlightenment Religion, and Non-Christian Faiths* (New York, 2000).

14. Much of the current literature on this topic demonstrates that many Natives in New England adopted a Christian identity as a strategy for communal survival in the face of settler colonialism. In light of this social context, scholars have debated whether Christian affiliation was merely a contingent adaptation to political circumstances or the creation of an "Indian" form of Christianity that encoded Protestant ideas of conversion in Native idioms. For the development of an Indian form of Christianity, which implied the salience of the term "conversion," see David J. Silverman, *Faith and Boundaries: Colonists, Christianity, and Community Among the Wampanoag Indians of Martha's Vineyard, 1600–1871* (New York, 2005), with a review of the literature on 8–11; Wheeler, *To Live Upon Hope*, 10–11; William B. Hart, "*For the Good of Their Souls": Performing Christianity in Eighteenth-Century Mohawk Country* (Amherst, MA, 2020); and Edwards E. Andrews, *Native Apostles: Black and Indian Missionaries in the British Atlantic World* (Cambridge, MA, 2013). For a critique of the term "conversion" and insistence on political motives: Linford D. Fisher, *The Indian Great Awakening: Religion and the Shaping of Native Cultures in Early America* (New York, 2012), 87–106. For other discussions of differences between Native and missionary versions of Christianity, see the essays in Joel Martin and Mark Nicholas, *Native Americans, Christianity, and the Reshaping of the American Religious Landscape* (Chapel Hill, 2010) and Jean O'Brian, "'They Are so Frequently Shifting Their Place of Residence': Land and the Construction of Social Place of Indians in Colonial Massachusetts," in Martin Daunton and Rick Halpern, eds., *Empire and Others: British Encounters with Indigenous Peoples, 1600–1850* (Philadelphia, 1999), 204–216. As used by contemporary missiologists and anthropologists, the term "conversion" encompasses adaptation, some syncretistic practice, and purposes for political survival: see Stanley H. Skreslet, *Comprehending Mission: The Questions, Methods, Themes, Problems, and Prospects of Missiology* (Maryknoll, NY, 2012), 97–134.

15. Jennifer Graber, *The Gods of Indian Country: Religion and the Struggle for the American West* (New York, 2018); and Kathryn Gin Lum, *Heathen: Religion and Race in American History* (Cambridge, MA, 2022). For the nineteenth-century story in America, see also Sean P. Harvey, *Native Tongues: Colonialism and Race from Encounter to the Reservation* (Cambridge, MA, 2015); and Claudio Saunt, *Unworthy Republic: The Dispossession of Native Americans and Their Road to Indian Territory*

(New York, 2020). This chapter omits discussion of Moravian missions, which differed markedly from English missions: see Wheeler, *To Live Upon Hope*, 80–104.

16. For histories of missions in the British Empire that stress contingency and difference: Norman Etherington, ed., *Missions and Empire* (Oxford, 2005); and Peggy Brock, ed., *Indigenous Peoples and Religious Change*, Studies in Christian Mission 31 (Leiden and Boston, 2005).

17. For examples from non-evangelicals who made conversion a central issue, see Charles Chauncy, *Twelve Sermons* (Boston, 1765), 338–339; and John S. Oakes, *Conservative Revolutionaries: Transformation and Tradition in the Religious and Political Thought of Charles Chauncy and Jonathan Mayhew* (Eugene, OR, 2016). 21–22, 173–183. For a cursory review of the different theological factions related to the revivals, see Brooks Holifield, *Theology in America: Christian Thought from the Age of the Puritans to the Civil War* (New Haven, CT, 2003), 127–128.

18. [Elisha Williams], *The Essential Rights and Liberties of Protestants* (Boston, 1744); for Gridley, the anonymous essay published under his editorship, "The Difference Between Popery and Protestantism," *The American Magazine* 3 (1746): 10–12; and Charles R. McKirdy, *The Last Great Colonial Lawyer: The Life and Legacy of Jeremiah Gridley* (Amherst, MA, 2018), 43–52; Samuel Johnson, definition of "liberty" in *A Dictionary of the English Language* (London, 1755); and [Caleb Fleming], *The Palladium of Great Britain and Ireland* (London, 1762).

19. Jonathan Mayhew, *Seven Sermons* (Boston; repr. London, 1750), 20, 43–45, 51.

20. Locke to William Molyneux, January 20, 1693, letter 1592 in E. S. De Beer, ed., *The Correspondence of John Locke*, 8 vols. (Oxford, 1976–1989), 4: 623–628, quotation from 625–626.

21. Solomon Stoddard, *A Treatise Concerning Conversion* (Boston, 1719); and Cotton Mather, *The Converted Sinner* (Boston, 1724).

22. The most concerted discussion is D. Bruce Hindmarsh, *The Evangelical Conversion Narrative; Spiritual Autobiography in Early Modern England* (New York, 2005). Hindmarsh provides a helpful description of the intellectual currents that formed a variety of evangelical conversion theologies. My purpose here is to account for a common thread among evangelicals and other Protestants from 1720 through 1760. See also Patricia Caldwell, *The Puritan Conversion Narrative: The Beginnings of American Expression* (New York, 1983); Mark A. Noll, *A History of Evangelicalism: People, Movements and Ideas in the English Speaking World*, vol. 1: *The Rise of Evangelicalism: The Age of Edwards, Whitefield, and the Wesleys* (Downers Grove, IL, 2003).

23. J. A. Robe, editor's "Preface" to *The Christian Monthly History* 1 (Edinburgh, 1743), 1–39; Timothy E. W. Gloege, "The Trouble with 'Christian History': Thomas Prince's 'Great Awakening'" *Church History* 82 (2013): 126–165; Jennifer Snead, "Print, Predestination, and the Public Sphere: Transatlantic Evangelical Periodicals, 1740–1745" *Early American Literature* 45 (2010): 93–118. Snead's language, p. 109, is helpful: London magazines displayed "an attempt to reconcile human use of agency and reason within the public sphere with the soteriological tenets that held faith in both to be useless."

24. Sarah Osborn, *Memoirs of the Life of Mrs. Sarah Osborn . . .* (Worcester, MA, 1799), 21–24. Osborn's biography and memoirs are discussed in Catherine A. Brekus, *Sarah Osborn's World: The Rise of Evangelical Christianity in Early America* (New Haven, 2013), esp. 93–118 on conversion. The interpretation here follows Brekus's biography of Osborn but suggests a different account of her conversion.

25. Osborn, *Memoirs*, 24, 26–30.

26. Sarah Osborn, *Familiar Letters, Written by Mrs. Sarah Osborn, and Miss Susanna Anthony* (Newport, 1807), 149–150, 152. In her *In the Neighborhood: Women's Publication in Early America* (Amherst, MA, 2016), 62–83, Caroline Wigginton gives a compelling reading of how multiple meanings of conversion and affection intersected in Osborn's life and particularly in her vexed relationship with an enslaved woman.

27. The diary of Hannah Heaton, a woman from rural North Haven, Connecticut, and Southampton, Long Island, further exemplified the perplexity around affections and will for New Englanders: Hannah Heaton, *The World of Hannah Heaton: The Diary of an Eighteenth-Century New England Farm Woman*, ed. Barbara E. Lacey (DeKalb, IL, 2003), esp. 8–10, 12, 14, 17, 138. The same could be said of Daniel Rogers, a Harvard graduate who despaired of his ability to choose Christ yet admired preachers who called for such decisions: Daniel Rogers, "Diary, 1740–175[3]," Rogers Family Papers, 1614–1950, ser. II, box 5B, New York Historical Society, New York.

28. Experience Mayhew, "A Discourse Concerning Human Liberty, or, an Essay on the Proposition that Man Is a Free-Agent," undated manuscript, Massachusetts Historical Society, Boston.

29. Jonathan Edwards, *A Careful and Strict Enquiry into . . . Freedom of the Will* (Boston, 1754).

30. Edwards, *WJE*, vol. 1: *Freedom of the Will*, ed. Paul Ramsey (hereafter *FW*), 137, 144. The following explication of Edwards relies heavily on Ramsey, "Editor's Introduction" to *FW*, 1–118; and Allen C. Guelzo, *Edwards on the Will: A Century of American Theological Debate* (Middletown, CT, 1989).

31. Edwards, *FW*, 162, 164, 346–347, 351. In a suggestive entry into his notebook of miscellanies, Edwards described Christ as elected by God and free as a moral agent at the same time, and he argued that the believer shared Christ's nature in this respect— predestined and capable of choice: Edwards, Miscellany no. 1245, in *WJE*, vol. 23: *The "Miscellanies" 1153–1360*, ed. Douglas A. Sweeney, 177–181.

32. Edwards, *FW*, 326; Guelzo, *Edwards on the Will*, 26, 51.

33. Edwards, *FW*, 162, 164.

34. Quoted and cited in Guelzo, *Edwards on the Will*, 38.

35. Edwards, quote from *Miscellanies* in Guelzo, *Edwards on the Will*, 48; also Edwards, *FW*, 351.

36. For the ecumenical, enlightened, and evangelical embrace of such claims: Isabel Rivers, *Reason, Grace, and Sentiment: A Study of the Language of Religion and Ethics in England, 1660–1780*, 2 vols. (New York, 1991, 2000), vol. 1: *Whichcote to Wesley*, 164–173. For rural Connecticut Calvinists who echoed Edwards on the will and conversion, we can point to Joseph Bellamy, "Theological Questions," Yale Divinity School library, New Haven, CT; Jeremiah Day, *The Ability of God to Restrain Sin, in*

a Way Consistent with the Liberty of the Creature (New Haven, 1774); and Levi Hart, "Diary, 1760–1807," Gratz Collection, sermons, box 7, vol. 2, Pennsylvania Historical Society, Philadelphia. Day was a part-time farmer and pastor who wrote hundreds of pages on divine providence and human liberty: "Metaphysical Essays," c. 1760, Connecticut Historical Society, Hartford, CT. For a statement on how evangelical Protestants in this period attempted to distance themselves from political coercion, see A. G. Roeber, "The Waters of Rebirth: The Eighteenth-Century and Transoceanic Protestant Christianity," *Church History* 79 (2010): 40–76.

37. Jonathan Mayhew, "Sermon IX," in *Sermons upon the Following Subjects* (Boston, 1755), 256–307, quote from 291–292. Many passages out of Mayhew on the nature of moral choice—in sum, that we must admit that God caused all that is, including our wills, but that people still had the power to do as they willed—sound very much like the evangelical Edwards and depend on the same reading of Locke and Hutcheson as Edwards gave. See Jonathan Mayhew, sermon "On Hearing the Word," in *Sermons upon the Following Subjects*, 296–303.

38. Ezra Stiles, *A Discourse on the Christian Union* (Boston, 1761; repr. Bookfield, MA, 1799), 65–66.

39. [John Edwards], *The Conversion of a Mehometan* (London, 1757; rep. New London, 1775), 17, 21. For John Edwards, no relation to Jonathan Edwards of Massachusetts: Jonathan H. Westaway, "Edwards, John (1714–1785)," *Oxford Dictionary of National Biography*, 60 vols. (New York, 2004) 17:939 (hereafter ODNB).

40. For the conversion especially of Native Americans and the Indians of the Asian subcontinent as an agenda of the SPG: the records of the SPG as excerpted in Charles Frederick Pascoe, *Classified Digest of the Records of the Society for the Propagation of the Gospel in Foreign Parts, 1701–1893* (London, 1893), 1–87 (quotation from 7–8); and, for a close narrative, C. F. Pascoe, *Two Hundred Years of the S.P.G.: An Historical Account of the Society for the Propagation of the Gospel in Foreign Parts, 1701–1900*, 2 vols. (London, 1901), vol. 1. In 1965 the SPG was renamed the United Society Partners in the Gospel (USPG). I have also consulted the U.S.P.G., Series A Letterbooks, 1702–1737, vols. 1–3 on microfilm (Film MS 88) at the Yale Divinity School library, New Haven, CT. These volumes contain dozens of letters between London and the colonies that promote the "propagation of the gospel" among Native inhabitants along with the enhancement of Anglican churches. For the numbers of SPG missionaries and history of the organization: Jean Fitts Hankins, "Bringing the Good News: Protestant Missionaries to the Indians of New England and New York, 1700–1775," Ph.D. diss., University of Connecticut, 1993. For recent scholarship on the SPG in America: Travis Glasson, *Mastering Christianity: Missionary Anglicanism and Slavery in the Atlantic World* (New York, 2012); Stevens, *Poor Indians*; and David Manning, "Anglican Religious Societies, Organizations, and Missions," in Jeremy Gregory, ed., *The Oxford History of Anglicanism*, vol. 2: *Establishment and Empire, 1662–1829* (Oxford, 2017), 429–527. On the decline of Native American slavery and missions: Margaret Ellen Newell, *Brethren by Nature: New England Indians, Colonists, and the Origins of American Slavery* (Ithaca, NY, 2015); and Wendy Warren, *New England Bound: Slavery and Colonization in Early America* (New York, 2016).

41. [Thomas Bray], *Missionalia: Or, a Collection of Missionary Pieces Relating to the Conversion of the Heathen; Both the African and American Indians* (London, 1727), 58–60. For an introduction to Bray and *Missionalia*: Samuel Clyde McCulloch, "A Plea fo[r] Further Missionary Activity in Colonial America—Dr. Thomas Bray's *Missionalia*," *Historical Magazine of the Protestant Episcopal Church*, 15 (1946): 232–245.

42. Bray, *Missionalia*, 60, 63.

43. Frederick V. Mills, Sr., "The Society in Scotland for Propagating Christian Knowledge in British North America, 1730–1775," *Church History* 63 (1994): 15–30. Many participants in mission beside members of the SSPCK also reflected ecumenical sentiments. A theologically diverse collection of ministers, for example, endorsed Experience Mayhew's work on Martha's Vineyard: the prefatory "Attestation" of Boston ministers to Experience Mayhew, *Indian Converts* (London, 1727), published in a modern edition as *Experience Mayhew's Indian Converts: A Cultural Edition*, ed., intro. Laura Arnold Leibman (Amherst, MA, 2008), 85–90. (Subsequent references to Mayhew's *Indian Converts* are made to the Leibman edition, noted as *IC*.) Leibman, editor's "Introduction," to *IC*, 15, indicates that Mayhew was indifferent to Old Light/New Light polemics.

44. Colin G. Calloway, *White People, Indians, and Highlanders: Tribal Peoples and Colonial Encounters in Scotland and America* (New York, 2007); and Laura M. Stevens, "The Souls of Highlanders, the Salvation of Indians: Scottish Mission and Eighteenth-Century British Empire" in Martin and Nicholas, eds., *Native Americans, Christianity, and the Reshaping of the American Religious Landscape*, 179–200.

45. Cotton Mather, *The Negro Christianized* (Boston, 1706), 39, (italics reduced). Edwards issued his warnings against the use of force in the context of the 1740 visit to Massachusetts of his cousin Eunice Williams, who had been captured by Mohawks, raised in a Mohawk village, and chose to remain with her Mohawk family: Mark Valeri, "Forgiveness: From the Puritans to Jonathan Edwards," in Laurie F. Maffly-Kipp, Leigh E. Schmidt, and Mark Valeri, eds., *Practicing Protestants: Histories of Christian Life in America, 1630–1965* (Baltimore, 2006), 35–48, esp. 45–46.

46. Mather, *The Negro Christianized*, 24. Tindal's *Christianity as Old as the Creation* (London, 1730), reprinted frequently, encapsulated deist arguments to the effect that religious conscience was natural and universal. Deists such as Tindal, however, took the implications of this logic in a different direction than did Protestant missionaries. He concluded that biblical revelation was redundant, orthodox Protestant doctrine misleading, and the evangelism of non-Christians an unnecessary imposition of accidental rather than essential theological tenets: see the discussion in Jonathan Z. Smith, "Religion, Religions, Religious," in Mark C. Taylor, ed., *Critical Terms for Religious Studies* (Chicago, 1998), 269–284.

47. Thomas Wilson, *An Essay Towards an Instruction for the Indians; Explaining the Most Essential Doctrines of Christianity* (London, 1740). Wilson welcomed dissenters, Quakers, and loyalist Catholics into his worship services and corresponded with the Moravian leader Zinzendorf about overseas missions. When James Oglethorpe asked Wilson for advice on the evangelization of Native Americans in Georgia, Wilson

produced his *Essay*: Carole Watterson Troxler, "Wilson, Thomas (1663–1755)," ODNB online.

48. Wilson, *Essay*, ii–iii, viii–ix, xi, xvi, xxxiii; for ignorant Britons, xxx.

49. Wilson, *Essay*, ix, 1; John Calvin, *Institutes of the Christian Religion*, ed. John T. McNeill, trans. Ford Lewis Battles, Library of Christian Classics, vols. 20, 21 (Philadelphia, 1960), Book 1, Chapters 2–5; esp. pp. 43–45 in the first volume of this edition. Wilson did entertain the possibility that the cosmological argument—that there must be a First Cause or power to the universe—might have some sway, certainly more than the rationalist abstractions of the ontological argument (the very idea of a god logically proves the existence of God) or the teleological argument (the design of the universe evidences an intelligent designer): Wilson, *Essay*, ix.

50. For the mission on Martha's Vineyard: Silverman, *Faith and Boundaries*; for Mayhew's translations and publications on language: Sarah Rivett, *Unscripted America: Indigenous Languages and the Origins of a Literary Nation* (New York, 2017), 108–208. For contrasting readings of missionaries' understanding of Indigenous cultures (and languages), see Linford D. Fisher, "'It Provd But Temporary, and Short Lived': Pequot Affiliation in the First Great Awakening," *Ethnohistory* 59 (2012): 465–488; and Stevens, *Poor Indians*.

51. This was included under a separate title in the original version of Mayhew's compilation of conversion stories from Martha's Vineyard and reprinted in *IC*.

52. Mayhew, *Discourse*, in *IC*, 2, 8. In this sense, these eighteenth-century missionaries did not deploy "reason" as a cudgel to claim White superiority, as did, according to Gin Lum, nineteenth-century missionaries to Hawaiian, Native North American, and Chinese people: Gin Lum, *Heathen*, e.g., 98–100.

53. Mayhew, *Discourse*, in *IC*, 6, 10–11.

54. For the creation of the Stockbridge mission: Wheeler, *To Live upon Hope*, 17–64, esp. 47 for Sergeant's preaching.

55. Jonathan Edwards, sermon on "The Importance of a Future State," c. 1723, in *WJE*, vol. 10: *Sermons and Discourses, 1720–1723*, ed. Wilson H. Kimnach, 357–358; Samuel Hopkins (1693–1755), *An Address to the People of New-England* (Philadelphia, 1757), 9, 16, 19. For Edwards's reliance on religious geographies: Edwards, *WJE*, vol. 9: *A History of the Work of Redemption*, ed. John F. Wilson (hereafter *HWR*), 408–409, 432–436. For Edwards, comparative religions, and natural consciousness as a preparation for conversion: the "Editor's Introduction" to Edwards, *WJE*, vol. 20: *The "Miscellanies" 833–1152*, ed. Amy Plantiga Pauw, 2–17. Edwards brought his thoughts to fruition in his treatise on "The Nature of True Virtue," where he commended many forms non-Christian moral reason as laudable in the civic realm even if deficient in a theological sense: *Two Dissertations, I. Concerning the End for Which God Created the World. II. The Nature of True Virtue*, published posthumously (Boston, 1765) and included in Edwards, *WJE*, vol. 8: *Ethical Writings*, ed. Paul Ramsey, 539–627.

56. For Edwards's and Brainerd's toleration of Native cosmologies: Rivett, *Unscripted America*, 151–184, esp. 159–160; and Grigg, *Brainerd*, 111–113. For these missionaries, the continuation of many traditional practices did not necessarily imply syncretism in the sense of the worship of several deities. For a broader discussion of

this issue: Douglas L. Winiarski, "Native American Popular Religion in New England's Old Colony, 1670–1770," *Religion and American Culture* 15 (2005): 147–186. New England missionaries, however, critiqued what they deemed to be the syncretism of Iroquoian Catholics who had converted under Jesuit missions because these converts retained shamanic practices: see, for a comparison, Allen Greer, *Mohawk Saint: Catherine Tekakwitha and the Jesuits* (New York, 2006). As a pastor among established Wampanoag congregations in which Christian rites were observed, Mayhew appears to have been less tolerant than were Edwards and Brainerd toward traditional practices.

57. Edwards, *HWR*, 434–435. See McDermott, *Jonathan Edwards Confronts the Gods*, 194–206.

58. It is striking that missionaries such as Mayhew, Brainerd, Edwards, and Smith, unlike Restoration-era observers, rarely mentioned Native physical characteristics. For colonial attention to indigenous bodies and the presumed superiority of western culture: David Spurr, *The Rhetoric of Empire: Colonial Discourse in Journalism, Travel Writings, and Imperial Administration* (Durham, NC, 1993).

59. For Sergeant and Edwards: Wheeler, *To Live upon Hope*, 213–218. Wheelock, an evangelical Calvinist who founded Dartmouth College as a school for Natives, stood out among his evangelical contemporaries for his rejection of Indigenous culture, disparagement of the Algonquian language, concern for the civilizing process, and promotion of imperial agendas: Baxter Perry Smith, *The History of Dartmouth College* (Boston, 1878), 1–22; James Axtell, "Dr. Wheelock's Little Red School," in Axtell, ed., *The European and the Indian: Essays in the Ethnohistory of Colonial North America* (New York, 1981), 87–109; John King Lord and Frederick Chase, *A History of Dartmouth College and the Town of Hanover, New Hampshire*, 2 vols. (Cambridge, U.K., 1891), 1: 82–87.

60. Edwards, sermon on 2 Peter 1:19, August 16, 1751, "To the Mohawks at the Treaty," in Wilson H. Kimnach, Kenneth P. Minkema, and Douglas A. Sweeney, eds., *The Sermons of Jonathan Edwards: A Reader* (New Haven, CT, 1999), 105–110 (quotations from 107, 109). For the Albany negotiations: Wheeler, *To Live upon Hope*, 175–186. For the contingency of loyalties to Britain, see the ample discussion in Christian P. Cuthbert, "'Your Most Humble Servant': The Public Service of John Stoddard as an Expression of the Religious Ideology of Jonathan Edwards," Ph.D. diss., Union Presbyterian Seminary, 2016, 223–242.

61. Edwards, Sermon on 1 Peter 4:7 (no. 1019), January 1, 1752, Works of Jonathan Edwards Online, the Jonathan Edwards Center at Yale University (hereafter WJEO), vol 70; for the quote on "Beasts": Edwards, sermon titled "To the Indian Children at Stockbridge," (no. 988), February 1751, WJEO, vol. 69. For Edwards's approach to preaching among Mohicans: Wheeler, "Edwards as Missionary"; and Wheeler, *To Live upon Hope*, 175–222. For Edwards and Mohican lands and settlements: Stevens, *Poor Indians*, 138–159.

62. Edwards, "To the Mohawks at the Treaty" (Edwards's double negative—"no better ... in no respect"—was not to be taken literally); and Edwards, *Original Sin* (Boston, 1758), in *WJE*, vol. 3: *Original Sin*, ed. Clyde A. Holbrook, 424. This paragraph relies on

Rachel Wheeler, "'Friends to Your Souls': Jonathan Edwards' Indian Pastorate and the Doctrine of Original Sin," *Church History* 72 (2003): 736–765, the characterization "egalitarian" from 765. As Sarah Rivett has contended, Brainerd and Edwards thought that Indians and Britons equally depended on human languages that could not capture divine realities: Rivett, *Unscripted America*, 159–160.

63. Brainerd, *Mirabilia*, cited and quoted in Grigg, *Brainerd*, 93–94; for Brainerd's aversion to Anglicization and warnings to the Delaware about land: Grigg, *Brainerd*, 86–127. The same could be said of Horton, an SSPCK worker on Long Island. By his account of his ministry among the Shinnecock, he advised those who inquired about salvation and baptized new believers with no mention of change in life ways, becoming literate in English, or other civilizing mandates: Azariah Horton, excerpts from his journals in *The Christian Monthly History*, 6, June 1742–first week of March 1743 (Edinburgh, 1744), from July 16, 1742, 8.

64. This biography taken from Smith's papers: Charles Jeffrey Smith, "A Brief Narrative of the Motions and Strivings of Gods Spirit," and "A Diary," Charles Jeffrey Smith Papers, 1758–1765, Yale University library, New Haven, CT.

65. Smith, "Diary," June 10 and July 26, 1763.

66. Smith, "Diary," October 16, 19, 1763.

67. Details about Kirkland are provided in Lord and Chase, *History of Dartmouth College*, 1: 85. During the American Revolution, Kirkland served as a diplomat from Continental forces to the Oneidas and Mohawks.

68. Samuel Kirkland, *The Journal of Samuel Kirkland, November, 1764–February, 1765* (Clinton, NY, 1966), 5, 6, 14.

69. Samuel K. Lothrop, "The Life of Samuel Kirkland," in Jared Sparks, ed., *The Library of American Biography*, vol. 25 (Boston, 1848), 139–364, quotation from 167 and the story of the funeral 169–172.

70. Charles Chauncy, *All Nations of the Earth Blessed in Christ* (Boston, 1762).

71. Chauncy, *All Nations*, 26–27.

72. Chauncy, *All Nations*, 30, 28–29 for quotations, also 12–13, 30–35. For the history of missions and establishment of a church at Oquaga, with reference to Forbes: Daniel R. Mandell, "'Turned Their Minds to Religion': Oquaga and the First Iroquois Church, 1748–1776," *Early American Studies* 11 (2013): 211–242.

73. This missionary agenda is admirably explained in David J. Silverman, *Red Brethren: The Brothertown and Stockbridge Indians and the Problem of Race in Early America* (Ithaca, NY, 2010), 39–40, 64–65; and illustrated in Brainerd, *Mirabilia*, 214–217.

74. Peter C. Mancall, "Illness and Death Among Americans in Bernard Picart's Cérémonies et Coutumes Religieuses," in Lynn Hunt, Margaret Jacob, and Wijnand Mijnardt, eds., *Bernard Picart and the First Global Vision of Religion* (Los Angeles, 2010), 271–287, 281 for Bernard.

75. Wilson, *Essay*, 1–3, 5–6.

76. Wilson, *Essay*, 13–14.

77. Wilson, *Essay*, 34, 44, 68. White's insistence on the social dimensions of Christianity and participation especially in the sacramental practices of the church set him apart from his dissenting contemporaries such as Brainerd, Edwards, and Smith.

78. Wilson, *Essay*, 78, 99.
79. Elam Potter, *The Author's Account of His Conversion and Call* (Boston, 1772), 9; and Mayhew, *Discourse*, in *IC*, 24, 27, 32. See also the evidence in Wheeler, *To Live upon Hope*, 48.
80. Leibman, "Introduction" to *IC*, 1–76, has informed much of the following.
81. Mayhew, *IC*, 267.
82. Mayhew, *IC*, 214–215.
83. Mayhew, *IC*, 198–199.
84. Mayhew, *IC*, 283.
85. Mayhew, *IC*, 148.
86. Quotations from Brainerd, *Mirabilia*, 232, 234; other material from Brainerd, *Life*, 300, 363–365; and Brainerd, *Mirabilia*, 202–204. Grigg, *Brainerd*, 86–127, esp. 98–99, shows that Brainerd overcame an initial revulsion against Delaware culture and manners as he settled into his mission.
87. Grigg, *Brainerd*, 96.
88. Quotations from Brainerd, *Mirabilia*, 229, 214–215; Brainerd, *Life*, 305, 309–310. Other material from *Mirabilia*, 208–215, 229–231; "Diary," 312.
89. Janice Knight, "Learning the Language of God: Jonathan Edwards and the Typology of Nature," *William and Mary Quarterly*, 3rd ser. 48 (1991): 531–551.
90. Wheeler, *To Live upon Hope*, 185.
91. Edwards, "To the Mohawks at the Treaty," 110.
92. Quoted and cited in Wheeler, *To Live upon Hope*, 180–181; Edwards, Sermon on 1 Cor. 6:11, (no. 859), March 1747, re-preached June 1755, WJEO, vol. 72. For Edwards's preaching on hellfire to Whites and divine benevolence to Natives, see Wheeler, *To Live upon Hope*, 175–222.
93. Quoted and cited in Wheeler, *To Live upon Hope*, 181, 216–217.
94. Charles Jeffrey Smith, "Diary," entry from October 13, 1763. Further information on Smith and his mission is given later in the chapter.
95. Smith, "Diary," July 15, 17, 1763.
96. Smith, "Diary," April 18, 1764; and July 19, 1764.
97. Both quoted and cited in Fisher, *Indian Great Awakening*, 88, 78–79. Fisher presents evidence that Native Americans differed among themselves about the nature of disaffiliation and the extent to which it implied a disavowal of traditional ways. The missionaries under scrutiny in this chapter drew the line at worship ceremonies conducted by Indigenous spiritual leaders (so-called powwows) and the invocations of non-Christian spiritual powers.
98. Gin Lum, *Heathen*.
99. Solomon Stoddard, *Question Whether God Is Not Angry with the Country for Doing so Little Towards the Conversion of the Indians?* (Boston, 1723), 8–9; Smith, "Diary," December 11, 1764; February 15, 17, 21, 26, 1765; and June 18, 1765. Smith admittedly found counterexamples as well. He lauded a Church of England vestry in Accomack County, Virginia, which allowed him to meet and pray with enslaved black people and to counsel a neighboring Presbyterian minister who had "been silenced" by Anglican priests: Smith, "Diary," January 20, 25, 1765. New England

laypeople such as the laborer Joseph Bean also used the tropes of cast-down idols, discarded weapons, peaceful relations, and expression of allegiance to the Trinitarian God to describe their conversion: Joseph Bean, "Diary, 1741–1744," Canaday Library, Bryn Mawr College, PA.

100. Daniel K. Richter, "'Some of Them . . . . would always have a minister with them': Mohawk Protestantism, 1683–1719," *American Indian Quarterly*, 16 (1992): 471–484, quotation from 475. For the prayerbook: The Church of England, *The Morning and Evening Prayer, the Liturgy . . .* (New York, 1715). This work was based on translations initially made by Dutch Reformed pastors in Schenectady. For an account of the translation, see John Wright, *Early Prayer Books of America* (St. Paul, MN, 1896), 27–29; and Rivett, *Unscripted America*, 136–137.

101. Edwards sermon on Acts 11:12–13, published as "The Things that Belong to True Religion, January 1751, in *WJE*, vol. 25: *Sermons and Discourses 1743–1758*, ed. Wilson H. Kimnach, 571.

102. For one description of Native Americans' choices in such terms, see [John Edwards], *The Christian Indeed* (London, 1757), reprinted with *The Conversion of a Mehometan*, 8–9. For other descriptions of Native Americans during the war, see Bickham, *Savages Within the Empire*; and Timothy J. Shannon, *Indian Captive, Indian King: Peter Williamson in America and Britain* (Cambridge, MA, 2018).

103. The Algonquian term "powwow" fits in many cases but not all. As an alternative term, shaman, and its correlate, shamanism, are vexed, modern anthropological interpositions. For a discussion of "shamanism," see William S. Simmons, "Southern New England Shamanism: An Ethnographic Reconstruction," *Papers of the 7th Algonquian Conference* (1975): 217–256.

104. Brainerd, *Life*, 326–327; *Mirabilia*, 220, 225.

105. Mayhew, *IC*, 223, italics reduced; Brainerd, *Mirabilia*, 155–158; and Brainerd, *Life*, 320; Edwards, Sermon on John 8:12, published as "Christ, the Light of the World," in *WJE* 10, 537. See Grigg, *Brainerd*, 111–112 and (for Edwards) Rivett, *Unscripted America*, 175.

106. Mayhew, *IC*, 171–172, italics reduced; and *IC*, 263.

107. Poohpoonue and Cornelius and Mary Munneweaunummic are cited and quoted in Wheeler, *To Live upon Hope*, 48, 221. The Uncas quotation is from the will of Benjamin Uncas II, Indian Papers, Connecticut State Library, Hartford, CT, quoted and cited in Linford D. Fisher, "Writing Histories: Empire, Religion, and the Production of Native American Manuscripts, 1600–1800," *Manuscripts* 63 (2011): 277–296, quotation on 283.

108. Mayhew, *IC*, 209–213; Brainerd, *Life*, 380–386; Smith, "Diary," July 21 and July 22, 1763, for baptism and marriage. Oneida and Mohawk converts eagerly sought baptism and sometimes complained about the paucity of Protestant ministers who celebrated the rite: Richter, "'Some of Them . . . . would always have a minister with them'"; Mandell, "'Turned Their Minds to Religion.'" For an extended study of Mohawk use of Christian ritual to "perform" Christianity, with a focus on SPG missionaries rather than on the missionaries discussed in this chapter: Hart, "*For the Good of Their Souls.*"

109. See, for further explication of this point, Avram Alpert, "Philosophy's Systemic Racism," *Aeon Essays*, online periodical, October 6, 2020. Literary scholars also point out that the type of the civil or good Indian itself imposed Anglocentric moral values and political agendas on fictionalized Native peoples: the good Indian was an ally of the British. See, e.g., Peter Way, "The Cutting Edge of Culture: British Soldiers Encounter Native Americans in the French and Indian War," in Daunton and Halpern, eds., *Empire and Others*, 123–148.

110. See Linford D. Fisher, "An Indian Bible and a Brass Hawk: Land, Sachemship Disputes, and Power in the Conversion of Ben Uncas II," *Journal of Social History* 47 (2013): 319–343. For an extended study of "freedom" as a vindication of racialized notions of hegemony: Tyler Stovall, *White Freedom: The Racial History of an Idea* (Princeton, 2021). For an anthropological analysis of how western missionaries' use of the idea of moral agency failed to account for local and communal concerns among indigenous communities, see Webb Keane, *Christian Moderns: Freedom and Fetish in the Mission Encounter* (Berkeley, 2007).

111. Aupaumet's request is cited and quoted in Wheeler, *To Live upon Hope*, 221.

Epilogue

1. Hannah Adams, A *Memoir of Miss Hannah Adams . . . with Additional Notices, by a Friend* (Boston, 1832) (hereafter, Adams, *Memoir*), 43 (her "preference"); 37 (Quincy and the endowment). For the other works mentioned here: Adams, *An Alphabetical Compendium of the Various Sects . . . with an Appendix, Containing a Brief Account of the Different Schemes of Religion Now Embraced Among Mankind* (Boston, 1784); *A View of Religions, in Two Parts*, 2nd ed. (Boston, 1791) (hereafter Adams, *View of Religions*); *A Summary History of New England* (Dedham, MA, 1799), published by an act of Congress (hereafter, Adams, *Summary History*); and *The Truth and Excellence of the Christian Religion Exhibited in Two Parts* (Boston, 1804) (hereafter, Adams, *Truth and Excellence*). For Quincy's father: Josiah Quincy (1744–1775), Diary (travel journal), March 1773, Quincy Papers, no. 61, Massachusetts Historical Society, Boston. The quotation from Zoroaster, which Quincy cited as "lib. lx. ch. 5," most likely came from Thomas Hyde's edition of the ethical sayings of Zoroaster, the *Sad dar*. See Guy G. Stroumsa, "Thomas Hyde and the Birth of Zoroastrian Studies," *Jerusalem Studies in Arabic and Islam* 26 (2002): 216–230. Other discussions of Adams are provided in Thomas A. Tweed, "An American Pioneer in the Study of Religion: Hannah Adams (1755–1831) and Her 'Dictionary of All Religions,'" *Journal of the American Academy of Religion* 60 (1992): 437–464; and Leigh E. Schmidt, "A History of All Religions," *Journal of the Early Republic* 24 (2004): 327–334.

2. Adams, *Summary History*, 102, 238–239, 350.

3. Adams, *Memoir*, 10–11. My interpretation here diverges especially from that of Tweed, "An American Pioneer," who downplays Adams's reliance on earlier writers such as Broughton and mentions nothing of the themes of religious choice and disestablishment.

4. Adams, *View of Religions*, 31, 45, 163, 169; 162–169, "Necessarians"; 96–104, "Hopkinsians."

5. Adams, *Truth and Excellence*, 5, 7, 73.

6. Adams, *View of Religions*, 330; 177–186 for "Papists"; 326–332 for "Italy." For her comments on French and Spanish assistance: *Summary History*, 398–403, 421. For changes in British policy on Catholicism: Evan Haefeli, "Protestant Empire? Anti-Popery and British-American Patriotism, 1558–1776," in Evan Haefeli, ed., *Against Popery: Britain, Empire, and Anti-Catholicism* (Charlottesville, Virginia, 2020), 203–233 For American views of Clement XIV: Michael D. Breidenbach, *Our Dear-Bought Liberty: Catholics and Religious Toleration in Early America* (Cambridge, MS, 2021), 116–230. American ambivalence toward Catholicism following the Franco-American alliance during the Revolution is discussed in Brendan McConville, "A Deal with the Devil: Revolutionary Anti-Popery, Francophobia, and the Dilemmas of Diplomacy," in Haefeli, ed., *Against Popery*, 234–256.

7. Adams, *Summary History*, 425–426 (on the war); and *A View of Religions*, 369–371, quotation from 369.

8. Adams, *View of Religions*, 373, 377, 385.

9. For an extended discussion of "liberty": J. C. D. Clark, *The Language of Liberty: Political Discourse and Social Dynamics in the Anglo-American World* (New York, 1994). On debates about the will and republican politics: Allen C. Guelzo, "From Calvinist Metaphysics to Republican Theory: Jonathan Edwards and James Dana on Freedom of the Will," *Journal of the History of Ideas* (1995): 399–418. For liberty and the mobilization of popular support for revolution: Alan Taylor, *American Revolutions: A Continental History, 1750–1804* (New York, 2016), 137–139. For a helpful analysis of religious language and the Revolution overall: John F. Wilson, "Religion and Revolution in American History," *Journal of Interdisciplinary History* 23 (1993): 597–613.

10. Adams referenced patriot preachers in several places in her *Summary History*, e.g., 297. For Cleaveland and Allen: Johannes Eremo [John Cleaveland], Essex *Gazette*, April 9, 1771, quoted in Stephen Botein, "Natural Rights Reconsidered," in Patricia U. Bonomi, ed., *Party and Political Opposition in Revolutionary America* (Tarrytown, NY, 1980): 13–34; and [John Allen], *An Oration upon the Beauties of Liberty*, 3rd ed. (New London, 1773). For Edwards the Younger, who had lived in Stockbridge and learned the Mohican dialect: Mark Valeri, "The New Divinity and the American Revolution," *William and Mary Quarterly*, 3rd ser. 46 (1989): 741–769; and (on re-nunciation of English identity) Jonathan Edwards, Jr., sermon on Ecc. 7:14, August 1774, in Jonathan Edwards, Jr., sermons, Box 166, folder 2735, item 75758, sermon #390, Hartford Seminary, Hartford, CT. For Langdon, who was instrumental in the founding of Dartmouth College and promoting its missionary agenda: John Langdon Sibley and Clifford K. Shipton, eds., *Sibley's Harvard Graduates*, 18 vols. (Boston, 1873–1999), 10:508–528; and Samuel Langdon, *Government Corrupted by Vice, and Recovered by Righteousness* (Watertown, MA, 1775). For West, who had served on Martha's Vineyard and was the son of a missionary among the Mashpee of Massachusetts: Sibley and Shipton, *Harvard Graduates* 13:501–510; and Samuel

West, *A Sermon Preached Before the Honorable Council* (Boston, 1776), reprinted in John Wingate Thornton, ed., *The Pulpit of the American Revolution: Political Sermons of the Period of 1776* (Boston, 1860).

11. For liberty and equality, see Michal Jan Rozbicki, *Culture and Liberty in the Age of the American Revolution* (Charlottesville, VA, 2011). For the general point about Enlightenment discourse and colonization: Linda Tuhiwai Smith, *Decolonizing Methodologies: Research and Indigenous Peoples* (New York, 1999), esp. 1–77. According to Smith, the idea of a universal humanity or rationality implied a single intellectual regime—a moral discourse—that validated imperial institutions.

12. See, e.g., David Chidester, *Savage Systems: Colonialism and Comparative Religion in Southern Africa* (Charlottesville, VA, 1996); Sylvester A. Johnson, *African-American Religions, 1500–2000: Colonialism, Democracy, and Freedom* (New York, 2015); Tisa Wenger, *Religious Freedom: The Contested History of an American Ideal* (Chapel Hill, 2017); and Kathryn Gin Lum, *Heathen: Religion and Race in American History* (Cambridge, MA, 2022).

13. See Joyce E. Chaplin, *Subject Matter: Technology, the Body, and Science on the Anglo-American Frontier, 1500–1676* (Cambridge, MA, 2003), which argues that race was an incoherent, rarely used idiom through the seventeenth century and had little to do with religion. Snait Gissis shows that racial identities were portrayed as fluid and unmoored to fixed categories until the development of biological taxonomies of race during the 1780s: Snait B. Gissis, "Visualizing 'Race' in the Eighteenth Century," *Historical Studies in the Natural Sciences* 41 (2011): 41–203. For a counterargument, which stresses the importance of Euro-centric notions of cultural supremacy as implicitly racist, even if unattended by scientific justifications for racial taxonomies based on physical characteristics, see Johnson, *African American Religions, 1500–2000*.

14. For a parallel account of intellectual exchange among European and indigenous peoples, see Steven Feierman, *Peasant Intellectuals: History and Anthropology in Tanzania* (Madison, WI, 1990).

15. Charles Taylor, *A Secular Age* (Cambridge, MA, 2007), esp. 1–22. Taylor's work offers a very helpful framework for understanding the transformations discussed in my study. For the emergence of autonomous moral judgment based on social opinion in the eighteenth century: Jürgen Habermas, *The Structural Transformation of the Public Sphere: An Inquiry into a Category of Bourgeois Society*, trans. Thomas Burger with Frederick Lawrence (1962; 1989; repr. Cambridge, MA, 1991). If by "secularism" we mean in part the idea that modern states were held together by moral conventions rather than by theological creed, this study confirms the interpretations discussed in the Introduction, such as Talal Asad, *Formations of the Secular: Christianity, Islam, Modernity* (Stanford, CA, 2003); Jonathan Z. Smith, "Religion, Religions, Religious," in Mark C. Taylor, ed., *Critical Terms for Religious Studies* (Chicago, 1998), 269–284; and Webb Keane, *Christian Moderns: Freedom and Fetish in the Mission Encounter* (Berkeley, CA, 2007).

16. The criticisms of the Whig narrative can be sampled in Alexandra Walsham, *Charitable Hatred: Tolerance and Intolerance in England, 1500–1700* (New York,

2006); Ethan H. Shagan, *The Rule of Moderation: Violence, Religion and the Politics of Restraint in Early Modern England* (New York, 2011); Ethan H. Shagan, ed., Introduction to *Catholics and the Protestant Nation: Religious Politics and Identity in Early Modern England* (Manchester, U.K., 2005), 1–21; and Benjamin J. Kaplan, *Divided by Faith: Religious Conflict and the Practice of Toleration in Early Modern Europe* (Cambridge, MA, 2007). For influential statements from postcolonial critics of secularization, see Asad, *Formations of the Secular*; Talal Asad, "Thinking About Religion, Belief, and Politics," in Robert A. Orsi, ed., *The Cambridge Companion to Religious Studies* (New York, 2012), 36–57, which includes a critical reading of Taylor; and Saba Mahmood, *Religious Difference in a Secular Age: A Minority Report* (Princeton, New Jersey, 2015). For the inferiority of "heathen" cultures, see Gin Lum, *Heathen*.

17. Richard White, *The Middle Ground: Indians, Empires, and Republics in the Great Lakes Region, 1650–1815* (New York, 1991).

18. Carlo Ginzburg, "Provincializing the World: Europeans, Indians, Jews (1704)," *Postcolonial Studies* 14 (2011): 135–150; Giovanni Tarantino, "From Labelling and Ridicule to Understanding: The Novelty of Bernard and Picart's Religious Comparison," in Giovanni Tarantino and Paola Wyss-Giacosa, eds., *Through Your Eyes: Religious Alterity and the Early Modern Western Imagination* (Leiden and Boston, 2011), 235–266.

19. Dipesh Chakrabarty, *Provincializing Europe: Postcolonial Thought and Historical Difference* (Princeton, 2000), esp. 3–96. The title of Ginzburg's essay, "Provincializing the World," reflects his use of Chakrabarty.

Index